MANAGING SYSTEMATIC
AND ETHICAL PUBLIC RELATIONS

MANAGING SYSTEMATIC AND ETHICAL PUBLIC RELATIONS

. . . . . .

Mark P. McElreath, Ph.D.
Towson State University

Madison, Wisconsin•Dubuque, Iowa•Indianapolis, Indiana
Melbourne, Australia•Oxford, England

Book Team

Editor *Stan Stoga*
Developmental Editor *Mary E. Rossa*
Production Editor *Kay Driscoll*

Vice President and General Manager *Thomas E. Doran*
Executive Managing Editor *Ed Bartell*
Executive Editor *Edgar J. Laube*
Director of Marketing *Kathy Law Laube*
National Sales Manager *Eric Ziegler*
Marketing Manager *Carla J. Aspelmeier*
Advertising Manager *Jodi Rymer*
Manager of Visuals and Design *Faye M. Schilling*
Design Manager *Jac Tilton*
Art Manager *Janice Roerig*
Production Editorial Manager *Vickie Putman Caughron*
Permissions/Records Manager *Connie Allendorf*

Chairman Emeritus *Wm. C. Brown*
Chairman and Chief Executive Officer *Mark C. Falb*
President and Chief Operating Officer *G. Franklin Lewis*
Corporate Vice President, President of WCB Manufacturing *Roger Meyer*

Cover design by Rebecca Lloyd Lemna

Copyedited by Patricia Stevens

Copyright © 1993 by Wm. C. Brown Communications, Inc. All rights reserved

Library of Congress Catalog Card Number: 91–77816

ISBN 0-697-10534-2

No part of this publication may be reproduced, stored in a retrieval system, or transmitted, in any form or by any means, electronic, mechanical, photocopying, recording, or otherwise, without the prior written permission of the publisher.

Printed in the United States of America by Wm. C. Brown Communications, Inc., 2460 Kerper Boulevard, Dubuque, IA 52001

10 9 8 7 6 5 4 3 2 1

Contents

Preface   xvii

PART ONE
Using Systems Theories and Ethical Guidelines to Manage Public Relations Campaigns and Programs   1

CHAPTER ONE
Introduction to Managing Systematic and Ethical Public Relations   2

Management Expectations for Public Relations Vary Dramatically   3
Systematic, Ethical Factors Affect Public Relations Management   4
Overview   6
A Brief, Systematic History of Public Relations   6
    Less Complex Times Had Fairly Simple Public Relations   7
    Simple Assumptions About Human Motives   8
    Modern Public Relations Born in Anti-Big-Business Period   9
    From Closed to Open Systems   11
    Managing Public Relations Today: Facilitating Relationships   12
General Systems Theory Explains and Predicts Public Relations   13
    Boundaries and Boundary Spanners   14
    Interdependent Organizational Subsystems   14
    Closed and Open Systems   15
    Structural Functionalism   16
    Systems Concepts Help Explain and Predict Public Relations   17
    Professional Roles of a Public Relations Practitioner   17
    Organizational Technology and Internal Structure   18
    Organizational Scope   19
    Four Basic Organizational Types   20
    Decision-Making Structures   21
    External Publics   22
    Organizational Environments   22
    Organizational Flexibility   23
    Linkage Between Senior Management and Public Relations Staff   23

Survey Research Results Confirm Value of System Concepts	23
The Size of an Organization Does Make a Difference	25
Business Functions Predict Public Relations Activities	25
Decision-Making Structures Also Make a Difference	30
Management's View of the World Predicts Public Relations	33
Public Relations Linkage to Top Management Is Vital	34
Conclusion: There Is No One Best Way to Manage Public Relations	34
Alternative Theoretical Perspectives Are Important	35
In Summary . . .	35
Study Questions	36
Four Mini-Case Studies For Classroom Discussion	37
Mini-case 1.1: The Traditional Organization	37
Mini-case 1.2: The Mechanical Organization	38
Mini-case 1.3: The Organic Organization	39
Mini-case 1.4: The Mixed Mechanical/Organic Organization	40
Recommended Readings	41

CHAPTER TWO

How to Define Problems and Opportunities, and Develop Measurable Goals and Objectives — 50

What Are Problems, Opportunities, Goals and Objectives?	51
Problems	52
Opportunities	52
Objectives	53
Process and Outcome Goals	53
Determining What's Right and What's Wrong with the Situation	54
Dominant Coalition's View of the World Sets the Agenda	56
Case 2.1: District of Columbia Statehood Campaign	58
Case 2.2: "Quality of Service" Campaign	61
Similarities and Differences Between the Case Studies	64
Identifying Problems and Setting Goals Are Basic Processes	64
Major Factors Affect Problem Definition and Goal Setting	68
Survey Research Results Support Predictions	68
How to Develop Theory-Based Goals and Objectives	69
Building Action-Oriented Theories	70
Theoretical Definitions	72
Link Operational Definitions to Create Practical Theories	73
Intervening and Moderating Concepts	74
Examples of Communication Theories in Action	74

Social Learning Theory	74
Case 2.3: The Norrell Business Theater 75	
Social Exchange Theory	76
Case 2.4: Alberta Government Telephones 77	
Hierarchy of Effects	79
Case 2.5: Bank of America Surprise Stock Awards to Employees 79	
How to Establish Goals	83
How to Write Goals	83
How to Determine Objectives	84
How to Assign Priorities to Goals and Objectives	86
Strategies for Building Consensus	86
Using Focus Groups to Develop Consensus	87
An Alternative: The Nominal Group Technique 87	
An Alternative: The Delphi Technique 88	
An Alternative: Force Field Analysis 88	
How Practitioners Get Involved with Goals and Objectives	88
An Alternative Theory: Problems as Garbage Cans	89
In Summary . . .	90
Study Questions	91

CHAPTER THREE

How to Define Publics and Relationships

How to Define Publics and Relationships	94
Several Approaches to Defining Publics	95
Going from Latent to Active Public—and Back Again	95
The Coorientation Model	96
A Situational Model of Public Relations	98
Markets and Publics Are Not Equivalent Concepts	99
Defining Publics as Nonvariables	99
Defining Publics Using Variables	100
Two Case Studies Illustrate How to Define Publics	102
Case 3.1: Freddie Mac's Person-to-Person Campaign 102	
Case 3.2: Job Corps Campaign 104	
Significant Differences	106
Guidelines for Defining Key Publics	108
Survey Results: Dominant Coalition's View of Publics Crucial	109
Alternative Theories of Publics	109
Communication Theories Help Define Publics and Relationships	109
Elaboration-Likelihood Theory	110
Case 3.3: State Bank Victoria of Melbourne, Australia 111	

    Agenda-Setting Theory   112
        Case 3.4: The Hawaii Business Roundtable Campaign   113
    Community Power Theories   116
        Case 3.5: Minnesota Heart Health Program   116
  The Plan Book: Part I   118
  A Framework for Analyzing Theories about Publics   119
  In Summary . . .   121
    Study Questions   121

CHAPTER FOUR
How to Plan Effective Public Relations   124
  Planning Characteristics   125
    Examples of Planning for Routine Events   126
        Case 4.1: A Small Association's Newsletter   126
        Case 4.2: Hosting a One-Day Career Conference   127
        Case 4.3: A Grand Opening for the Metrorail   129
    Similarities and Differences   129
    Calendarizing   130
    Timelines and Gantt Charts   130
    Project Flow Charts and PERT Diagrams   132
    Routine vs. Nonroutine Events: "Closed" vs. "Open" Systems   132
    *Professionals React to Two Fictionalized Case Studies: One Routine,
      and One Nonroutine*   134
        Case 4.4: A Routine Newsletter   134
        Case 4.5: A Nonroutine Seminar   134
    Similarities and Differences   135
  Planning for Nonroutine Events   135
    Examples of Planning for Nonroutine Events   136
        Case 4.6: A Public Relations Agency Plans an Economic Development
          Program for a Complex Region   137
        Case 4.7: The Same Public Relations Agency Plans Another Economic
          Development Program for Another Client   138
    Similarities and Differences   139
    Two Additional Examples of Planning for Nonroutine Events   139
        Case 4.8: Public Relations Long-Range Planning   139
        Case 4.9: Emergency or Crisis Communication Planning   141
    Similarities and Differences   141
    Characteristics of Planning for Nonroutine Events   142
  Steps in the Planning Process   142
  Survey Research Findings   147

The Plan Book: Part II	151
An Alternative—Pessimistic—Theory of Planning	151
In Summary . . .	154
Study Questions	155

CHAPTER FIVE
How to Budget and Perform Cost-Benefit Analyses — 156

Budgeting: Negotiating about Organizational Resources	158
Unsophisticated Budgets Are Common in Public Relations	159
Standard Approaches to Public Relations Budgeting	161
Standard Categories within Budgets	161
Standard Budgets in Public Relations	162
Narrative Budgets Are the Workhorses in the Field	164
Three Case Studies	169
An Example of Corporate Public Relations Budgeting	169
Case 5.1: Blue Cross and Blue Shield Communication Plan for Corporate Clients 169	
Two Examples of Budgeting by Public Relations Agencies	170
Case 5.2: Media Relations for the Roman Catholic Pope's Tour of the United States 170	
Case 5.3: Porter/Novelli and the International Apple Institute 172	
Similarities	173
Differences	174
Additional Budgeting Strategies	174
What-If-Not-Funded Scenarios	174
Benefit Shadow Pricing	179
Cost-Benefit Compensation Estimation	183
Benefit-Cost Remainders (Net Value) and Benefit-Cost Ratios	186
Expected-Value Analysis	188
Factors Associated with Public Relations Budgeting	193
The Plan Book: Part III	194
In Summary . . .	195
Study Questions	195

CHAPTER SIX
How to Select a Research Design and Conduct Research to Help Plan and Evaluate Public Relations — 198

What Is Research?	199
What Is a Research Design?	200
Basic Steps in the Research Process	200

What Gets Measured?	203
Who Gets Measured?	204
When to Measure?	208
How to Select an Appropriate Research Design	209
Nine Evaluation Research Designs	214
Design A: Before-After with No Control Publics	215
Design B: Before-After with True Control Publics	216
Design C: Before-After with Nonequivalent Control Publics	216
Design D: After-Only	217
Design E: After-Only with True Control Publics	218
Design F: After-Only with Nonequivalent Publics	218
Design G: A Single Time-Series	219
Design H: A Time-Series with True Control Publics	219
Design I: A Time-Series with Nonequivalent Control Publics	220
The "Garbage Can" Theory of Research Design	221
Wide Range of Research Methodologies Available	222
Four Case Studies about Media Content Analysis	223
Case 6.1: Porter/Novelli's Background Review Service 224	
Case 6.2: Gatekeeper Audit and Publicity Evaluation 224	
Case 6.3: Publicity Evaluation and Tracking Service 226	
Case 6.4: Issues and Market Monitoring 227	
Two Case Studies about Focus Groups	227
Case 6.5: Focus Groups Used for a Formative Evaluation 227	
Case 6.6: Focus Groups Used for a Summative Evaluation 230	
Systematic Use of Press Clippings	232
Case 6.7: Content Analysis Using an After-Only Research Design 232	
Quantitative Research Means Using Statistics and Samples	234
Random Samples Reduce Sources of Error	238
Three Case Studies Involving Quantitative Research	239
Case 6.8: Black and Decker Campaign: A Before-Only Design 240	
Case 6.9: D.C. Statehood Campaign by David Apter & Associates: A Before-After Design 243	
Case 6.10: "McGruff" Crime Prevention Campaign: A Before-After Quasi-Experimental Design with Controls 247	
Checklist for Conducting Research	248
Survey Results	250
The Plan Book: Part IV	252
Alternative Reasons for Conducting Research	252
Ethics in Public Relations Research	253

In Summary...	254
Study Questions	255

CHAPTER SEVEN
How to Analyze and Evaluate Public Relations Using Systems Concepts—and a Master Checklist

	258
Strengths and Weaknesses of Checklists	258
The Master Checklist	259
Two Case Studies Compared	264
Case 7.1: Towson State University's Publications 264	
Case 7.2: Giant Food's Publications 264	
Key Factors	265
The Similarities	265
The Differences	266
Public Relations at the University	267
Public Relations at the Grocery Store Chain	267
Planning and Production Schedules	268
How the Grocery Store Chain Published Its Employee Newspaper	268
How the State University Published Its Alumni Magazine	269
Common Steps in Publishing	270
How the Grocery Store Chain Evaluated Its Publications	271
How the State University Evaluated Its Publications	271
Common Evaluation Criteria	272
Two Unique Yet Predictable Solutions	272
A Revised Checklist for Publications	274
Two Case Studies Involving the Same Agency	277
Case 7.3: The National Coffee Association 277	
Case 7.4: The Papal Visit 277	
Key Factors	278
The Similarities	278
The Differences	279
Media Relations for the Coffee Association	280
Media Relations for the Papal Visit	282
Crucial Steps in Conducting Media Relations	284
A Revised Checklist of Media Relations	285
Similarities and Differences in Revised Checklists	290
The Plan Book: Part V	290
Alternative Approaches to Evaluations	291
In Summary...	292
Study Questions	292

PART TWO
Using Research Priorities and Ethical Theories to Guide Professional Development in Public Relations 295

CHAPTER EIGHT
How to Identify and Investigate Priority Research Questions in Public Relations 296

- Top Priority Research Questions in Public Relations 297
- How to Conduct a Delphi Study 298
- Two Delphi Studies Identify Priority Research Questions 300
  - *Results of 1980 Study Used in 1990 Study* 302
  - *The Key Question: What Is the Best Way to Evaluate Public Relations?* 302
- In Summary... 309
  - *Study Questions* 310

CHAPTER NINE
How to Conduct Ethical Public Relations, Considering Intrapersonal, Interpersonal, Small Group, and Organizational Factors 318

- Defining Ethics 320
  - *What Is Right? What is Good?* 320
- Meta-Ethics: The Logic of Ethics 321
  - *Applying Rules* 322
  - *Living with the Consequences of Your Actions* 323
- Ethical Relativism 324
- A Model of Ethical Decision-Making 326
- The Potter Box 326
- Ethical Decisions at Different Levels of Analysis 329
  - *Intrapersonal Ethics* 329
    - Stages in Moral Development 330
    - Differences Between Men and Women 330
  - *Interpersonal Ethics* 332
  - *Small Group Ethics* 333
  - *Organizational Ethics* 335
    - Size Measured in Terms of People and Money 335
    - Technology 336
    - Rules and Regulations 336
    - Rewards and Sanctions 337
    - Hierarchy 337
    - Roles and Relationships 337

      Boundary Spanning Relationships   338

      Management Strategies for Dealing with the Environment   339

      Cooperation as a Strategy   340

      Organizational Strategies for Improving Ethics   342

      Steps in Preparing and Communicating Codes of Ethics   345

      Two Approaches to Corporate Ethics Training   346

      Monitoring and Enforcing Codes of Ethics   347

      U.S. Defense Industry Initiatives on Business Ethics   348

      Call for Multinational Corporate Communicator Codes of Ethics   349

  A Contingency Model of Ethical Decision-Making in Public Relations   349

Personal Interviews Used to Examine Factors in Model   351

      Case 9.1: An Individual Is Affected by Not Having All the Facts to Answer Media Inquiries about a Crisis   351

      Case 9.2: Interpersonal Relationships Affect Press Interviews   353

      Case 9.3: A Small Group of Elite Decision-Makers Determines the Right Amount of Information to Release to Stockholders   355

      Case 9.4: Organizational Factors Affect Establishing an Independent Voice for the Company Newsletter   356

  Conclusions from Personal Interviews   358

Two Controversial Alternative Explanations   358

  The Evolution of Consciousness—and Conscience   359

In Summary . . .   359

  Study Questions   360

Additional Cases   361

How the Practitioner's Relationship with the Sponsoring Organization(s) or Client(s) Affects Ethical Decision-Making in Public Relations   361

      Case 9.5: The Right Location for a Press Conference   361

How Interpersonal and Small Group Factors Affect Ethical Decision-Making in Public Relations   362

      Case 9.6: Assigning Responsibility for Last-Minute Changes in a Special Event   362

How Intrapersonal Factors Affect Ethical Decision-Making in Public Relations   364

      Case 9.7: Disclosing Insider Information to Friends   364

CHAPTER TEN

How to Conduct Ethical Public Relations Considering External Publics, Laws, Public Policies and Cultural Factors   370

Many Factors Affect Ethical Decision-Making in Public Relations   371

Defining Factors Outside the Control of the Organization   372

    External Consumer and Activist Publics   373
    Radical and Mainstream Activist Publics   374
    Competitors   375
    Investors and Ethical Corporate Decision-Making   376
    Professional Associations   376
        State Licensing of Professions   377
        Voluntary Professional Associations   378
        Award Programs Recognize Professional Norms   378
        Accreditation of Professionals   378
        Professional Codes of Ethics   379
Systems-Based Comparison of Public Relations Codes of Ethics   379
    Practitioner's Relationship with Cultural Values, Beliefs   379
    Practitioner's Relationship with Laws and Public Policies   381
    Practitioner's Relationship with Publics Outside the Immediate Control of the Sponsoring Organization or Client   381
    Practitioner's Relationship with the Sponsoring Organization or Client   383
    Practitioner's Relationship with Other Individuals and Small Groups within the Sponsoring Organization or Client   384
    Practitioner's Relationship with the Self   385
    Similarities and Differences   386
Laws and Public Policies   387
Cultural Values   389
Solutions to Ethical Dilemmas in Public Relations   391
Survey Results   391
How Cultural Values Affect Ethical Decision-Making in Public Relations   392
    Case 10.1: Shock Radio Advertising on TV, and a Calculated Public Relations Response   392
How Laws and Public Policies Affect Ethical Decision-Making in Public Relations   394
    Case 10.2: Releasing Public Information about a Top-Secret Organization   394
How External Publics and Other Organizations Affect Ethical Decision-Making in Public Relations   395
    Case 10.3: Hype Versus Solid News Value—How to Get the Media to Pay Attention   395
Alternative Explanation   397
In Summary . . .   398
    Study Questions   398

Additional Cases   399

    Case 10.4: When a Local Catholic Church Wants to Support a Pro-Life Political Candidate   399

    Case 10.5: Balancing Customer Confidentiality with the Public's Right to Know and the Organization's Best Interests   400

    Case 10.6: When a Vendor Fires a Very Popular Employee   402

    Case 10.7: When a Hospital Cancels Its Treatment Program for the Homeless   403

    Case 10.8: Putting a Money-Losing Fund-Raising Event in a Favorable Light by Shading the Truth   405

    Case 10.9: Reciprocity between an Organization and a Local Television Station   406

    Case 10.10: Informing the Public about a Product's Harmful Side-Effects   408

    Case 10.11: Informing the Public about an Unsafe Bridge   409

    Case 10.12: Disclosing Donor Information to Third Parties in a Fund-Raising Campaign   410

CHAPTER ELEVEN
How to Get a Good Job and Advance in the Field of Public Relations   414

    Today's Job Market   415
        Entry-Level Public Relations Positions   415
        Middle-Management Public Relations Positions   416
        Senior-Level Public Relations Positions   418
    Experienced Professionals Offer Career Advice   419
        For Women Entering the Field   419
        For Minorities Entering the Field   420
        For Any Individual Entering the Field   421
        For Entry-Level Applicants   421
        For People Wanting to Leave an Entry-Level Position   422
        For Women Advancing in the Field   423
        For Minorities Advancing in the Field   424
        For Any Individual Advancing in the Field   424
        For Someone No Longer Satisfied at an Entry Level   425
        For People Wanting to Leave Middle and Senior Management   425
    Ethical Guidelines and Career Advice   426
    Factors Affecting Ethical Decisions Vary from Level to Level   428

Applying for the Job ... 429
   Advice on how to Prepare a Resume ... 429
      Functional Resume   430
      Chronological Resume   430
      Combination Functional/Chronological Resume   431
   Advice on How to Write a Cover Letter ... 433
   Advice on How to Have a Successful Job Interview ... 434
An Alternative Explanation for the "Glass Ceiling" in Public Relations ... 437
In Summary 437
   Study Questions ... 439

APPENDIX
A. How to Use *Systematic Public Relations Software* (SPRS) Version 1.0 ... 442
B. Code of the Public Relations Society of America ... 444
C. Code of the International Association of Business Communicators ... 454
D. Code of the International Public Relations Association ... 460
E. International Bill of Rights of the United Nations ... 464

Index ... 470

Preface

This book, designed as an advanced college textbook for courses in public relations campaigns and public relations management, has three purposes. The first is to provide the reader with an understanding of current communication theories and state-of-the-art techniques for managing effective public relations. The second is to present an in-depth treatment of ethical decision-making in public relations that goes beyond a discussion of professional codes of conduct and examines ethics as they apply to individuals, small groups, organizations, publics, societies, and cultures. The third purpose is to provide computer-generated forms and lists that can be used to plan, implement, and evaluate both short-term programs and long-term campaigns.

Using a systems approach to the analysis of organizational behavior, the author presents more than fifty case studies which allow the reader to compare and contrast public relations activities sponsored by dramatically different types of organizations in dramatically different situations. The case studies illustrate the influence of the following factors on day-to-day management of public relations: organizational size, technology, internal structures, external environments, senior management perceptions and goals, the linkage the public relations manager has to the organization's dominant coalition, the location of the public relations department within the hierarchy, and the roles and orientations assumed by the public relations practitioner.

In Part One of the book, the first chapter presents an overview of general systems theories as they apply to public relations. Subsequent chapters explain how to define problems and opportunities, how to develop measurable goals and objectives, how to define key publics, how to plan campaigns for routine and nonroutine events, how to budget and perform cost-benefit analyses, how to design and conduct both qualitative and quantitative research, and how to evaluate public relations programs and campaigns.

In addition to the systems approach to organizational behavior, with its implied emphasis on functionalism and behaviorism, the book will present a number of alternative—some would say "radical"—perspectives, such as those offered by critical, interpretive and sociobiological analyses of organizational communication. While exploring alternative explanations and novel theories, the emphasis of this book is on empirical, applied communication theories useful to public relations practitioners.

Throughout the book, research results are presented based on a series of original studies, conducted by the author, that involved both mail surveys and in-depth personal interviews with more than 250 public relations practitioners. The results allow the implications of various theoretical propositions developed from the case studies and elsewhere to be explored in greater detail.

In Part Two, the systems perspective is used to present and analyze the results of a series of Delphi studies the author conducted which identify priority research questions and trends within the field of public relations. More than 70 sets of provocative research questions are presented, with citations that could be used to investigate answers to these important questions. The expectation is that readers will appreciate seeing the range of provocative questions that require investigation, and that some readers will be interested in pursuing answers and adding new knowledge, and new questions, to the field. The list of public relations educators and senior practitioners who participated in the Delphi study is a list of elite influencials in public relations research and education, and I am deeply grateful to them:

James Anderson, University of Florida; Joseph F. Awad, Reynolds Metals Company; Robert K. Berry, Berry Associates Public Relations; Nancy E. Blethen, The Blethen Group; Carl Botan, Purdue University; E. W. Brody, Memphis State University; Glen M. Broom, San Diego State University; Mary P. Caldwell, University of South Carolina; Robert O. Carboni, Northwestern Mutual Life Insurance Company; Roberta L. Crisson, Kutztown University; Hugh Culbertson, Ohio University; David M. Dozier, San Diego State University; Joe S. Epley, Epley Associates, Inc.; Dennis R. Felts, Kutztown University; Rick Fisher, Memphis State University; Margaret Fitch-Hauser, St. Olaf College; Ralph E. Frede, Consultant; Donald H. Frenette, 3M Company; Paul Fullmer, Selz, Seabolt and Associates; Walter G. Gray, Arizona Department of Transportation; Larissa A. Grunig, University of Maryland; James E. Grunig, University of Maryland; Mary J. Hart, St. Olaf College; Charlotte Hatfield, Ball State University; Robert L. Heath, University of Houston; Todd Hunt, Rutgers University; James E. Hunt, James E. Hunt and Associates; Frank Kalupa, University of Texas, Austin; Elaine Falk Katz, Communication research specialist; Jan Kelly, University of Scranton; Robert Kendall, University of Florida; Dean A. Kruckeberg, University of Northern Iowa; Mark A. Larson, Humboldt State University; Chester K. Lasell, Deere & Company; Peter Lazar, Professional Public Relations, Ltd.; Philip Lesley, The Philip Lesley Company; Curtis G. Linke, Pratt & Witney; John R. Lueke, University of Wisconsin, Whitewater; Elizabeth M. Lynn, GMI Engineering and Management Institute; Dan Millar,

Indiana State University; Debra A. Miller, Florida International University; Ellis Murphy, Murphy and Murphy Marketing Communications; Priscilla Murphy, University of Delaware; Bonita Neff, Public Communication Associates; Anne L. New, Timmerman and New, Inc.; Lloyd Newman, The Newman Partnership, Ltd.; Douglas Ann Newsom, Texas Christian University; Cyndi Bowers Nicholas, The Marcus Groups, Inc.; Jennifer Nichols, Otterbein College; Garrett O'Keefe, University of Wisconsin-Madison; John L. Paluszek, Ketchum Public Relations; Susan C. Paul, Decatur Federal Savings and Loan Association; John V. Pavlik, Columbia University, David Pincus, University of California, Fullerton; Marion K. Pinsdorf, Hill and Knowlton, Inc.; Mary Ann Pires, The Pires Group; Cornelius Pratt, Michigan State University; Ron Price, Cameron University; Shirley A. Ramsey, University of Oklahoma; Carol Reuss, University of North Carolina, Chapel Hill; Donna Rouner, Colorado State University; Maria P. Russell, Syracuse University; Charles Salmon, University of Wisconsin-Madison; Linda Scanlon, Norfolk State University; Tracy A. Schario, Otterbein College; Thomas A. Schick, College of Mount St. Joseph; Margaret L. Stacey, C. W. Post/Long Island University; Douglas P. Starr, Texas A&M University; Dulcie Straughan, University of North Carolina; James B. Strenski, Public Communications, Inc.; Kathryn Theus, Rutgers University; Elizabeth Lance Toth, Syracuse University; Alma Triner, Corporate Initiatives; Judy Van Slyke Turk, University of South Carolina; James K. Van Leuven, Colorado State University; Gerald J. Voros, Ketchum Communications; Gay Wakefield, Butler University; Albert Walker, Retired; Al Weitzel, San Diego State University; Paul M. Werth, Paul Werth Associates, Inc.; Anna L. West, Kerns & West; Dennis L. Wilcox, San Jose State University; Betty Winfield, Columbia University; Donald K. Wright, University of South Alabama; and, Frank W. Wylie, California State University, Long Beach.

Because the hallmark of the true professional is an adherence to high standards, two chapters in Part Two are devoted to ethics. The first of these two chapters deals with how individual, small groups and organizational factors affect ethical decision-making in public relations, including how organizations go about developing corporate codes of ethics. The second deals with how external publics, organizations and cultural factors influence public relations ethics, including, of course, codes of conduct established by associations of public relations professionals. This in-depth discussion of ethics focuses on practical guidelines public relations practitioners can use to make ethical decisions. The author presents the results of more than two dozen personal interviews with practitioners who described ethical dilemmas in public relations.

Because the book is expected to be used by advanced public relations students interested in pursuing careers in the field, the final chapter is devoted to current job descriptions and career advice from a wide range of public relations professionals. This career information is presented in the context of the systems analysis used throughout the book, so the reader can see how to match personal strengths and professional skills with the needs and expectations of specific types of organizations. Special checklists will help readers prepare effective resumes.

The book has been designed for upper-level undergraduate and graduate-level public relations campaigns and public relations management courses, with the expectation that material in Part One could be used in the first half of the course and tested with a midterm examination. The final chapter in Part One, Chapter 7, serves as a summary of the previous six chapters. The priority research questions identified in Part Two could be used to stimulate student research projects.

SUGGESTED COURSE OUTLINE

The following is one way the chapters could be assigned for a 15-week course:

PART ONE

Week 1 Chapter 1: Introduction
Week 2 Chapter 2: How To Define Problems and Opportunities, and Develop Measurable Goals and Objectives
Week 3 Chapter 3: How To Define Key Publics and Relationships
Week 4 Chapter 4: Planning Characteristics
Week 5 Chapter 5: How To Budget and Perform Cost-Benefit Analyses
Week 6 Chapter 6: How To Select a Research Design and Conduct Research To Help Plan and Evaluate Public Relations
Week 7 Chapter 7: How To Analyze and Evaluate Public Relations Using Systems Concepts—and a Special Checklist

PART TWO

Week 8 Chapter 8: How To Identify and Investigate Priority Research Questions in the Field of Public Relations
Week 9 Chapter 9: How To Conduct Ethical Public Relations, Considering Intrapersonal, Interpersonal, Small Group and Organizational Factors
Week 10 Chapter 10: How To Conduct Ethical Public Relations, Considering External Publics, Laws, Public Policies and Cultural Factors
Week 11 Student Case Presentations and/or Research Projects
Week 12 Student Case Presentations and/or Research Projects
Week 13 Student Case Presentations and/or Research Projects
Week 14 Chapter 11: How To Get a Good Job
Week 15 Review and Final Examination

APPLICATIONS SOFTWARE

A reader can profit from this book without using the unique computer program designed to augment and reinforce information, techniques, and strategies presented in each chapter. However, it is expected that most readers will use and appreciate *Systematic Public Relations Software* (sPRs), explained in greater detail in the appendix. sPRs Version 1.7. allows the user to generate checklists, budgets, and other planning documents that can aid in the management of specific public relations programs and campaigns. sPRs 1.7 also contains a program that can produce comprehensive proposals, reports, and a variety of customized professional resumes.

A Personal Note of Thanks

Graduate and undergraduate students at Towson State University assisted the author in conducting research reported in the book, and I very much appreciated their serious efforts and refreshing enthusiasm: Monica Acarese, Catherine Crawford, Shawn Donahue, Mark Eber, John Goucher, Christy Haugh, Susan Kamachatis, Cindi Larson, Michelyn Pantaro, Susan Miller, Shannon Smith, Inge Van Trigt, and Scott Warren.

Special thanks go to my colleagues at Towson State University who were members of the "writers' group" which met informally several times each year to review each others writings, and who were so encouraging of my work, especially Barbara Bass, Fil Dowling, Sharon Gibson, Carolyn Hill, and Linda Mahin of the Department of English; Linda Sweeting of Chemistry; Karl Larew of History; and, Joan McMahon of Health Sciences. I also appreciate the strong support of other TSU colleagues: Tom Basuray, chairman of the Department of Management; Alice Feeney, associate director of the Career Placement Center; and, Dan McCarthy, vice president of institutional development and university relations.

This book would not have been possible without the support of the public relations professionals who participated in the research and who provided the many case studies presented throughout the book. My thanks to Marc Apter of David Apter & Associates, Washington, D.C.; Catherine Barham of The Ryland Group, Columbia, Maryland; Jennifer Berk of the National Aquarium in Baltimore; John H. Boyd, Carlton Caldwell, Philip Giaramita, and Charles Manor of Martin Marietta Corporation; Camilee Bryant and Susan J. Hamilton of Blue Cross and Blue Shield, Washington, D.C.; Debby G. Butcher of Blue Cross and Blue Shield, Maryland; Barbara Burns of the International Public Relations Association; Michael C. Burton of Baltimore Gas and Electric Company; Helen Dale of the Baltimore Mass Transit Administration; Gary Edwards of the Ethics Resource Center in Washington, D.C.; Robert A.

Ellis of PHH FleetAmerica; John R. Finnegan, Jr. of the Minnesota Heart Health Program; Terri Freeman and Kathy A. Whelpley of Federal Home Loan Mortgage Corporation; Marguerite Gee, communication consultant, of Oakland, Calif.; Zack Germroth of the City of Baltimore; Robert J. Gould, Pattie Yu Hussein, and Jerry Franz of Porter/Novelli, Washington, D.C.; Andrea L. Just of CSX Corporation; Clifton Kagawa of Hill and Knowlton/Communications Pacific; Elizabeth Ann Kovacs of the Public Relations Society of America; Domenic LaPonzia of the U.S. Internal Revenue Service; Abbey Lazarus of the March of Dimes in Baltimore; Norm G. Leaper of the International Association of Business Communicators; Sy Leon of Sy Leon Associates, Baltimore; Barbara Lucus of Black and Decker; Robert Mead of SmithMead and Associates, Baltimore; Nancy Moses of Potomac Electric Power Company; John Nelson of The Right Brain, Minneapolis, Minn.; Ron Rhody of the Bank of America, San Francisco; William C. Rolle of Rolle Communications, Bethesda, Maryland; Barry Sher of Giant Food; Peter J. Stanton of Stanton Communications, Washington, D.C.; Janet Tom, consultant, of San Francisco, Calif.; and, Harland Warner of Manning, Selvage, and Lee/Washington. This list does not include the dozens of professionals who participated by sharing ethical dilemmas which were presented as fictionalized case studies to protect the confidentiality of these thoughtful, candid individuals. You know who you are. Thank you!

I would also like to thank the manuscript reviewers for their thoughtful and incisive comments: Ron Anderson, University of Texas-Austin; Bill Baxter, Marquette University; Richard Dubiel, University of Wisconsin at Stevens Point; Guy Meiss, Central Michigan University; Michael G. Parkinson, Southern Illinois University, Carbondale; David Pincus, California State University, Fullerton; Karyn Rybacki, Northern Michigan University; Robert Vivian, California State University, Chico; and Don Wright, University of South Alabama. Many of their suggestions have been incorporated into the book, and it is a better book for their efforts. Also, a special thanks to other educators in this field: William P. Ehling (retired) and Elizabeth Lance Toth of Syracuse University; James and Larissa Grunig of the University of Maryland; and Marilyn Kern-Foxworth of Texas A&M.

My deepest appreciation goes to my principal and principled cohort and delightful companion in life, Linda McElreath, who edited the manuscript more than once and patiently listened, challenged, and encouraged me throughout the several years it took to research and write this book.

Mark McElreath
Towson, Maryland

PART ONE:

Using Systems Theories and Ethical Guidelines to Manage Public Relations Campaigns and Programs

. . . . . .

CHAPTER ONE

Introduction to Managing Systematic Ethical Public Relations

. . . . . .

Susan had very little trouble getting her company to pay for her to attend today's professional workshop. As manager of media relations for the city's gas and electric company, all she had to do was mention it once informally to her boss who suggested she put the request in writing, which she did, and it was approved. So, here she was, with thirty other professionals attending a workshop titled "Measuring the Effectiveness of Public Relations and Organizational Communication." It was the mid-morning coffee break before Susan had her first real opportunity to talk with her colleagues. Sipping her coffee, she stepped into one small group. There was a quick round of introductions; Susan's coffee clutch included the director of community relations from the mayor's office, an employee newsletter editor from the local bank, and the assistant director of a national association.

"You wouldn't believe the hassle I had getting management to approve this workshop," the woman from the bank said. "You would think a bank, of all places, would be quick to say 'yes' to a workshop like this—the bottom line, and all. But, no. I had to submit my request three different times. It took months. Two managers and one committee had to sign off on it. I hope it's worth it."

"Fortunately, our agency has personnel policies that encourage us to go to professional workshops like this," the man from the mayor's office said. "Besides, the mayor intends to make some cuts. A lot of us downtown are worried. I hope to get some clues today about how to keep the axe from falling on my head. I would have paid for this out of my own pocket, but I didn't have to."

"I had to," the man from the association said. "There's no money for anything like this. We're cutting back publications, dropping services. It's hard. I'm on the job market, looking around. But, before I go, I want to learn better ways to document and evaluate what we're doing; I mean, we need to. I want to know how others do it. I know there are better ways to do it. Susan, I hear you guys do all kinds of evaluations."

"Yes, we do. But, you would be surprised. I remember one manager from one of our engineering groups saying, 'You can't measure public relations. It's not a product. It's an idea—an attitude. It's more of an art than a science.' I told him we needed to operate with as much accuracy as possible, and then I explained what we did—focus groups, surveys, measurements and number crunching of all kinds. He had no idea that public relations people talked like that, or that his company was doing it. It was fun watching his face. I expect to learn a lot today. There is so much going on in this area now."

. . .

MANAGEMENT EXPECTATIONS FOR PUBLIC RELATIONS VARY DRAMATICALLY

While the opening vignette is fiction, it's typical of numerous conversations the author has witnessed as professionals discuss the difficulty they have in getting management's support for evaluating public relations campaigns. Almost all professional communicators acknowledge the importance of measurement and evaluation; but, few do it. One major reason is because different organizations have different levels of management expectations for public relations.

For example, consider the organizations represented in the vignette. It's predictable that each of these organizations would support their public relations professional in different ways. Because utilities often are major institutions within their communities and regulated by public commissions, they are fairly sophisticated in their public relations and genuinely seek feedback from their publics. Banks are more traditional in their decision making, particularly when it comes to public relations, which is viewed too often as the weak partner of marketing. Many government agencies are required by law to regularly assess the need for and to justify public information programs, but government communication activities not mandated are vulnerable to budget cuts. The lifeblood of most associations is the steady flow of information among members; so, despite limited resources, public relations remains a central responsibility of association management.

The professional communicator recognizes these differences and knows that there is no one best way to manage public relations—that while effective management varies from organization to organization, from one situation to the next, there are basic principles of fairness and truth that cut across all situations. The professional public relations practitioner recognizes that making decisions about what is right and what is wrong is not easy. Professionals know that you don't answer all ethical questions with a wishy-washy statement about how "it all depends on the situation." The best public relations managers are those who have a clear understanding of their values, principles, and loyalties. And, they know both when and why to use certain communication strategies in specific situations for different clients and organizations.

SYSTEMATIC, ETHICAL FACTORS AFFECT PUBLIC RELATIONS MANAGEMENT

Public relations is viewed today as a management function that uses communication to facilitate relationships and understanding between an organization and its many publics. This book presents more than fifty case studies that describe numerous ways public relations managers make ethical decisions and effectively manage public relations programs and campaigns. The distinction between a program and a campaign is subtle yet important; it's determined by the initial mandate authorizing the set of public relations activities. A program is a sustained public relations effort that often has an ongoing mandate, such as an employee communication program, a stockholder relations program, or a community relations program. A public relations campaign, on the other hand, has a fixed time period in which to accomplish its goals, such as a campaign to reduce employee absenteeism, a campaign to have drivers use their safety belts, or a campaign to influence legislation. Both programs and campaigns are composed of a variety of communication activities.

Because public relations programs are maintained over sustained periods of time, they represent an ongoing commitment by an organization to a particular set of stakeholders. Consequently, programs generate a special set of expectations by management, and by the targeted stakeholders, that an effective public relations manager will take into consideration. Because campaigns have a definite time period in which to achieve specific goals, they reflect sensitive, timely issues affecting an organization, which also affect how the campaign is managed.

Public relations managers are being held to ever higher standards of ethics and accountability. As the cases and research presented in this book will illustrate, there are a variety of ways a professional can meet the increasing demands for more accountable, ethical public relations programs and campaigns.

A number of factors help explain and predict why ethics and accountability are becoming increasingly important in public relations. For example, the degree of competition within a marketplace can force some organizations to increase their investment in public relations because it gives them the necessary edge on their competitors. Along with additional staff time and money devoted to public relations come more bottom-line questions such as, "What is the return on our investment?" However, the same competitive pressures can force the same organizations to make unethical decisions, because they think it will help them beat the competition.

Similarly, the sophistication of an organization's technology—the essential work of an organization—can affect public relations programs and campaigns. Consider a hospital versus a pizza franchise. Hiring specialists and transforming raw materials into either health care services or pizzas are dramatically different examples of technology; consequently, public relations programs and campaigns for these two types of organizations will differ, primarily because of management's expectations for the role of public relations. For example, a hospital's public relations might be judged effective if it increases the public's perception of the quality of health services and the medical community's willingness to practice at the hospital. For a pizza franchise, an effective public relations campaign might be the one that uses special coupons and incentives to sell the most pizzas. The differences between the complex hospital technology and the relatively routine technology of the pizza franchise also affects ethical decision-making in the two organizations: there will be more complicated ethical dilemmas within the nonroutine technology because there are so many more exceptions to the rules.

Another factor that differs from organization to organization and affects the management of public relations campaigns is the frequency of involvement senior public relations professionals have in crucial policy decisions by top management. As the public relations person's role in senior management increases, it is likely that the scope of the public relations function will increase also. With those additional duties there will be additional responsibilities to explain and predict the organization's public relations.

The hallmark of professionals is their adherence to a common set of values, principles and loyalties—to a common set of ethics. Professional medical specialists, despite pressures from patients, hospitals, insurance companies or others, will prescribe treatment programs that meet high standards. Professional lawyers, despite a variety of pressures, will defend their clients to the best of their abilities so long as it is within the law; their primary allegiance is to the justice system, not to the client. In the same way, professional public relations specialists have an allegiance to truth and effective communication; but, because they are involved in establishing and facilitating hundreds of relationships, public relations practitioners experience pressures from various stakeholders that create serious ethical dilemmas.

OVERVIEW

The purpose of this chapter is to present a brief history of public relations and to relate this history to developments in the management sciences, particularly structural functionalism and general systems theories as they apply to organizational behavior. The major assumption of systems theories is that the structure of the relationships that define an organization is based on the functions performed by those relationships for the organization. A structure can be defined as a set of relationships—an edifice made up of bricks and boards, or an organization made up of people working together to achieve a common goal. According to structural functional theories of management, the sets of relationships that define an organization—its structure—also serve to define the function of public relations. And, visa versa: the function of public relations is to identify, clarify, modify, and maintain sets of relationships of importance to the organization.

After discussing the major concepts and variables used in the management sciences to explain and predict public relations, survey data will be presented to illustrate key relationships among certain factors that affect the management of systematic, ethical public relations. The following history of public relations also will highlight key ethical issues affecting the practice of public relations, which will be examined in much greater depth in later chapters.

While the book emphasizes structural functionalism and general systems theories, each chapter ends with a discussion of alternative approaches to the analysis of public relations. This chapter concludes by acknowledging the importance of critical analyses of the history of public relations.

A BRIEF, SYSTEMATIC HISTORY OF PUBLIC RELATIONS

Public relations, as an identifiable management function, began prior to the beginning of the 20th century when it was viewed primarily as a way for an organization to generate positive publicity that might offset public pressures to regulate big business. One hundred years ago people did not expect a lot from a public relations practitioner. Our expectations for public relations, then and now, are linked to our expectations of organizations. People today expect a lot more from their organizations. They are turning to the institutions in their lives not only for essential services but also for social enhancements.

It has not always been so. For centuries, public relations was thought of—if people thought about it at all—as a way for an organization to tell the public what the organization thought best. Until the 1920s, the primary purpose of public relations was publicity.[1] For good reasons, which will be discussed in this chapter, press agentry was the most appropriate public relations activity for most organizations to engage in at the time. But, people's attitudes and expectations have changed. Organizations today, and their environments, are dramatically different than they were a century or more ago. Attitudes toward public relations today are equally different, and for similar reasons: the pressures for organizations to be responsive to publics have changed.

The basic notion of relating to publics and being concerned about public opinion was first discussed by philosophers and statesmen who wrote about the importance of public opinion, primarily as it related to government.[2] From the days of Caesar and Cleopatra to Thomas Paine and Benjamin Franklin, there always have been men and women who were good at relating to publics. They knew how to stage an event and how to use the media of the day to influence public opinion. The founding fathers of many nations, including the United States of America, were masters at publicity and public relations.[3] Former U.S. President Richard Nixon once complimented former U.S.S.R. President Mikhail Gorbachev by acknowledging that the Soviet leader had earned an undergraduate degree in law but was "born with a master's degree in public relations."[4]

Less Complex Times Had Fairly Simple Public Relations

Public relations a century or more ago was less complex than it is today. People prior to the 20th century were dealing with relatively simple organizations existing in fairly abundant times—lots of available labor, lots of raw materials, plenty of consumers, very little competition or government regulation. In earlier times, people decided who said what to whom according to royalty and family ties; little or no concern was paid to factors outside the immediate network of individuals involved in an organization. Organizations were then viewed as closed systems; self-contained and fairly self-sufficient, successful organizations concerned themselves primarily with internal matters and a limited number of external publics. There were fairly simple expectations for organizations in those days.

"Public relations" as a term didn't occur until the late 1800s.[5] Few businesses paid much attention to public relations prior to the 1700s. Before then, people were most often organized according to the divine rights of royalty and by kinship. Citizens yielded to regal authority; nepotism was rampant; most organizations were very small and, in many instances, were operated as extended families. Prior to the Industrial Revolution, agrarian life focused most organizational goals on efficient uses of agricultural resources. Little or no attention was paid to public relations and other "boundary-spanning" activities.

With the Industrial Revolution, the focus shifted to include the efficient use of labor and capital.[6] The advent of the twentieth century saw more attention paid to public relations as labor and raw materials became more difficult to obtain and people became better educated—and more difficult to manage. As the twentieth century marketplace became saturated with goods and services, organizations had to spend more time relating to the growing network of publics.

Up until the late nineteenth century, a "public be damned" notion on the part of business and industry was defended by many of society's opinion leaders. During the time of slavery in the United States, some people thought industrial organizations, including their sweatshops, were appropriate ways to evolve a better race. The theory of Social Darwinism said that some people might not be fit for industrial life, but that was okay. If some people didn't fit, others would; it's the strong ones, the argument went, the ones who can "go along with the program," who will improve the quality of the species.[7]

Simple Assumptions About Human Motives

At the turn of the twentieth century, it was argued that the best way to manage was to be authoritarian—to assume that people did not like to work, that people were motivated almost exclusively by basic needs, and that they needed to be told what to do all the time. From the heyday of the Industrial Revolution on into the twentieth century, chief executive officers assumed that the most efficient way to manage was to break down tasks into small components and mini-tasks and to have people do just the work they were hired to do. Measuring and figuring out how best to get work broken down and done on schedule paid off for many manufacturing firms in the United States at the beginning of this century. "Scientific management," as it was called, became one of the most widely used theories of management in the early 1900s, primarily because it was so appropriate for the non-complex, routine technologies of its day.[8] It still is an appropriate management theory, particularly when designing workstations and performing time-and-motion studies. However, classical management theories such as scientific management paid little or no attention to public relations.

In the early 1900s, when economic and social forces created a hostile public opinion toward big business, managers were forced to consider improving their public relations. The labor movement in the United States and elsewhere, and communism and socialism worldwide, were significant forces working against the doctrines of Social Darwinism, laissez-faire capitalism, and free enterprise. Workers were no longer content to let managers dictate what had to be done. Workers began to demand and negotiate for better working conditions. Top management began to recognize they needed cooperation if they were to achieve their goals.

Managers in the early part of the twentieth century came to realize that legitimate power rested with the lower participants in the organization; willing workers cooperating toward the achievement of a set of goals gave real power to management. According to AT&T's Chester Barnard, a highly respected chief executive officer in the early part of this century, the function of management in such a cooperative system is to inculcate and indoctrinate the workers with the mission and goals of the organization.[9] Only by managers effectively communicating with workers about goals and objectives is it possible for workers to cooperate willingly toward the achievement of those goals and objectives. Internal public relations became an important function of management when organizations were viewed less as closed systems and more as open systems interacting with their environments, as systems where the cooperation of the workers was not assumed but actively sought out.

External public relations became more important to managers in the early part of the twentieth century when people began to question and resist the tactics of the monopolies and cartels running major industries. Anti-trust legislation—the reality of it and the prospect of having it—forced big business to think seriously about government relations and public relations.[10] With increasing pressures from an organizing workforce and with increasing pressures from suppliers, customers and regulators, big business turned to media specialists and lobbyists to get their message across and to get public support.

Modern Public Relations Born in Anti-Big-Business Period

The modern roots of public relations were established in this anti-big-business environment. Ivy Lee, an enterprising ex-newsman whom some call the father of public relations, made his money and his reputation providing public relations services to major business institutions.[11] Lee told his clients that big business could not remain silent in the face of growing public opposition; it had to present its point of view to the public, for only then would the public understand and be more supportive. Lee embraced the idea that an informed public was society's best safeguard against social ills. He aggressively demonstrated to the managers of a variety of major organizations how they could win public support over time by consistently providing the publics with accurate information. He was one of the first practitioners to hand out a press release. One of the most successful public relations practitioners of his day, Lee specialized in counseling management about its options and about the necessity of putting out accurate information. He had a great deal of faith in the value of an informed individual in a free society.

Some executives sought out and took Lee's advice; most others ignored him. Traditional management at the beginning of the twentieth century continued to assume that the general public's welfare and goodwill were not its concern and that the individual worker was no more than a machine to be used and, if necessary, discarded and replaced.

Yet, the social ideologies and economic forces emerging during the early 1900s contradicted these assumptions by emphasizing improved working conditions and the social well-being of individuals. Management theories that focused on "human relations" were developed in reaction to the impersonal, authoritarian management styles prevalent at the time, and because the human relations approach worked sometimes for some organizations.[12] The increased emphasis by human relations specialists on leadership styles and improved working conditions were based on assumptions that individuals liked to work, that they were driven by more than money, and that when left unsupervised, motivated workers would be productive.

Many other assumptions about the role of the worker in society were undergoing changes in the early part of the twentieth century. One assumption that changed was that government should no longer take a hands-off attitude about big business and the social problems blamed on industry. As social scientists and historians would say later, a paradigm shifted at the beginning of the twentieth century: we went from an acceptance of the assumptions underlying Social Darwinism to an appreciation for the assumptions underlying greater government intervention and involvement in the conduct of business and in social welfare.[13] Landmark legislation in the areas of labor, anti-trust, and women's right to vote marked this dramatic shift.

Public relations campaigns also changed during this "paradigm shift." More than 100 years ago, only big businesses, loose associations of concerned citizens, such as farmers or women, and more organized associations of workers, such as labor unions, engaged in public relations campaigns. Governments then did not support or engage in public education campaigns as we know them today. Then, as now, associations had to turn to the media to get their message of reform across to other citizens and to legislators. Testifying before legislative bodies and staging protests to generate publicity were standard campaign techniques of early public relations campaigns.[14]

From the 1900s to the 1940s, a time when broadcasting and modern mass communication techniques were developed, the government passed numerous pieces of social legislation which assumed that certain aspects of social life "ought" to occur: workers, particularly children and women, should not be abused; stockholders should not be swindled; consumers should not have to worry about food and product safety. Some of this legislation mandated public disclosure and public information campaigns. During this time, the government's role in authorizing and funding public relations campaigns became firmly established.

During the 1940s and 1950s, managers and organizational specialists began to see that authoritarian management techniques worked better for some organizations than for others, that human relations approaches to management worked better for some organizations, than for others. They found out there was no one best way to manage, and that the management technique that worked best depended on a variety of contingencies.[15]

During this time period, social psychologists were humanizing the bare bones of the authoritarian structure of classical management by recognizing that the decision-making processes of an organization were limited by the decision-making of individuals. According to this view, human decision-making traits, with all their strengths and weaknesses, were at the base of all organizational decisions.[16] The quality and kinds of information available to people, and what people did with information, were important contingencies.

During the first half of the twentieth century, particularly during the world wars, organizations developed sophisticated communication hardware and learned sophisticated ways to disseminate information and be persuasive. Much of the early research in persuasion and the mass media was funded by the military. With fairly sophisticated communication hardware and with new and more powerful theories about communication, the persuasion industry flourished.[17]

From Closed to Open Systems

During the 1950s and 1960s, the concept of the complex organization completed its shift from that of a closed system to that of an open system. With this shift came a renewed interest in public relations. Management specialists recognized in the early 1960s that certain effective organizations were the ones best able to integrate and coordinate their operations in accordance with the organization's technology and in keeping with the organization's environment.[18] Other researchers found out that in many cases, the kinds of organizations that survived, the ones that grew and prospered were the ones that best matched their operations to environmental pressures. It was Social Darwinism applied to organizations: the survival of the fittest organizations depended in part on how effective organizations were in adapting to changes and demands in the environment.[19]

With the dramatic increases in world populations and the number of global networks of organizations that occurred during the middle of the twentieth century, the reality of organizational life in post-industrial societies shifted, and with it came a dramatic shift in people's expectations for what constitutes effective public relations. Organizations reacted to these growing expectations by increasing the amount of organizational resources spent on "boundary spanning activities," including public relations. As it became more important for an organization to have effective two-way communication across its boundaries, the prestige and power that went to those in boundary spanning positions increased.

This shift in the reality of organizational life can be seen in the different career paths of chief executive officers of major corporations over the past few years. In the early 1950s, most top executives of the big organizations, and almost all of the leaders of small businesses, were technical experts in the core technology of their organization; many were engineers. The leaders of many of today's major corporations have been trained formally in negotiation, conflict resolution, and the strategic management of public affairs; many are lawyers. The penultimate career path for many of today's chief executive officers includes a stint as vice president of public relations.

During the 1960s and 1970s, public relations campaigns became more sophisticated. Not only were the media more sophisticated, and communication theories more precise, but federal, state, and local governments funded major public education campaigns and required that a certain percent of public funds be spent on research and evaluation. The knowledge gained about public communication campaigns from the government-funded research and development projects not only helped make the campaigns more effective, but also contributed significantly to the body of knowledge in public relations.[20]

In the 1970s and 1980s, management theorists and administrators began to seriously consider the organization's "ecosystem"—the network of social relationships in which the organization was embedded.[21] They recognized that a group of people working together is essentially a social system within a network of other social systems within economic systems within larger political and cultural systems. They recognized that the actions of organizations were often reactions to external pressure groups and other social forces. The ecological approach to the analysis of organizational behavior looks upon public relations as one way an organization adapts to its environment.

Managing Public Relations Today: Facilitating Relationships

Public relations today is defined as "a management function that identifies, establishes and maintains mutually beneficial relationships between an organization and the various publics on whom its success or failure depends."[22] Managing public relations means researching, planning, implementing and evaluating an array of communication activities sponsored by the organization—from small group meetings to international satellite-linked press conferences, from simple brochures to multimedia national campaigns, from open houses to grassroots political campaigns, from public service announcements to crisis management. An almost endless array of communication techniques and strategies are used by public relations professionals today to facilitate relationships and improve understanding.

Anyone who works for an organization operates within a complex network of relationships among employees, groups and publics. An organization can be defined as a system of relationships operating to achieve a goal. What holds this system together is communication: it's the vital link among all parts. While some managers—for example, in engineering or retail sales—can do a good job by staying focused on fairly narrow areas of concern, public relations managers, to be effective, must see the "big picture" that encompasses all relationships affecting the organization. An effective public relations manager is concerned with how and why communication activities can affect significant relationships so that organizational goals can be achieved. An organization, if it strives to be rational, will strive to achieve a predictable set of ongoing relationships. It is the purpose of public relations professionals within that system to help the organization achieve that rational goal by properly managing communication activities.

GENERAL SYSTEMS THEORY EXPLAINS AND PREDICTS PUBLIC RELATIONS

One of the most useful theories in the applied social sciences—which, of course, includes the field of public relations—is General Systems Theory.[23] Developed decades ago as a way to link various scientific disciplines, general systems theory can be used to describe organizations as dynamic (some would say, "living") organisms. The analogy is that an organization is a living entity because it has boundaries, inputs, outputs, "through-puts," and enough feedback from both internal and external environments so that it can make appropriate adjustments in time to keep on living. Economist Kenneth Boulding gave such an analogy when he said organizations are like birds and bees.[24] Imagine, he said, if all the birds and bees in the world, except for those on the east coast of the United States, were destroyed by some global catastrophe. Assume, he said, that whatever caused this near extinction of the birds and bees was corrected so that the Earth would begin to rebuild itself. Slowly, the birds and bees would take flight. It might take decades, centuries, or more, but in time, the world again would be populated by birds and bees.

This would be the case, too, Boulding said, if all the organizations in the world were destroyed, except those on the east coast of the United States. Eventually, they too would expand, establish foreign subsidiaries, make new trade agreements, merge, build up their databanks of information, sell copyrights, trademarks, and patents, and otherwise reproduce themselves until the world was again populated by organizations.

Critics point out that although this organization-as-organism image is powerful, it undervalues the role of the individual and overvalues the role of market forces.[25] Nevertheless, from general systems theory a number of important concepts have emerged that help explain and predict organizational behavior. Because public relations is one form of organizational behavior, the systems concepts are useful when examining public relations management.

Boundaries and Boundary Spanners

Two important systems concepts that apply to public relations are: (1) organizations have boundaries, and (2) certain people serve as "boundary spanners."[26] What are the boundaries of an organization? Of course they are not the walls of the buildings in which the organization is housed. But, are they defined by the geographic or technological limits of the marketplace? Are organizational boundaries somehow described by the total number of employees? If so, what about part-timers, consultants, and people who have retired or have left the organization? What about primary suppliers, major customers, and principal regulators? Do all stakeholders fall within the boundaries of the organization? Which stakeholders do not?

Reaching consensus on what relationships best define an organization is very difficult. Even among members of the organization's major decision-makers—called by some the "dominant coalition"—it is difficult to determine the most important set of relationships that define the organization. Yet, it is precisely this role of helping an organization's members recognize and facilitate important relationships that constitutes the core responsibility of the public relations manager.

In addition to public relations professionals, various organizational members, serve as boundary spanners. They are people who because of their role responsibilities, experiences, skills or personal insights are able to understand various points of view. They can explain corporate policies and organizational actions to others. They know how to communicate, and sometimes translate, information from one group to another. The higher the person's position in the organizational hierarchy, the more boundaries that are spanned. Because the function of public relations is to span boundaries, the organization's more senior managers have the most public relations responsibilities. Most chief executive officers spend most of their time on boundary-spanning public relations activities.

Interdependent Organizational Subsystems

Another important concept from systems theory that helps clarify the function of public relations is that an organization is made up of a set of interdependent subsystems. For example, every organization has a core technology in which the essential work of the organization is performed. It has an inner-directed management subsystem which coordinates internal operations. It has another management subsystem that is responsible for establishing overarching goals and objectives for the organization, securing basic resources, distributing goods and services, evaluating overall corporate performance, and buffering and protecting the organization from unwanted changes. There also are human culture and machine-oriented technological subsystems, along with an environmental subsystem composed of the networks of relationships the organization has with other organizations and members of the public. The public relations manager must understand and facilitate relationships among these various subsystems.[27]

It is easy to see how the role of the public relations person within a large organization is illuminated by general systems theories. But, these concepts also help to explain how and why public relations professionals can operate effectively "outside the system." Systems strive to achieve a steady state. For an organization, achieving this steady state means operating successfully. It means that changes are predictable; its future survival is not in jeopardy; and, its members are content with the status quo, whether it be aggressive, rapid growth or no growth at all. If a public relations person is working to affect changes in any system, big or small, simple or complex, the facts remain: it is the set of relationships that defines the system. Change these relationships and the system changes. For example, public relations practitioners working for a small, little-known grassroots political organization might engage in an effective campaign to change major corporations by focusing their grassroots efforts on vulnerable relations that the giants have with critical stakeholders—stockholders, customers, regulators and other important "players" in the system.

Closed and Open Systems

Some systems are said to be "closed," whereas others are "open." These are important general systems concepts for public relations professionals because they stress the importance of management's expectations and perceptions. There is an unfortunate tendency with systems theories to describe organizations as entities unto themselves. As a colleague once said, "Long after you and I, and all the students and faculty, have come and gone from this university, it's still going to be here, churning away without us—and probably doing just fine without us, too!" In a manner of speaking, organizations do have "lives" that outlive individual members. But, in very practical terms, organizations are made up of people, and it's how these people view themselves and others that strongly predicts and explains organizational behavior. Some groups within an organization may see themselves as self-contained and satisfied with the situation; they are closed to considering options. Other groups may view the situation differently and be more open to new possibilities. Whatever the views of the various groups, it is the dominant coalition of decision-makers within the organization which sets the organization's agenda. If public relations is able to influence an organization's view of itself and its relationships with others, it can only do so by significantly changing the views of the dominant coalition.

Structural Functionalism

The major assumption of systems theories is that the structure of the relationships that defines the organization is based on the functions performed by those relationships for the organization.[28] For example, the essential work of the organization will determine whether decision-making is centralized or decentralized. If the organization's function is to operate a routine technology, then centralized decision-making is appropriate. If its function is to generate innovative solutions, then decentralized decision-making would be appropriate. The assumption is that significant role relationships are determined primarily by the function those relationships have for the organization. If the function of the public relations department is to generate publicity in support of marketing, efforts to make it otherwise are not necessarily doomed to failure, but they will be met with reluctance, if not opposition. In this example, to structurally change the relationship between public relations and marketing requires redefining their functions.

Structural functionalism works both ways. Sometimes the structure predicts the function; at other times, function predicts structure. For example, if the public relations department is persistent in, and good at, communication activities other than generating publicity that supports the marketing function, the new relationship between the departments may cause management to redefine both functions. Similarly, if management has high expectations for the public relations function, but the performance is below expectations—due, for example, to such structural factors as the qualifications of the practitioner, the location of the department in the hierarchy, or the status of the position—then, management may redefine the function to fit the reality of the situation. On the other hand, improving these structural factors could improve the organization's public relations so as to better fulfill its expected function.

The yin and yang aspect of structure and function suggests another important perspective that systems theories give to public relations. General systems theories assume that any one organization is greater than the sum of its parts. It assumes there are subtle yet significant interactions among an organization's various subsystems that are not easily identified. Keep this in mind while you read this book. Each theoretical perspective examined will have strengths and weaknesses; none will capture the full complexity of most organizations. The major weakness of most systems theories, in the author's opinion, is the assumption that no single individual is crucial to the behavior of any complex system. Systems theories play down or ignore the power of individual free will and leadership. They are based on the notion that the most important factors explaining and predicting organizational behavior are structural and functional variables.

Systems Concepts Help Explain and Predict Public Relations

A number of structural and functional variables can predict and explain public relations. One of the most obvious structural characteristics of an organization is its size, which can be measured in a number of ways, including number of full-time employees, sales or assets. The structure and function of public relations for organizations with large workforces predictably would be different than for smaller organizations because (1) the greater number of employees would require more mass communication among members (for example, more company publications, newsletters, and employee relations activities), and (2) its economic impact would require more outward expressions of social responsibility (for example, more community relations and crisis communication activities).

Another example of the impact of size on the management of public relations programs is presented in Chapter 7. In that chapter, one case study describes a publicity and media relations campaign designed by an agency for a coffee industry trade group. The second case describes another campaign designed by the same agency, only this time it was to handle publicity and media relations for a visit to the United States by the Roman Catholic Pope. While the two campaigns had the same basic purposes—establish and maintain good media relations and generate lots of favorable publicity for the client—the two accounts were dramatically different in terms of size, i.e., number of "critical players" in the client's dominant coalition, budget, media sophistication, and number of markets. Recognizing this difference, the agency structured the campaigns differently. For the smaller account, fewer professionals worked on it and more informal contacts were made with the media. For the larger account, a larger team of professionals was assembled and a formal planning document was prepared. Affectionately called "the bible" by agency people, the planning document was several inches thick and had to meet the guidelines of U.S. Catholic bishops, Vatican officials, and the U.S. Security Service. The Pope's visit required the use of press pools; the coffee account did not. As these examples indicate, the size of an organization (or the client) influences the management of its public relations campaigns.

Professional Roles of a Public Relations Practitioner

Another factor that will affect the management of public relations campaigns is the professional roles assumed by the public relations practitioner. Research indicates that there are two basic roles assumed by practitioners: technician or problem-solver.[29] The research indicates women are more likely to assume the technician's role of providing public relations services such as producing publications, while men are more likely to assume the problem-solving role of asking clients or senior management to rethink or clarify problems and to look for innovative solutions.

There are obvious differences between roles performed by public relations practitioners working within an organization and those performed by practitioners working within a public relations agency. The question is: Do these two types of roles require different management strategies when researching, planning, implementing and evaluating public relations activities? The most likely answers: yes and no.

Yes: there will be more similarities than differences in the way they manage campaigns because management expectations, whether from a set of at-arms-length clients or from a set of close-at-hand colleagues, would be the driving force behind role performance by public relations practitioners in either situation. For example, the frequency with which certain public relations activities are engaged in by these two types of practitioners most likely would be the same, if the organization and need for the public relations campaign were basically the same. Whatever differences there might be between outside counsel and in-house professional public relations roles would depend more on the characteristics of the client or sponsoring organization and the need for the public relations campaign than on individual differences between public relations practitioners.

Or, no: agency and in-house practitioner roles are not the same for equally qualified public relations managers. Compared to in-house public relations specialist practitioners, agency practitioners often do not have as much access to or experience with the client's organization, so they are more likely to engage in more research and planning activities than their in-house counterparts. Agency practitioners often need to know a variety of research and planning strategies suitable for meeting the array of management expectations they experience from their clients. Case studies of agency and in-house public relations practitioners using a variety of planning and research strategies are presented in several chapters. While individual differences in terms of education, gender and work experience do make a difference in the performance of public relations roles, more powerful influences come from an organization's technology, decision-making structure, and core set of management expectations.

Organizational Technology and Internal Structure

If the basic technology and internal structure of an organization can be accurately determined, then predictions can be made about its public relations.[30] Technology is more than just hardware and machinery used within an organization; it is the essential work of the organization. This can range from the very routine (a state agency processing fishing licenses) to the very nonroutine (a hospital treating patients in an emergency room).

The complexity of an organization's technology is reflected in the number of exceptions encountered in making day-to-day decisions within the organization. For example, undoubtedly there are exceptional applications for fishing licenses. Because these exceptional cases and other problems will need to be resolved by managers within the organization, there most likely will be a set of standard operating procedures (SOPs) for managers to use in resolving the problems. In some bureaucracies, these SOPs would be found in manuals; in others, the SOPs would be built into computer programs, "kicking out" exceptions so that they are handled separately. Routine technologies are characterized by standardized rules and regulations. In the case of bureaucracies, the rules are necessary because the organization must handle a tremendous volume of requests for services every day; it's the only efficient way the job can get done on time.

Public information campaigns and employee relations programs for a routine government agency would be different than public relations activities for a more complex organization such as a hospital.

The technology of a hospital is complex because a wide variety of nonroutine and routine decision-making occurs on a daily basis. Within the hospital's emergency room, dramatic rapid-fire decisions are made so often they seem routine; but, this is definitely the area of the hospital where decisions are made hands-on and on a case-by-case basis. Medical staff first perform triage by using established criteria for admitting and initially treating incoming emergency cases. This form of routine decision-making is minor compared to the volume of nonroutine decisions made by the medical staff in the emergency room. Down the hall from the emergency room are excellent examples of routine decision-making. Wherever the "hotel" aspects of the hospital are managed—food preparation, general admissions, or the gift shop, for instance—fairly bureaucratic techniques will be used to make most decisions. The public relations activities of a hospital—community relations, employee relations, patient relations, fund raising, and volunteer services—will reflect the organization's complex technology.

Organizational Scope

Another structural characteristic that helps predict and explain public relations is the scope of the organization, the size and domain of its marketplace. For example, conducting economic development campaigns for two clients—one a major research center with an international reputation, the other a rural, relatively unknown area of the country—would be done differently because while there might be similarities, there would be significant differences. One difference between these two campaigns would be the number of critical publics which thought they might have a stake in the success of the campaign. The greater the scope, size and diversity of the stakeholders, the more likely the client or sponsoring organization is to engage in a greater variety of public relations activities.

Four Basic Organizational Types

An organization's technology, internal decision-making structure, and scope of marketplace have been used to identify four basic types of organizations: traditional, mechanical, organic and mixed mechanical/organic. According to structural functionalism, public relations for these four types of organizations vary in predictable ways.[31]

Traditional Organizations are characterized by small scope and low technological complexity. A good example would be a financially secure family-owned-and-operated department store serving a relatively small market. Decision-making would be centralized through family members. Even though retail sales is a relatively routine set of tasks, decision-making would not be impersonal because the small size of the staff would allow individual attention to customers and employees. Public relations for a traditional organization like this would be minimal. While a full range of public relations activities may be used for various special events and circumstances, the least amount of resources possible would be invested. This minimalist approach to public relations is predictable for traditional organizations primarily because the dominant coalition—in our example, the family—sees the organization as a comfortable, closed system.

Mechanical Organizations are characterized by large scope and low technological complexity. For example, consider an international pizza franchise company. Running an efficient pizza franchise may look busy, but it is clearly routine technology; standardized rules and regulations govern almost all decisions, particularly if the organization prides itself in having each franchise look and operate in the same way, and in having the pizzas made and delivered in the same fashion. The larger the organization, the more emphasis that is likely to be placed on bureaucratic, mechanistic ways of making decisions. Because so many people are involved, the organization is likely to depend on mass communication for much of its internal public relations activities. Because it is sales oriented, the pizza franchise organization would link its public relations closely to its marketing. While the scope of most mechanical organizations is large enough to require fairly sophisticated public relations, their low technological complexity allows reliance on print media and more traditional, "low tech" approaches to public relations.

Organic Organizations are characterized by small scope and high technological complexity. One way to measure the complexity of an organization is to look at the educational level of the employees. The higher the education level of the workforce, the more complex the decision-making within the organization. It takes bright, educated people to make good decisions about complex matters. Small groups of professional lawyers, accountants or doctors would be good examples of organic organizations. A relatively small computer software company that specializes in custom-designed programs for a fairly small set of clients would be another good example. Because the dominant coalition sees the organizations as an open system, public relations is characterized by an emphasis on quick feedback from stakeholders; interpersonal, informal communications wherever possible; and a willingness to use a full range of sophisticated public relations activities.

Mixed Mechanical/Organic Organizations are characterized by large scope and relatively complex decision-making. A modern medical facility owned by a national chain of hospitals would have characteristics of both the mechanistic bureaucracy and the innovative organic organization. Because of their size and scope, these organizations have large numbers of stakeholders who demand fairly sophisticated public relations. Because the hospital has a complicated set of overlapping hierarchies—senior medical staff, health care support staff, and administrative staff—a full range of public relations activities is normally associated with hospital public relations. Because there are so many educated and involved stakeholders, public relations practitioners for mixed mechanical/organic organizations often spend more time researching, planning and evaluating public relations activities than do their counterparts conducting similar campaigns in traditional or mechanical organizations. This means public relations practitioners working for these organizations need more skills in research, planning and evaluation. The practitioner also gains experience asking for, and more often than not receiving, management approvals. The complicated, bureaucratic hierarchy of these types of organizations often works to constrain certain types of public relations activities, making public relations campaigns less innovative than they might be for smaller, more purely organic organizations. Despite these complications, and because the stakes are so high, some of the most challenging, sophisticated and professionally rewarding public relations work is done for large-scale, complex organizations. Dozens of case studies throughout this book will illustrate this point.

Decision-Making Structures

Classifying organizations by decision-making structures offers additional insights into the practice of public relations beyond those gleaned by classifying organizations by type of business (for example, profit-making, not-for-profit; or, government agency, hospital, university, etc.). While public relations activities vary from one type of business to another, within any one type of business several decision-making structures may exist. Consequently, classifying organizations by decision-making structure generates additional predictions and explanations about public relations activities.

External Publics

Another concept from systems theories which helps explain and predict public relations is the predictability of external publics. If management views certain publics as major concerns for the organization, then it is likely that public relations campaigns will be targeted to these publics. And, if the members of the dominant coalition view their environment as turbulent and unpredictable, public relations for these organizations will involve more two-way communication. Two cases presented in Chapter 2 illustrate these points. In one case, an insurance company had to prepare a promotional campaign that their customers would use to persuade customer employees to participate in a benefits program. In another case, a public relations agency had to develop a campaign designed to influence delegates to the Democratic National Convention. The first case involved very predictable, indeed, passive publics. The second case involved very active publics. Faced with very predictable publics, very little research or evaluation was conducted. Faced with very volatile, active publics, much more attention was given by the public relations staff to research and evaluation.

Organizational Environments

An important distinction exists between what really is going on in the environment and what members of the dominant coalition or senior management think is going on. Sometimes, management's perception fits reality; sometimes, it doesn't. Often it is the responsibility of senior public relations managers and outside counselors to double-check management's perception and, if necessary, educate members of the dominant coalition. When public relations professionals are "out of the loop" and not involved in management deliberations, such reality checks cannot be performed. One of the strongest predictors of how an organization will manage its public relations is the collective perception by senior management of what the organization is doing, what it is facing, and why. The ability of members of the dominant coalition to recognize problems varies not only from organization to organization, but also from moment to moment, as various members of the organization are considered in or out of the dominant coalition, depending on the topic or issue being considered.

Organizational Flexibility

The willingness and capability of management to consider alternatives also varies from organization to organization. How problems and opportunities facing the organization are perceived by the dominant coalition will influence such practical, structural matters as how readily management approves public relations plans, the location of the public relations department within the hierarchy, the use of outside counsel, and the salary and status of the public relations practitioners. If the dominant coalition views certain publics as being of more concern than others to the organization, then more public relations activities will be targeted toward these publics. When the perception of top management does not match reality, numerous organizational actions, including public relations, will be inappropriate.

Linkage Between Senior Management and Public Relations Staff

Two closely related factors help predict and explain public relations. One is the frequency of contact public relations professionals have with members of the dominant coalition. The percent of staff time devoted to research and planning will be greater for those organizations that include public relations professionals within the dominant coalition. Closely associated with the practitioner's frequent contact with top management is the location of the public relations department within the hierarchy. Frequency of involvement by public relations professionals with the dominant coalition is positively related to the number of levels of management between the senior public relations professional and the chief executive officer. For example, in Chapter 7, the public relations department of a major grocery store chain revamped the flagship employee publication without having to seek numerous management approvals, because the senior public relations manager was a member of the organization's elite dominant coalition.

In summary, the following system concepts, among others, are logically related to the practice of public relations: the size of an organization, its function and internal decision-making structure, the expected and assumed roles of the public relations managers, the dominant coalition's perception of the environment, and the linkage between public relations practitioners and elite members of the dominant coalition.

SURVEY RESEARCH RESULTS CONFIRM VALUE OF SYSTEMS CONCEPTS

To further investigate specific propositions discussed above, and to examine in greater depth other aspects of public relations, the author conducted a set of mail surveys and personal interviews with a large sample of public relations professionals.[32] Two assumptions were made when designing the research: one, that there is no single best way to engage in public relations; and, two, that different organizations engage in public relations in different ways for a variety of understandable reasons. The purpose of the research was to examine in-depth these reasons.

A sample of more than 400 professional public relations practitioners received the initial survey instrument in the fall of 1988. Members of the sample were selected purposefully, not randomly. Because they constituted a judgmental sample, the survey results cannot be generalized to a larger population, such as all the members listed in the directories of the Public Relations Society of America (PRSA) or the International Association of Business Communicators (IABC).

See Chapter 6 for a more technical explanation of scientifically random and judgmental samples. Suffice it to say here that each type of sample has its strengths and weaknesses. Because it is doubtful that there can ever be a definitive list of all organizations or of all public relations practitioners, properly selected judgmental samples are commonly used for organizational research studies such as those reported here.

More than two-thirds of the sample was made up of members of PRSA and IABC, selected primarily from the Baltimore-Washington, D.C. area, which allowed for relatively inexpensive follow-up interviews that were conducted personally by the author and his assistants. Also, award-winning members of both PRSA and IABC from throughout the United States and Canada were included in the sample. Professional communicators listed in business directories and mass communication graduates of the author's university who were employed in the communication field also participated in the research. More than 140 useable mail surveys were returned in the 1988 survey. The size and diversity of this judgmental sample afforded an excellent opportunity to examine how and why different types of organizations and people engage in such a variety of public relations activities.

Following an initial analysis of the results, more than two dozen personal follow-up interviews were conducted with selected respondents to explore in greater depth the strategies and techniques these practitioners used to research, plan, implement and evaluate their public relations campaigns. A follow-up Delphi survey conducted in 1990 involved more than 80 members of the original sample and other public relations professionals. Both mail questionnaires and personal interviews of selected members of the sample were used in the 1990 study.

The Size of an Organization Does Make a Difference

According to the professionals surveyed, the public relations activities most frequently engaged in are: writing press releases, editing publications, staging special events, and managing employee and community relations. See Table 1.1. Other important activities are: holding press interviews, setting up conferences and meetings, and establishing and updating crisis communication plans (" . . . hoping they're never used," as one professional commented about her crisis plans). Activities less frequently engaged in are: investor relations, consumer affairs, fund raising and holding press conferences.

Percentages presented in Table 1.1 can be used to compare the frequency of public relations activities engaged in by practitioners working for large and small organizations. Public relations agencies were excluded from the sample for this analysis. Organizations with fewer than 125 employees were selected because these organizations would be too small to be true bureaucracies. When the workforce includes more people than any one person reasonably can know on a first-name basis, organizations normally will—even if they don't want to—establish rules and regulations typical of bureaucracies. Because they are dealing with a larger workforce, public relations practitioners working for large-scale organizations engage in more employee relations than do their counterparts in smaller organizations. Also, larger organizations engage more frequently in consumer affairs and community relations, as befits their institutional character.

Large organizations use more mass media for both internal and external public relations. For example, practitioners for large firms spend more time editing and producing publications and print advertisements than do practitioners working for smaller firms. Smaller organizations, often because they lack the institutional clout and slack resources of larger organizations, engage more frequently in staging special events, holding meetings, and trying to raise funds.

Business Functions Predict Public Relations Activities

As Table 1.2 indicates, the function or purpose of an organization makes a big difference in how public relations will be performed. Profit-making organizations engage in more sales promotion and employee relations. Not-for-profit organizations engage in more fund raising. Hospitals and universities are more involved in fund raising than profit-making organizations. In an era of increased public concern about the environment and industrial accidents, government public affairs specialists are as involved in crisis communication planning as are colleagues who work for profit and not-for-profit organizations.

TABLE 1.1:

Frequency of Engaging in Public Relations Activities by Size of Organization.[a]

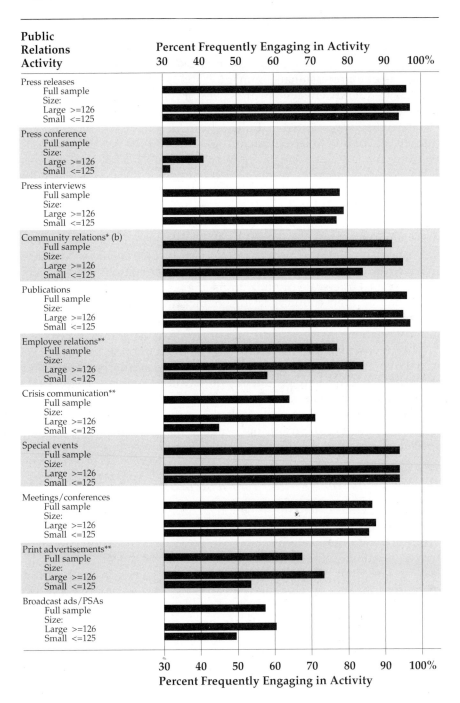

TABLE 1.1 Continued

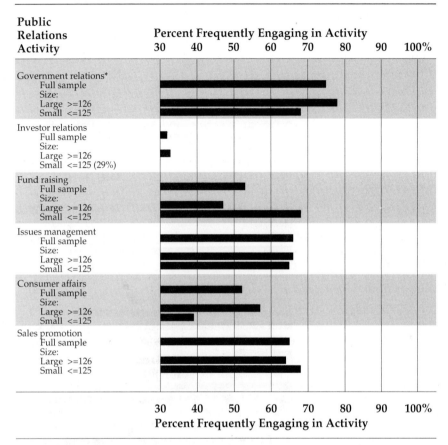

Full sample n = 116
Large organization sample n = 85
Small organization sample n = 31

[a]Percent engaging in activities based on respondents indicating "very frequently" or "sometimes" to four-point scaled question that included "rarely" and "never."

[b]Significance of difference determined by t-test; reported is the probability of difference due to chance: * = .05; ** = .01.

Professionals working for public relations agencies and government public affairs specialists spend more time setting up press conferences and holding press interviews than do their counterparts in industry. Public relations agencies get more directly involved in designing and producing print and broadcast advertisements, including public service announcements, than their colleagues in industry or government.

TABLE 1.2:

Frequency of Engaging in Public Relations Activities by Type of Organization.[a]

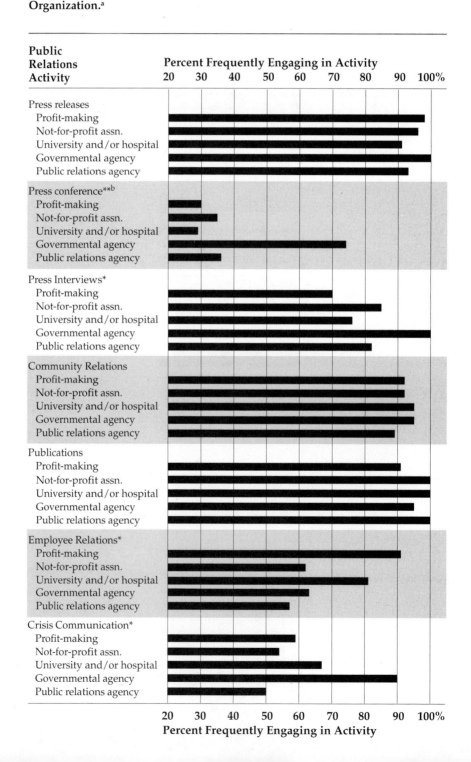

TABLE 1.2 Continued

TABLE 1.2 Continued

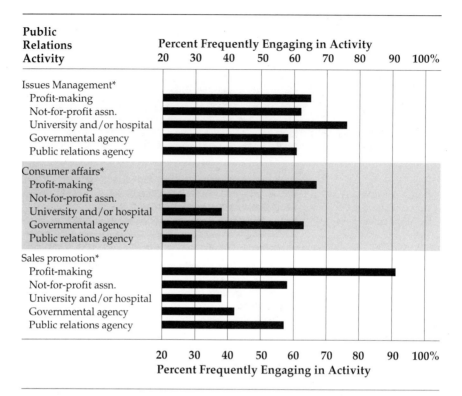

Sample sizes: Profit-making business (n=43)
Not-for-profit association (n=28)
University and/or hospital (n=21)
Governmental agency (n=19)
Public relations agency (n=28)

[a]Percent based on respondents who indicated they engaged in these activities either "very frequently" or "sometimes" to on a four-point scale that included "rarely" and "never."

[b]Significant difference determined by F-test; reported is the probability of difference due to chance: * = .05; ** = .01.

Decision-Making Structures Also Make a Difference

Several factors were used to sort the organizations studied into four different decision-making structures. See Table 1.3. One factor was size, which we already have seen can impact an organization's public relations. Another factor was the number of significant business units within an organization. The fewer divisions, major groupings or profit-centers within an organization, the more centralized the administration. The more significant business units there are within an organization, the more decentralized its management.

Two other factors used to classify the organizations were the educational level of the workforce and the scope of the marketplace. The educational level is indicative of decision-making complexity: the

TABLE 1.3:

Percent Engaging in Public Relations Activities by Type of Organizational Structure[a]

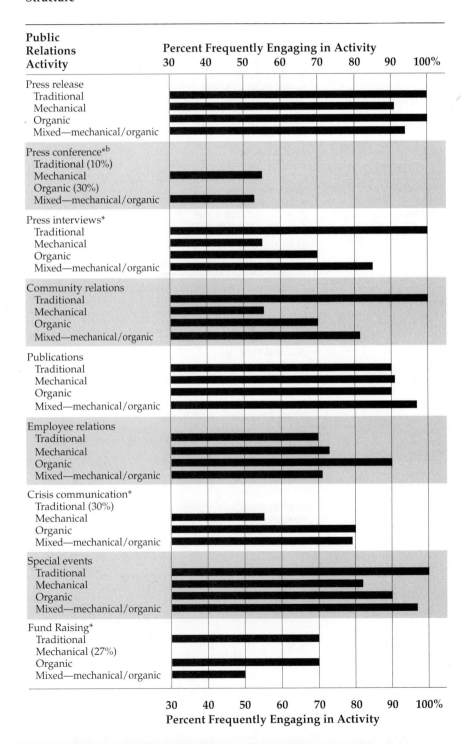

TABLE 1.3 Continued

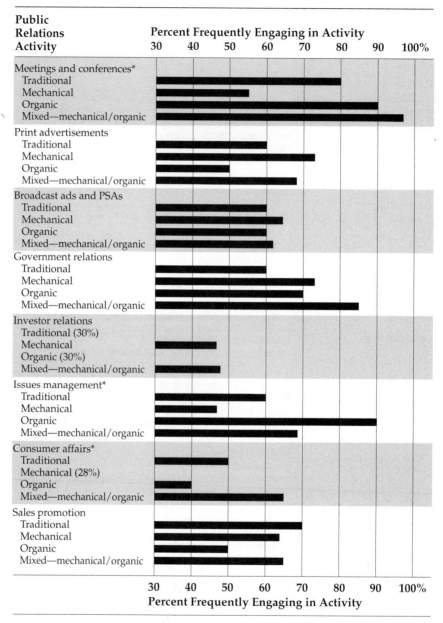

Sample sizes: Traditional (n=10)
 Mechanical (n=11)
 Organic (n=10)
 Mixed—mechanical/organic (n=34)

[a]Percent based on respondents who indicated they engaged in these activities either "very frequently" or "sometimes" to on a four-point scaled that included "rarely" and "never."

[b]Significant difference determined by F-test; reported is the probability of difference due to chance: * = .05; ** = .01.

higher the educational level, the more complex the decision-making. The greater the scope of the marketplace, the greater the scope of the organization's public relations. For example, public relations for a locally-owned restaurant will differ in significant ways from that conducted by an international fast-food chain.

Small, centralized organizations are traditional because they are relatively closed systems using routine decision-making within a local or regional marketplace. From among the organizations surveyed, the following were classified as traditional: a regional bank, a radio station, and a real estate firm.

Mechanical organizations are similar to traditional organizations, only larger, with a broader marketplace. These organizations were classified as mechanical: a grocery store chain, a government printing office, and a major insurance company.

Organic organizations are decentralized, have an educated workforce making complicated decisions, and most often focus on a fairly well-defined marketplace. In this study, a state teachers' association, a community college, and a local credit union were classified as organic.

Mixed mechanical/organic organizations are generally large-scale organizations which may be centralized or decentralized and have a national or international marketplace. In this study, a national association, an international bank, and a major university were classified as mixed mechanical/organic.

Table 1.3 indicates that among the four types of organizations traditional organizations are least likely to engage in press conferences or crisis communication. Mixed mechanical/organic organizations are most likely to engage in meetings and conferences. When compared to mechanical or mixed mechanical/organic organizations, traditional and organic organizations are more likely to engage in fund raising activities. Mechanical organizations are least likely to engage in consumer affairs or issues management.

The significant differences among these four types of organizations indicate that decision-making structures influence the frequency with which public relations activities are engaged in by an organization. Specifically, mixed mechanical/organic organizations will engage more frequently in a greater array of public relations than will traditional, mechanical or organic organizations.

Management's View of the World Predicts Public Relations

The dominant coalition's view of the organization's overall environment—competitors, regulators, customers, stockholders and other significant stakeholders—definitely influences decisions to engage in certain types of public relations activities. Research results presented in Chapter 2 indicate that if members of the dominant coalition view the environment as full of change, the organization will more often engage in community relations and will spend more time editing and producing publications. When the environment is seen as more consistent and predictable, the organization is more likely to engage in employee and investor relations. An even stronger indication of the power of the dominant coalition's perspective to influence public relations is seen in research results presented in Chapter 3, which indicate that if a public is deemed a major concern to the members of the dominant coalition, then it is very likely that there will be a special public relations program targeted toward that public.

Public Relations Linkage to Top Management Is Vital

The distance separating one manager from another can be counted in the number of people separating the two in the formal chain of command. If the manager of public relations has to see the department head and a senior vice president before he can speak to the chief executive, then there are two people—or levels of management—separating these two individuals. The closer the linkage is between the senior public relations manager and the chief executive officer, the more frequent the contact is between the two and the more each is influenced by the other. Research results reported in Chapter 4 indicates that the more closely linked the public relations practitioner is to senior management, the more staff time will be spent evaluating public relations activities, particularly media and employee relations. The more distant the public relations function is from senior management, the more likely public relations is to be involved in sales promotion.

Conclusion: There Is No One Best Way to Manage Public Relations

While a number of important factors which help explain and predict public relations have been discussed in this chapter, it is important to realize that organizations, while they can be described in cold, rational terms, are systems made up of warm, often emotional and, at times, irrational individuals. Like ordinary people, organizations often are too complex for simple descriptions. While a person's weight, education, thought processes, and physical abilities can be measured and observed, the full complexity of any one person remains elusive and unmeasured. Just like people, each organization is unique. The chemistry of people working together to achieve a common goal is difficult to measure; but, it is real, and it affects how organizations are managed.

Three factors which help predict and explain public relations are the size of the organization, its basic purpose, and its decision-making structure. Even more important are the perceptions of top management toward the world in general, and of key stakeholders in particular. The attitudes and opinions of top management are crucial elements in defining an organization's culture—that rich mixture of ideas, symbols, customs and beliefs that summarizes how a group is organized, and that somehow is passed on to each new member of the organization. Consequently, public relations managers who are closely linked to members of top management will be in a better position to influence, and be influenced by, the corporate culture.

ALTERNATIVE THEORETICAL PERSPECTIVES ARE IMPORTANT

In addition to the theoretical perspective of organizations as systems, with its emphasis on functionalism and behaviorism, alternative and perhaps controversial theories will be presented throughout the book that will help further explain and predict public relations. For example, an alternative to the systems-oriented history of public relations presented in this chapter is the critical analysis of the history of public relations by Marvin Olasky. A libertarian conservative, Olasky has focused on how major public and private institutions in society used public relations to establish and maintain a status quo favoring big government and big business, preventing ideal free-market enterprises. His thesis is that "many major corporate public relations leaders have worked diligently to kill free enterprise by promoting big government-big business collaboration."[32] Such a macro-level analysis uses structural functionalism by focusing on the role of public relations in facilitating relationships among economic institutions. Olasky's theory is that the railroad, steel and oil industries used public relations at the end of the nineteenth and beginning of the twentieth century to eliminate competition—all in the name of social responsibility.[33]

The advantage of Olasky's type of analysis is that it focuses on global economic patterns. The major weakness of critical, macro-level theories—the same as with general systems theories—is that the role and power of individuals, especially leaders, are devalued. Using such a critical perspective, the contributions of such important figures in public relations history as Ivy Lee and Arthur Page would be placed in the broader context of the times by explaining that these individuals were responding to the political and economic realities of the times. The assumption of the critical theorists is that economic viability of major systems within the marketplace is a compelling, if not overwhelming, factor that helps predict and explain public relations.

IN SUMMARY . . .

This opening chapter has presented numerous concepts which can be used to explain and predict public relations and organizational behavior. We emphasized, above all, that an organization should be viewed as a system, and that public relations is a subsystem that facilitates relationships and understandings between the organization and its many publics. We pointed out how the image of organizations as living systems has implications for public relations managers. We also acknowledged that critical theorists draw ugly images of public relations practitioners as obsequious functionaries serving base economic interests of major institutions.

We will present these and other images of organizations and public relations throughout this book. The key question remains: What are the images of organizations and public relations within the minds of the members of the dominant coalition? The answers to this question will suggest the working hypotheses of senior management. Knowing the expectations and often unstated theories of the dominant coalition and others will help the practitioner better manage public relations for that organization. This book presents a range of case studies and highlights a number of factors that will help in-house specialists, agency consultants, and independent counselors be more systematic, and ethical, in their analysis and management of public relations programs and campaigns.

Study Questions

1. Agree or disagree with the following statement: utilities and nonprofit associations are more likely to support professional development of public relations managers than banks or government agencies. Explain your answer.
2. How has the development of public relations been related to economic, social, and political developments?
3. How was public relations defined 100 years ago? How is public relations defined today?
4. What is meant when an organization is called a "closed system" or an "open system"?
5. Give three examples of how general systems theories can be used to explain and predict public relations.
6. How do public relations specialists serve as "boundary spanners"?
7. What is structural functionalism, and how does it apply to public relations?
8. What are the two major roles performed by public relations practitioners?
9. Give at least four different examples of organizational technology, and explain how each affects the practice of public relations.
10. How important is the linkage between senior management and the public relations staff? How can this linkage be used to predict or explain the function of public relations?
11. Agree or disagree with the following statement: there is no one best way to manage public relations. Explain your answer by giving at least two examples.
12. How important is management's worldview in explaining and predicting public relations? Give examples of the relationship between management's perceptions and public relations.

Four Mini-Case Studies for Classroom Discussion

The four mini-cases that follow can form the basis of a public relations campaign exercise for out-of-class work. You are encouraged to work in teams to develop a proposal. The proposal may be developed over a several week period, with each week's class discussion and set of exercises focusing on topics related to the proposal.

Instructors may provide special guidelines for the proposal, or students may use the following outline to prepare a 9 or 10 page proposal neatly typed and professionally presented:

1 page	Statement of the problem/situation
1 page	Campaign goals and objectives
1 page	Target public(s) characteristics
1 page	Media characteristics
1–2 pages	Campaign strategies, including research, planning, implementation, and evaluation activities
1 page	Timeline
1 page	Narrative budget
1 page	Cost-benefit analysis
1 page	Summary statement of benefits of campaign

Compare and contrast the four campaign proposals. Discuss the impact of organizational and environmental factors on the management of the public relations campaigns.

. . .
MINI-CASE 1.1:
The Traditional Organization

A local department store, established in the 1930s, has the good fortune of being located on a street where a major shopping mall is also located. This is a family-owned company with 125 employees, most of whom have no more than a high school education or are earning their way through college. The store carries a full line of moderately priced men's and women's clothing, and a modest array of other items found in most department stores. Among the customers, the company has a reputation for quality service and affordable prices. Among the current and potential employees, it has the reputation of being a good place to work for steady wages, but not offering much upward mobility. It's looked upon as a good training ground by young buyers. Too often, the brightest employees see the lack of career advancement potential and leave the company for promotion, often to stores located in the nearby mall. Two months ago, the head of public relations did just that and is now working for a national chain located in the mall.

As a recent college graduate who specialized in public relations, you eagerly accepted the position at the family-owned department store. Your boss, the president's son, has been working for the company for the past twenty years and currently is vice president of marketing. All the company's advertising is performed by an agency which has managed this account for the past twenty-five years. Your job description includes media relations, editing the employee newsletter, staging special events, and community relations.

One major project was being discussed with the former head of public relations when she left: how to deal with the growing crime problem in and around the store. Over the past few years, there has been a steady increase in shoplifting, and an increasing number of cars parked near the store have been broken into. A few months ago, an employee was raped after dark in the parking lot; a suspect has been charged in the crime, and a trial is scheduled to begin in about six months. The vice president tells you that discussions with the former head of public relations did not produce any specific plan, and that you should take this problem on as your first major assignment. In a fatherly way, he tells you the crime problem has taken years to develop and that any public relations solution also will take time. Then, as your new boss, he says he would like a detailed proposal, "with some kind of cost-benefit statement in it," by the end of the week.

Prepare and present this proposal.

. . .

MINI-CASE 1.2:
The Mechanical Organization

Pizzas are one of the healthiest and most popular of fast foods, and you're proud of it because you've been in the business for ten years. You earned your way through college working as a driver and then became assistant store manager for the international pizza franchise company. After graduation, you advanced to the company's regional office in Los Angeles, where you served as director of marketing and public relations. Then, two years ago, you were promoted to vice president of marketing and public relations and joined the headquarters staff in Chicago. Currently, the company employs more than 8,000 full- and part-time workers at more than 400 pizza stores located primarily in North American and European markets. Some of the franchises seat and serve customers in the store; most are take-out and delivery only. All of the stores brag about their speed of delivery and give refunds if pizzas are delivered late. There has been a growing public concern, with opinions expressed on editorial pages and at civic associations, primarily in the United States, that drivers are being unsafe as they speed deliver their pizzas. There have been several automobile accidents nationwide that involved drivers employed by the company, and many of the news reports of these accidents have mentioned the company. The claim is that because most of the company's delivery personnel are young and inexperienced drivers, and because the company has a policy of paying drivers incentives for the total number of pizzas delivered during a shift, the company is responsible. A suit has been filed in civil court against one of the company's drivers, and the suit requests that damages be paid by the driver's insurance company and the pizza company. The suit will be argued before a judge later this year.

In the meantime, you want to mount a public relations campaign designed to deal with this situation. You want to develop a plan that will be implemented at the franchise level. Your staff at headquarters will develop and coordinate regional broadcast and print advertising through the international advertising and public relations agency which handles your account. What you want to produce is a plan of action, and a set of materials (press kits, ideas for special events, coupons, etc.), which can be used by local franchise owners. A significant portion of the cost of the campaign must be paid for by the local franchises, so an essential part of the proposal is a cost-benefit analysis. At the most recent stockholders' meeting, the chairman of the company clarified policy concerning what he called "the speedy, safe delivery of pizzas." He said it was a long-standing position of the company that no driver ever is encouraged to drive in an unsafe manner and that incentives are paid only to drivers who maintain safe, good driving records.

Prepare a complete campaign proposal that you will present for formal review to your staff this week. Your final proposal will be delivered at the next quarterly meeting of the franchise owners, to be held in Chicago next month.

. . .
MINI-CASE 1.3:
The Organic Organization

You are director of marketing and public relations for a software design shop, located in the nation's capital. This relatively young company specializes in writing and producing customized software and computer-assisted video training materials. Most of the clients are small business owners, primarily lawyers, doctors, accountants, association managers and other professionals. Some clients, especially those solely interested in computer-assisted video, are major corporations and government agencies. The five original founders are equal partners in this privately owned enterprise, which was recently profiled in the region's business journal as "one of the busiest and most profitable software shops in town." The owners have focused their energies on regional sales and have not encouraged or sought business elsewhere. In addition to the partners, there are five programmers (and an equal number of part-timers and consultants on-call), five computer system experts, five specialists in video production, five sales people, and ten support staff. At staff meetings you have discussed the possibility of developing a public relations campaign that would address the growing public awareness and concern about computer viruses—the safe-looking but nasty little programs that are embedded into existing programs and later emerge to cause harm to databases and other computer software. Your original idea was to use corporate advertising to position the company as a source of information and innovative ideas about establishing and maintaining virus-free computer environments.

However, before you have had a chance to do anything with your idea, your worst nightmare happens. One of your clients is hit by a computer virus, and your new software is believed to be the source of it. Although the incident makes the business section of the local newspaper, your company is not mentioned in the news story. The senior partners investigate and discover that it is true: there was a virus in the program. By a process of elimination, it was discovered that a part-time programmer may have done it. When confronted with the evidence, the programmer admitted that his section of the program had the virus in it, but he said he had no knowledge of the virus or how it got into the program. While the in-house investigation continues, legal counsel is preparing to file a suit against the part-time programmer. Fortunately, no damage was done to the client's business by the virus; it was only a nuisance. Your company's computer specialists already have removed the virus and enhanced, at no cost, the client's computer system.

In the meantime, you must quickly design and conduct a public relations campaign to deal with the situation. The senior partners want a proposal this week that deals with both the short-term and long-term issues surrounding the computer virus.

. . .

MINI-CASE 1.4:
The Mixed Mechanical/Organic Organization

An inner city hospital was faced with serious problems: crime in the nearby streets was affecting not only employee morale but also the willingness of area doctors and their patients to use the medical facility. For decades, the hospital had a fine reputation, but in recent years, two factors changed the fortunes of the hospital. First, the neighborhood around it changed, with the flight of middle class blacks and whites to suburban areas. An influx of unscrupulous real estate brokers then sold homes to people unable to afford them, foreclosed, and sold them again to others also unable to afford the mortgage payments. Eventually, federal housing authorities and the local newspaper brought the housing scam to light, but the damage already had been done. Second, an influential group of doctors associated with the inner city hospital established a new hospital in the suburbs and took most of their patients to the newer facility. The board of directors of the inner city hospital initially supported the doctors' efforts and discussed plans for joint ownership, but those plans collapsed. Civil suits were considered by the boards of both hospitals, but not pursued. Instead, the inner city board accepted an offer from a national chain of privately-owned hospitals, and the hospital was sold.

Throughout all these years, there has been one public relations director who was responsible for patient, employee, and community relations. The new management group offered the public relations director an early retirement plan which was accepted. The senior administrator of the hospital screened numerous candidates and selected you to be the new director of public relations.

Your mandate: develop a public relations campaign that improves employee morale and increases the willingness of doctors and residents to use the facility. You request and receive authorization to hire immediately an assistant who will be primarily responsible for the employee, patient, and community newsletters. You are told to develop a public relations campaign and budget for the next year and to present it to the board members at their next meeting.

Prepare this campaign proposal.

Recommended Readings

The recommended readings that follow are based on the public relations activities reported in the survey results and listed in Tables 1.1 to 1.3. The recommended readings are articles from DIALOG, one of the world's largest databases. DIALOG is made up of hundreds of separate databases. It includes, for example, all the periodicals in the *Reader's Guide to Periodicals,* all the major daily newspapers, and thousands of other publications.

The reader is encouraged to update the articles listed below by accessing DIALOG either through the services of a librarian or by personal computer. For more information about DIALOG, call 1–800–334–2564.

The reader can access DIALOG through a personal computer by using an appropriate modem, communication software package, and a gateway service such as CompuServe Information Service (CIS). For more information about CIS, call 1–800–848–8199.

Other gateway services to major databases are: NEXIS (1–800–543–6862), EasyNet (1–800–327–9638), and Dow Jones News/Retrieval (1–800–334–2564).

Once DIALOG is reached through a gateway service, the user must present a password and then specify the database(s) within DIALOG to be searched. Next, the user must specify search terms and indicate the type of output—for example, basic citation of article title, name of publication, pages and date; full citation including abstract; or, for some databases, full text.

The cost of the search depends on the amount of time spent on-line conducting the search and producing the output. The cost of the transaction is presented on-line at the end of the search. The cost of the search and listing of basic citations for each of the following sets of readings was approximately $10 in 1990.

With each set of readings is the search term used with the term "public relations" to capture citations from the ABI/INFORM database, accessed through DIALOG. The reader is encouraged to use these search terms when updating the recommended readings.

1. Press Releases

Levy, Ronald N. "Successful techniques of food public relations," *Public Relations Quarterly,* Vol. 36, No. 1, Spring 1991, pp. 36–38.

Adams, William C. "Turn your expert's knowledge into cash," *Public Relations Quarterly,* Vol. 36, No. 1, Spring 1991, pp. 31–33.

Rubin, Maureen. "Avoid truthful but incomplete press releases," *Public Relations Journal,* Vol. 47, No. 3, March 1991, pp. 26–27.

White, Alix. "Press releases: Don't keep a dog and then do your own barking," *Business Marketing Digest* (UK), Vol. 16, No. 1, First Quarter 1991, pp. 111–114.

Francis, Chris. "Why throw away the chance of free publicity?" *Business Marketing Digest* (UK) Vol. 16, No. 1, First Quarter 1991, pp. 107–110.

2. Press Conferences

Lehrman, Celia K. "Videoconferencing comes down to earth," *Public Relations Journal*, Vol. 45, No. 4, April 1989, pp. 23–27.

Elsberry, Richard B. "It doesn't have to be a dud: Your new product press conference," *Business Marketing*, Vol. 73, No. 10, October 1988, pp. 96–101.

Hogtgan, Karen. "Public relations: A change of pitch," *Marketing* (UK), Vol. 25, No. 5, May 1986, pp. 16–17.

Shawe, Jan. "Public relations: A place to add pace," *Marketing* (UK), Vol. 25, No. 5, May 1986, pp. 47–48.

3. Interviews

Zetlin, Minda. "Meet the press—and survive!" *Management Review*, Vol. 77, No. 12, December 1988, pp. 35–40.

Melymuka, Kathleen. "Close encounters of the fourth-estate kind," *CEO*, Vol. 1, No. 8, July 1988, pp. 14–20.

Howards, Carole M. "How to say 'no' without alienating reporters," *Public Relations Quarterly*, Vol. 31, No. 4, Winter 1986/87, pp. 25–28.

4. Community Relations

Katella, Kathleen M. "Outstanding chain store managers: Community relations," *Progressive Grocer*, Vol. 70, No. 4, April 1991, pp. 56–60.

Wold, Marjorie. "Outstanding independents: Community relations," *Progressive Grocer*, Vol. 70, No. 3, March 1991, pp. 58–64.

Johnson, Donald E. "CEO interview: Martin H. Diamond—award showcases programs," *Health Care Strategic Management*, Vol. 9, No. 3, March 1991, pp. 8–11.

"Utility system calms fears, trains teens," *Electrical World*, Vol. 205, No. 2, February 1991, pp. 21–22.

Hathaway, Fred. G. "Franchises juggle national name with local idiosyncrasies," *Commercial Lending Review*, Vol. 6, No. 1, Winter 1990–1991, pp. 68–72.

5. Publications

Johnson, Donald E. "Communicate your hospital's quality by writing, speaking," *Health Care Strategic Management*, Vol. 9, No. 4, April 1991, pp. 2–3.

Wylie, Kenneth. "Broadening pr's reach," *Business Marketing*, Vol. 76, No. 1, January 1991, pp. 18–19.

Geddie, Tom. "Write face-to-face," *Communication World*, Vol. 7, No. 9, September 1990, pp. 30–32.

Thaler-Carter, Ruth E. "The winner's edge—'cascading management,' attention to employee needs spell success for these Gold Quill recipients," *Communication World*, Vol. 7, No. 12, 1990, pp. 6–8.

"AT&T revamps employee communications to emphasize 'new direction' for 1990," *Public Relations Journal*, Vol. 46, No. 11, November 1990, p. 26.

6. Employee Relations

McKeand, Patrick J. *Public Relations Journal*, Vol. 46, No. 11, November 1990, pp. 24–26.

Pujol, Juan L., and Edward Tudanger. "Employee relations: A vision for excellence," *HRMagazine,* Vol. 35, No. 6, June 1990, pp. 112–116.

"Once the ESOP is established, then what?" *Employee Benefit Plan Review,* Vol. 44, No. 11, May 1990, pp. 39–42.

Shell, Adam. " 'Channel 12' delivers company news into employees' living rooms," *Public Relations Journal,* Vol. 46, No. 23, March 1990, pp. 10–11.

Murino, Catherine, Stephanie Lawrence, and Allan Halcrow. "What benefit is communication?" *Personnel Journal,* Vol. 69, No. 2, February 1990, pp. 64–69.

7. Employee Communication

"Ron Martin, ABC, discusses IABC and the profession," *Communication World,* Vol. 7, No. 8, August 1990, pp. 14–17.

Frieden, Joyce. "Getting your flexible benefits program under way," *Business & Health,* Vol. 7, No. 10, October 1989, pp. 44–47.

Drennan, David. "Are you getting through?" *Management Today* (UK), August 1989, pp. 70–72.

Cayer, Shirley. "Suppliers 'on stage,' on target at Allen-Brady," *Purchasing,* Vol. 107, No. 2, July 20, 1989, pp. 100a10–100a15.

"Restructuring: Good and bad news for employee communications," *Public Relations Journal,* Vol. 45, No. 4, April 1989, pp. 6–10.

8. Employee Benefits

Fitzsimmons, David J. "From paternalism to partnership," *Journal of Compensation & Benefits,* Vol. 6, No. 5, March-April, 1991, pp. 48–51.

Rogerwick, Edward A. "A strategic approach to communication management," *Journal of Compensation & Benefits,* Vol. 6, No. 6, January-February 1991, pp. 59–61.

Phillips, Kenneth F. and Ruth M. Bramson. "Packaging work/family benefits to create maximum impact," *Compensation & Benefits Management,* Vol. 7, No. 1, Autumn 1990, pp. 86–87.

Siegelman, Stanley. "Communicating the bad news," *Business & Health,* Vol. 8, No. 11, November 1990, pp. 12–19.

Lynons, Nancy J. and Bruce G. Posner. "Executive compensation: Q & A in hard times," *Inc.,* Vol. 12, No. 11, November 1990, pp. 80–87.

9. Management of Crisis

Gordon, Judy A. "Meeting the challenge of risk communication," *Public Relations Journal,* Vol 47, No. 1, January 1991, pp. 28–29.

Lukaszewski, James E. "Good news about bad news," *Security Management,* Vol. 34, No. 12, December 1990, pp. 60–67.

Nash, Tom. "Tales of the unexpected," *Director* (UK), Vol. 43, No. 8, March 1990, pp. 52–56.

Barton, Laurence. "Crisis management: Selecting communications strategy," *Management Decision* (UK), Vol. 28, No. 6, 1990, pp. 5–8.

O'Rouke, A. Desmond. "Anatomy of a disaster," *Agribusiness,* Vol. 6, No. 5, September 1990, pp. 417–424.

10. Crisis Communication

Harrison, E. Bruce. "Lemons and litigation," *Public Relations Journal,* Vol. 42, No. 6, June 1986, pp. 20–24.

Leavy, Dennis P. "Crisis communications: A planning checklist," *Credit*, Vol. 12, No. 2, March/April 1986, p. 13.

11. Special Events

Korenchen, James. "Generating leads through public relations," *Cellular Business*, Vol. 8, No. 3, March 1991, pp. 68–71.

Fry, Susan L. "Reaching Hispanic publics with special events," *Public Relations Journal*, Vol. 47, No. 2, February 1991, pp. 12–14.

Martin, Don. "Motivating employees with the 4Rs," *American Agent & Broker*, Vol. 62, No. 10, October 1990, pp. 20–21.

Cipalla, Rita. "When staging public events, the Smithsonian reaches for the moon," *Communication World*, Vol. 7, No. 10, October 1990, pp. 28–31.

Penzer, Erika. "Incentives marketing: Measuring special events." *Incentive*, Vol. 164, No. 10, October 1990, pp. 162–166.

12. Meetings

Welch, Andrea. "The lowdown on the hoedown," *Successful Meetings*, Vol. 39, No. 11, October 1990, pp. 63–68.

MacLean, Daniel. "Communication: Rocky roads," *Successful Meetings*, Vol. 39, No. 9, August 1990, pp. 101–102.

Borchardt, John K. "Improve in-house communications," *Chemical Engineering*, Vol. 97, No. 3, March 1990, pp. 135–138.

Rand, Lawrence A. "If you're such a great merchant, why can't you sell on Wall Street?" *Retail Control*, Vol. 58, No. 2, February 1990, pp. 15–18.

Raimondi, Ann. "Speaking out: A troubled future for the professional planner?" *Successful Meetings*, Vol. 38, No. 12, November 1989, pp. 45–46.

13. Conferences

Brookes, Adam. "Confer in peace," *Management Today* (UK), August 1990, pp. 75–80.

Winter, Grant. "Improving broadcast news conferences," *Public Relations Journal*, Vol. 46, No. 7, July 1990, pp. 25–26.

Darwent, Charles. "Changing the conventions," *Management Today* (UK), September 1989, pp. 113–117.

Lehrman, Celia K. "Videoconferencing comes down to earth," *Public Relations Journal*, Vol. 45, No. 4, April 1989, pp. 23–27.

14. Newspaper Advertising

Kerwin, Ann M. "Reaching out to advertisers," *Editor & Publisher*, Vol. 124, No. 13, March 30, 1991, pp. 16–17.

Marsh, Winston. "Getting your name in the papers," *Australian Accountant*, Vol. 60, No. 3, April 1990, pp. 34–39.

Boscarino, Joseph A. "Hospital wellness centers: Strategic implementation, marketing, and management," *Health Care Management Review*, Vol. 14, No. 2, Spring 1989, pp. 24–29.

15. Magazine Advertising

Neal, Craig. "Hooking your share of the national advertising pie," *Folio: The Magazine for Magazine Management*, Vol. 19, No. 12, December 1990, pp. 127–128.

Cappo, Joe, Fred Danzig, and Scott Donaton. "Value-added—the new medium," *Advertising Age*, Vol. 61, No. 15, April 1990, pp. s36–s38.

Sabolik, Mary, James F. Plante, and Bill Patterson. "Media relations: What's news?" *Public Relations Journal*, Vol. 45, No. 11, November 1989, pp. 14–22.

16. Television Advertising

Levin, Gary. "PR gives new life to rejected TV ads," *Advertising Age*, Vol. 61, No. 42, October 1990, p. 76.

Plachta, Joan. "Public relations/corporate communications: A survival guide to sponsorships," *Marketing* (UK), September 27, 1990, pp. 31–34.

Seecunda, Eugene. "Is TV addicted to drug company pr?" *Business & Society Review*, No. 73, Spring 1990, pp. 11–14.

17. Radio Advertising

Pasley, Kathleen A. "Cause-related marketing bolsters image," *National Underwriter*, Vol 94, No. 2/34, August 20, 1990, pp. 13, 38–39.

Gates, Michael. "Gulf oil: Pumping up sales," *Incentives*, Vol. 164, No. 4, April 1990, pp. 115–116.

Lewis, Jan. "How to write corporate ads," *Public Relations Journal*, Vol. 44, No. 9, September 1988, pp. 45–46.

18. Public Service Announcements

Taylor, William H. "Insurer risk classification under gun," *National Underwriter*, Vol. 91, No. 34, August 24, 1987, pp. 8–10.

Davids, Meryl. "Doing well by doing good," *Public Relations Journal*, Vol. 43, No. 7, July 1987, pp. 17–21.

Bivins, Thomas H. "Applying ethical theory to public relations," *Journal of Business Ethics* (Netherlands), Vol. 6, No. 3, April 1987, pp. 195–200.

19. Consumer Advertising

Liesse, Julie. "Kodak brand calls retreat in the battery war," *Advertising Age*, Vol. 61, No. 43, October 15, 1990, pp. 3, 69.

Bogren, Peter A. "Put the quality in before the message goes out," *MarketFacts*, Vol. 9, No. 1, January/February 1990, pp. 26–29, 32–42.

Greer, Thomas V., and Michael J. Chattalas. "The role of the promotion fund of the International Coffee Agreement," *International Marketing Review* (UK), Vol. 6, No. 3, 1989, pp. 47–61.

20. Government Relations

Kiener, Robert. "Business and government: Beyond the lobby," *World*, Vol. 24, No. 3, 1990, pp. 29–35.

James, Michael. "Corporate communications: Positive vibes," *Marketing* (UK), June 21, 1990, pp. 29–30.

Newman, Rebecca. "The lobbying coalition that wasn't," *Public Relations Journal*, Vol. 46, No. 5, May 1990, pp. 40, 39.

21. Lobbying

Rubin, Bennett. "Campaign opens door to safety issue," *Public Relations Journal*, Vol. 47, No. 2, February 1991, pp. 28–29.

Mallarid, Vincent. "Good exposure," *American Printer*, Vol. 206, No. 2, November 1990, pp. 54–57.

Choate, Pat. "Political advantage: Japan's campaign for America," *Harvard Business Review*, Vol. 68, No. 5, September/October 1990, pp. 87–103.

22. Investor Relations

Lowengard, Mary. "Business as not-so-usual," *Institutional Investor*, Vol. 25, No. 3, March 1991, pp. 146.

St. Goar, Jinny. "What price investor relations?" *Across the Board*, Vol. 28, No. 3, March 1991, pp. 36–39.

Calise, Angela K. "Investor relations importance soaring," *National Underwriter*, Vol. 95, No. 5, February 1991, pp. 57–61.

Galant, Debbie. "Investor relations: Battling the bear," *Institutional Investor*, Vol. 25, No. 1, January 1991, p. 139.

Karp, Richard. "The six most improved IR programs," *Institutional Investor*, Vol. 24, No. 10, August 1990, pp. 78–83.

23. Fund Raising

Harrison, Thomas A. "Six PR trends that will shape your future," *Nonprofit World*, Vol. 9, No. 2, March/April 1991, pp. 21–23.

Bailey, Willard. "Writing and development—'You just can't raise money for free care'," *Fund Raising Management*, Vol. 21, No. 13, March 1991, pp. 65, 72.

Gerhart, G. David, and Michael Bexilla. "Fund-raising success takes teamwork," *Fund Raising Management*, Vol. 21, No. 12, February 1991, pp. 64, 66.

Johnson, Eugene M., and Andrew Laviano. "Telemarketing and fundraising: Ethical and legal issues," *Nonprofit World*, Vol. 9, No. 1, January/February 1991, pp. 34–35.

24. Issues Management

Hing, Amy. "Issues management and influencing decisions," *Practical Manager* (Australia), Vol. 11, No. 1, Summer 1990, pp. 42–44.

Eisenstadt, David. "Measuring public relations effectiveness," *Sales & Marketing Management in Canada*, Vol. 31, No. 6, June 1990, pp. 22–23.

Oliver, William H. "The quality revolution: Internal first, externally second," *Vital Speeches*, Vol. 56, No. 20, August 1, 1990, pp. 625–628.

Stout, Daniel A. "Internal process of corporate advocacy," *Public Relations Review*, Vol. 16, No. 1, Spring 1990, pp. 52–56.

Nelson, Richard Alana. "Bias versus fairness: The social utility of issues management," *Public Relations Review*, Vol. 16, No. 1, Spring 1990, pp. 25–32.

25. Strategic Management

Clapham, Stephen E., and Charles R. Schwenk. "Self-serving attributions, managerial cognition, and company performance," *Strategic Management Journal* (UK), Vol. 12, No. 3, March 1991, pp. 219–229.

Halperin, Fred. "How valuable is excellence in communication?" *Executive Speeches*, Vol. 5, No. 5, December 1990, pp. 19–21.

Grunig, James E. "Theory and practice of interactive media relations," *Public Relations Quarterly*, Vol. 35, No. 3, Fall 1990, pp. 18–23.

Craig, S. Russell. "How to enhance customer connections," *Journal of Business Strategy*, Vol. 11, No. 4, July/August 1990, pp. 22–26.

Band, William. "Benchmark your performance for continuous improvement," *Sales & Marketing Management in Canada*, Vol. 31, No. 5, May 1990, pp. 36–38.

26. Consumer Affairs

Huyse, Luc, and Stephan Parmentier. "Decoding codes: The dialogue between consumers and suppliers through codes of conduct in the European community," *Journal of Consumer Policy* (Netherlands), Vol. 13, No. 3, September 1990, pp. 253–272.

Bunn, David, Gail Feenstra, Lori Lynch, and Robert Sommer. "Consumer acceptance of cosmetically imperfect produce," *Journal of Consumer Affairs*, Vol. 214, No. 2, Winter 1990, pp. 268–279.

Sherlock, John J. "Sensational service: Wow your members by exceeding their expectations," *Association Management*, Vol. 42, No. 11, November 1990, pp. 68–72.

Grant, Ruth A. "Joining service and quality strategies," *Trustee*, Vol. 43, No. 10, October 1990, p. 18.

27. Sales Promotion

Stanton, Edward M. "PR's future is here: Worldwide, integrated communications," *Public Relations Quarterly*, Vol. 36, No. 1, Spring 1991, pp. 46–47.

Nakra, Prema. "The changing role of public relations in marketing communications," *Public Relations Quarterly*, Vol. 36, No. 1, Spring 1991, pp. 42–45.

Tortorici, Anthony J. "Maximizing communication through horizontal and vertical orchestration," *Public Relations Quarterly*, Vol. 36, No. 1, Spring 1991, pp. 20–22.

McElnea, Jeffrey K. "We've reached the crossroads: Which path will we take?" *Marketing News*, Vol. 25, No. 8, April 15, 1991, p. 22.

Hastings, Hunter. "Introducing new products without advertising," *Journal of Consumer Marketing*, Vol. 7, No. 3, Summer 1990, pp. 19–25.

Endnotes

1. Two textbooks with excellent chapters on the history of public relations are: Scott M. Cutlip, Allen H. Center, and Glen M. Broom, *Effective Public Relations*, 6th edition (Englewood Cliffs, N.J.; Prentice-Hall, 1985); Dennis Wilcox, Phillip H. Ault, and Warren K. Agee, *Public Relations: Strategies and Tactics*, 2nd edition (New York: Harper and Row, 1989).

2. According to the Encyclopaedia Britannica (Chicago: William Benton, Publishers, 1979, 15th edition, vol. 15, pg 39): "The systematic, detached, and deliberate analysis of propaganda, in the West, at least, may have begun in Athens about 500 B.C., as the study of rhetoric (Greek: 'the technique of orators')."

3. Nevins, Allan, "The Constitution makers and the public: 1785–1790," *Public Relations Review*, vol. 4, Fall, 1978, pp. 5–16.

4. Nixon, Richard, "By what honorific in the year 2000?," essay published in *The Washington Times*, January 31, 1990.

5. Bernays, Edward L., "Emergence of the public relations counsel: Principles and recollections," *The Business History Review*, vol. 45, Autumn, 1971, pp. 296–316.

6. Boulding, Kenneth, *Ecodynamics: A New Theory of Societal Evolution* (Beverly Hills, CA: Sage, 1978).

7. For an excellent explanation and critique of Social Darwinism, see Charles Perrow, *Complex Organizations: A Critical Essay*, 3rd edition (New York: Random House, 1986, pp. 55–56).

8. Taylor, Frederick W., *Principles of Scientific Management* (New York: Harper & Row, 1911).

9. Barnard, Chester, *The Functions of the Executive,* (Cambridge, MA: Harvard University Press, 1938).

10. Tedlow, Richard S., *Keeping the Corporate Image: Public Relations and Business, 1900–1950* (Greenwich, Conn.: JAI Press, 1979) pp. 25–59.

11. Hiebert, Ray Eldon, *Courtier to the Crowd, the Story of Ivy Lee and the Development of Public Relations* (Ames, IA: Iowa State University Press, 1966).

12. Roethlisberger, F. J., and William J. Dickson, *Management and the Worker* (Cambridge, MA: Harvard University Press, 1947).

13. Kahn, Thomas, *The Structure of Scientific Revolutions* (Chicago: University of Chicago Press, 1962); Robert L. Heath and Richard Alan Nelson, *Issues Management* (Beverly Hills, CA: Sage, 1986). p. 51.

14. Paisley, William, "Public communication campaigns: The American experience," in *Public Communication Campaigns* 2nd edition, edited by Ronald E. Rice and Charles K. Atkin (Newbury Park, CA: Sage, 1989) pp. 16–17.

15. Lawrence, Paul R., and Jay W. Lorsch, *Organization and Environment* (Cambridge, MA: Harvard University Press, 1967; and Charles Perrow, "A framework for comparative organizational analysis," *American Sociological Review,* vol. 32, April, 1967, pp. 194–208.

16. March, James G., and Herbert A. Simon, *Organizations* (New York: John Wiley, 1958).

17. Cutlip, Scott M., "Public relations in American Society," *Public Relations Review,* vol. 6, Spring, 1980, pp. 3–17.

18. Emery, Fred E., and E. L. Trist, "The causal texture of organizational environments," *Human Relations,* vol. 18, 1965, pp. 21–32; and, same authors, *Toward a Social Ecology* (London: Tavistock, 1973).

19. Hannan, Michael T., and John Freeman, "The population ecology of organizations," *American Journal of Sociology* vol. 82, March, 1977, pp. 929–966; and, Michael Micklin and Harvey Choldin, editors, *Sociological Human Ecology: Contemporary Issues and Applications* (Boulder, Colo: Westview Press, 1984).

20. Suchman, Edward A., "Action for what? A critique of evaluative research," in *Evaluating Action Program,* edited by Carol H. Weiss (Boston, Mass.: Allyn and Bacon, 1972); PRSA Task Force, "Public relations body of knowledge task force report," *Public Relations Review* 14, 1, Spring, 1988, p. 30.

21. Perrow, Charles, *Complex Organizations: A Critical Essay,* particularly the chapter on the environment (New York: Random House, 1986, pp. 178–218.

22. Walker, Albert, "The evolution of public relations according to Cutlip and Center," *Public Relations Review,* Summer, 1986, pp. 28–31; see also, Scott M. Cutlip, Allen H. Center, and Glen M. Broom, *Effective Public Relations,* 6th edition (Englewood Cliffs, N.J.; Prentice-Hall, 1985, p. 4).

23. von Bertalanffy, L., *General Systems Theory: Foundations, Development, Applications* (New York: Braziller, 1968); Russell L. Ackoff and Fred E. Emery, *On Purposeful Systems,* (Chicago: Aldine, 1972); and, Glen M. Broom, "Public relations and systems theory: Functional and historicist causal models," paper presented to the International Communication Association, Chicago, 1986.

24. Boulding, *op.cit.*

25. Morgan, Gareth, *Images of Organizations,* especially the chapter on organizations as organisms (Beverly Hills, CA: Sage, 1986, pp. 39–76).

26. Thompson, James D., *Organizations in Action,* (New York: McGraw-Hill, 1967).

27. Aronoff, Craig, and Otis Baskin, *Public Relations: The Profession and the Practice,* especially chapter 4, 2nd edition (Dubuque, Iowa: William C. Brown Publishers, 1986); and William P. Ehling, "PR administration, management science, and purposive systems," *Public Relations Review,* vol. 1, Fall, 1975, pp. 15–54.

28. Prior-Miller, Marcia, "Four major social scientific theories and their value to the public relations researcher, in *Public Relations Theory,* edited by Carl H. Botan and Vincent Hazleton, Jr., (Hillsdale, NJ: Lawrence Erlbaum, 1989).

29. Broom, Glen M., and David M. Dozier, "Advancement for public relations role models," *Public Relations Review,* vol. 12, Spring, 1986, pp. 37–56.

30. Theus, Kathryn T., "Organizational ideology, structure and communication efficacy: A causal analysis," paper presented to the Association of Education in Journalism and Mass Communication, Washington, D.C., 1989.

31. Grunig, Larissa S., "Power in the public relations department as a function of values, professionalism, and organizational structure," paper presented at the 16th annual communication conference at Howard University, Washington, D.C., 1987.

32. McElreath, Mark P., "Using systems concepts to explain and predict public relations: management perceptions are keys," paper presented at the Association for Education in Journalism and Mass Communication, August, 1990.

33. Olasky, Marvin N., *Corporate Public Relations: A New Historical Perspective* (Hissdale, NH: Lawrence Erlbaum, 1987).

CHAPTER TWO

How to Define Problems and Opportunities, and Develop Measurable Goals and Objectives

. . . . . .

*I*n *the small conference room on the tenth floor, Steve stood next to a flip chart at the end of the long table. It was mid-morning, and he was thirty minutes into the meeting. His staff of three public relations professionals and two other managers from outside the department had agreed to meet for two hours this morning to work out plans for a public relations campaign designed to facilitate the introduction of the corporation's new policy on smoking: in six months, all cigarette and tobacco smoking in the building would be banned, and a new outdoor pavilion was to be provided for smokers to use during breaks and meal times. The agenda for the first part of the meeting, Steve had announced, was to identify all of the forces working for and against the introduction of this new policy. He had filled three flip chart sheets with his colleagues' ideas and had taped the sheets onto a nearby wall. Steve carefully removed another sheet from the flip chart, taped it on the wall near the others, and called for another idea: "So, what other forces are working against us?"*

"It's the older folks. Some of our most senior people still smoke. They're not going to like it," Steve's assistant public relations manager said. On the flip chart Steve wrote, "Some senior people still smoke. Next?" he said.

"The vending machines, the company with the cigarette vending machines," the director of human resources said. "I think we should get all those machines out of the building."

Steve liked one part of the statement but wanted to delay considering another part, so he said, "Okay, I'll write 'vending companies' up here, but let's wait until the next hour to talk about getting rid of the machines or negotiating a new contract with the vendors. Let's stay focused for now on forces working against us. We'll think of solutions after we've done this." Steve turned to his other colleagues, "Next?"

"Not everyone in the union is convinced, even though it was agreed to in the new contract," the head of health services commented. *"Some employees are going to complain about it to their union reps,"* she said.

Steve wrote, *"Complaints through union reps,"* on the flip chart. *"Okay. Is that all? Any other ideas about forces working against us?"*

"Yes," his assistant said. *"The coffee shop people. They have a separate rental contract with the building's owners. They're not affected by the smoking ban. I'm not sure if they will be with us or against us on this."*

"I agree," Steve said. *"Until we know, let's list them on both sides. He wrote "Coffee shop owners" at the bottom of the last page, removed the sheet from the flip chart and taped it on the wall. Then, on a new sheet, he wrote, "Forces working for us," and under it, "Coffee Shop Owners." Turning to his colleagues, he said, "Okay. Now, let's list some more forces working in our favor."*

Before the hour was over, more than three dozen favorable and unfavorable forces were listed on flip chart pages. Steve went to the erasable board on one side of the room and rewrote the lists, combining and collapsing certain ideas so his colleagues could better see the conflicting and parallel forces affecting the campaign. He summarized by naming the publics associated with each of the forces, and he pointed out that some of the publics aligned themselves together, while other publics were more isolated.

Shifting the focus of the meeting, he said, "Now let's talk about targeting our campaign to these people. Let's talk about solutions. What do you recommend?" He sat down at the end of the conference table and listened, confident that the discussion this morning would address important, practical campaign issues.

. . .

WHAT ARE PROBLEMS, OPPORTUNITIES, GOALS AND OBJECTIVES?

As this vignette illustrates, an effective manager knows how to set the agenda for what others will think about. Managers do not necessarily try to decide how others should think about something, but they select those topics or aspects of the situation that should be considered. Often, the manager does this by asking crucial questions: Is this situation a problem or an opportunity? Are we part of the problem or part of the solution? Do we act now or wait until we know more facts? Do we make all these decisions ourselves or bring in others? Can we put some of these issues off for a while? What happens if we don't do anything? How will we know we have made the right decision? Once we make a decision, who do we need to convince that we are right? Is this the best decision we can make? What are our options?

If organizations operated as logically as computers, then defining problems and opportunities, and developing goals and objectives, would be rational and simple matters of assessing facts and drawing conclusions. But while managers strive to be as rational as possible, they usually do not have enough information to make ideal decisions. Consequently, most decisions within an organization will be less than ideal; they will be "satisficing" decisions which are appropriate given the circumstances and amount of information available at the time the decisions are made.[1] Effective managers know both when to take risks and how to make judgments based on intuition and less-than-perfect information. Effective managers know how to define problems and opportunities, because that is the essential work of a manager. Effective managers do not avoid problems; they deal with them. As the sign by the desk of one public relations manager reads: "I eat problems for breakfast. What can I do for you today?"

Problems

The word problem comes from the Greek word meaning "to throw forward." The logical extension of the idea is that throwing something forward means someone has to catch it. A problem is something to be solved. In math, a problem is a statement of something to do. The flip side of a problem is a goal statement. To catch something is a goal. To solve a problem is a goal.

Defining problems and opportunities is logically linked to goals and objectives. How problems are defined, and how people think about defining problems, strongly influences their choice of solutions. If, after discussions, they don't consider it a problem but an opportunity, that's a significant shift in attitude which will permeate all other decisions about the situation. Unfortunately, many discussions of problems too quickly shift to talk of solutions, and the full range of possible solutions are not considered because the problem has not yet been defined completely. Too often, there is not enough group discussion. Someone in the group will say, "The problem is . . ." and immediately someone else will say, "Well, what we should do about it is . . . ," and the group's focus shifts to solutions. One of the strategies to be discussed in this chapter is the deliberate delay of discussion of solutions until the full ramifications of the problem, or opportunity, are understood.

Opportunities

Two individuals looking at the same situation could each define it differently, as a problem or an opportunity, depending on how they defined the circumstances. An opportunity can be defined as a favorable circumstance—a chance to attain a goal, to advance or make progress. Opportunities are occasions when an advantage can be made of a situation. Problems are looked upon as unfavorable circumstances.

How someone does or does not take advantage of a situation is an ethical issue. Someone who takes advantage of opportunities with little regard for ethical principles is an opportunist. An ethical manager is not an opportunist. A professional public relations manager knows how to define problems and opportunities in ways that generate ethical solutions. Ethical dilemmas in public relations will be discussed in greater detail in Chapters 9 and 10.

The function of management is to establish goals—to point out the place or places toward which the organization is going. Goals are end points toward which effort is directed. An important strategy in achieving higher order goals is to establish and clearly spell out mid-level and lower-order goals and objectives.

Objectives

Some people say goals and objectives are one and the same. In certain ways, they are. But, in this book, a clear distinction will be made between goals and objectives. Goals are relatively abstract and may be difficult to quantify—for example, "We need to increase our sales." Objectives are more concrete statements of goals and are measurable—for example, "We need to increase our sales by ten percent." An objective is something that can be documented; it's factual and observable, especially by scientific means. Any one goal can have a series of objectives related to it—for example, "Our objective this month is to increase sales by two percent; and next month, by three percent; and the following month, by four percent; and so on, until we reach our goal." A set of goals is achieved only by achieving a subset of interrelated objectives, even if those objectives are not clearly stated or articulated. Therefore, an objective is a strategic step along the way toward achieving a desired goal.

It is also possible for an organization to have both official and unofficial goals and objectives. Complex organizations will have scores of official goals and hundreds, if not thousands, of related official objectives. But, there also will be unofficial goals and objectives. For example, the official, publicly stated goal may have been to establish a new program within the corporation, while the unofficial goal was to provide a safe "pasture" for a soon-to-retire senior executive. Hidden agenda abound in organizational life and sometimes dramatically affect problem definition and goal-setting processes.

Process and Outcome Goals

There are two basic types of goals: process and outcomes. *Process goals* describe means, the processes used before and during the public relations campaign. It is critical that managers monitor process goals so that appropriate adjustments can be made during the planning, production and early stages of the campaign. An example of a process goal for a campaign using direct mail would be receiving on time from the printer 10,000 brochures ready to be mailed. *Outcome goals* are the desired ends toward which a campaign is aimed. Outcome goals are useful for evaluating the overall impact of a program. An example of an outcome goal for a lobbying campaign would be passage of favorable legislation.

Because most discussions about problems and opportunities quickly become discussions about goals and objectives, an effective manager knows how to direct a group discussion so that clear distinctions are made. Without a solid understanding of a problem or opportunity, it is unlikely that appropriate goals and objectives will be established. Effective public relations managers know how to ask probing questions which make it easier for others to see the connection between problems and opportunities, and between goals and objectives.

DETERMINING WHAT'S RIGHT AND WHAT'S WRONG WITH THE SITUATION

The first time public relations practitioners encounter an ethical dilemma when managing a new public relations program and campaign is when they try to define the problem or opportunity confronting their client or employer. To do this, they must determine what is right and what is wrong about a situation—which is, in fact, a very good definition of ethics. More detailed definitions and explanations of ethics will be presented in Chapters 9 and 10. Here, let us define ethics in two ways: 1) it is a branch of philosophy that is concerned with ethical and moral reasoning; and 2) it is, for an individual, a small group, an organization, or society, the set of criteria by which decisions are made not only about what is right and wrong, but also about what is good and bad.

Defining a public relations situation always generates a discussion about what is right, wrong, good, and bad, because all public relations situations involve two or more publics, each of whom has a unique perspective on the situation. Because there may be two or more valid points of view, it is doubtful that any one stakeholder's definition of the situation would be comprehensive and accurate.[2] Consequently, the ethical dilemma is: what is the right way to "frame" the situation in terms of rightness and wrongness?

For example, consider the situation of restricting the sale and use of tobacco products. Here is how a variety of stakeholders could define the situation:

Stakeholder	Definition of situation
Tobacco grower	It is a legitimate product, with federal crop subsidies and agricultural services; therefore, tobacco should be allowed to be grown and marketed as any other legal product in this country.
Tobacco industry	Corporate free speech, including marketing and public relations, should not be restricted for corporations producing legal products and services; to produce and use a legal product is a basic right.
Tobacco smoker	An adult's right to free choice should not be restricted; if adults want to consume a legal product, they should be allowed to do so.
Passive smoker	My life is being affected by the choices made by smokers to smoke in my presence; therefore, my rights and the rights of smokers need to be balanced and fairly judged together.
Lung association	Medical costs of treating lung and smoking-related diseases, plus the number of lives lost each year to these diseases, outweigh the negatives caused by limiting the rights of smokers, tobacco growers, and the tobacco industry.
Government health officials	Lawmakers have decided tobacco is a legal product; therefore, research and public education about tobacco and the health risks of smoking are our only legitimate roles.

Notice how these various points of view can be used to contrast one public against another: the tobacco smokers vs. the lung association; the tobacco grower vs. the government health official; etc. When defining public relations situations, decision-makers often ascribe points of view to different publics in terms of "us" versus "them," or one public versus another public, because it helps them clarify the various positions and better understand the situation. It is common for practitioners to frame the issues not only as one public versus another public, but also as "good guys" versus "bad guys." Whichever set of decision-makers is able to establish the criteria by which others determine who are the good guys and who are the bad guys has effectively and advantageously framed the issue.[3] For example, the coalition of like-minded stakeholders in the tobacco situation which is able to convince the most number of legislators, consumers, and taxpayers of the rightness of their position—and the wrong-headed, bad ways of the opposition—will "win" the public debate about tobacco and smoking.

Defining the situation as something that needs to be changed means whatever public relations program or campaign is developed to effect these changes must infringe on the rights of those who like the status quo. Even if the decision is to resist changing the current situation—to maintain the status quo—the public relations program or campaign will be designed to offset pressures from individuals and publics working for change. Whenever rights conflict like this, there are ethical dilemmas. Is it a win-lose situation? A win-win situation? Is compromise possible? Will one set of rights prevail over another? How will the public relations program or campaign be justified to those who think it is unnecessary or, worse yet, unethical? How will the various stakeholders' points of view be taken into account when describing the situation?

Within any public relations situation, there will be a dominant coalition of decision-makers—individuals, publics and organizations—which will be in a position to answer most, if not all, of these questions; they will frame the issues and, by so doing, define the problem. Knowing the values, principles and loyalties of the dominant coalition helps to explain and predict how they will frame issues and define problems.[4] (More information about how values, principles and loyalties are used in ethical decision-making will be presented in Chapters 9 and 10.)

DOMINANT COALITION'S VIEW OF THE WORLD SETS THE AGENDA

When confronted with a problem, Japanese managers are known to spend a great deal of time analyzing circumstances before making a decision about a possible solution. Faced with a similar problem, U.S. managers would be more likely to try out a variety of solutions and only reexamine the problem if initial solutions did not work.[5] Such differences in management styles exist not only between national cultures but also between corporate cultures. Indeed, even within the same corporation, dramatic differences often exist between the ways in which various members of the dominant coalition define problems and generate solutions.

Knowing how the members of the dominant coalition perceive problems and opportunities helps to explain and predict communication behavior. For example, if the President of the United States were to call for new taxes, he would capture the headlines of the major media and set the public's agenda; people would talk about what the President said because it would be prominently displayed in the media. Leaders do not necessarily tell people what specifically to think about a subject, but by gaining access to the public through the media, leaders are able to focus people's topics of conversation.[6] The President's "bully pulpit" is an example of a leader being able to influence the communication behavior of individuals and organizations, including the media.

Similarly, in corporations and organizations, leaders are in positions to influence the topics of conversation. The larger the organization, the more likely it is that the leader will set the agenda by using internal mass media, such as policy manuals, special memoranda, news bulletins or company publications.

If members of the dominant coalition view a certain issue as a problem, they are more likely to engage in communication that will influence others within the organization. There is a rippling effect throughout the organization as opinion leaders express their concerns. People do not communicate in a vacuum nor do they communicate without a reason. The research of James Grunig and his associates indicates that if people perceive something as a problem and if they think they may be in a position to do something about the situation, then they are more likely to engage in communication.[7] Leaders are in powerful positions so that once they have recognized and identified problems, they can communicate their perspective on this information to others. Effective leaders know that they must first make others recognize the problem as being relevant and important, and then make people think that something practical can be done about it. When people both recognize a problem and believe a solution can be found, they will be open to communication. They'll say, "Let's talk about it." If a person either does not recognize a problem as a major concern, or does not think anything can be done to solve a problem, the possibility of communication will be closed. The conversation is over before it begins.

The problem-recognition ability of people is related to the amount of information and knowledge the people have about a situation. For example, if a person is uncertain about the effects of passive smoking but works around a number of people who do smoke, that person will be eager to talk to others or to read about the effects of passive smoking. On the other hand, a person who is convinced that passive smoking is not harmful, or who doesn't care if it is, will not be bothered by working around others who smoke and will not communicate a great deal with others or read or listen to media reports about passive smoking.

Organizations, like people, are not likely to communicate about something unless the members of their dominant coalitions see the relevance to the organization and the possibility of doing something about the situation. For example, organizations which are highly constrained by regulations and public policies and do not see potential taxes as affecting their business will not be likely to engage in any unusual public relations activities. On the other hand, fast-growing companies in an unregulated industry that see taxes as a major threat are likely to engage in a range of public relations activities designed to garner public support for changes in the tax laws.

Because they perceive too many constraints and have limited expectations about changing their environments, some organizations engage primarily in one-way communication with their publics. According to Grunig, traditional publicity and one-way communication roles are engaged in by organizations with a certain management mindset or world view.[8] They think the organization is always right. They think publics must be "sold" the organization's position before the publics will cooperate. Members of the organization's dominant coalition view themselves as "us" versus "them," the external publics. These types of organizations have an insular, closed-system perspective. They value efficiency more than innovation. They are conservative and consider change undesirable. They believe in a centralized authority structure, and their culture emphasizes tradition for the sake of tradition.

According to Grunig, organizations likely to support genuine two-way public relations would have worldviews that assume that communication leads to understanding. Managers would recognize that their organizations, as systems, are more than the sum of their parts; that there is a special chemistry among the members of their organization. They would see their organizations as open systems that freely exchange information among all stakeholders. They would see the desirability of stable sets of relationships but recognize that they don't want the status quo to become permanent; they want to create a moving equilibrium. They would stress equality, autonomy, and decentralized management structures. They would place more emphasis on innovation than on tradition. They would consider conflict best resolved through negotiation and compromise. And, they would encourage, rather than discourage, interest groups.

Effective public relations managers learn how to accurately assess the attitudes and opinions of the dominant coalition. They know that how the leadership of an organization views the world strongly indicates how they will address and resolve public relations problems. As will be discussed in the next section, the attitudes and opinions of top management predict and explain not only how problems and opportunities are defined but also how goals and objectives for public relations campaigns are developed.

. . .

CASE 2.1:

District of Columbia Statehood Campaign

One year before the 1988 presidential election, the District of Columbia Statehood Commission issued a Request for Proposal (RFP) that called for a campaign "to provide public relations support and educational outreach" for the Commission, which was established at the District of Columbia

Results of the DC statehood campaign. Reprinted with permission of David Apter and Associates.

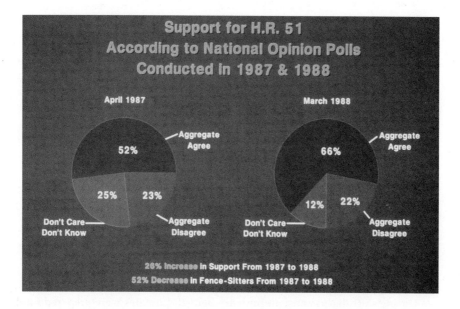

Constitutional Convention "to advocate, educate, and promote D.C. statehood locally and nationally." The Commission, which convened at least once a month, was composed of twenty-four part-time commissioners—three from each of the eight wards of the District. The RFP called for proposals from "District of Columbia public relations firms" that would include a workplan outlining the services to be delivered, objectives, periodic milestones and a timetable, including a detailed description of staff resources. The RFP also stated "unnecessarily elaborate brochures or other presentations beyond those sufficient to present a complete and effective response to this solicitation are not desired and may be construed as an indication of the offeror's lack of cost consciousness." Specifically, the Commission's RFP called for:

1. Further implementing its local educational program;
2. Creating and implementing a minimum of two major and four minor media events;
3. Preparing and disseminating press releases, editorials, op-ed pieces, letters to the editor, and video news releases;
4. Outreaching to appropriate columnists and editorial boards;
5. Monitoring media coverage; and,
6. Developing distinctive, original and effective programs to further the Commission's purposes.

Because the Commission received federal funds, it was prevented from engaging in lobbying activities. This meant that a public relations campaign for the Commission could not include such activities as direct mail to, or personal contact with, members of Congress. The Commission legally could engage in public information and education campaigns.

Here is how the seven-person agency won the contract:

1. Although the head of the agency knew that several other proposals would be submitted to the Commission, he felt confident his agency would prepare the winning proposal because his agency already was doing work for the Commission. In fact, some of the activities requested in the RFP were a continuation of services currently being provided by the agency, such as preparing press releases and managing press conferences for the Commission. For more than a year, the Commission had granted a number of short-term contracts to his agency which had allowed the Commission to engage in a limited national public relations campaign that was in progress at the time the RFP was circulated.
2. The head of the agency met with two senior members of the Commission and the Commission's legal counsel to discuss the proposed campaign. From this discussion, the head of the agency estimated that a budget of approximately $250,000 for an 18-month campaign would be available.
3. The head of the agency and others on his staff talked with politicians and political analysts to determine the best way to increase public awareness of the D.C. statehood issue. It was determined that local news coverage, grassroots networks, and national public opinion polls would all be helpful.
4. During staff discussions, preliminary budget estimates were prepared for a range of different activities. It was determined that there were insufficient funds for advertising. Limited campaign funds required using standard publicity techniques: special events, press releases, and other media relations activities.
5. The head of the agency prepared an initial draft of the proposal that included a statement of the problem, a set of goals, an outline of services to be provided, timetables and a budget. The key goals were to generate as much publicity as possible so that delegates attending the Democratic National Convention would pass a resolution in favor of D.C. statehood and presidential candidates would address the issue.
6. Several days were spent in staff discussions, breaking down individual activities, and collecting cost estimates so that an accurate budget could be constructed of both production and administrative costs.
7. The final proposal met all specifications in the 12-page RFP. It was submitted on time by hand to the designated member of the Commission. A month later, the contract was awarded.

After winning the contract, the agency implemented its campaign by engaging in the following activities:

1. Commissioned a national opinion poll to measure public awareness of D.C. statehood issues;
2. Established a nationwide toll-free number for people to call with questions concerning D.C. statehood;
3. Coordinated the creation of a D.C. Statehood Coalition comprised of various groups interested in the statehood issue;
4. Coordinated and publicized media events planned around major holidays or celebrations, such as "Mend the crack in the Liberty Bell," for the

opening ceremonies of the Constitutional bicentennial in Philadelphia; a memorial to D.C. war dead who "died defending a democracy in which they did not fully share," for a Memorial Day event at the Vietnam Veteran's Memorial; and, staging an event in front of the U.S.S.R. Embassy on Soviet Constitution Day that emphasized the irony of the U.S. denying equal representation for the citizens of the nation's capital.
5. Coordinated D.C. statehood booths at area fairs and festivals;
6. Designed and distributed a D.C. Statehood Coalition press kit; wrote and distributed press releases treating statehood-related matters;
7. Held editorial board meetings with newspapers;
8. Distributed op-ed pieces and letters to the editors;
9. Coordinated outreach to appropriate columnists;
10. Wrote and distributed sample feature stories about statehood;
11. Monitored media coverage;
12. Commissioned the printing of collateral materials;
13. Coordinated the implementation of a two-week educational effort in seven states just prior to the Democratic National Convention; and,
14. Prior to the national conventions of both political parties, commissioned a second national poll asking the same questions about public awareness of D.C. statehood issues that were asked in the first national poll.

Because the agency conducted two national polls—one at the beginning and one near the end of the campaign—there was solid, scientific evidence of their campaign's effectiveness. More details about how these two surveys were conducted will be presented in Chapter 6. While the data generated from the surveys provided excellent evidence that specific objectives were met, that was not the reason for conducting the surveys. The agency's primary rationale for the surveys was the generation of press releases that could be localized to various media markets, particularly highlighting public opinion in the home districts of delegates to the Democratic National Convention. Convincing evidence of the campaign's effectiveness was the strong endorsement by the Democratic Party and its presidential candidate of statehood for the District of Columbia. For campaign excellence, the agency won an award from the International Association of Business Communicators.

CASE 2.2:

"Quality of Service" Campaign

Baltimore Gas and Electric (BG&E), one of the nation's largest—and its oldest—utilities, had an excellent reputation for both service and commitment to its customers. With more than two dozen professional communicators on staff who were specialists in dealing with both internal and external public relations, the publicly owned corporation was highly sensitive to changes in its environment. Responding to the potential of government deregulations that would encourage competition by allowing utilities to generate and sell power to other companies and to offer additional services to their customers, BG&E senior management recognized that they had to make some strategic changes in how the organization operated in an increasingly competitive market. With local utility rates still being controlled by a state public service commission, management realized that they were going to have to improve employee productivity and the organization's quality of service to customers, if they were going to increase profits. Management's resolve to improve quality of service was reinforced when the results of a nationwide public opinion poll conducted by the electric industry trade association indicated public trust and confidence in utility companies was decreasing. The survey showed that the public wanted more reliable service and enhanced billing effectiveness.

A senior vice president of the company discussed the survey results with the manager of customer relations and asked him to develop a set of criteria by which the company's quality of service to customers could be monitored. BG&E had a formal set of goals which was regularly updated and published for all employees, along with standard operating procedures and related manuals. The vice president indicated he wanted to include the new set of Quality of Service criteria in the next revised edition of the corporate goals, which was to be published in six months.

With this mandate from senior management, the manager of customer relations decided to present the issue as an assignment to the corporate-wide Customer Planning Group, which he chaired. The group, comprised of members of management from various divisions within the company, was responsible for forecasting trends and developing recommendations for corporate policies that would affect customer relations.

The manager of customer relations wrote a memorandum, attaching a copy of the survey results, to the members of the planning group, "to shape their thinking about these issues." His memo noted that the survey's two major indicators—service reliability and billing effectiveness—should be included in the proposed new set of criteria. Based on suggestions from the vice president, the manager of customer relations suggested that these additional criteria be considered: corporate image, appliance sales and service, industrial/commercial service, and stockholder relations.

Under normal circumstances, the committee met every other month. Because the vice president wanted the criteria developed in six months, it was decided that there would be twice-monthly meetings over a five-month period. These were the steps the manager of customer relations took, through this special committee, to better define the problem and develop measurable goals and objectives:

1. The first set of meetings reached consensus on six major areas of concern: service reliability, bill effectiveness, corporate image, appliance sales and service, industrial/commercial service, and stockholder relations. No special small group techniques were used to facilitate the group's consensus. They met once to discuss the vice president's mandate, and once to discuss in greater detail how to implement the mandate. Following each meeting, the manager of customer relations wrote a memo summarizing the meeting and setting the agenda for the next meeting.
2. The committee developed specific measurable targets within each of the six areas of concern by preparing draft documents and circulating them among committee members. The drafts were reviewed, revised and recirculated.

3. Eventually, within three months, the iterations evolved into a consensus document approved by senior management; an agreement was reached to measure twenty-four objectives, unevenly spread over the six major areas of concern.
4. The committee recommended that the twenty-four objectives, which they called "targets," be introduced to the employees through an appropriate public relations campaign. The committee also recommended that only after careful study should the targets be included as measures of work unit productivity or individual performance.
5. The manager of customer relations and the manager of corporate communications, who served on the Customer Planning Group, and his staff, developed a public relations campaign to introduce the new "Quality of Service to Customers and Stockholders" goal. It focused on three levels:
    a. Corporate-wide activities:
        1) Quarterly communication meeting of top 250 managers in the company, addressed by CEO, included discussion of Quality of Service goal.
        2) Bulletin boards uniformly displayed, within each department, information about Quality of Service goal.
        3) "Infoline," a telephone message service for employees, included messages about the Quality of Service goal.
        4) Features in monthly and quarterly publications discussed Quality of Service goal.
        5) Executive speeches at service club dinners included remarks about Quality of Service.
        6) Special videotape about Quality of Service goal was produced for playback within departments.
        7) Presentations at annual meeting of stockholders included discussion of Quality of Service; it was also mentioned in the annual report.
        8) Tie-ins were made with corporate advertising.
    b. Managerial level: Quality of Service goal and targets discussed with department managers in staff meetings.
    c. Employee level: Employees encouraged to use the "Good Neighbor" telephone line, a special phone number established and advertised by the company for employees to report customer complaints which might be given to the employees by friends, neighbors, and acquaintances. Prior to the campaign, approximately 50 calls to Good Neighbor line were made yearly by employees; after campaign, goal was set at 315. After one year of the campaign, approximately 525 calls by employees were made. A new goal of 750 calls was set, with the ideal of having all 9,000 employees make at least one call a year to the Good Neighbor telephone service.
6. A special monthly report was prepared by the manager of customer relations. This report, titled "Corporate Performance Goal Three: Quality of Service to Customers and Stockholders," was distributed to managers who were members of the Customer Planning Group. The external and internal indicators of Quality of Service Goal performance were reviewed quarterly with all managers and officers of the company. This report,

prepared by the manager of customer relations, was titled "Quarterly Quality of Service." It included statistics, representative samples of customer compliments and criticisms, and copies of news articles.

SIMILARITIES AND DIFFERENCES BETWEEN THE CASE STUDIES

These two cases share a number of similarities. Both campaigns were sophisticated, large-scale operations. A significant amount of time and money was spent on each. The senior public relations practitioners in both cases were seasoned professionals who managed the campaigns smoothly. The sponsors of both campaigns were large bureaucracies, each with its own set of red tape and standard operating procedures; yet, both organizations responded flexibly to the unusual demands put upon them. Both campaigns were focused on narrowly defined publics. The gas and electric company focused its campaign on employees. The D.C. Statehood Commission campaign focused on public education.

There were also significant differences between the campaigns. One, aimed at external publics, was developed by a small agency working for an organization funded by taxpayers. The other, aimed at internal publics, was developed in-house by a private corporation with quasi-public responsibilities. The sponsors of the public education campaign for the government agency had a worldview that supported two-way asymmetrical public relations, which can be described as unbalanced communication between perceived unequals.[9] They conducted surveys to gather feedback from target audiences primarily because they wanted to use the information to reinforce existing beliefs that the organization was right and that the public needed to be convinced of it.

The worldview of senior management of the gas and electric utility was more supportive of two-way symmetrical public relations, which can be described as balanced communication between perceived equals.[10] They encouraged a consensus-building process within the company when developing the new set of Quality of Service goals, and they institutionalized new ways to gather reliable feedback from customers and stockholders.

IDENTIFYING PROBLEMS AND SETTING GOALS ARE BASIC PROCESSES

Because each organization has its own corporate culture, organizations often have unique approaches to identifying problems and opportunities and to developing goals and objectives. Yet, despite these differences, most organizations share a remarkable number of commonalities in how they make decisions. Management specialist Gareth Morgan points out that there are striking similarities among people who work for large organizations throughout the world, because people are participating in decision-making processes influenced by similar structural, economic and political factors.[11] Mid-level managers in a large organization in Moscow, or Toronto, or Mexico City, or Beijing, or anywhere else in the world, experience many common decision-making situations. Two of the most common decision-making processes within organizations are: defining problems and opportunities, and developing goals and objectives.

For public relations managers, these are the basic steps in defining problems and opportunities and developing goals and objectives; the first two are interchangeable:

1. Recognize key publics and stakeholders.
2. Explore knowledge, gather information.
3. Identify priorities, place situation in context.
4. Generate possible solutions, specify outcome goals.
5. Select a specific solution, specify process goals.
6. Acknowledge (sometimes in writing) the relationships among campaign activities, strategies and outcome goals.
7. Implement campaign and evaluate process goals.
8. Implement campaign and evaluate outcome goals.

1. Recognize key publics and stakeholders. Break down "general public" into specific target publics.

    In Case 2.1, the key publics were identified by the head of the agency in discussion with his own staff, the client, politicians and others involved in the D.C. statehood issue. In Case 2.2, three levels of employees were identified as key publics by the Customer Planning Group and the public relations staff. Chapter 3 discusses in greater detail how to define key publics.

2. Explore knowledge, gather information.

    In Case 2.1, the head of the public relations agency had a long-standing relationship with the client and agreed with them about the D.C. statehood issues. To convince both the general public and target publics, the agency conducted a national poll to document public opinions about D.C. statehood. In Case 2.2, the national survey conducted by the electric industry association provided ample evidence to top management of the need to establish a set of objectives to measure the quality of service to customers and stockholders. See Chapter 6 for more information about how to conduct qualitative and quantitative research.

3. Identify priorities, place the situation in context. Discuss both short-term and long-term implications for the organization. Recognize how key publics perceive the situation and acknowledge the worldview and assumptions of critical members of the dominant coalition.

In Case 2.1, a close prior relationship between the head of the agency and members of the D.C. Statehood Commission meant that he was, in fact, a member of the commission's dominant coalition. Together, they recognized the uphill battle that had to be fought to gain statehood for the District of Columbia; they knew they were in the minority and had a lot of people to convince. In Case 2.2, the members of the Customer Planning Group represented a cross section of the corporation. The iterative process they went through to develop and approve drafts of the specific objectives allowed others within the company to express both short-term and long-term concerns.

4. Generate possible solutions, specify outcome goals. Remember: goal statements should be the flip sides of problem statements. After determining appropriate actions to take, figure out several ways to measure the impact of those actions; these are the desired outcomes.

In Case 2.1, the public relations agency knew that the ultimate goal was Democratic Party delegate votes on the D.C. statehood plank, and that lots of favorable publicity was the key. There was no requirement by the D.C. Commission for the agency to spend any specific portion of the budget on evaluation; research was done primarily for the sake of the publicity that survey results would generate. The agency regularly collected news clippings and monitored broadcast coverage. In Case 2.2, the senior members of management knew that customer satisfaction based on job performance was the key and that employee acceptance of the new goal and set of objectives was crucial. To facilitate employee understanding and acceptance, they involved lots of people in the development of the goal and objectives.

5. Select a specific solution, specify process goals. Explain in greater detail the activities planned for the campaign. Break down activities into manageable tasks and assign people appropriate responsibilities. Determine costs and timetables for completing each task.

In Case 2.1, the RFP from the D.C. Statehood Commission specified a number of activities that needed to be performed by the public relations agency. The head of the agency and his staff generated several additional activities and, together, determined a budget and timetable for the campaign. In Case 2.2, there were two sets of activities: developing the Quality of Service goal and its twenty-four objectives; and conducting a public relations campaign in support of the goal. For both sets of activities, the principal managers charged with developing budgets and timetables served on the Customer Planning Group, the committee responsible for overseeing the campaign.

6. Acknowledge (sometimes in writing) the relationships among specific activities, strategies and outcome goals. Remember: during difficult budget discussions, funds for activities acknowledged to be closely linked to outcome goals will be maintained or increased; whereas, funds for activities perceived as loosely linked to outcome goals may be reduced or eliminated. Sometimes powerful statements of relationships between activities and goals may be expressed as benefit statements in this form: if we engage in X, then we will get Y.

   In Case 2.1, the public relations agency's proposal, as requested in the RFP, contained a list of services to be provided. In Case 2.2, the assumption made in developing the twenty-four objectives was that reports based on these performance measures would influence future job performance. It also was assumed that the process of setting the goal and determining the objectives would influence the job performance of participating managers and their employees.

7. Implement the campaign, evaluate process goals. Expect to make mid-course corrections during a public relations campaign.

   In Case 2.1, the public relations agency made a variety of changes in plans in response to changes in the political environment and in response to media coverage. In Case 2.2, after the initial set of twenty-four objectives was approved and in place, the reactions of department managers to monthly progress reports suggested additions and modifications to the original twenty-four objectives; these changes were made.

8. Implement the campaign, evaluate outcome goals. To improve chances for success, set mid-range achievable goals.

   In Case 2.1, the short-term goals of the campaign were achieved, but the long-term goal of statehood for the District of Columbia remained; consequently, the need for an effective public relations campaign was ongoing. In Case 2.2, the use of the quarterly progress reports and discussions about incorporating the Quality of Service objectives into individual job performance and work unit productivity measures indicated that the goal had been institutionalized. Certain components of the public relations campaign—such as awards programs and items in company publications—were ongoing, designed to maintain employee interest and understanding of the Quality of Service goal.

MAJOR FACTORS AFFECT PROBLEM DEFINITION AND GOAL SETTING

These two case studies illustrate a number of factors that influence the processes of defining problems and opportunities and developing measurable goals and objectives. The views of the client or senior management toward the problem or opportunity are crucial to understanding or predicting how the organization will act in any given situation. The closeness of the senior public relations practitioners to the dominant coalition helps predict and explain how and why organizations define problems/opportunities and do or do not develop measurable goals and objectives.

The potential and actual impact of the problem or opportunity on the organization also will predict and explain how many resources in terms of dollars and staff hours will be devoted to the campaign, including the initial time spent clarifying the problem and, later, developing goals and objectives. The organization's familiarity and experience with similar problems and opportunities also will influence how it goes about problem definition and goal setting. The more experience the organization has, the fewer resources it will spend planning. In Chapter 4, there will be more discussions of planning for routine and nonroutine events.

The expertise and experience of the public relations practitioner also can influence these processes. Less experienced managers than those illustrated in the two cases in this chapter might not have been as sensitive to the expectations of others or have been as capable in dealing comfortably with the complexities of the campaigns.

SURVEY RESEARCH RESULTS SUPPORT PREDICTIONS

The survey conducted by the author, and explained in detail in Chapter 1, asked public relations professionals whether members of the dominant coalition viewed "competitors, regulators, customers, stockholders and significant others" as being full of change or as being predictable. They also were asked to indicate the frequency with which their organizations engaged in certain types of public relations activities. See Table 2.1.

Two of the most significant results presented in Table 2.1 are: 1) if an organization's top management views its principal publics as being predictable, then the organization will engage more frequently in government relations and fund-raising activities, and 2) if top management views its principal publics as being full of change, then the organization will engage more frequently in a wide range of public relations activities, including employee relations, consumer affairs, and crisis communication.

TABLE 2.1:

Percent Engaging in Public Relations Activities by Dominant Coalition's View of External Publics.[a]

Public Relations Activities	Dominant Coalition's View of Overall Environment: Competitors, Regulators, Customers, Stockholders and Significant Others.		
	Full of Change (n = 58)	Predictable (n = 33)	Significant Difference[b]
Press release	98%	97%	
Press conference	46	46	
Press interviews	83	82	
Community relations	97	94	*
Publications	98	94	*
Employee relations	83	73	**
Crisis communication	74	67	**
Special events	95	97	*
Meetings/conferences	90	79	**
Print advertisements	68	58	**
Broadcast ads/PSAs	58	49	**
Government relations	75	88	**
Investor relations	30	30	
Fund raising	44	64	***
Issues management	68	64	*
Consumer affairs	54	46	**
Sales promotion	65	58	**

(a) Percent engaging in public relations activities based on respondents indicating either "very frequently" or "sometimes" to four-point scaled question that included "rarely" and "never."

(b) Significance of difference determined by t-tests based on four-point scale; reported is the probability of difference due to chance: * = .05; ** = .01; and, *** = .001.

The main conclusion from this set of survey results is that the dominant coalition's view of key publics definitely will influence the frequency with which the organization engages in different types of public relations activities targeted toward these publics. The effective public relations manager will be sensitive to how top management views key publics.

HOW TO DEVELOP THEORY-BASED GOALS AND OBJECTIVES

Public relations campaigns are theory-based, even when practitioners managing the campaigns do not know the definition of "theory." Public relations managers design campaigns to have an impact, even though they might say half jokingly, "Whether it does or not is another question." Professionals assume there is a relationship between their efforts and expected outcomes. That assumption is a theory.

TABLE 2.2:

Types of Theoretical Concepts in Public Relations

Nonvariables	Variables
Public	Public's level of knowledge
Organizational action	Organization's frequency of advocacy advertising
Communication	The degree of exposure to a message

A theory is a statement of relationship between two or more concepts that helps explain or predict a phenomenon.[12] If the theory is scientific, it must be a statement about the observable world that can be documented, verified, or falsified. A theory-based public relations campaign is one where you can state:

> "If we do this kind of activity, we can expect to get this kind of reaction."
>
> "If we increase our media buys in radio, we will penetrate the market better."
>
> "Because these people want this information, when we give it to them, they are going to consider it, act on it, and appreciate that we gave them the information."

Public relations managers know they have developed a theory-based public relations campaign or program when they can make testable statements of relationships between communication activities and expected results.

BUILDING ACTION-ORIENTED THEORIES

Action-oriented theories are not abstractions created mysteriously out of vague concepts. Theoretical statements can be constructed by writing sentences that contain appropriate clauses or concepts that are connected with verbs.

Theories are made out of two types of concepts: nonvariables and variables. Look at Table 2.2. Nonvariables are concepts such as "public," or "organizational action," or "communication." Variables are concepts such as "the public's level of knowledge," and "an organization's emphasis on advocacy advertising," or "the degree of exposure to a message." Nonvariables are categories that describe things in either/or terms: things either fit into a category or they don't; an

TABLE 2.3:

Types of Theoretical Statements in Public Relations

Either/or statements	Public relations is a management function.
	There is no one best way to manage an organization; there is no one best way to engage in public relations.
	If a person is highly involved in a situation, then that person will appreciate information about that situation.
Continuous statements	The more local news in a press release, the more likely that release will be used by the local media.
	Increasing the frequency of exposure will increase the public's level of knowledge.
	If you increase—by training—an employee's awareness of problems affecting the company, then you will increase that person's appreciation for company-related information.

individual is either in a public or not; an organization either commits some action or it does not; one is either engaged in communication or one is not.

Nonvariable concepts are useful, but you can build more useful theories with variables. For example, using the nonvariable concepts in Table 2.3, the following theoretical statements are possible:

"The public will be influenced by that communication."

"This organizational action will influence the public."

Both are scientific theoretical statements; they specify a relationship between two or more concepts and can be documented as being true or false. But, from a manager's point of view, they are weak and not action-oriented. Stronger theoretical statements are possible if the concepts are described as variables. For example:

"The public's level of knowledge will increase if we increase their exposure to this particular message."

"Increasing our organization's frequency of advocacy advertising will increase our public's level of knowledge."

Notice that theoretical statements containing variables require a sentence structure with a verb in the future tense that indicates direction; they are predictions; they explain what happens when things change.

Theories can be made up of either/or statements or continuous statements. Table 2.3 contains six theoretical statements illustrating these two basic forms. One easy way to tell the difference is to notice the parts of speech: theoretical statements that contain some form of the verb "to be" are expressing either/or connections. Sentences suggesting some kind of mathematical formulation are expressing continuous connections by suggesting that you can add, subtract, multiply or otherwise manipulate certain factors in the relationships.

To develop a theory-based public relations program you have to develop operationally-defined concepts relating your public relations activities to specific, operationally-defined characteristics of the public. To develop theory-based public relations programs you need to conceive of theoretical and operational relationships between what you plan to do and what you expect to happen.

Theoretical relations have two components—an independent concept and a dependent concept. An independent concept influences in some way the dependent concept. The dependent concept, in other words, depends for its own value on the value of the independent concept. For example:

Independent concept . . .	(Verb) Dependent concept
The public relations program . . .	(will create) a favorable public opinion for our client.
A series of training sessions . . .	(will reduce) in the long-run the number of employee questions about new procedures.
If we distribute this brochure . . .	then the public (will know) more about our program.

One way to build a theory-based public relations program is to start out by indicating which are the independent and which are the dependent concepts; then, specify concept names and theoretical and operational definitions.

Concept names are labels, such as "the general public," "the company," "the media," or "opinion makers," and are used to describe components or factors affecting a public relations campaign.

Theoretical Definitions

Definitions are the core of any formal theory. A theoretical definition imparts meaning to the concept: it describes the concept in such a way that other people can understand it. Theoretical definitions are fairly easy to spot: look for the synonyms—phrases or clauses—that describe the concept in equivalent ways, often by comparing or contrasting the concept to something else. Such equivalent phrases or clauses can be substituted for the concept; they imply definitions. For example, "Our corporate advertising, patterned after the Mobil Oil op-ed ads, seems to be working." This is a theoretical statement (with an either/or

TABLE 2.4:

Concepts Used to Build Theories About Public Relations

Concept	Independent Variable	Dependent Variable
Name	The public relations program	Public goodwill
Theoretical definition	A specific set of management activities designed to facilitate relationships and understanding	Public opinion about our organization
Operational definition	Running a series of full-page ads in area newspapers about our new quality control program	Responses to a telephone survey asking for opinions about our organization and the quality of our products and services

construction) in which the concept of the public relations campaign has been defined more precisely by comparing it to another campaign.

Operational definitions describe concepts in very specific, concrete, practical terms so that someone else can see them. Operational definitions make a theory testable. For example, look at the levels of theoretical statements possible from the concepts in Table 2.4. By connecting just concept names with an appropriate verb, this sentence is created: "The public relations program . . . will influence . . . public goodwill." This is an abstract and almost useless theoretical statement because the concepts are so vague. It's also one of the most common theoretical expressions in the field of public relations.

Link Operational Definitions to Create Practical Theories

Linking the two theoretical definitions of these same concepts creates a more useful sentence: "A specific set of management activities . . . will influence . . . public opinion about our organization." While this statement has more substance to it than simply stating that the public relations program will influence public goodwill, it still lacks a certain degree of specificity: it needs operational definitions.

Linking operationally-defined concepts creates a powerful, provocative sentence: "Running a series of full-page ads in local newspapers about our new quality control program . . . will influence . . . responses to a telephone survey asking for opinions about our organization and the quality of our products and services, with the survey based on a random sample of our target audience." This is a statement with a lot of substance. It is a hypothesis: it can be tested. Not only is this a scientific, theoretical statement, but also it is action-oriented: it identifies the administrative "handles and knobs" that a manager can turn and adjust in a campaign to make improvements.

Intervening and Moderating Concepts

In addition to independent and dependent concepts, two other important concepts enter into theory building: intervening and moderating concepts. An *intervening concept* is one that is assumed to occur between the independent and the dependent concepts. For example, a news release, printed in a local newspaper, may be expected to influence public knowledge about an organization; but, a media gatekeeper, probably a city editor, is an intervening factor. Before the news release can influence public knowledge, it must go to the city editor and be selected for publication.

A *moderating concept* is one that helps define when and where and how much an independent concept will influence the dependent concept. It somehow moderates the influence of the independent concept. For example, a certain media mix for a public relations campaign might work in one region and not in another because there are economic and political differences. Here, the moderating concept would be regional differences.

Building a good, practical theory about a public relations program or campaign is hard mental work. It's easy to have vague public relations goals and objectives, but it's hard to precisely define critical concepts and make clear-cut statements of relationship between what will be done and what is expected.

EXAMPLES OF COMMUNICATION THEORIES IN ACTION

Three communication theories will be used to demonstrate how effective public relations programs and campaigns incorporate communication theories—even when the managers don't label them as such. The three are: social learning theory, social exchange theory, and the hierarchy-of-effects theory. A different award-winning campaign will be used to illustrate each theory.

Social Learning Theory

The assumption of social learning theory is that we learn by modeling our behavior after others—not only by watching our teachers, peers, parents, and friends, but also by watching TV and movie stars, and reading about fictional and nonfictional characters in books.[13] Social learning theory assumes the following sequence of events: we notice a particular behavior; we admire it; we wish to emulate it; so, we act in this new way; and, if we like it, we integrate the behavior, and related attitudes, into our way of thinking and behaving. The theory assumes learning is a social process involving modeling of admired behaviors.

If there is positive feedback, there will be an adoption of appropriate attitudes about the behavior which will predispose the person to act again in this new way, given similar circumstances.

. . .

CASE 2.3:

The Norrell Business Theater

The fifth-largest temporary services company in the United States, Norrell, contracted with Ketchum Public Relations for the agency to produce a special trade show exhibit at the annual convention of the American Society of Personnel Administrators (ASPA). This convention normally attracts 4,000 professionals, most of whom place orders on a regular basis for temporary services. Here are the steps the agency went through to research, plan, implement, and evaluate the trade show event:

1. Norrell senior executives were convinced that the company needed to set itself apart from its competition at the trade show. They told the account executives with Ketchum Public Relations that they wanted something "to cut through the convention show 'clutter' and simultaneously attract sales leads." Specifically, the contract with the agency stated the company wanted "to establish a unique identity and generate 250 qualified sales leads for Norrell at ASPA through creative booth concept, design and implementation."
2. The account team at Ketchum used computerized databases to search for characteristics noted in the trade press and elsewhere of Norrell's and their competitors' temporary services. They discovered that Norrell's Office Automation training program was a point of differentiation from the competition.
3. The account team brainstormed exhibit ideas and came upon the notion of producing live comedy theater to illustrate what it is like to train temporary employees. They presented the concept to the client, who endorsed it.
4. The account executives developed specific objectives for the live-theater booth:
   - Differentiate Norrell from the competition.
   - Increase qualified booth traffic from 200/day at the previous ASPA convention to 250/day.
   - Generate 250 qualified sales leads.
   - Create opportunity for audience involvement.
   - "Keep" decision-makers in the booth long enough to expose them to Norrell without losing their attention.
   - Support Norrell's Office Automation training program.
5. A budget was established and approved by the client for three actors, a producer, booth construction, shipping, set-up, exhibit coordination and supervision.
6. In 45 days, the account team in Atlanta had designed and constructed the booth, scripted the play, hired actors, and rehearsed the world première of *Temporary Insanity or How I Got Over My Temporary Fears with*

Norrell Employees. The booth was designed as a mini-theater, complete with ticket window, elevated stage and stage curtain. Because only 30 seats would fit into the small trade-show exhibit space, the front wall of the booth was designed to stop at knee level so others outside the booth could see the production. Both playbills and tickets, distributed throughout the convention hall, had built-in lead response identifiers which attendees could fill out. The comedy called for audience participation. At the end of each 15-minute production, the audience was asked to rise and recite the Temps Anonymous Pledge, a wonderfully funny parody that was printed inside the playbill.

7. The account team ran the theater production every half hour on the hour for the duration of the 2 1/2-day conference. Prior to each show, tickets were collected from those in attendance.
8. The results were impressive: Norrell's was the only theater at the convention, and standing room only was normal for each show, with four-to-five people deep standing outside the booth watching the production. Members of the audience, even those standing outside the booth, repeated the Temp Pledge, in mock seriousness and good humor at the end of each production. Compared to the previous year's exhibit, three times the number of convention attendees viewed the Norrell booth, and more than 500 qualified sales leads were generated. Furthermore, long after the convention, people continued to contact Norrell saying, in good spirits, that they had "temp fear" and needed Norrell's services.

. . .

Key to the success of this exhibit was the audience's modeling of behaviors presented by the actors in the play. By encouraging members of the audience to react to the actors, by having the members of the audience repeat the Temp Pledge, and by rewarding such behaviors with good humor and camaraderie, the public relations specialists who created and executed this special event made the same set of assumptions that social learning theory does. In other words, social learning theory assumes that some people, even when they are reluctant to hold a certain attitude, can be persuaded to behave in an appropriate manner; then, when they are rewarded for this behavior, they will adopt attitudes which predispose them to act in a similar way the next time it seems appropriate. In the Norrell case, social learning theory, and the public relations professionals responsible for the Norrell Business Theater, predicted accurately that if some of the people could be persuaded to act in a certain way, then appropriate attitudes and long-term learning would be sure to follow. For this successful special event, the public relations agency received an IABC award of merit.[14]

Social Exchange Theory

This theory is based on the power of reciprocity in human relationships. In other words, people don't like to feel beholden; they like to be in balanced relationships.[15] Based on studies of individuals in relationships, the theory has been applied to the study of organizational behavior.[16] At an organizational level of analysis, the theory assumes that rational organizations work to achieve equity in resource exchanges.

These exchanges occur among organizations and publics. The assumption is that when exchanges of resources result in a perceived imbalance, tensions among managers within the organization or among members of the public who are experiencing the imbalance will reach such a point that they will do something about it. They might rationalize the imbalance and decide to live with it for a while longer; they might exchange resources in such a way as to balance the relationship; or, they might break off the relationship. One prediction of the social exchange theory is that whenever a relationship is not perceived as being equitable and balanced, communication among rational individuals, organizations, and publics will occur.

. . .

CASE 2.4:

Alberta Government Telephones

The primary supplier of telecommunications products and services to more than two million customers in western Canada, Alberta Government Telephones (AGT) was seeking "to strengthen the understanding and support of Albertans at a grassroots community level" when the company decided to launch a community relations program targeted at public schools.[17] After its first year of operation, the new community relations program received an IABC award of merit. Here are the steps the public relations specialists went through during the first year:

1. The need for the program was recognized when it became apparent that there were too many individual requests from teachers for out-of-service telephones, old telephone directories and miscellaneous obsolete phone equipment which could be used in life-skills courses in elementary and kindergarten schools. The head of AGT community relations said that although individual teachers expressed appreciation for the materials, "responding to ad-hoc requests was time-consuming, inconsistent, and provided little tangible return to the corporation."
2. The community relations staff decided to package sets of the requested old equipment and teaching tools, and to distribute them at one time, throughout the province, to more than 1,000 teachers who would reach more than 32,000 children and, by extension, their parents.
3. They established the following goals for the campaign:
    a. To channel AGT resources toward the creation of a beneficial, consistent educational program identifiable with the corporation.
    b. To enhance AGT's corporate image by visibly responding to an identified need of children and the educational community, and by promoting a program which needs this need.
    c. To produce an effective, continuing corporate vehicle for grassroots contacts with Alberta teachers and school children.
4. The community relations staff met with school officials to develop learning objectives and program components. The teachers wanted materials and equipment that could be used to instruct students on

making emergency telephone calls, on using the alphabet and numbers, and on communicating properly and politely over the telephone and elsewhere.
5. All school boards throughout the province were contacted and presented the company's plan, and all endorsed the program before it was distributed to the schools.
6. Each "Communikit" included: two nonworking telephones, specially designed student directories similar to the "White Pages," a set of current telephone books for the school's area, and a colorful poster with friendly, talkative animals portraying proper telephone techniques.
7. Paid actors and employee volunteers dressed as mascots similar to the animals on the poster and were sent to participating schools to demonstrate how to use the equipment.
8. The campaign was "rolled out" first in the province's largest school district, and thereafter by geographic region, so that the community relations department could properly staff and supervise the introduction and implementation of the campaign.
9. On the launch dates in each geographic region, press announcements and copies of the telephone courtesy poster were "paw" delivered to local media by animal mascots.
10. Newspaper advertisements explaining the program were placed in local media.
11. Response to the campaign was as follows: ad hoc requests from teachers dropped significantly; teacher response was 96% positive; publicity about the program reached a combined media audience of approximately two million; and, many unexpected requests for the kits were received from private schools, churches and children's groups.
12. Formal evaluation of the campaign, using mail questionnaires to participating teachers, not only indicated high use and appreciation but also generated many suggestions on how to use the kits. The teacher suggestions were incorporated into an instructor's manual which was distributed to participating teachers and in all new Communikits.

. . .

The public relations campaign occurred because the corporation perceived an imbalance in its relationships with the school: there were too many uncoordinated requests for old equipment, and not enough of a return on the corporate investment in responding to the ad hoc requests from the teachers. The campaign was a success because the corporation gave to the teachers such a well-designed package of materials, plus collateral activities, that the teachers felt, in turn, that the relationship was out of balance—they received more than they expected. In such an imbalanced yet advantageous situation, the teachers obviously would not break off the relationship; nor could they exchange resources in some way to bring the relationship back

FIGURE 2.1

A public relations hierarchy of effects model.

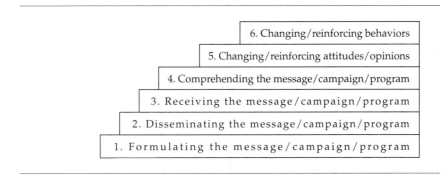

into balance. Consequently, they rationalized the relationship by adopting very positive attitudes toward the company and sharing these attitudes not only with the students but also with the students' parents.

Hierarchy of Effects

Most public relations campaigns and programs use the hierarchy-of-effects theory, because most public relations managers assume that their first job is to get people to listen to, think about, understand, and agree with the information being presented in the campaign or program; then, maybe, the target audience will act on the information. Early communication theorists assumed learning new behaviors occurred logically through a hierarchy of effects: first, awareness; then, comprehension; then, acceptance; and, finally, retention.[18] Building on this model, communication researchers, looking at the diffusion of innovations, identified a similar hierarchy: awareness, interest, evaluation, trial and adoption.[19] Neither of these two earlier versions of the hierarchy-of-effects model takes into consideration message formulation or information dissemination—the basic work of the communicator. The earlier versions of the hierarchy-of-effects model were receiver oriented; they were not producer-oriented. Incorporating these producer-oriented steps into the hierarchy-of-effects model makes it more applicable to public relations managers, because formulating and disseminating messages to key publics are two tasks often spelled out in detail in a practitioner's job description. See Figure 2.1 for a staircase illustration of the public relations hierarchy-of-effects theory.

The front page of the employee newsletter announces stock awards to employees. Reprinted with permission of Bank of America.

. . .

CASE 2.5:

Bank of America Surprise Stock Awards to Employees

For two years during the late 1980s, the Bank of America lost almost two billion dollars. They were hard years; the corporation had to suspend issuing dividends to stockholders, sell properties and assets, restructure and downsize the employee workforce, and fight off a hostile takeover attempt. But, under new management, they emerged on the other side of this period in much stronger financial shape. While highly secret discussions were underway among senior management about reinstating dividends to their long-patient stockholders, the new management group asked the Corporate Communication Division to develop and implement a campaign designed to boost employee morale and productivity. Senior management had just received an employee audit they had commissioned that revealed only 53% of the restructured 50,000 workforce were satisfied with the recognition they received for doing a good job, and that two-thirds of the employees disagreed with the statement that the new management group had a sincere interest in employee satisfaction and well-being. Here are the steps the bank's corporate communications department took:

1. Because the senior public relations manager was a member of the small group of senior managers considering when and how to reinstate dividends to stockholders, the day that the new dividends were to be announced was considered in planning the employee morale campaign.

Because the discussions about the dividend were confidential, the head of corporate communication instructed the staff to keep plans of the employee campaign secret also.

2. Brainstorming was limited to a small group of managers and communication specialists, who came up with a bold and expensive idea: award shares of stock, complete with dividends, to all 50,000+ employees worldwide!
3. A senior member of the brainstorming group presented the proposal to the bank's highest management committee, which liked the idea and asked for a feasibility study.
4. When this study was completed, the program was not only approved, it was expanded. The new management group wanted to add more bonuses to the employee recognition program: one extra vacation day in the next year for each employee, and cash awards to those who were newcomers or part-time workers. The total cost, including ten shares of stock per employee, was approximately $20 million.
5. With senior management's final approval, specific communication strategies were developed:
    a. Keep the awards secret until the moment of announcement.
    b. Hold simultaneous staff meetings worldwide (coordinated through time zones) two days after current stockholders, and the financial community, are informed of the reinstated dividends, and give each employee a letter from the CEO announcing the award and thanking the employee for helping make the turnaround possible.
    c. Follow up immediately through bank publications and a video with employee reactions to the program.
    d. One month after the announcement, hold special staff meetings where individual certificates would be distributed to employees by their supervisors.
6. Here is what the corporate communication staff did to implement the program:
    a. In secrecy, thousands of information packets for managers to use at the surprise staff meetings were prepared. Each packet included announcement letters, suggested remarks for the manager, and a list of anticipated questions and answers.
    b. Human resource managers in the United States, and senior bank managers in other nations, were briefed in confidence, with special instructions to those managers whose units had union and labor contracts requiring prior notification.
    c. The day before the surprise staff meetings, all managers were contacted by electronic mail or by telephone and told to expect a special mailing the next day. A coordinated worldwide mail delivery put the packets on managers' desks at the same time.
    d. As planned, all employees met with their managers and received the good news.
    e. During the day of the announcement, corporate communication staff conducted an informal telephone survey of employees, and overnight, produced and distributed an employee newsletter featuring employee comments and reactions.

f. One month later, a video, featuring the staff meetings where the stock certificates were presented, was produced and distributed throughout the corporation. The stock certificate meetings also were covered in the employee publications.
7. Senior managers did not evaluate the employee recognition program formally or attempt to link its success quantitatively to measures of employee productivity or corporate performance. Rather, by considering informal feedback from employees, which was overwhelmingly positive, senior managers judged the program a success, particularly in light of the bank's continuing financial growth and healthy profits.

Here is how the hierarchy-of-effects model—and social exchange theory—can be used to analyze the Bank of America campaign:

Formulating the message:
  Senior managers developed and approved the concept, and the corporate communication staff produced information packets.

Disseminating the message:
  Corporate communication staff coordinated worldwide distribution of packets, and managers held simultaneous staff meetings with their employees.

Receiving the message:
  50,000+ employees received personal letters and heard about the bonuses from their supervisors.

Comprehending the message:
  In addition to the letter from the CEO, the remarks from the manager, the articles in publications, and the feature stories on videotape, each employee also had the opportunity to address individual concerns by asking questions of his or her supervisor; this increased the likelihood that each employee would fully comprehend the message.

Changing or reinforcing appropriate attitudes:
  Social exchange theory helps explain why positive attitudes about the company and employee productivity would be generated by the bank's generous bonus. The periodic dividends of the stock awards would function as a stimulus-response reinforcement schedule to then extend the impact of the program and increase the probability of long-term attitude change or reinforcement.

Changing or reinforcing appropriate behaviors:
  Managers were encouraged to praise specific contributions of members of their staffs so employees would associate the awards with specific approaches to job assignments and other on-the-job behaviors.

. . .

Implied within any set of goals and objectives for a public relations program or campaign is one or more theories. It does not matter if public relations managers are aware of the academic labels used to describe the theories; all public relations programs and campaigns are based on theories—statements of relationship that help explain and predict what is going on. Some theories are better than others. The social learning, social exchange, and hierarchy-of-effects theories are some of the most powerful theories in communication; they help explain and predict a lot of what happens in many public relations campaigns and programs.

HOW TO ESTABLISH GOALS

Establishing appropriate goals is not an easy task. There often are differences among members of the dominant coalition about what should constitute appropriate goals and outcomes for a campaign, and what are appropriate ways to achieve those outcomes. The goal-setting process often sparks conflicts. If the experienced public relations specialist is aware of this potential going into a situation, appropriate strategies can be used to alleviate the conflict and facilitate group consensus. The goal-setting process itself is an important public relations activity because, properly managed, it facilitates relationships and understanding.

Here are a few points to consider when establishing goals:

1. Make goals specific and understandable. Don't use jargon. Express goals in everyday language.
2. Don't confuse outcome and process goals. They are related, but they should be considered separately.
3. Get some kind of consensus on the goals from among those most affected by the activity—particularly from members of the dominant coalition—and, if possible, get it in writing. Goals become the standards by which the effectiveness of the activity will be judged. If consensus on the goals is not achieved, another set of criteria may be used by others at a later time to evaluate the effectiveness of the campaign, and this can be counter productive. When consensus is not possible, solicit and acknowledge dissenting opinions, and carefully consider these critical comments when later examining the achievement of both process and outcome goals.

HOW TO WRITE GOALS

Goals for public relations campaigns should be expressed in easily understood terms, and they should be agreed upon not only by the public relations professionals but also by many others within the organization. Consensus building around public relations goals is important for two reasons: first, because the impact of most campaigns affects many publics within an organization; second, because without support from many internal publics, it is difficult to develop most campaigns.

Goals can be expressed in one of two formats—as statements or as questions.[20] Here are some examples of goals expressed as statements:

The campaign is designed to influence key decision-makers.

Our goal is to increase attendance at these town meetings.

We want to create a favorable climate for our client. The employees will appreciate the company's position after they read this information.

Before a campaign gets underway, goals are often expressed as statements. Once underway, goals are often reexpressed as questions along the lines of, "Have we achieved what we set out to accomplish?" Here are the same set of goals mentioned above, now expressed as questions:

Did the campaign influence key decision-makers?

Did attendance at the town meetings increase?

Is there a favorable climate for our client?

Do the employees appreciate the company's position after they read this information?

HOW TO DETERMINE OBJECTIVES

Objectives are goals expressed in concrete, measurable terms. Objectives are not abstract: someone can actually go out and see whether or not an objective has been achieved. Goals specify means and outcomes. Objectives specify nuts and bolts. Objectives indicate how and when to turn administrative handles and knobs. They explain specifically what needs to be done to complete the job. Managers can use objectives as indicators of subordinate job performance.

The theory-building techniques discussed in the previous section are useful in the goal-setting process. Testable statements of relationship between a public relations program and its desired outcomes are hypotheses: they can be tested, verified or falsified. You cannot engage in a theory-based public relations activity without considering goals and objectives. Similarly, you cannot seriously consider the relationship between public relations goals and objectives without being theoretical, because theories underlie all goals and objectives.

Objectives are expressed in practical terms but in various ways. The level of specificity will depend upon the organization's willingness or ability to collect specific data. There is little purpose in spending time specifying objectives and collecting data that will not be used later on. The members of the dominant coalition who will be making the decisions about the public relations campaign should be involved early on in determining the campaign's goals and objectives. During and after the campaign, these decision-makers should be presented with the kind of information they need. That means finding out what these critical decision-makers want to know before engaging in the campaign; that means finding out what they think should be the goals and objectives for the campaign.

Still, you need to be practical. If you are the only one who will make judgments about the activity, then you should decide what constitutes specific objectives. If several people are involved, they should be consulted; but, if they are only interested in certain outcomes, only those outcomes should be operationally defined with concrete objectives. There can be dozens of objectives generated about any one activity, and there is no point in collecting data about them all, for not everyone will care if they are achieved. You must set priorities. How you can do this will be discussed shortly. In the meantime, here are some guidelines to use in developing objectives:

1. Don't confuse the process, what the public relations person does, with the outcome, what you want publics to do. Most public relations objectives focus on outcomes.
2. Develop objectives that reflect the complexity and various stages of the activities and expected outcomes. For example, if voting for your client is the ultimate objective, what are intermediate objectives (awareness of candidate, accuracy of perception about the candidate's position, interest in voting, etc.)? What is an appropriate hierarchy of importance for these objectives? Does the hierarchy of objectives accurately reflect the range and scope of activities engaged in?
3. Develop objectives for both specific publics and for the campaign itself. Goals and objectives that focus on publics are outcome goals and those that focus on the campaign are process goals. Goals and objectives can be focused on primary and secondary publics. For example, you might state that your goal is to influence the voters and that your objective is to get at least a plurality of the votes cast. Both of these statements focus on the publics involved. Or, goals and objectives can be focused on the program itself. For example, you might state that your goal is to contact every voter in the area and that your objective is to give each voter a piece of literature.
4. When you write objectives, use action words. Be direct; be specific; be brief. Objectives should create word pictures about what is to be done and what is to be expected. Edit and re-edit objectives until they are unmistakably clear. Remember that these objectives will be used to evaluate the effectiveness of the program; be precise and realistic.
5. Don't develop a measure, indicator, or questionnaire item without relating it to a specific goal. All objectives should be goal-related. Don't create objectives in a vacuum.
6. Recognize that objectives are hypotheses based on a theory about why the public relations campaign is expected to influence targeted publics. Objectives can be expressed as stimulus-response statements; the public relations campaign is the stimulus, and the public's reaction is the response.

HOW TO ASSIGN PRIORITIES TO GOALS AND OBJECTIVES

Almost all public relations campaigns have numerous goals. From just a few goals, dozens of specific objectives can be generated. There comes a time when it will be necessary to assign priorities to these goals and objectives. In many instances, practitioners do not have the time, money or inclination to accurately assess the likely achievements of all campaign goals and objectives. The question for these practitioners then becomes, "How do you assign priorities to goals and objectives?"

There are two ways to assign priorities. One is to do it yourself. As experts and public relations technicians, you can act alone, or you and a small group of public relations specialists can select the most important campaign goals and objectives.

The other way is to involve others. As problem-solving or process facilitators, you and your associates of public relations specialists can involve a variety of other people in making these decisions about campaign goals and objectives.

When all goals are about equal in importance, you can elect not to set priorities but to select a representative sample from the full set of objectives. Randomly selecting a set number from a long list of objectives may be appropriate, particularly when you want to save money on collecting data and monitoring results. If certain goals have been identified as top priority, you might randomly select objectives from this pool of top priority goals.

The difficult question is: How do you get a group of people to reach consensus on top priority goals and objectives? It is fairly easy as an individual to make the decisions, and it is relatively easy with just a few specialists. But, when a number of people representing a variety of publics are involved, how can you get them to agree on one set of goals and objectives?

STRATEGIES FOR BUILDING CONSENSUS

You can ask various key individuals to rank order sets of goal statements or sets of objectives clustered according to goals. This is how the customer relations manager for the gas and electric company reached consensus on the set of twenty-four objectives. There were six major categories of objectives and an initial set of objectives per category. Through the process of circulating working documents and holding small-group discussions, the various suggestions were rank ordered and a consensus was reached on priority objectives to include under the Quality of Service goal.

Another procedure is to type all the goals and objectives on cards, asking individuals to pick out the most important cards and stack them in order of importance. If you use such a card method, remember to keep goals and objectives separate. Remember that goals, because they are broad statements, sound more important and are selected first. Consequently, you should make sure that the statements to be ranked all have the same sound to them, that they have the same level of specificity, and that they are, in fact, comparable. If both goals and objectives are to be considered, select first the most important goals; then, from the top priority goals, select the most important objectives related to these goals.

Using Focus Groups to Develop Consensus

Another technique used to develop consensus is to conduct a formal meeting focused specifically on identifying top priority goals and objectives. Focus group exercises among colleagues are most effective when the group is comprised of equally informed, mutually respectful individuals who have the time to give the issue a fair discussion. If the group's discussion is rushed, if personalities in the group don't mix well, if hidden agenda are operating, then focus groups among work associates do not function well. More information about conducting focus groups is presented in Chapter 6.

An Alternative: The Nominal Group Technique   One focus group procedure that helps reduce the potentially negative influences of individual personalities and hidden agenda is the Nominal Group Technique (NGT), which is described in a case study in Chapter 6. Modified for a goal-setting process, the NGT can be used in two ways: one, it can be used to identify goals and objectives; and two, it can be used to rank order predetermined goals and/or objectives.

The key steps in the NGT are:

1. The posing of a single question for the group to consider;
2. Silent writing of ideas by each individual (this is why it is called a nominal group—the work is in silence, with each individual working alone most of the time);
3. A round-robin listing by the group leader of each individual's ideas, one at a time, until all ideas are listed on flip charts, the pages of which are often taped around the meeting room like wallpaper;
4. After all ideas are listed, reading aloud the ideas and asking the group to decide which should be considered most important;
5. Each individual looking over the entire list and selecting the most important items; and, finally,
6. The group leader recording and tallying the rank orders assigned by each individual to the various statements so that everyone sees which are the most important ideas as judged by the group.

An Alternative: The Delphi Technique A variation of the nominal group format is the Delphi technique, which is explained in detail in Chapter 8. It relies on the same techniques of listing rank-ordered ideas as the NGT, only the Delphi technique uses the mail system as its forum for discussion instead of a small-group meeting. The procedure is the same: to have participants select, as individuals, top priority statements, to summarize the individual rankings, to inform the group of what everyone else has suggested, to ask for priorities to be assigned to each suggestions, and, to go through this process until all participants have had a chance to vote on what they consider to be the most important ideas. What emerges from the Delphi technique is a priority listing.

Sometimes, participants are not convinced that the focus group's priorities are an accurate reflection of what they consider to be priority concerns. In such cases, it is wise to include these dissenting opinions and concerns as additional criteria by which the effectiveness of the campaign will be judged. Conflicts regarding priorities should be explored and not ignored because they clarify the assumptions and theories underlying the public relations activity.

An Alternative: Force Field Analysis This chapter's opening vignette illustrates how force field analysis works. A small group of people interested in identifying a problem or opportunity—or interested in engaging in a new project or set of activities—is brought together and asked to focus attention on one topic: forces working for and against whatever is of concern to the group.[21] The leader makes two lists based on suggestions from the group. Some leaders begin the process by making a central list of basic characteristics of the problem/opportunity/situation. Then, to either side of each characteristic, a force working for it and a force working against it are listed.

The assumption in force field analysis is that most political, economic and organizational forces are vectored against other forces. The practical implication of force field analysis is that an effective manager can use it to identify varied and often conflicting forces before introducing a public relations campaign into a situation. Using the technique of force field analysis has the added benefit of keeping the group discussion from focusing too quickly on solutions; it keeps the discussion focused on problems.

HOW PRACTITIONERS GET INVOLVED WITH GOALS AND OBJECTIVES

Entry-level practitioners too often are brought into the goal-setting process as an afterthought. Novices often are assigned the role of the technician. If the goals and objectives set for the entry-level practitioner are appropriate, there should be little or no problem. However, if the goals and objectives do not reflect the reality of the problem, the entry-level practitioner may be caught in a bind: technically, tasks can be completed, but completing the tasks may not be the best way to solve the problem. A common mistake on the part of novices is to work diligently to meet specific objectives without questioning how achieving objectives relates to overarching goals. While being sensitive to the political realities of the corporate culture, entry-level practitioners can double check the appropriateness of the goals and objectives of specific public relations activities by discussing these issues with colleagues and associates.

Mid-management public relations practitioners focus much of their attention on process-oriented goals and objectives, making sure work is coordinated and on schedule. Campaign and project specific objectives must be integrated with overall corporate goals and objectives. Goal-setting procedures are often linked with the budget review and authorization procedures. Mid-management public relations practitioners often concern themselves with this linkage between the budget-review process and the goal-setting process. More information about the budgeting process is presented in Chapter 5.

At the senior management level, the practitioner is highly involved in the budgeting process. At this level attention turns more toward evaluating complete public relations campaigns and determining overarching goals and objectives for the organization. At this level, it is readily apparent that organizations are shifting coalitions of individuals and groups, and that these coalitions differ according to goals and objectives. At this senior management level, the skills of defining publics and establishing goals and objectives are crucial.

AN ALTERNATIVE THEORY: PROBLEMS AS GARBAGE CANS

The structural-functional theory underlying the analysis of the case studies presented in this chapter emphasizes the rationality involved in identifying problems and setting goals. The lists of steps that are used to chronicle each case make the processes appear even more logical and sequential. The survey statistics suggest that the decision-making processes are not only quantifiable but also predictable.

An alternative approach to problem identification and goal setting is the "garbage can" theory of organizational behavior.[22] This theory recognizes the apparent irrationality involved when people come together to solve problems. Management professor James G. March noted that people are hired by organizations because they have knowledge and skills which can be used to solve problems. The assumption, he said, is that employees have solutions within them, ready to come out at the right moment. Organizations, from this point of view, are made up of people with solutions who need problems to justify their salaries. Without problems to solve, most employees, particularly members of senior management, wouldn't have anything to do. Consequently, when problems occur, employees throw solutions at them. Problems become the garbage cans for the organization's solutions.

This garbage can quality of problems accounts for the apparently irrational behavior so often seen in organizations at the onset of a problem or first glimmer of an opportunity. Initially there is great enthusiasm while people brainstorm solutions, with lots of key players jockeying for position. But, when the solution is implemented, enthusiasm fades and support disappears, even though there hasn't been enough time for the solution to have a major impact on the problem.

From a public relations manager's point of view, one of the implications of the garbage can theory is that sustaining the interest and support of staff and colleagues is easiest during the process of problem identification, when everyone is tossing about solutions, and more difficult during the process of setting goals and objectives.

IN SUMMARY . . .

Defining problems and opportunities are common activities—and ethical dilemmas—for all organizations. How the members of the dominant coalition view potential problems and opportunities has a major influence on the organization's public relations. The closeness of the senior public relations person to the members of the dominant coalition strongly influences how problems will be defined, and how goals and objectives for public relations campaigns will be determined. The basic steps in defining problems and developing goals and objectives are: to recognize key publics; to explore knowledge; to identify priorities; to generate and select solutions; to acknowledge the relationships between activities, strategies and outcome goals; to implement the campaign; and, to evaluate both process and outcome goals.

Effective public relations campaigns are based on practical theories. Effective public relations managers know how to link specific public relations activities and specific public perceptions and actions that help the organization achieve its goals. This chapter has presented a number of planning strategies and techniques public relations managers can use to define problems and opportunities, and to develop measurable goals and objectives. In the next chapter, more information will be presented about how to define publics and relationships.

Study Questions

1. What are the relationships between problems, opportunities, goals, and objectives? Be sure to define each term.
2. What is the difference between process goals and outcome goals? Give examples of each.
3. When and how do ethical considerations become involved in defining a problem or opportunity?
4. What steps do most public relations practitioners go through when defining problems and opportunities and developing goals and objectives? Give examples for each of the steps.
5. Briefly describe the D.C. statehood campaign and the BG&E quality-of-service campaign. What similarities and differences were there between these two campaigns in terms defining problems/opportunities and developing goals and objectives?
6. Write a statement of relationship between a public relations program and its expected impact, and label the parts of the sentence that are the independent and dependent variables. Is what you have written a theory? Why do you think so?
7. Briefly describe a social learning theory, and explain how it might be used to explain or predict a public relations program.
8. Briefly describe a social exchange theory, and explain how it might be used to explain or predict a public relations program.
9. Briefly describe a hierarchy-of-effects theory, and explain how it might be used to explain or predict a public relations program.
10. What advice would you offer someone who was preparing to write a set of goals for a public relations program?

Endnotes

1. Simon, Herbert *Administrative Behavior*, 3rd edition (New York: Free Press, 1976).
2. Salmon, Charles, "Campaigns for social 'improvement': An overview of values, rationales and impacts," in *Information Campaigns*, edited by C. Salmon, (Beverly Hills, CA: Sage, 1990) pp. 23–26.
3. Salmon, *op.cit.*
4. Salmon, *op.cit.* pp. 24–26.
5. Ouchi, William, *Theory Z* (Reading, Mass.: Addison-Wesley, 1981) pp. 30–35.
6. McCombs, Maxwell, "Agenda setting function of mass media," *Public Relations Review*, Vol. 3, Winter, 1977, pp. 89–95.
7. Grunig, James E., "Organizations, environments, and models of public relations," *Public Relations Research and Education*, Vol. 1. No.4, 1984, pp. 6–29.
8. Grunig, James E., "Symmetrical presuppositions as a framework for public relations theory," in *Public Relations Theory*, edited by Carl Botan and Vincent Hazelton, Jr. (Hillsdale, NJ: Lawrence Erlbaum Associates, 1989) pp. 17–44.
9. Grunig, James *op.cit.*, 1989.
10. *ibid.*
11. Morgan, Gareth, *Images of Organization* (Beverly Hills, CA: Sage, 1986) pp. 111–140.

12. Hage, Jerald, *Techniques and Problems of Theory Construction in Sociology* (New York: Wiley & Sons, 1972).

13. Bandura, Albert, *Social Learning Theory* (Englewood Cliffs, NJ: Prentice-Hall, 1977); and, Peter, J. P. and J. C. Olson, *Consumer Behavior* (Homewood, Ill.: Irwin, 1987).

14. *IABC Gold Quill Award Winning Case Histories*, Vol.6 (San Francisco, CA: International Association of Business Communicators, 1990) pp. 15–19.

15. Prior-Miller, Marcia, "Four major social scientific theories and their value to the public relations researcher," in *Public Relations Theory* edited by Carl Botan and Vincent Hazelton, Jr. (Hillsdale, NJ: Lawrence Erlbaum Associates, 1989) pp. 71–73.

16. Blau, Peter M., *Exchange and Power in Social Life* (New York: Wiley, 1964); and, Hall, Richard H., *Organizations: Structure and Process* 3rd edition (Englewood Cliffs, NJ: Prentice-Hall, 1982).

17. *IABC Gold Quill Award Winning Case Studies*, op.cit., pp. 3–6.

18. Hovland, C., I. Janis, and H. Kelley, *Communication and Persuasion: Psychological Studies of Opinion Change* (New Haven, CT: Yale University Press, 1953).

19. McGuire, William, "Theoretical foundations of campaigns," in *Public Communication Campaigns*, 2nd edition, edited by Ronald Rice and Charles Atkin (Beverly Hills, CA: Sage, 1989) pp. 43–66.

20. Morris, L. L., and Carol T. Fitz-Gibbon, *How To Deal With Goals and Objectives*, part of the *Program Evaluation Kit*, edited by Morris and Fitz-Gibbon (Beverly Hills, CA: Sage, 1978).

21. Simmons, Robert E. *Communication Campaign Management* (New York: Longman, 1990) pp. 50–54.

22. March, J. G., and J. P. Olsen, *Ambiguity and Choice in Organizations* (Bergen, Norway: Universitels Forlaget, 1976).

CHAPTER THREE

How to Define Publics and Relationships

. . . . .

*S*orting through his mail at home that night, Bob, 33, director of communication for a major insurance company, sat down at the sleek kitchen table in his $200,000 townhouse, delighted with all the "junk" mail he had received. He and his wife, also a professional, liked to joke about their junk mail. With no children, it was a fun little ritual they went through when they got home at night.

Bob liked it because it gave him an opportunity to see the direct mail business in action. He always said that if you wanted to see the cutting edge of marketing, look at direct mail. He freely allowed his name to be used by mailing-list firms. He even deliberately misspelled his name on certain magazine subscriptions so he could track where his name was sold and by whom.

A two-color brochure from the city's symphony was addressed to "Occupant," so Bob figured it probably was mailed to everyone in his upscale neighborhood.

A solicitation for a magazine subscription used a misspelled version of his name that he had used for a technical publication he no longer subscribed to or read. He spent some time looking over the material, because he did like the subject matter.

A computer-generated sales letter from a local Volvo dealership had his name spelled correctly and integrated throughout the letter, even though he had never owned a Volvo. He and his wife owned two Toyota MR2s. He didn't know how the car dealership obtained his name, but he knew it wasn't that difficult to find.

A two-color handsome newsletter from an international environmental group made him smile like a wry detective. The mailing label used his first name and a fictitious middle initial he had used only once when he filled out a questionnaire and donated money to a very persuasive door-to-door solicitor from a local social action group. "Gotcha," he thought: this time he knew how they had found his name.

Here is Bob's profile:
- *is young upwardly mobile professional—a YUPpy;*
- *is married without children, Bob and his wife are DINKS—Double Incomes, No Kids;*
- *lives in an expensive home with upscale ZIPcode;*
- *owns two sports cars;*
- *reads technical publications;*
- *is willing to sign petitions for and give money to social action groups;*
- *likes junk mail.*

While that last bit of information makes Bob fairly unusual, his profile illustrates how publics may be defined. Publics may be defined by some combination of the following possibilities: roles (occupation, marital status), socio-economic status (cost of home), demographics (age, gender), geographics (neighborhood), psychographics (opinions), "infographics" (readership), and lifestyles (sports car enthusiast).

. . .

SEVERAL APPROACHES TO DEFINING PUBLICS

A public is more than just any group of individuals. A public is a group of people who are aware of shared interests and common concerns. Just any list of people does not constitute a public. For example, all the people who answer the phone when telemarketing operators call them from a randomly generated set of phone numbers do not constitute a public because the group is not aware of any shared interests. An effective public relations campaign, however, could make all individuals on this list well aware of their common interests. For example, the telemarketer, by placing ads in papers, identifying "winners," and requiring winners to find their prizes listed in these newspaper ads, might be able to make this group of people become aware of themselves as a public, and act as a public. An effective public relations campaign can generate publics from groups, sometimes making the publics so active they become organizations in their own right. Or, deliberately working in the opposite direction, an effective public relations campaign might change active publics into aware but much less active publics, making them less of a threat to certain organizations.

Going from Latent to Active Public—and Back Again

A latent public is a group whose members are unaware of their common interests. For example, voters who are unaware of their stake in the passage of certain legislation constitute a latent public. Often it is the job of the public relations professional to make members of this latent public more aware of their common interests so that they will become an aware and active public.

An example of moving a latent public to the active level would be a grassroots effort by a few individuals who stage events and generate publicity to raise public awareness to the point at which community leaders emerge to organize a political action group. On the other hand, an example of deactivating an active public would be an industry, faced with an organized consumers' boycott and potentially restrictive legislation, having its trade association establish a quasi-independent commission to investigate the public's concerns and to serve as an industry watchdog. From the industry's point of view, this would diffuse the active publics by providing a more manageable, predictable forum for public discussion, and it might eliminate calls for restrictive legislation. Because an organization is an active public, the job of the public relations practitioner often can be described as helping certain publics to become better organized and dissuading other publics from becoming too organized. The public relations professional needs to know how to organize and communicate with groups and publics that are at various levels of awareness.[1]

The Coorientation Model

Two key ingredients in a public's awareness are its degree of self-awareness and its degree of orientation toward shared interests. The greater the public's self-awareness and orientation toward shared interests, the easier it is to communicate with that public. For example, it is much easier to communicate with employees than it is with potential customers. Employees live and work together; they share numerous interests. While potential customers may share certain needs, they do not have the degree of shared interests that current customers do, nor do potential customers have the same sense of self-awareness as current customers.

Self-awareness and coorientation by members of a public are necessary conditions for communication to occur at all.[2] Because communication is the transfer of meaning between two entities, it is necessary for those entities to share something in common before they can communicate; otherwise, they are like ships passing in the night, each without notice of the other. The two entities need to sense a certain degree of perceived agreement or congruency between what they think and what they think the other entity thinks. The more perceived agreement and self-awareness, the easier it is for these individuals and publics to communicate with each other and with other publics.

A public's awareness and coorientation are not constants. Figure 3.1 diagrams the coorientational model of communication. To better understand the dynamics of this model, you should imagine meeting a

FIGURE 3.1

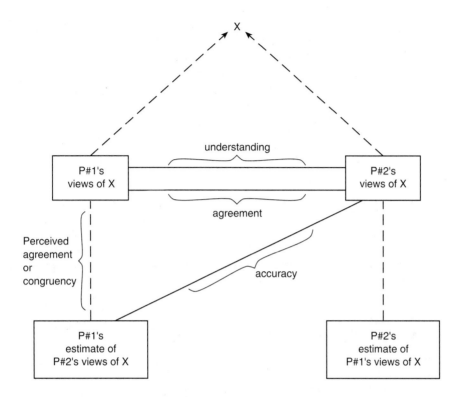

new person, maybe at a party, and that you both are represented in the model. You are P#1; the new person you have just met is P#2. Notice in the figure that P#1 and P#2 are communicating and that they are cooriented toward something called X. Notice the dotted lines indicating that P#1 can have a perception about what P#2 is thinking about X, and that P#2 can have a perception about what P#1 is thinking about X. Let us say that you and this other person strike up a conversation and, as luck will have it, the conversation turns to the subject of public relations. The X toward which you and this other person are coorientated is "public relations."

Here is how the coorientation model works. You have an idea in your mind about the concept of public relations. The other person has an idea about public relations, too. Judging by the other person's initial comments and nonverbal cues, you might guess or think you know what the other person thinks about public relations. With the same amount of limited information and cues, the other person will think, probably as you are talking, that he or she knows what you think about public relations. If you are both right, then you have accurate perceptions; if not, then your perceptions are inaccurate. As the two of you continue to talk about public relations, your perceptions will become more accurate. You may not like what the other person thinks about public relations, and the other person might not like what you have to say about public relations either; but at least, the result of your communication is more accurate perceptions. As a result of your conversation, you might agree to disagree, but you both will understand each other better.

If you substitute Public #1 and Public #2 for P#1 and P#2 in Figure 3.1, the model is useful for describing relationships and perceptions among various publics. The coorientational model of communication emphasizes the importance of accurate communication. It is the hallmark of the professional public relations practitioner to facilitate communication and understanding among various groups and publics so that there are at least more accurate perceptions of other people's points of view. People may well agree to disagree as the result of increased communication; but, at least they will better understand each other. One implication of the coorientation model is that understanding does not mean necessarily being in agreement; it means having accurate perceptions.

A Situational Model of Public Relations

American philosopher John Dewey and sociologist Herbert Blumer defined publics in similar ways.[3] According to these two scholars, members of a public have three basic characteristics:

1. Its members are faced with similar problems or opportunities.
2. They recognize and are willing to discuss these problems or opportunities.
3. They want to organize themselves better to deal with these problems or opportunities.

Building on this three-part definition of a public, Grunig and his associates have conducted a series of research studies designed to explore and develop a situational model of public relations.[4] According to this model, three factors help explain and predict the communication behavior of publics. Members of the public must recognize the problem; they must perceive the problem as being relevant to their lives; and, they must feel they can do something about the problem. Using each factor as a variable, a number of provocative theoretical statements can be developed about communication behaviors of publics. For example, the more a public recognizes a problem, perceives the problem as being relevant to their lives, and feels that they can do something about it, the more likely members of the public will appreciate and participate in communication about the problem.

The situational model of public relations suggests that each of these factors can be influenced by an effective public relations manager. A public's problem recognition ability and perception of the problem's relevance can be influenced through education. The public's feeling that something can be done about the situation also can be affected by education and by changing the availability of options for the public. The model also suggests that certain publics in certain situations will be more appreciative of and responsive to public relations campaigns than will others. For example, if a management group does not think the European market affects their marketing, does not see any linkage between their organization and the European market, and does not have any slack resources, then they are not likely to care about or respond to a public relations campaign about investment opportunities in Europe.

Markets and Publics Are Not Equivalent Concepts

Markets and publics are not identical concepts, although they both describe segments of a population. An implication of the situational model is that publics are defined by their problems and their approaches to dealing with their problems. Because publics recognize a common set of problems and want to be better organized to do something about their situation, publics turn to organizations for solutions; publics seek out organizations.[5]

Organizations, on the other hand, seek out markets. Markets are segments of the population that have desired characteristics that can help an organization achieve its mission. The decisions that define a market are made by management. Marketing managers can identify a large segment of the population as a potential market then, for whatever reasons, choose not to enter it. Publics, on the other hand, even if initially ignored, often have a way of pushing themselves into the picture and making people take notice. The transition from latent, to aware, to active public is an organizing process. When a public has become active, it has become an organization: it is a group of individuals working together to achieve a common goal. It will seek out other organizations and publics to help achieve its goals. Markets can be developed and refined, but they do not transform themselves into organizations; publics do.

Defining Publics as Nonvariables

Traditional publics have been classified into fairly broad categories: employees, stockholders, management, customers, community groups, men, women, union members, whites, blacks, Hispanics, old, young, etc. Such broad categories of publics often are named first, then described with appropriate demographics and psychographics. Using this procedure, a public is given a label; then, it is described by finding out as much as possible about its members—income, age, gender, religion, likes, dislikes, where they live, where they work, etc. Naming a public and then describing its characteristics is the conventional way to define a public. Such a definition is a nonvariable: an individual is either in or out of the public, whatever its name.

"The general public" is a nonvariable. Such a mass audience is rarely used as the target audience for a public relations campaign; it's too broad. Within the general public are not only better defined target publics, but also unintended publics which, if exposed to a campaign, may react in unexpected ways.

Geographic markets also are nonvariables. Often defined as the organization's domain or area of influence, geographic markets are filled with groups which are not publics. True publics emerge from geographic markets once they become aware of themselves, coorientate toward common interests, and form relationships with other publics.

Other nonvariable definitions of publics are demographic and socioeconomic categories such as gender, age, race and income. Also, roles or positions such as community leader, home owner, father, editor, legislator, stockholder, and college student are nonvariable definitions of publics.

Readership or viewership of selected media also can be used to define publics as nonvariables. For example, subscribers vs. nonsubscribers; viewers vs. nonviewers; or, people exposed to a campaign message vs. those not exposed to it.

A variation on this approach to defining publics is to cluster subsets of nonvariables. For example, certain members of an occupation, in certain age brackets, in certain markets, who subscribe to certain publications, might be defined as one public. It is a narrowly defined public that is still a nonvariable: an individual is classified as either being in this public or not.

Defining Publics Using Variables

Another approach is to define publics using variables. Most nonvariable publics can be transformed into variables by classifying them according to the degree to which an individual or group possesses the nonvariable characteristic. Gender and race often are used to classify people as nonvariables; yet, these classic nonvariables can be transformed into variables by considering an individual's degree of masculinity or femininity, or the person's degree of ethnic identity. As another example, instead of either/or differences in socioeconomic status, a public can be described by degrees of income and education.

For publics to be defined using variables, there need to be more than one basic category; there need to be at least two, if not many more, degrees or levels of measurement. A variable—for example, a public's degree of education—can be ranked: sixteen years of education is more than twelve years of education; a college degree is more than a high school degree. Variables used to define publics have scales indicating priority differences among members of the public; for example, this public has more of this characteristic than another. Interval and ratio scaling are more precise ways to classify publics; for example, the proportion of income spent on housing, the amount of money spent per year on car repairs, the degree of favorable impression of a candidate, the amount of time spent watching television, etc.

Another approach to defining publics as variables is to identify clusters of people with similar reactions to certain issues of concern to the client or sponsoring organization, and to conduct research to find out more about these individuals. The approach is to research the public—using geodemographic, psychographic and lifestyle studies—and then, to label the public. First intended publics are surveyed to determine who among the members would appreciate communication about the subject matter; then, the campaign is targeted to them; labeling them is the least concern and is done last, if at all. The approach here is to recognize important traits and predispositions for favorable communication, search out the people with these traits, and target activities to these preferred publics. Following are two examples of this approach.

Employees were surveyed about their company's internal communication media.[6] They were asked what they liked and disliked about the various internal media, how often they thought about certain issues, and how much influence they thought they had on organizational matters. Those employees who responded in similar ways were clustered together, and the communication patterns of these people were identified. When demographics were linked to these publics, it became evident where consistent publics were within the organization. The editor of the company's newsletter used this approach to identify the mix or proportion of high-interest readers in various locations within the organization, so that internal media could be designed to better serve those publics.

A similar approach to defining publics—first, with variables, then with nonvariables (labels)—was used in an advocacy advertising campaign.[7] Pretests of readers of selected publications were conducted to determine the proportion of readers who are predisposed to agree or disagree or feel neutral about certain key issues identified by the corporation as important public affairs issues. Those publications without the preferred mix of readers are eliminated from the campaign. Posttests are conducted to monitor shifts that occur in the mix of readers for the targeted publications. As one director of public relations, said it is better to target information and activities at "friendlies" than it is to waste time, money and effort on publics not likely to be influenced by the advocacy advertising.

Two Case Studies Illustrate How to Define Publics

Two campaigns illustrate how to define publics using occupational roles, geodemographics, psychographics, infographics and lifestyles. The choices and consequences—in terms of usefulness, explanation and prediction—are examined.

. . .

CASE 3.1:

Freddie Mac's Person-to-Person Campaign

Freddie Mac is a stockholder-owned corporation chartered by Congress in 1970 to facilitate the flow of funds to mortgage lenders who, in turn, would loan the funds to those interested in owning homes and apartments. Over the years, Freddie Mac has helped finance one in every eight American homes, including more than half a million apartment units. In the late 1980s, the corporation experienced phenomenal growth; in five years, it increased by 500 percent its issuance of mortgage-backed securities, introduced new securities, and increased its customer base by 100 percent. This dramatic growth, combined with the physical separation of a large home office from more than five regional centers throughout the nation, a relatively high turnover rate among employees, and frequent changes in the structure of senior management, produced, according to the director of employee communications, a "shell-shocked staff, wary of new initiatives."

These are the steps the director of employee communications took to research, plan, implement and evaluate an internal public relations campaign:

1. She commissioned an internal communication audit by an international consulting firm that specialized in employee communication.
2. The consulting firm had two representatives conduct personal interviews with all members of senior management. They also conducted eight employee focus groups: three at headquarters (one with directors, one with managers, and one with staff-level employees), and one each at five different regional centers, with groups that included a mix of managers and nonmanagers.
3. The audit results were reported for two occupational roles: members of management and all other employees, both at headquarters and at regional centers. When asked questions about sources of corporate information, both managers and employees indicated that face-to-face meetings were their preferred choice of communication.
4. Objectives for a person-to-person communication campaign were developed: 1) to facilitate candid, face-to-face encounters between employees and senior management; 2) to convey corporate goals, industry events and organizational changes to employees; 3) to give executives a means to gain feedback from employees on corporate activities and issues; and 4) to improve staff-management relationships. The person-to-person campaign goals complemented other corporate objectives, among them, enhancement of the corporate culture by building a common understanding of corporate goals and directions, reduction of employee turnover rates, and increased interaction between executives and employees.

A packet of materials was distributed to employees. Reprinted with permission of Freddie Mac.

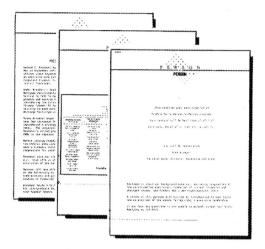

5. The campaign involved inviting, in the course of one year, all 2,000 employees to participate at least once in a series of four-hour person-to-person sessions between employees and managers. Each session included six to eight discussion groups composed of one member of senior management and from five to eight employees. Following an introduction, there were group discussions and a break; then, the executives, as a panel, answered questions from participants. A dozen such person-to-person events were held during the first two years, and more than 500 employees participated. RSVP invitations were mailed to employees three weeks before each event. One week prior to the event, participants were mailed packets of information that included biographies of the participating executives, an organizational chart, and summaries of current corporate issues.
6. Employees were asked to evaluate the person-to-person campaign by completing short questionnaires at the end of the sessions. Approximately 90 percent of the participants had returned questionnaires by the end of the first year of the campaign. A majority of employee respondents indicated that they thought the executives spoke candidly. They appreciated the executives' willingness to share their insights on corporate events and agenda, and most said that their understanding of corporate goals was enhanced. Executives said they appreciated the opportunity to hear employee concerns firsthand.

. . .

Notice that the design of the communication audit, which divided employees into two publics, was based on discussions between the consultants and the director of employee communication, and other senior managers. In this case, members of the dominant coalition defined internal publics as being either managers or nonmanagers.

CASE 3.2:

Job Corps Campaign

The Job Corps of the U.S. Department of Labor (DOL) offers basic education and job training to teenagers. Operating through a partnership with private employers and labor organizations, the Job Corps particularly targets low-income black teenagers who have exceptionally high rates of unemployment. Major corporations and nonprofit organizations manage and operate seventy-five Job Corps centers under DOL contractual agreements. At certain centers, labor unions and trade associations provide special training. Each center operates seven days a week. The centers subcontract to local organizations the tasks of recruiting and screening eligible trainees.

When the number of female trainees dipped well below the number of teenage women who could be trained within one Job Corps region, the agency hired a public relations firm to design and implement a campaign to boost enrollments. The region served a five-state area where there were thirteen training centers, approximately 5,000 training slots and a $60 million annual budget. The centers were located in urban, suburban and rural settings.

The public relations agency which won the contract had conducted other public relations work for the Job Corps in this region. Practitioners were familiar with the local directors of the training centers and other Job Corps officials.

Here are the steps the public relations agency took to research, plan, implement and evaluate the Job Corps campaign:

1. While preparing their proposal in response to the federal agency's RFP, the public relations firm conducted informal research by contacting training center directors and asking them to identify major problems in recruiting black teenage women into their programs.
2. With the cooperation of the center directors, the public relations agency surveyed approximately 200 black females who were current Job Corps trainees, selected randomly from nine different centers in the region. The purpose of the survey was to find out the young women's motivation for being involved in the program; major persons of influence affecting their decision to enroll in the program; interest in earning a high school diploma through the Job Corps; immediate plans after graduation; and, description of Job Corps benefits, particularly what they would tell others about the program.
3. The public relations agency analyzed research reports from the U.S. Census Bureau and DOL to determine areas within the region that were more heavily populated by the target groups.
4. The agency also perused an in-depth evaluation of the Job Corps training program that had been conducted almost ten years earlier, but which still had pertinent insights into why black women often were too discouraged to enroll.

5. Informal discussions with recruiters also revealed information about changes in family structures that were affecting teenage female enrollments.
6. The agency incorporated this research into its proposal. Several other public relations firms also bid on the contract.
7. Upon winning the contract, the public relations agency commissioned a survey by a professional polling organization that interviewed a sample of eligible young women in shopping malls in three cities. Interviewers encountered young women randomly in the shopping areas, prequalified them by asking economic and age questions, and proceeded with the interview in a quiet location within the shopping area. The survey measured, among other factors, interest in job training, awareness of the Job Corps, relative importance of training benefits, and the type of influential people the women turned to when they were making personal decisions.
8. From this combination of informal and formal research, the agency developed the following profile of the target audience:
   - is an 18–year-old female high school dropout;
   - reads at an elementary-school level;
   - comes from a poor family headed by a woman;
   - never has held a full-time job;
   - does not want to leave her neighborhood to receive job training; and,
   - looks to her parents and family when making important decisions.
9. The agency interviewed a sample of editors and reporters working for weekly and daily newspapers in the region. They discovered that only a few had more than basic knowledge about the Job Corps, and that many were not aware that the program, which had begun as all-male in the 1960s, now accepted females.
10. With this information, the agency designed a campaign targeted at three publics:
    1) Eligible youth 16 to 21 years of age were chosen as the primary public, with priority given to females.
    2) Families and adult influencers of potential enrollees were a secondary public that included school guidance counselors, ministers, social service workers, media, and opinion leaders.
    3) Job Corps directors and personnel who specialized in recruiting and screening enrollees also were targeted.
11. The agency set specific objectives for the campaign: to create awareness, encourage enrollment, counter misinformation, and foster greater cooperation within the Job Corps to boost female recruitment.
12. Planning the campaign involved a series of staff meetings and monthly conference calls with center directors, as media and staff training materials were developed and implemented.
13. Implementation included training all urban-area recruiters and screeners. The training included explaining results of geodemographic research that indicated where potential enrollees were most likely to be found; how to best present the benefits of Job Corps training; how to maintain contact with potential enrollees; where to locate secondary publics and how to address their concerns; and, how to build on the mass media campaign being executed by the public relations agency.

14. Counsel provided to center staffs included how to generate the regular flow of hometown press releases; how to arrange for favorable center publicity in local media; how to prepare for difficult situations which might generate unfavorable publicity; how to use media materials produced by the public relations agency.
15. Editorial service to the centers included the agency's writing and distributing hometown press releases during the first few months of the campaign, and assisting center staffs in developing in-house expertise necessary to continue the flow of hometown press releases featuring current enrollees.
16. The centerpiece of the media campaign was a ten-minute video featuring singer Michael Jackson's recording of his smash-hit, "Man in the Mirror," which featured the refrain, "Make that change!" Other elements of the media campaign included TV and radio public service announcements based on the video. Also included in the media campaign were brochures and posters carrying the theme "Make that change!"
17. Special events included fashion shows in shopping malls and promotion leveraged through tie-ins with urban contemporary radio stations.
18. Extensive radio advertising during one recruiting period included a media buyer's analysis of the radio markets in the region and purchases of time on the stations which were listened to most frequently by the primary target audience.
19. Media monitoring and editorial clipping services were used to track media placements. Follow-up surveys with enrollees, school guidance counselors, center staff, and others, indicated that campaign objectives were met. Within twelve months of the start of the campaign, total enrollment in the region was increased by 10 percent, to 104 percent of capacity.

. . .

Although the primary target public of unemployed young black women ages 16 to 21 was specified in the government agency's initial Request for Proposal, the extensive amount of research conducted for this campaign yielded useful geodemographic, psychographic, infographic and lifestyle information not only about the primary target public but also about secondary and tertiary publics.

Significant Differences

The most obvious difference between these two cases is that one campaign focused exclusively on internal publics and the other focused on both internal and external publics. Another obvious difference is that the employee population was easy to find; young unemployed black women were much more difficult to locate.

One campaign focused, from the beginning, on active publics; while the other began with latent and aware publics and ended by creating more active publics. Employee publics are active publics: all of its members are, by definition, members of an organization. Members of management are likely to be more active than nonmanagers, but all groups of employees can be considered active publics. They are well aware of each other as members of a public, and they want to better organize themselves to deal with the problems and opportunities they confront. However, most young unemployed black women are not active; many are aware, but many others are latent. The goal of the Job Corps campaign was achieved by effectively motivating latent and aware publics into becoming active publics. The young black women recruited into the Job Corps program as a result of their exposure to the public relations campaign constituted an active public because, by enrolling in the training program, they demonstrated their willingness to do something about the problems they confronted.

Using concepts from the coorientational model of communication, the degrees of congruency, accuracy, agreement, and understanding varied between the two cases. The degree of congruency between what members of the target employee public thought, and what they thought members of management thought, was closer for employees but more distant for unemployed young black women. Employees are more socialized into the sponsoring organization and identify themselves with management more readily than do potential recruits for a training program. Because they are more socialized into their system, employees had more accurate perceptions of what management thought than did potential recruits. Consequently, the level of understanding at the beginning of the communication campaign was higher among employees and management than it was between potential recruits and management.

The levels of involvement, problem recognition and perceived options of stakeholders were also different for these two cases. The employees recognized the problems they faced; they knew they had a major stake in the success of the organization and were eager to discuss their options. Consequently, they appreciated the person-to-person communication campaign. While unemployed black women obviously knew they had problems finding jobs, most needed to be convinced that they could do something about their situation; consequently, they were fairly fatalistic in their communication behavior.

One of the most significant differences between these two cases was the use of nonvariables and variables to describe key publics. Freddie Mac management commissioned a communication audit that had the potential to refine if not redefine internal publics; yet, simple categories of managers and nonmanagers were used before, during and after the audit. Prior to the beginning of the Job Corps campaign, the public relations agency conducted economic, geodemographic and psychographic analyses of the target public. During the planning stages of the campaign, the agency also conducted infographic and lifestyle studies. Eventually, they developed a sophisticated profile of the target audience that included a number of variables including the degree of willingness to relocate to take job training, closeness to family, frequency of contacts with school counselors, and personal responsibility for making changes.

GUIDELINES FOR DEFINING KEY PUBLICS

Here are three basic guidelines for defining key publics:

1. Identify who is affected by the problems or opportunities. Focus only on significant relationships.

    In Case 3.1, the director of employee communication recognized that all employees, both managers and nonmanagers, were affected. Part-time and temporary employees were not considered. In Case 3.2, the members of DOL who wrote the original RFP stated that unemployed black women 16 to 21 years of age were the primary target audience. While they wanted the program to continue targeting young black men, the most significant relationship they wanted to establish in this campaign was with unemployed young black women.

2. Name the public and then conduct research, if needed or better yet, conduct research and then name the public.

    In both Case 3.1 and 3.2, the public was named and then research was conducted. In Case 3.2, the extensive amount of research that focused on the target audience also yielded information about secondary publics. In this case, the research led to the identification of adult influencers as a significant public.

3. Pretest campaign materials or implement the campaign and then evaluate the usefulness of definitions of key publics by asking, Do these definitions help us predict or explain communication behaviors of the publics?

    In Case 3.1, no pretesting of campaign materials occurred. The communication audit indicated that employees wanted more person-to-person communication; so, such a campaign was implemented. Because both managers and nonmanagers later indicated the campaign was a success, there was no reason to think that more precise definitions of their internal publics were needed. In Case 3.2, both the Job Corps managers and the staff of the public relations agency knew that the target audience would be hard to reach and difficult to persuade, so campaign materials were pretested among current trainees and center staff. Also, during the campaign, adjustments were made in placement of hometown news releases, staging special events and making specific media buys, based on initial reactions by samples of the target publics.

TABLE 3.1:

Probability of Engaging in Public Relations Activity Based on Whether or Not Dominant Coalition Views the Target Public as a Major Concern.[a]

	Dominant Coalition Views Public as Major Concern		
Target for Public Relations Campaign	Yes (n = 71)	No/ Don't Know (n = 23)	Sign.[b]
New business	63%	39%	***
The competition	37	18	***
Major suppliers	33	18	***
Current customers	70	44	***
Employees	60	37	***
Stockholders/investors	51	22	***
Government officials			
Local	50	30	***
State/regional	56	27	***
National	35	20	**
International	20	15	
Media representatives	69	49	***
Local			
State/regional	62	45	***
National	40	31	
International	22	18	

(a) Percent of respondents indicating "probability that your organization will initiate and target a new public relations campaign directed at the following publics within the next month," based on 10–point 0%-to-100% scale.

(b) Significance of difference determined by t-test; reported is probability of difference due to chance: ** = .01; *** = .001.

SURVEY RESULTS: DOMINANT COALITION'S VIEW OF PUBLICS CRUCIAL

The public relations professionals who participated in the survey conducted by the author were asked to indicate whether or not the dominant coalitions in their organizations viewed certain publics as being a major concern. They also were asked to indicate the frequency with which their organizations engaged in public relations campaigns targeted toward these same publics.

Table 3.1 indicates a strong relationship between the dominant coalition's view that a public is a major concern and the likelihood that the organization will target a public relations campaign toward that public. Across the board—for new business, the competition, major suppliers, current customers, employees, stockholders, government officials and media representatives—if respondents said that the dominant coalition thought a certain public was a major concern, there was a very high probability that there would be a campaign targeted toward that public. The implication of these findings for public relations managers is: *Knowing the views of the dominant coalition toward key publics will help predict and explain an organization's public relations.*

ALTERNATIVE THEORIES OF PUBLICS

The main reason that public relations managers define publics is to better understand the communication behavior of the publics. If labeling an employee a member of management helps explain and predict how that person will respond to employee communication, it is a useful definition. If describing the target public as unemployed black teenage women does not help the public relations manager design an appropriate campaign, then more research and a better profile of the target audience is required. A useful definition of a public provides insights into a public's communication behavior. Implied within these definitions are theories that help explain or predict the behavior of publics.

COMMUNICATION THEORIES HELP DEFINE PUBLICS AND RELATIONSHIPS

Three communication theories have been especially useful for predicting and explaining the behavior of publics: the elaboration-likelihood, agenda-setting, and community-power-structure theories. Three case studies will illustrate how public relations managers can use these theories in defining publics and relationships.

Elaboration-Likelihood Theory

This theory assumes that persuasion and long-term change in attitudes occurs more often when a person not only focuses on a message but also elaborates upon it while thinking about it.[8] The theory predicts that certain aspects of a public relations program or campaign are more likely than others to elicit this desirable message-elaboration from individuals. Using this theory, publics can be defined by the degree to which they are likely to elaborate upon messages sent to them.

This theory is similar to Grunig's situational model, because it classifies publics by their cognitions about issues and problems. But, it is more, because this theory not only predicts *when* publics will process information but also *how* publics will process information they receive. For example, the theory predicts that if the quality of the message is high (that is: clear, coherent, logical), and it is very relevant to members of a target public, then it is likely that the information will be focused on seriously and processed centrally: elaboration and persuasion can be expected.⁹ If, on the other hand, the message quality is low, or it has little immediate relevance, then it is likely that the information will be lightly considered and processed peripherally. In such a case, if persuasion is to occur, it will not be because the message was elaborated upon by the receiver but because there were sufficient cues (such as source credibility, pleasing design, or third-party endorsements) embedded within the message to evoke an appropriate response in the receiver. Using this theory, publics can be defined by the degree to which they would be intellectually engaged in by certain messages. The practical implications for public relations managers are to know how to identify publics most likely to centrally process and elaborate upon certain information, and to know the salient cues that can enhance messages not likely to be given serious consideration by target publics.

. . .

CASE 3.3

State Bank Victoria of Melbourne, Australia

There were more than 525 bank branches of State Bank Victoria, headquartered in Melbourne, Australia. Senior bank officials had developed a new investment product, called a High Yield Call Account, which they wanted to introduce to the public. Prior to the public announcement, they wanted to educate branch managers and other bank employees about the new product, so that they would properly explain and sell it to bank customers. The senior officials asked the manager of marketing and public relations to design an internal communication program that would help the bank introduce the product to its employees. Here are the steps the communication manager took:

1. She knew that the program had to meet two well-established corporate goals:
   - For staff to be knowledgeable about all products and services offered by the bank.
   - For staff to be able not only to handle all customer inquiries but also to identify how bank products and services could meet the needs of potential customers.
2. After discussions with senior management and her staff, she established two objectives for the program:
   - To have at least 60 percent of the bank's branches conduct training sessions for staffs to ensure basic product awareness.
   - To attract one million dollars in deposits before the external launch to the general public.
3. Her strategy was to use specific target publics, and to stratify messages so each public received only the information it needed. Four target publics were identified: senior regional managers, branch managers, branch staff, and all staff. She worked with the bank's training department to prepare some program material. Separate messages and media were used for each public:
   - For senior regional managers, a personal letter from their supervisor, the chief general manager, was prepared that gave background

information on the product, launch details, strategic implication of the product for the bank's portfolio, and predictions about how branch managers and staff would be affected by the product introduction.
- For branch managers, a launch kit was prepared that included: 1) a letter from the chief general manager to branch managers that was similar to the one sent to the regional managers; 2) a comparison chart listing all the bank's products that demonstrated each product's unique selling points; 3) a training booklet so that the branch manager could conduct a training session for branch staff; 4) a detailed list of the product features; and, 5) an easy reference list of selling points. The kit was designed to generate "tactile involvement." While it contained five interesting-looking pieces, the kit could not be expensive-looking. As the public relations manager said,

> "Branch managers are very cost-conscious; to make the communication work, it had to be low-cost and look low-cost. Otherwise, they would possibly reject the message. However, it was also essential that the communication be eye-catching and that it be addressed to the branch manager. Otherwise, the kit may have been overlooked in the multitude of paper managers receive every business day."

- For branch staff a memorandum with procedural information was distributed.
- For all staff, articles were published in the bank's employee newsletter.

4. More than 80 percent of the branch managers conducted training sessions for their staffs prior to the public announcement, and 10 percent conducted training sessions after the launch date. In the ten business days prior to the external launch, more than two million dollars in deposits to the High Yield Call Accounts had been made, all generated by personal selling efforts of the bank staff.

. . .

The elaboration-likelihood model would have predicted the success of this Australian public relations program, which won an award of merit from the International Association of Business Communicators. The key to the program's success was the information kit to the branch managers, which was designed to facilitate tactile involvement and to meet the low-cost expectations of the target audience. The quality of the message was high, and its relevance to branch managers was very high, primarily because the kit contained lists of selling points and a discussion of how the new product would affect staff members. Given the intended audience—and these message characteristics—persuasion and elaboration were to be expected.

Agenda-Setting Theory

The agenda-setting theory assumes a two-step flow when public relations programs and campaigns use mass communication: 1) from public relations specialists to the media, and 2) from the media to target publics. The assumption is that the media serve to set the agenda for what members of the public discuss. The theory does not assume that the media affects what the public will think about certain topics and issues; rather, it assumes that the media affects, to a significant degree, what topics and issues the public will think about.[10] The theory predicts that the longer specific topics and issues appear in the media, and the more prominently they are displayed in the media, the more likely the media's publics will recall reading or hearing about the topics and issues, and discussing them with others.[11]

One of the practical implications of the agenda-setting theory is that public relations managers should not expect to dramatically affect target publics with messages that have received only limited media coverage; desired items in the media need to be prominently displayed over a long period of time (3–6 weeks for certain issues, much longer for other issues) before it will be possible to measure public opinion and find indications that specific mediated messages have been received and comprehended by target publics. The theory underscores the importance of properly defining and understanding intermediary publics such as reporters, editors, and publishers, and of meeting their needs and interests not once, or twice, but many times, over a sustained period of time.

. . .

CASE 3.4:

The Hawaii Business Roundtable Campaign

Hawaii's public school system was of increasing concern to a few parents, students, school officials, and some civic organizations in the late 1980s, when the Hawaii Business Roundtable, an association of twenty senior business executives, decided to take action. They commissioned a comprehensive study by an internationally recognized educational consulting group which researched the situation and prepared a report, called "The Hawaii Plan: Educational Excellence for the Pacific Era." The report contained a significant set of recommendations on how to reform Hawaii's educational system. So impressed were the members of the business association with the report that three months before the legislative session was scheduled to begin, they authorized a major public relations and legislative lobbying campaign. Here are the steps the Hawaii Business Roundtable took to conduct their very successful campaign:

1. They authorized the establishment of a special council made up of public relations and communication professionals from the member organizations in the Business Roundtable, and from Hill and Knowlton/Communications-Pacific, the Hawaii office of the international public relations agency.
2. They established the following goals for the campaign:
   - To convince a cynical public of the importance of and possibilities for educational reform.

Publicity generated by The Hawaii Plan. Reprinted with permission of Hill and Knowlton, Inc. Copyright January 1991 by Hill and Knowlton, Inc.

- To gain the support of the governor and state administration officials and to convince them to place educational reform high on the legislative agenda.
- To encourage state legislators to introduce bills designed to change the educational status quo.
- To involve school administrators and elected boards of education in the change process.

3. The committee identified six target publics: the governor and members of his administration; state legislators; senior state education officials, including members of boards of education; principals, teachers, and students; and, business and community leaders.

4. Research was conducted on each of the target publics to determine their positions on educational reform. A list of volunteers willing to contact members of the target publics and to personally present campaign information to them was developed.
5. The implementation of the campaign relied heavily on the media:
   - The Hawaii Plan was formally presented to the governor at a press conference, which was attended by key legislators, education officials, and community leaders.
   - An information kit was prepared and distributed statewide to all media, and others.
   - Members of the Business Roundtable, education specialists, and community leaders discussed The Hawaii Plan on public television.
   - A speaker's bureau, composed of members of the Business Roundtable, volunteers, and others involved in the campaign who participated in TV and radio talk shows and made speeches to community groups, was established.
   - Public service announcements were aired on radio and TV, urging people who wanted improvements in Hawaii's schools to call in their support. Those who called heard a taped message from the governor, and later they received a personal call from a volunteer, who suggested appropriate action plans.
   - A weekly newsletter updating educational reform actions and legislation was published and distributed to media, interested groups, and individuals within the state.
   - Experts who supported The Hawaii Plan testified before legislative committees and provided documentation useful in drafting new legislation.
6. From the initial press conference to the opening day of the legislative session, and beyond, the campaign generated daily media coverage of educational reform issues promoted by The Hawaii Plan.
7. Letters to the editors of newspapers indicated tremendous grassroots support for the campaign. Companies volunteered to form partnerships with local schools (one of the major recommendations of The Hawaii Plan). Community groups staged rallies on the steps of the state capitol. The Hawaii Plan became the blueprint for educational reform in the state legislature. The governor's state-of-the-state address recommended reforms modeled on those in The Hawaii Plan. Several significant legislative bills were introduced, and two were enacted. The campaign was such a success that the Business Roundtable continued the campaign for the following year, primarily because more reforms were needed. Many editorials and letters to editors appeared in the media praising the role of the business community in improving Hawaii's public schools.

. . .

The agenda-setting theory helps explain the success of this campaign. Because the campaign generated media coverage of The Hawaii Plan recommendations for a sustained period of time, the campaign was successful in setting the agenda for public discussion of education reforms not only among civic and community groups but also among legislators, elected officials, and school administrators. The elaboration-likelihood model helps explain why the message was so successful. The Hawaii Business

Roundtable campaign contained messages of quality and substance that were relevant to key publics; therefore, the publics elaborated upon campaign messages, making them their own, and were persuaded to act on the campaign's recommendations.

Community Power Theories

Public relations programs and campaigns aimed at affecting lifestyles—such as risk communication campaigns aimed at stopping people from smoking or getting people to check their cholesterol levels—must assume that members of the target public will turn to family, friends, and others in the community, and listen to their advice about what to do.[12] Community power theories assume that no individual will change a significant aspect of a lifestyle, and maintain the new behavior, unless there is a very supportive network of people and organizations in that person's life.[13]

Proponents of the theory argue that lifestyle campaigns should target first the community power structure, then individuals. They point out that successful campaigns designed to change lifestyles will first increase a community's capacity for social action by reinforcing local values, building coalitions, and encouraging participation in community decision-making; then, or simultaneously, they will target information to individuals. Community power theories look upon communities as change agents in the lives of individuals. Community power theories emphasize the importance of identifying, researching, and getting to know the leadership of community-based organizations most likely to support, with money and staff time, the purpose and activities of the campaign. The theories also emphasize the importance of incorporating community values within campaign messages and activities targeted at individuals.

. . .

CASE 3.5:

Minnesota Heart Health Program

The Minnesota Heart Health Program (MHHP) was funded by the federal government to research and demonstrate techniques in managing public health campaigns designed to impact lifestyles in three communities in Minnesota, North Dakota, and South Dakota. Changes in lifestyles of residents in these communities was measured over time and compared to residents living in three matched communities not receiving the campaign. The purpose of the campaign was to identify the incidence of risky behaviors within these communities, and to develop community-specific communication

campaigns designed to improve the lifestyles of individuals engaged in such risky behaviors as smoking, eating improperly, drinking too much alcohol, not exercising, and not having regular medical checkups. A key component of each community's campaign was the establishment of an advisory board of local leaders who not only helped design the campaign but also participated visibly in it, primarily by giving personal testimonials about healthy lifestyles in media messages and before community groups, and by encouraging others to participate in policy-making discussions about health issues. Here is a summary of the community analysis activities that the campaign planners engaged in within each community:

1. Two months were spent conducting personal interviews with approximately 500 randomly selected individuals in each community to determine health behaviors, medical histories, and demographics. The sample data were generalizable, within appropriate scientific margins of error, to the entire population of each community.
2. Three months were devoted in the campaign communities to conducting interviews, in person and over the telephone, with community officials and "reputed influentials" who, in turn, nominated other community leaders to participate in the interviews. The purpose of the interviews was to identify powerful relationships among health-oriented organizations and individuals within the community and to develop a list of names of possible members for advisory boards and task forces.
3. Using public records from libraries, government agencies, and health organizations, plus the original data generated by the above surveys, the planners spent two months analyzing all of the information and writing a report describing community characteristics, risk behaviors, structure, history, and special health concerns.
4. Planners reviewed local directories from churches, service groups, business associations, recreational groups, professional societies and health-related public agencies. Interviews with officials of these organizations, plus their publications and news clippings, were used to prepare a detailed inventory of organizations interested in improving health and reducing specific risk behaviors. It took three months to prepare the "community casebook," which was used extensively by planners, and others, as they continued their assessment of the community.
5. Planners wrote an analysis, based on the above information and additional interviews with community leaders, that described the community's resources and capacity for implementing a public health campaign. This information was included in the community casebook.
6. Surveys of officers from selected organizations were conducted to ascertain their awareness of the incidence of risky behaviors in the community. The information was summarized and incorporated into the community casebook.
7. Special surveys were conducted based on issues of concern within each community, such as food buying habits and membership activities for specific organizations. This information, too, was incorporated into the community casebook.

8. Community advisory boards were appointed, and special task forces were formed, to help design the public health campaign for their community. The community casebook became the central planning document in this process.
9. During implementation, community analysis activities continued. Relying primarily on weekly staff reports, unobtrusive measures, and anecdotal information, the progress and initial impact of campaign activities were tracked.
10. After the campaign, both qualitative and quantitative data were collected to analyze the impact of the campaign on individual behaviors and on the community's power structure.

. . .

The Minnesota Heart Health campaign, which is similar to public health campaigns in California, Rhode Island, and Pennsylvania, was successful, as were the campaigns in these other states, because campaign planners devoted an extraordinary amount of time and monies researching the communities and getting to know the leaders—and involving these leaders in a variety of ways in the planning and implementation of the campaign. The assumption of the planners was that by first establishing a broad base of support for individuals interested in changing risky behaviors, the probability of getting individuals to adopt new lifestyles when they were exposed to campaign messages, would be improved.

THE PLAN BOOK: PART I

As the last case indicated, the planning document that results from the efforts to define the problem, key publics, and relationships can become a focal point for the ongoing development of the public relations program or campaign. Often this document is called The Plan Book. As the program or campaign develops in complexity, so does The Plan Book.

In this chapter we will discuss briefly the purpose and look of The Plan Book when it is developed during the very initial planning stages. In Chapters 4, 5, 6, and 7, more information about The Plan Book will be presented.

At the earliest stages, when campaign managers are defining the problem (or opportunity), identifying publics, and clarifying relationships, the primary purpose of The Plan Book is to help build consensus among key decision-makers about the goals, objectives, and strategies of the program or campaign. Because individuals often review and comment on plan books developed during the early stages, most are prepared with plenty of "white space" for marginal comments and notes, and most start new topics on new pages, which makes the report appear even more spacious. Most plan books are written in a crisp, business-like fashion, using short paragraphs, lists, and lots of "bulleted" items.

A FRAMEWORK FOR ANALYZING THEORIES ABOUT PUBLICS

Communication scholar William McGuire developed a framework for analyzing the dynamic aspects of persuasion that can be used to explain and predict the communication behavior of publics.[14] See Figure 3.2. His basic four-cell framework is determined from two sets of factors: motivations that initiate communication, and end states of communication. McGuire recognized that initiation of communication, indeed all human action, springs either from a need for either growth or stability. He classified two end states of communication: cognitive or affective. Cognitive states are informational, full of thought; affective states are emotional, full of feelings. From this framework, four sets of theories were identified: cognitive stability theories, cognitive growth theories, affective stability theories, and affective growth theories.

The coorientation model of communication, presented earlier, is analogous to a cognitive stability theory. It is based on balance theories that predict that communicating parties will seek to achieve a balance of ideas and feelings about each other and the ideas and issues toward which they are cooriented. The assumption of a cognitive stability theory is that the parties involved in communication want a consistent or balanced set of ideas and feelings. Cognitive dissonance results when thoughts and feelings among the communicating parties are not attuned to each other. Because this dissonance is an uncomfortable state, the communicating parties will change ideas, feelings, or their relationships to each other in order to achieve a stable and balanced set of ideas and feelings.

An example of a cognitive growth theory is Grunig's situational model that assumes members of a public are problem solvers. According to this model, publics communicate when they think they are in a position to solve a problem. Members of publics will communicate in situations which are favorable to cognitive growth. But, if members of the public don't recognize a problem or see that they can do anything about it, then they will be fatalistic in their communication behavior.

Affective stability theories can be used to explain and predict the behavior of latent publics. Ego-defensive mechanisms within certain publics might make them selectively avoid certain messages and selectively attend to others. For example, personal pride and self-images of unemployed individuals may prevent them from tuning into campaign messages about job training programs. Effective public relations campaigns need to consider these ego-defensive mechanisms that give the person a sense of emotional stability. One way the Job Corps campaign addressed the need for affective stability among members of the target public was to channel information to adult influentials who could be compassionate and understanding when presenting the job training information to the unemployed young women.

FIGURE 3.2

Framework for developing theories about publics. Based on William J. McGuire "Theoretical foundations of campaigns," in *Public Communication Campaign*, edited by Ronald Rice and Charles Atkin (Beverly Hills, CA; Sage: 1989).

		Initiation of human communication	
		Stability	Growth
End state of human communication	Cognitive	Cognitive stability theories	Cognitive growth theories
	Affective	Affective stability theories	Affective growth theories

Affective growth theories assume people want to mature emotionally and that they will model their behavior on and learn from others whom they admire. Campaigns that use peer pressure as a motivation (for example, anti-drug campaigns) assume members are motivated to grow and mature in ways that are acceptable to their peers. When a campaign illustrates or demonstrates appropriate coping skills, for example, the assumption is that the target audience will learn the new skills by modeling, by comparing current behaviors with those depicted in the campaign. Affective growth theories assume members of the public will adapt new behaviors when doing so will make them feel they are growing emotionally and maturing as they should.

The communication behavior of a target public may be explained by several or all of these theories. It is very possible that a member of one public may be experiencing cognitive dissonance, high problem recognition, ego-defensiveness, and peer pressures. The effective public relations manager knows how to define publics and design campaigns so that all relevant aspects of the public's communication behavior are addressed. One purpose of presenting this theoretical framework is to highlight the variety of theories that are possible to explain and predict publics. Effective public relations managers do not rely on any one theory; they explore all possibilities for explaining and predicting their target publics.

IN SUMMARY . . .

While publics can be defined in numerous ways, the two basic characteristics of any public are that it is a group of people who share common concerns and who are aware of themselves. By focusing on these basic characteristics, a public relations specialist can increase the power of a public by conducting campaigns that increase a public's problem recognition ability and awareness of each other as members of a public. An effective public relations campaign can make a latent public become an aware public, and it can make an aware public become an active public.

The key to precisely defining a public is to conduct research before, during and after a campaign to determine exactly who is affected by the problem (or opportunity) and how they communicate about it. Underlying the research, and built into definitions of publics, are theories that help explain and predict the communication behavior of publics. Top management's definitions of publics definitely influence how public relations campaigns are planned and managed.

In the next chapter, more information is presented about how to plan effective public relations campaigns.

Study Questions

1. What are the similarities and differences among target audiences, markets, and publics? Be sure to define each.
2. Agree or disagree with the following statement: self-awareness and coorientation by members of a public are necessary conditions for communication to occur in any public relations campaign or program. Explain your answer.
3. Give examples of how publics can be described with nonvariables. Give examples of how the same public could be described with variables. Which is the most useful way to describe publics? Which is the most common way to describe publics? Why?
4. What are appropriate guidelines for defining key publics? Describe how the Freddie Mac campaign and the Job Corps campaign followed these guidelines.
5. Briefly describe an elaboration-likelihood theory, and explain how it might be used to explain or predict a public relations program.
6. Briefly describe an agenda-setting theory, and explain how it might be used to explain or predict a public relations program.

7. Briefly describe a community-power-structure theory, and explain how it might be used to explain or predict a public relations program.
8. Give examples of cognitive stability and cognitive growth theories of communication; and, give examples of affective stability and affective growth theories of communication.

Endnotes

1. Grunig, James, and Todd Hunt, *Managing Public Relations* (New York: Holt, Rinehart and Winston, 1984) pp. 145–160.

2. McLeod, Jack M., and Steven H. Chaffee, "Interpersonal approaches to communication research," *American Behavioral Scientist*. Vol. 16, No. 4, March/April, 1973, pp. 483–488; see also, Broom, Glen M., "Coorientational measurement of public issues," *Public Relations Review*. Vol. 3, No. 4, Winter, 1977, pp. 110–119.

3. Dewey, John, *The Public and Its Problems* (Chicago, Il: Swallow, 1927); and, Blumer, Herbert, "The mass, the public, and public opinion," in Bernard Berelson and Morris Janowitz (ed.) *Reader in Public Opinion and Communication*, 2nd edition (New York: Free Press, 1966) pp. 43–50.

4. Grunig, James, and Larissa Grunig, "Toward a theory of the public relations behavior of organizations: Review of a program of research," *Public Relations Research Annual*, edited by James Grunig and Larissa Grunig, Vol. 1 (Hillsdale, NJ: Lawrence Erlbaum, 1989) pp. 27–66.

5. Grunig, James, "Publics, audiences and market segments: Segmentation principles for campaigns," in *Information Campaigns*, edited by Charles T. Salmon (Newbury Park, CA: Sage, 1990) pp. 197–226.

6. Grunig, James E., "Some consistent types of employee publics," *Public Relations Review*, Vol.1, Winter, 1975, pp. 17–36.

7. Sethi, S. Prakash, "Advocacy advertising: A novel communication approach to building effective relations with external constituencies," *International Journal of Advertising* Vol. 6, No. 4, 1987, pp. 279–298.

8. Petty, R. E., and J. T. Cacioppo, *Communication in persuasion: Central and peripheral routes to attitude change* (New York: Springer/Verlag, 1986).

9. Devine, Patricia G, and Edward R. Hirt, "Message strategies for information campaigns: A social psychological analysis," in *Information Campaigns*, edited by Charles T. Salmon (Newbury Park, CA: Sage, 1989) pp. 236–238.

10. McCombs, Maxwell, and David L. Shaw, "The agenda-setting function of the media," *Public Opinion Quarterly*, Vol. 36, 1972, pp. 176–188.

11. Maxwell E. McCombs, "Agenda-setting function of mass media," *Public Relations Review*, Vol. 3, Winter, 1977, pp. 89–95.

12. Fischhoff, Baruch, "Risk: A guide to controversy," in *Improving Risk Communication* (Washington, D.C.: National Academy Press, 1989) pp. 211–319.

13. Finnegan, John. R., Neil Bracht, and K. Viswanath, "Community power and leadership analysis in lifestyle campaigns," in *Information Campaigns*, edited by Charles T. Salmon (Newbury Park, CA: Sage, 1990) pp. 54–84.

14. McGuire, William J., "Theoretical foundations of campaigns," in *Public Communication Campaigns*, 2nd edition (Newbury Park, CA: Sage, 1989) pp. 43–66.

CHAPTER FOUR

How to Plan Effective Public Relations

. . . . .

When she put the phone down, the public relations manager for the national association knew she had more to do that day than she had time. She had to work on the monthly newsletter, plan an annual conference, and prepare publicity for a "grand opening"—not to mention attend several meetings and respond to a stack of phone messages and correspondence on her desk. It was going to be a busy day.

If she were an inexperienced manager, she might approach each task that day on a first-come-first-served basis. She would start by writing copy for the newsletter until she ran out of time. Then she would go to the annual conference planning meeting where she would probably take on even more gotta-do-today tasks. Later, she would try to write press releases for the grand opening, and this would leave her with very little time to return phone calls or write letters. If she focused her energies on each task in the same earnest yet naive way, she might not be able to sort out the various pressures on her. As the day wore on, she would probably begin to feel less and less in control of her job. It would be a hectic and frustrating day.

If she were an experienced manager, she would know how to devote a different amount of her time and energies to each task depending on whether the task was routine or nonroutine. She would recognize the newsletter as a routine event and plan accordingly: she would prepare a list of activities, with deadlines, and distribute it to the people involved. She would walk into the annual conference planning meeting knowing that this was a routine but complex event requiring more sophisticated planning efforts on her part and a greater number of planning meetings. She would view the grand opening as a fairly complex but, nevertheless, routine event, requiring various planning charts and another series of meetings. She would know that her major responsibilities as the manager for all these tasks would be to establish agendas for each activity, and to make assignments—for herself and others—so that each activity was both effective and efficient. It would be a busy, productive day, but because she knew how to plan she would feel in control of it.

. . .

PLANNING CHARACTERISTICS

Public relations programs which are not planned properly are often reactive—driven by the demands of others. Some reactive public relations programs, depending on the situation and pure luck, may be successful. But more often than not, reactive public relations are ineffective because they lack direction and do not reinforce or help redirect the mission of the client or sponsoring organization.

Planned public relations programs and campaigns are proactive: they are systematically designed to meet specific goals and objectives of the client or sponsoring organization.

At a minimum, planning means acknowledging the current state of affairs, recognizing what is desired, and figuring out what it takes to get there. While some public relations plans may be informal, even unwritten, procedures for doing work; others are highly detailed formal documents. Regardless of the specific nature of the event or set of activities being planned, there are basic steps common to the planning process:

1. Recognizing and defining the problem or opportunity, and deciding—often getting a mandate from top management or a client—to do something about it.
2. Determining goals and objectives.
3. Generating ideas and alternatives.
4. Developing and coordinating an action plan, including production of campaign materials.
5. Implementing the plan: conducting the program or campaign.
6. Evaluating and refining the campaign.

These generic steps in the planning process are emphasized in varying degrees by public relations managers depending on the nature of the event being planned. Because routine events are recurring or relatively predictable, planning public relations programs and campaigns for them often involves relatively quick and straightforward decision-making techniques that primarily focus on synchronizing activities. On the other hand, planning public relations programs and campaigns for nonroutine events often involves more lengthy and unusual decision-making techniques that help to generate innovative solutions; then, once innovative solutions are generated, the planning becomes more "routine," focusing on synchronizing and completing the planned set of activities.

The major value of systematically planning for routine events is that it helps efficiently allocate organizational resources by identifying and emphasizing appropriate administrative controls. Lists of activities are prepared which allow detailed staffing arrangements to be made, budgets to be prepared, and deadlines to be discussed. Without such lists, it is possible to get some of the jobs done, but not as efficiently.

The perception of an upcoming event by top management or by the public relations manager strongly influences how and why a manager will plan public relations campaigns. If an event is perceived as being predictable because it is recurring or thought to be relatively routine, then planning for it most likely will involve some form of calendarizing: the practitioner may list planned activities, establish milestones or prepare flow charts and graphs about the scheduled activities. The primary focus of this type of planning is getting the job done on time.

If the event involves a great deal of uncertainty or is perceived as being nonroutine, planning for it most likely will involve more people and more time than if the event is perceived as routine. If the event is seen as nonroutine, the initial stage in the planning process will emphasize generating new ideas and identifying new possibilities. Once a manageable set of activities is identified, the planning shifts its focus to getting the job done on time.

Examples of Planning for Routine Events

The following three case studies illustrate planning for routine events. One case illustrates how to prepare a simple list of things-to-do. Another case illustrates how to use a timeline. The third case illustrates how to develop combinations of timelines and project flow charts.

. . .

CASE 4.1

A Small Association's Newsletter

One of dozens of tasks the program chairman had volunteered to do for the Public Relations Division of the Association for Education in Journalism and Mass Communication that year was to publish two issues of a simple four-page newsletter for the division's 300 active members. It would be done informally on a shoestring budget. One unusual aspect of this year's communication effort with members was the desire on the part of the program chairman to "upload" the newsletter onto a national electronic bulletin board that could be accessed through personal computers. To help accomplish these tasks, the program chairman prepared a list of things-to-do. Here are the steps he went through:

1. He recognized that the newsletter was one of his tasks as program chairman; the division always published a newsletter three or four times each academic year.
2. He called members of the executive committee to find out what needed to go in the newsletter—what the audience, the association members, wanted or needed to know—and they discussed copy deadlines and publication dates.
3. He prepared copy deadlines and a production schedule which he included as an article in the first issue of the newsletter.

4. He gathered news and wrote other newsletter copy.
5. He made appropriate arrangements with the printers and mailroom personnel.
6. He had the first issue printed as a self-mailer.
7. He had the newsletter mailed.
8. He uploaded the newsletter onto CompuServe's PRSIG.

. . .

CASE 4.2

Hosting a One-Day Career Conference

When Maryland's second largest university, Towson State University, decided to host a day-long career conference for college students in the Baltimore metropolitan area interested in careers in the communication field, it began planning for the event more than a year in advance. These were the planning steps the TSU Department of Speech and Mass Communication went through:

1. The department chairman requested that a communication career day be held on campus and gave the task of conference coordinator to one member of the faculty.
2. A steering committee was formed which included faculty and administrators, staff specialists in career placement and university relations, and one student.
3. First, monthly, then bi-weekly, and finally, weekly meetings were held to adjust and coordinate plans.
4. Research was conducted to determine conference themes, topics, speakers, opinions about career opportunities, and expected attendance at the conference. Part of the research effort included using the Nominal Group Technique (NGT) with conference planners to help identify priority issues and topics of importance to key publics.
5. A schedule of activities, including a flow chart, was developed. See Figure 4.1.
6. Speakers were invited, the conference was publicized, and the conference was held.
7. Data were collected before, during, and after the conference that could be used to evaluate the current conference and help plan the next one.
8. A final meeting of the steering committee was held to critique the conference and discuss future events.

FIGURE 4.1

Gantt chart for Case 4.2: Communication Career Day

Activity	Sept	Oct	Nov	Dec	Jan	Feb	Mar	Apr	May
Mandate to plan event	X								
Form Steering Committee	X								
Hold 1st meeting		X							
Reserve facilities		X							
Focus groups		X--X							
Solicit speaker/participant nominations		X----X							
Hold 2nd meeting			X						
Conduct mail survey, soliciting participants			X----X						
Hold 3rd meeting, select speakers				X					
Invite speakers/participants				X---X					
Hold 4th meeting					X				
Confirmation letters to speakers/participants						X			
Confirm facility/food arrangements						X			
Prepare publicity						X--X			
Print materials						X----X			
Hold 5th meeting							X		
Distribute publicity							X		
Reminder letters to speakers/participants							X		
Hold event								X	
Analyze feedback								X	
Hold 6th (and final) meeting									X
Activity	**Sept**	**Oct**	**Nov**	**Dec**	**Jan**	**Feb**	**Mar**	**Apr**	**May**

CASE 4.3

A Grand Opening for the Metrorail

The Maryland Transportation Authority, the agency responsible for the Baltimore metropolitan rail system used by more than 300,000 people daily, had to plan a public relations campaign for two new terminals and a new line connecting one of the area's suburbs to the inner city. They planned to have "open houses" one weekend at both terminals, and a grand opening for the new completed line later that week. The purpose of the public relations campaign for the new terminals and commuter line was to increase public awareness and ridership of the metrorail, and to say "thank you" to the communities experiencing inconveniences during construction. Here are the steps the public relations department went through to plan for the open houses and grand opening:

1. They established a task force, which would meet more than ten times before the campaign ended.
2. The task force developed specific goals and objectives for the campaign. They also developed a calendar of meeting dates for the task force and an agenda for each of the meetings.
3. They gathered and coordinated background information for press kits and press conferences. They determined appropriate dates and times for various speeches and press conferences.
4. They requested lists from management and staff for invitations to community leaders and others thought appropriate to attend the opening functions.
5. They held formal meetings to generate ideas and alternatives. They requested at those meetings, as well as by memo, budget estimates. From this information, they prepared a detailed budget and timeline for the campaign.
6. They had informal discussions with local merchants and others to generate ideas and promotional options.
7. They made arrangements for VIP receptions.
8. They collected information for press releases, how-to-ride-and-use brochures, a souvenir newsletter and slide shows.
9. They researched local media and prepared appropriate advertisements and public service announcements.
10. They determined how best to evaluate the campaign.

Similarities and Differences

Planning activities in these three case studies were similar because the events were similar; they were regular, recurring events for which members of the organization and target audiences had built-in expectations and which the public relations professional staff had experience managing. While some time was spent at the beginning of the planning process to generate new ideas, the primary emphasis was to get the job done on time. Timelines and deadlines were established, and most of the meetings focused on making assignments and hearing progress reports on the completion of these assignments. Because the number of meetings and the sophistication of the planning documents increased as the events became more and more complex—from simple newsletter, to career conference, to grand opening—there were differences in the planning activities. Still, the major goal of planning all three of these public relation campaigns was efficiency.

Planning for routine events assumes a closed system: all the major activities of the campaign (the "system") are not only known and predictable but also are under the control of the public relations manager. Obviously, the degree of control that the manager may have over the various people and events involved in the campaign will vary. Consequently, the manager needs to be ready to adjust the planning emphasis to fit the situation. The effective planner will identify those elements of the campaign which can be described as "under the control of the public relations manager" and plan and schedule these activities accordingly.

Typical planning activities that are used to plan for routine events include preparing chronological lists, milestones, timetables and more sophisticated production schedules, such as Gantt charts and PERT networks, which will be explained below.

Calendarizing

Listing activities to be performed in a campaign by calendar dates—and getting people involved in the campaign to agree to these dates—is one of the most common planning methods used in public relations. It's not always the easiest, however. Listing the activities is not difficult; what is difficult is developing consensus about the dates and what should happen if "due dates" are not met.

Timelines and Gantt Charts

A more sophisticated approach to calendarizing campaign activities is to construct a timeline called a Gantt chart. This procedure requires the manager to list campaign activities in chronological order down the left side of the chart and to indicate graphically across the chart how long it will take to complete each activity. Read from left to right, the chart often looks like descending stairs, with the campaign "stepping off" with the first activity and ending up at the bottom by finishing the last activity of the entire campaign. The width of each step in the descending stairs often is shown in proportion to the estimated time required to complete the designated activity. Figure 4.2 lists the steps in constructing a Gantt chart.

FIGURE 4.2

How to prepare a Gantt chart

---

1. Make a list of things-to-do for the campaign or program. Initially write down all activities in whatever order they occur to you. Then, rewrite and rearrange items on the list into a chronological sequence. Rewrite the items so that they are expressed in parallel sentence structures. It is best to begin each item with an action verb: Make... Coordinate... Plan... Prepare... Arrange... Meet... Receive... Implement... Evaluate... Develop... etc. The action verb clearly indicates the activity has a definite starting point. An acceptable alternative is to use the past tense of the verb: Made... Coordinated... Planned... Arranged... etc. The past tense clearly indicates the completion of an activity.

2. Prepare the L-shaped shell of the Gantt chart by listing down the left side of the page, in a narrow column, the things-to-do, with the first activity listed at the "top of the L." Across the bottom of the page, draw a line—the bottom of the "L." Mark off on this line in units of time—hours, days, weeks, months, years—using the most appropriate unit of time for your program or campaign. Label the column, the top of the L, "Activities." Label the line, the bottom of the L, "Time [insert precise unit of time] To Complete Activities." Note: If preparing the Gantt chart by hand, it is best to work with graph paper. If preparing the chart using a typewriter or word processor, it is best to mark the units of time along the bottom of the chart in standard symbols for keystrokes, such as:

   x x x x   x x x x   x x x x   x x x x   x x x x   x x x x   or,

   /●●●●/ /●●●●/ /●●●●/ /●●●●/ /●●●●/ /●●●●/   or,

   I----I----I----I----I----I----I----I----I----I

3. On an imaginary horizontal line extending from a specific item, mark the place on the chart above the appropriate time period for that activity. Some Gantt charts indicate either starting or ending dates. Other Gantt charts indicate both starting and ending dates for activities, with the length of the line connecting these two points indicating the length of time to complete the activity.

4. Recognize that it is normal for certain activities to "overlap" because they will be performed during the same time period. It would be unusual for a complex set of activities not to have some activities that overlap. It would be unusual for a Gantt chart to have the following appearance:

   Activities

   ```
   Item 1    X---X
   Item 2        X------X
   Item 3              X--X
   Item 4                 X-------X
   Item 5                         X------X
   Item 6                                X--X
             /●●●●/●●●●/●●●●/●●●●/●●●●/●●●●/●●●●/●●●●/●●●●/
                        Weeks To Complete Activities
   ```

   It would be more normal for a Gantt chart to have the following appearance, with certain activities overlapping:

   Activities

   ```
   Item 1    X---X
   Item 2        X------X
   Item 3          X--X
   Item 4              X-------X
   Item 5                  X-------X
   Item 6                         X--X
             /●●●●/●●●●/●●●●/●●●●/●●●●/●●●●/●●●●/●●●●/
                        Weeks To Complete Activities
   ```

5. Be prepared to revise the Gantt chart, for the process of preparing the chart will often suggest new activities, conflicting time schedules for different activities, and other issues which should be addressed. Look upon a Gantt chart not as a pretty picture but as a working document—and expect to work on it.

Project Flow Charts and PERT Diagrams

An even more advanced form of calendarizing is to design a flow chart that indicates the network of activities, often described as a "critical path" or PERT (for Program Evaluation Review Technique) diagram. This procedure requires the manager to list campaign activities in the order in which they must be done. This facilitates the identification of activities that should be completed before other activities can begin. The list is usually more complicated than a straight listing of activities in chronological order, because some activities have similar "start dates" but different "end dates"—with the completion of some activities being more critical than others.

The manager makes a list of activities, estimating the date at which each activity will start and end. The manager then draws a PERT diagram of circles and lines indicating connected activities, with the line between each activity indicating the start and end dates; in other words, each line indicates the length of time it takes to complete an activity. The circles (or "nodes") in the diagram represent the beginning or end of a particular activity. The advantage of the PERT network is that it identifies the critical path of essential activities that must be done for the project to be completed on time. It highlights for a manager the set of activities that must be closely monitored and supervised if the complete set of activities is to be conducted as planned and on schedule. If adjustments need to be made in the amount of time allowed for completion of any activity, the "critical path" or PERT procedure allows a public relations manager to calculate the consequences. Figure 4.3 lists the steps in preparing a PERT chart.

Routine vs. Nonroutine Events: "Closed" vs. "Open" Systems

If a public relations problem or opportunity is perceived as being routine, planning an appropriate public relations campaign will focus on calendarizing and getting the job done on time. The more the event being planned for is perceived as being nonroutine, the more emphasis will be devoted to generating new ideas and innovative campaign strategies.

Routine events, assumed to be part of a predictable "closed system," are most often planned by preparing production schedules, timelines and milestones. Sometimes very little, if any, formal planning seems to take place for routine events, because everyone knows what to do—it's that predictable. Sometimes more sophisticated production schedules, such as Gantt and PERT charts, are used to plan for more sophisticated routine events. The more complex the "routine" event is, the more complex the planning procedures will be.

As will be discussed later in this chapter, nonroutine events are assumed to be part of an unpredictable "open system" and are often best

FIGURE 4.3

Steps in drafting project flow charts and PERT diagrams.

---

1. Prepare a chronological listing of project activities, similar to what is prepared for a Gantt chart. See Figure 4.2, step #1.

2. Next to each activity indicate the hour, day, week, month, year—whatever is an appropriate unit of time—that the activity will begin.

3. Next to each activity list antecedent activities that must be completed before this particular activity can begin. This means you would not list activities that could occur simultaneously or overlap with this particular activity.

4. Estimate the amount of time it will take to complete each activity. Next to each activity, beside the start time, list the exact time the activity will be finished or stopped.

5. Use the following symbols in preparing the PERT diagram:

    *   absolute beginning of project

    O   beginning or ending point of specific task

    - - -   length of time it takes to complete task

    @   absolute ending of project

6. Draw the project flow chart by marking the absolute beginning of the project, followed by a line indicating the very first task or acitivity—which may be a single line representing one task or a set of parallel lines representing an initial set of activities being performed simultaneously. Continue drawing the diagram by using small circles to indicate start dates of activities, and lines to indicate the length of time to complete the activity. Label the small circles (called "nodes") with exact dates. Label the lines with the name of the activity. Mark the absolute ending of the project.

    NOTE: Work in pencil—and, have an eraser handy. PERT diagrams are conceptually and graphically challenging, for drafting them requires rethinking the expected sequence of project activities—and drawing them so that they are easy to read and understand requires design skills.
    Example:

7. Highlight the "critical path" of activities that requires the greatest amount of time for the project to be completed. This is the set of activities that needs to be monitored closely, for any delay of any one of these activities will delay the entire project. Recognize slack time also: these are the activities that have similar start times as other activities but can be completed prior to the completion of other activities which must be completed before the next set of activities can begin.

8. For more information, refer to technical articles about preparing PERT charts and critical path diagrams.[1]

9. Transfer the above information into one of several off-the-shelf software programs available in project management. This will free you from the laborious calculations of time estimates and resource allocations, and it will allow you, as a manager, to creatively consider a variety of "what if" options.

---

[1] Allen, T. Harrell, "PERT: A technique for public relations management," *Public Relations Review* Vol. 6, Summer, 1980, pp. 38–49; Moder, J. J., C. R. Phillips, and E. W. Davis. *Project Management with CPM. PERT and Precedence Diagramming* 3rd edition (New York: Van Nostrand Reinhold, 1983): and, Meredith, Jack R., and Samuel J. Martel, Jr. *Project Management: A Managerial Approach* 2nd edition (New York: John Wiley and Sons, 1989) pp. 327–372.

planned for by using unusual group decision-making techniques and out-of-the-ordinary idea-generation strategies.

The experienced public relations manager knows the value of systematically planning for routine events: it helps save time, money, and energy—all which may be better spent planning for more exceptional, nonroutine events.

Professionals React to Two Fictionalized Case Studies: One Routine, and One Nonroutine

To examine how planning public relations varies depending on whether or not the event prompting the program or campaign is routine or nonroutine, the following two case studies were presented in personal interviews to eighteen public relations professionals. For each case study, the professionals were told, "Imagine that you are the public relations professional in the following situation. How would you go about planning an appropriate public relations response?"

. . .

CASE 4.4:

A Routine Newsletter

An association of firefighters and fire prevention administrators has decided to produce a new monthly newsletter for its members, in addition to the association's quarterly magazine. The association's board recommends that they publish an eight-page, one-color newsletter as soon as possible. An experienced public relations specialist, who has been with the association for years, agrees to write and produce the newsletter.

. . .

CASE 4.5:

A Nonroutine Seminar

An association of firefighters and fire prevention administrators has decided to establish a quarterly training institute for its members, and to include a week-long series of lectures and course materials designed to help the members manage effective public relations for their own organizations. The association's board has asked the public relations specialist, who has just joined the association, to serve on the new institute's steering committee and to prepare both a comprehensive public relations campaign for the institute, and with input from experts, appropriate public relations instructional materials.

FIGURE 4.4

Parallel PERT charts for two public relations programs: one developed in response to a routine event, one in response to a nonroutine event.

DEVELOPMENT OF PROGRAM IN RESPONSE TO PERCEIVED ROUTINE EVENT: Total of six meetings over 20-day period

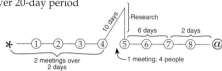

DEVELOPMENT OF PROGRAM IN RESPONSE TO PERCEIVED NONROUTINE EVENT: Total of eight meetings over 50-day period

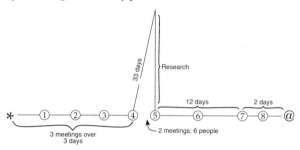

Legend: * = mandate
  1 = establish planning committee
  2 = clarify the problem/opportunity
  3 = determine goals and objectives
  4 = generate ideas and solutions
  5 = make action plans
  6 = coordinate production
  7 = implement program
  8 = evaluate program
  @ = end of project

Similarities and Differences

A series of questions was asked of each professional interviewed to determine how he or she would manage various planning activities. Half the professionals were asked questions about Case 4.4, and half were asked questions about Case 4.5. Figure 4.4 presents parallel PERT charts developed from an analysis of their responses.

In both cases, the mandate to prepare the public relations program was clearly stated by the board of the association. The key difference between the cases is that Case 4.4 describes a relatively routine event involving an experienced public relations professional, while Case 4.5 is a nonroutine event involving a public relations person new to the organization.

As indicated in Figure 4.4, when compared to the routine newsletter, the week-long nonroutine seminar required twice the amount of time to plan and implement and fifty percent more time for staff meetings. Also, a greater proportion of time was devoted to research and generation of new ideas for the nonroutine event than for the routine event.

Planning for Nonroutine Events

Many, though certainly not all, public relations programs and campaigns are unique: they have never been done before. A unique program or campaign requires planning strategies that are different from those used in routine campaigns, because almost everyone involved has had little or no experience with such an event. From the public relations manager's point of view, what is needed initially is a general, overarching plan for developing a specific plan of action. Once a manageable set of activities is identified, routine planning procedures—calendarizing and synchronizing—can take place, making sure the it's-never-been-done-before campaign gets done on time.

What separates planning for nonroutine events from planning for routine ones is that time-consuming and special decision-making techniques are often used to define the problem, determine goals and generate innovative solutions. After an innovative set of solutions is generated, planning becomes more routine and focuses on synchronizing activities.

The two major values of systematically planning for nonroutine events are: (1) it helps to allocate internal and external resources to the advantage of the organization—in the long-run, it's efficient; and (2) in the short-run, systematically planning for nonroutine events helps to establish, maintain, and protect relationships of importance to an organization—it keeps a variety of people alert to the nuances of ongoing relationships and to the possibilities of new ones.

Examples of Planning for Nonroutine Events

The next two cases involve the public relations agency of Manning, Selvage, and Lee/Washington and two of the agency's clients. Both clients were seeking an economic development program. Since neither client at the outset had a specific campaign in mind, something new and special for each client was developed. However, one of the clients had more experienced senior managers and their focal community was within a more developed, complex region than was the other client; consequently, planning for this more complex economic development campaign was more time-consuming and complicated.

. . .

CASE 4.6:

A Public Relations Agency Plans an Economic Development Program for a Complex Region

A simple list of things-to-do would not work for the major public relations agency that wanted to win the contract from the local Chamber of Commerce. The Chamber had requested proposals from more than 50 public relations agencies that would outline how the Chamber could develop and implement a multi-year public relations campaign designed to improve economic development in a small city overshadowed by its "sister city." Both were part of an internationally famous "research triangle" of three cities and major universities in the South. This was the problem: if the public relations agency was to win this important account, an innovative and novel approach to the public relations campaign would be needed. Even though the agency had extensive experience designing and implementing economic development programs, it would have been inappropriate to foist on one client what might have worked well with another client; the campaign needed to be unique to this specific client and economic region.

The agency won the contract by doing extensive preliminary research and investing staff time in planning efforts that involved anonymous participant observations, personal interviews with scores of community leaders, and dozens of meetings with the client. What emerged from this process was an award-winning public relations campaign that dramatically increased the international reputation of the community and began a sustained surge of economic development in the region. Here are the steps the Manning, Selvage, and Lee/Washington professionals went through in planning this campaign:

1. A request for a proposal was received by the agency—and more than 50 other public relations agencies.
2. Agency professionals were assigned to an account team; they conducted preliminary research, including on-site visits to the community; and, they determined appropriate goals and objectives for the campaign.
3. In a series of staff meetings and discussions with the client, the agency team identified an appropriate campaign theme, publicity possibilities, a preliminary budget, and a timetable.
4. The team prepared a draft proposal and circulated it among other staff members for their comments and suggestions.
5. The team prepared and rehearsed their presentation to the client.
6. Team members—along with members of the agency from other offices who had conducted successful economic development programs—made the presentation to the client.
7. The agency was awarded the contract.
8. Team members designed and conducted more research, including personal and telephone interviews with selected members of the community.
9. The team refined the theme, publicity and media options, and prepared a detailed budget and production schedule.

10. The team coordinated production of media materials, including a film and print advertisements.
11. The campaign was implemented.
12. The team established a number of ways to measure the effectiveness of the campaign, even as it was underway; as a result, they were able to make within-campaign adjustments as well as conduct post-campaign analyses.

. . .

CASE 4.7:

The Same Public Relations Agency Plans Another Economic Development Program for Another Client

Manning, Selvage, and Lee/Washington had to plan a similar economic development campaign for another client. But, this time they engaged in different research and planning efforts because the client and the economic situations were different.

From the agency's perspective, the initial problem with the second client was the same as for the first: to win the contract. The second client was comprised of two counties which had joined together in underwriting a regional economic development program. Since this client had limited resources and relatively limited experience in economic development, the agency's planning efforts could be streamlined by performing less research and holding fewer meetings with the client. Nevertheless, the focus of the planning was on generating an innovative program unique to the client. The exact shape of the campaign was not determined until completion of sufficient research. This research, coupled with a series of meetings and consultations with the client, enabled the agency's planning process to evolve through stages designed to encourage innovation:

1. The agency was approached by the client, and a team of agency professionals was assigned the task of preparing a proposal for the client.
2. The agency's team conducted preliminary research and determined goals and objectives for the campaign.
3. In a series of meetings, the team spent time brainstorming, developing a campaign theme, and identifying ways to use innovative publicity and media for the campaign.
4. The team prepared a proposal, with specific budget and project milestones, and presented it to the client.
5. The contract was awarded to the agency.
6. The team did more original research but kept costs down by relying heavily on their professional experience planning and executing similar economic development programs for other clients.
7. They held telephone and in-person meetings with the clients, who approved the final campaign plan.
8. The team coordinated the production of campaign materials.
9. The team implemented the campaign.

10. Similarly to the way they had evaluated other economic development campaigns, the team evaluated this one by monitoring media placements, public opinion, requests for more information, and interest in starting new businesses in the region.

Similarities and Differences

In the preceding two cases, action plans for nonroutine, innovative campaigns were generated for nonroutine events. In both cases, there were time pressures on the agency professionals to develop and implement the campaigns, because both clients were eager for results.

The constant factor in both cases was the public relations firm, its staff and resources. The major difference was the nature of the agency's relationship with its clients, which was affected primarily by the differences in each client's management expertise and the amount of resources available to implement the campaign. Although the same planning steps were followed for both clients, Manning, Selvage, and Lee/Washington invested more time, energies and resources in the more complex campaign, because the client expected it and was willing to pay for it. The client in the less complex region had fewer resources which could be devoted to the campaign and less experience managing economic development programs. Consequently, the client for the two counties relied heavily on the agency's in-house expertise in planning and executing the campaign.

Two Additional Examples of Planning for Nonroutine Events

The last two cases in this chapter illustrate more than planning for nonroutine events. They not only are good examples of planning which generates new ideas and innovative solutions, they are excellent examples of strategic planning which focuses on questions about the basic purpose and mission of the organization and how the organization can help prepare for, shape and take advantage of significant relationships and future events.

· · ·

CASE 4.8:

Public Relations Long-Range Planning

Martin Marietta, a major defense contractor, convened quarterly long-range strategic planning meetings to discuss public relations goals and objectives for the corporation's various divisions and plant locations. Prior to these meetings, participants would prepare documents describing their public

relations goals and objectives. Each public relations director determined the appropriate format of his or her documents and style of presentation. At these meetings, plans were discussed, ideas were shared and, in the process, consensus was facilitated about long-range and short-range public relations goals and objectives. Following the meetings, some public relations directors modified and changed certain aspects of their public relations programs. If there were any program changes, these changes were incorporated into updated versions of formal corporate-wide planning documents, so others within management knew of the changes. In some instances, as a result of these meetings, new public relations programs were developed. As an on-going process, the defense contractor's long-range public relations planning went through certain stages:

1. Senior management at the corporate level established the importance of the strategic planning process by making it an essential element of the corporate culture. Without being dictatorial, senior management regularly expected that significant business units (divisions, subsidiaries, and other major profit centers) would update appropriate long-range planning documents. By doing this, senior management, in effect, mandated that long-range planning be considered a serious and important activity throughout the corporation. Specifically, senior management set the agenda and specified deadlines for the corporation's long-range planning process.
2. Senior management at the corporate level reviewed and revised existing strategic plans and updated goals for the organization. As part of this process, senior public relations planners at the corporate level developed long-range public relations goals.
3. Senior management for strategic business units reviewed their specific long-range plans and identified specific objectives that helped meet the overarching corporate goals of the organization.
4. Public relations directors within specific business units prepared appropriate goals and objectives by conducting brainstorming sessions with their staff and others.
5. The long-range public relations goals and objectives were discussed within each unit's senior management, and if necessary, adjustments were made.
6. On-going and special public relations programs were implemented as called for in each unit's plan.
7. The on-going planning cycle would begin to repeat itself when each unit's public relations long-range plans and current activities were discussed at the next regularly scheduled corporate-wide meeting involving all public relations managers. Following these meetings, appropriate refinements were made in public relations plans and specific programs, if needed.

C A S E   4.9:

Emergency or Crisis Communication Planning

An item on the agenda of one of the defense contractor's quarterly corporate-wide meetings of public relations directors was to discuss emergency or crisis communication plans. At this meeting, the public relations directors who had recent experiences dealing with emergencies (such as a fire at one location, or sudden unexplained illnesses at another) would present each unit's crisis communication plan and discuss how it was implemented during the most recent emergency. The following steps were taken at one unit to develop its crisis communication plan:

1. Senior management encouraged the public relations director for this strategic business unit to develop an emergency communication plan and to have this plan be reviewed and revised, if necessary, and integrated into the corporation's long-range planning process.
2. The public relations director met with outside experts and company specialists to discuss appropriate corporate responses to possible emergencies or crises.
3. The unit's public relations director, working with others, determined a chain of command responsible for disseminating information during an emergency and drafted a set of guidelines that were circulated for approval by all those involved in executing the plan.
4. The emergency or crisis communication plans at this unit were implemented only in response to crises. At other units, crisis communication plans were rehearsed.
5. The unit's crisis communication plans were discussed and evaluated at one of the regularly scheduled corporate-wide meetings of public relations directors.

Similarities and Differences

There were a number of similarities between these two planning efforts by the defense contractor. They were both focused on creating and protecting internal and external relationships, and they both helped allocate organizational resources to these important relationships. Both planning efforts were strongly supported by top management. The corporate culture expected, indeed mandated, all strategic business units to have long-range public relations plans and detailed crisis communication plans.

The major differences between these two planning efforts were the number of issues, the number of "players," and the amount of time spent identifying, selecting and evaluating alternatives. Although both planning efforts were complex, developing specific crisis or emergency communication plans was less complex than developing long-range public relations plans because fewer resources were devoted to it, less time was required to conduct it, and fewer people were involved.

Characteristics of Planning for Nonroutine Events

Planning for nonroutine events assumes an open system, which means that all the major activities of the campaign are not known at the beginning of the planning process. Planning for nonroutine events means acknowledging that there are factors affecting the campaign which are not under the direct control of the client or sponsoring organization. In planning campaigns for nonroutine events, public relations managers need to develop and plan campaigns that fit special, often unique, requirements. In these situations, no one really knows at the beginning of the planning process what the public relations campaign will look like, but by the end of their planning efforts, there will be a custom-designed campaign. The key is identifying what is special about a situation and planning a campaign that uniquely fits that situation.

Crisis communication planning differs from long-range strategic planning in that it does not ask questions about the basic purpose of the organization, its mission, or its function in society. Consequently, crisis communication planning is less comprehensive than strategic planning.

STEPS IN THE PLANNING PROCESS

Depending on circumstances and the perceived routineness of the event being planned, the following steps are appropriate for planning public relations programs and campaigns.

A. Recognize and define the problem (or opportunity)
   1) The public relations professionals make no concerted effort to further define the problem or opportunity; they just do what's expected.

   In Case 4.1, the program chair recognized that the newsletter was one of the tasks to be done that year. Since its beginning, the public relations division of this association had published a newsletter; someone had to do it, so he did it.

   2) A problem or opportunity is recognized by the public relations professionals, who independently prepare a document that outlines the situation and solicits from the client or senior management a mandate to more extensively plan an appropriate public relations program or campaign.

   In all the cases presented in this chapter, the public relations staff was asked by top management or the client to develop an appropriate public relations activity. In other cases—for example, soliciting new business from a client or initiating a new public relations program within an organization—a planning document might be prepared independently by the public relations staff and then authorized by the client or senior management for further development.

3) A problem or opportunity is recognized and discussed among members of the dominant coalition, including the client and members of the public relations staff, and an official mandate is received from top management to develop a more specific proposal. The public relations staff then meets to decide how best to respond to this request.

In Case 4.2, the department chair requested that a communication career day be held on the campus; he gave the task of coordinating the conference to one member of the faculty.

In Case 4.3, the public relations staff was told by top management to prepare the grand opening when construction was finished on the new commuter line.

In both Case 4.6 and Case 4.7, the agency received the RFP—Request For Proposal—from the client.

In Case 4.8, principal members of senior management consistently reviewed their strategic plans which generated an unofficial mandate within the corporate culture for significant business units to regularly update long range plans.

In Case 4.9, the public relations staff received an official mandate from senior management to prepare a crisis communication plan.

B. Determine goals and objectives:

1) Hold quick, informal discussions with the client or key members of the organization—primarily over the phone or, briefly, in person—to determine goals and objectives.

In Case 4.1, the program chair called members of the executive committee to find out what needed to go into the newsletter, copy deadlines and publications dates. The characteristics of the audience were not discussed because the audience was small and fairly well understood; the medium—the newsletter—was not discussed because "that's how we've always done it."

In Case 4.2, informal discussions were held with students, faculty, staff and alumni.

In Case 4.3, community leaders and others were consulted about promotional activities.

2) Hold more formal meetings to determine campaign goals and objectives, using any of the following strategies:

   a. Send appropriate documents and reading materials to participants prior to formal meetings.

   b. Use relatively unstructured decision-making techniques during the meeting, such as listing suggestions and having one member summarize the group's consensus.

c. Use fairly structured decision-making techniques during the meeting, such as the Nominal Group Technique, or force-field analysis.

In Case 4.2, at first monthly, then bi-weekly, and finally, weekly meetings were held to adjust and coordinate plans, including some fairly structured meetings using the Nominal Group Technique that helped identify and clarify goals, objectives and audience characteristics.

In Case 4.3, a formal task force was established and devoted several hours to developing specific goals and objectives.

In Case 4.6 and Case 4.7, the agency, in concert with the clients, defined goals and objectives and researched the situation to determine if the goals and objectives were realistic.

In Case 4.8, other members of management became involved in reviewing planning documents and reaffirmed the corporate mission, goals, and objectives.

In Case 4.9, public relations managers, working with other members of management, identified appropriate goals and objectives for crisis communication within each strategic business unit.

C. Generate ideas and alternatives:

1) Consider no alternatives; just do what's expected.

   In Case 4.1, the tradition of publishing a newsletter would continue; the only innovation was "uploading" the newsletter onto a computer network's bulletin board.

2) Prepare, with a minimum of input from others, a document by the public relations staff specifying appropriate program or campaign ideas and circulate it for review and comment.

   In Case 4.1, the editor of the newsletter discussed with the executive board, by telephone, the types of articles that would be appropriate. He also published an article in the newsletter that detailed copy deadlines and called for suggestions from readers.

3) Conduct research to determine audience characteristics, media options, campaign messages, themes and strategies.

   In Case 4.2, research was conducted to determine conference themes, topics, speakers, opinions about career opportunities, and expected attendance at the conference.

   In Case 4.3, data were collected for press kits and press conferences, and local media were researched to determine ideal placement.

4) Hold formal meetings and discussions with the client or senior management to discuss campaign ideas and alternatives, using any of the following strategies:

   a. Send appropriate documents and reading materials to participants prior to the meeting.
   b. Use standard decision-making techniques during the meeting.
   c. Use unusual decision-making techniques during the meeting.

   In Case 4.2, the conference steering committee spent several meetings discussing various ideas, primarily examining what had and had not worked in the past at similar conferences.

   In Case 4.3, the task force solicited ideas and suggestions from not only themselves at formal meetings but also from community leaders and others within the agency.

   In Case 4.6 and 4.7, the agency conducted additional research to determine if the goals and objectives were realistic.

   In Case 4.8, public relations managers within strategic business units developed unit-specific public relations goals and objectives in accordance with overall corporate goals and objectives.

   In Case 4.9, the public relations staff explored knowledge with specialists in the field to find out how others were prepared to deal with similar crises.

D. Develop and approve an action plan:

   1) Develop very few, if any, formal plans; assume everyone knows what to do.

   In Case 4.1, while the editor prepared copy deadlines which he included as an article in the first issue of the newsletter, no other formal planning document for the newsletter was prepared.

   2) Prepare and distribute a document from the public relations staff that specifies deadlines and a schedule of activities—including, if appropriate, timelines, milestones, Gantt charts, and PERT diagrams.

   In both Case 4.2 and 4.3, Gantt charts were prepared by the steering committee and revised regularly.

   3) Hold meetings, encourage maximum input from others, and prepare a comprehensive campaign proposal, with a specific budget and timetable, to be presented for approval by the client or senior management.

In Case 4.3, following a series of meetings by the task force, a schedule of activities, including a flow chart and budget, was developed.

In Case 4.6 and Case 4.7, the agency figured costs and established milestones and timetables for implementing and evaluating the campaigns. When this last step in this process was completed—when the budget and timetables were approved—the planning efforts shifted from generating ideas to getting the job done on time.

In Case 4.8, management within each unit analyzed gaps between projected performance and anticipated resources. With an approved budget, public relations managers coordinated production of campaign materials and activities.

In Case 4.9, the public relations staff developed internal and external support and resources for implementing the plan. With these commitments from others for both money and staff time, the public relations staff coordinated production of crisis communication documents and materials.

4) Develop and produce materials and activities for the campaign and if necessary, conduct pretests of these materials and activities before full field implementation.

In all but the most routine case (4.1), most of the final meetings of the planning committees were devoted to monitoring and coordinating production of program and campaign materials.

E. Implement and evaluate the program or campaign.

In Case 4.1, the association published the newsletter the required number of times. Because it was mailed on time, and the editor heard no complaints, and there was no discussion of the newsletter at the executive board meeting, it was considered a success.

In Case 4.2, the university held the career day as planned. More than 300 students attended, and more than 80 professional communicators participated in the day-long event. Attendees who completed an evaluation form were eligible for a dinner for two, which was donated by one of the professional participants. Evaluation forms from students and professionals indicated the program was a success. The cost of the program was within projected budgets. The Steering Committee met once after the career day and recommended that future career days be planned.

In Case 4.3, the opening of the metrorail station was held as planned, with good weather boosting the number of people in attendance. Local newspapers and media gave good coverage. All materials produced for the opening were distributed. The cost of the opening was within the projected budget.

Case 4.4 and 4.5 were fictitious, so we can assume they were implemented and evaluated in storybook fashion.

In Case 4.6 and 4.7, the agency regularly presented progress reports to their clients. A final report to the client documented the impact of the campaign in terms of press coverage, business inquiries and new economic developments generated during the campaign.

In Case 4.8, management regularly reviewed the progress of specific public relations campaigns in terms of costs, benefits and its relationship to other corporate activities and needs.

In Case 4.9, following any crisis or emergency, the effectiveness of the public relations plan would be determined by the quality of media coverage, employee opinions, staff time and costs required to meet the needs of the specific crisis.

SURVEY RESEARCH FINDINGS

As noted in previous chapters, the survey of public relations professions, which was conducted by the author, indicated that an organization's decision-making structure does influence the frequency with which certain public relations activities are engaged in by certain organizations. For example, mixed mechanical/organic organizations are more likely than traditional organizations to engage in crisis communication.

Public relations professionals who participated in the survey were asked to indicate the percent of staff time devoted to various phases of managing campaigns by answering the following question: "Textbooks in this field often emphasize four stages in the public relations process: research, planning, implementation and evaluation. What percentage of your organization's staff time is normally devoted to these stages for each of the following activities? [Note: the total for each activity should equal 100 percent.]" Responses to this question, classified according to four decision-making structures (traditional, mechanical, organic, and mixed mechanical/organic) are presented in Table 4.1.

The results indicate a remarkable consistency in the percent of staff time spent researching, planning, implementing and evaluating public relations activities across all four types of decision-making structures. There were only two significant differences. Public relations staffs for mechanical organizations spend more time planning and implementing publications than do staffs working for traditional, organic or mixed mechanical/organic organizations, which is understandable given the large size and routine nature of mechanical organizations. Public relations staffs for mixed mechanical/organic organizations spend less time researching and evaluating meetings and conferences than do their colleagues in other types of decision-making structures.

TABLE 4.1:

Frequency of Engaging in Public Relations Activities and Percent of Staff Time Spent Researching, Planning, Implementing and Evaluating Public Relations Activities by Type of Organizational Structure.[a]

Public Relations Activities	Traditional (Low Scope, Low Complex) (n = 10)	Mechanical (High Scope, Low Complex) (n = 11)	Organic (Low Scope, High Complex) (n = 10)	Mixed Mech/Organic (High Scope, High Complex) (n = 34) SD[b]
Press release	100%	91%	100%	94%
Researching	14	25	23	24
Planning	22	35	27	35
Implementing	52	38	41	44
Evaluating	9	16	9	8
Press conference	10%	55%	30%	53%*
Researching	8	10	16	20
Planning	23	48	33	36
Implementing	18	35	39	25
Evaluating	9	8	12	12
Press interviews	100%	55%	70%	85%*
Researching	16	19	23	24
Planning	28	26	21	26
Implementing	36	44	35	39
Evaluating	10	11	9	10
Community relations	90%	73%	100%	97%
Researching	14	16	15	19
Planning	32	35	38	32
Implementing	43	27	35	32
Evaluating	11	10	12	14
Publications	90%	91%	90%	97%
Researching	22	15	31	30
Planning	23	42	23	25**
Implementing	28	38	35	34
Evaluating	18	6	8	11
Employee relations	70%	73%	90%	71%
Researching	23	8	10	15
Planning	15	36	21	24
Implementing	34	40	58	45
Evaluating	16	11	6	15
Crisis communication	30%	55%	80%	79%*
Researching	8	11	18	21
Planning	12	35	33	24
Implementing	59	38	38	37
Evaluating	17	16	12	17
Special events	100%	82%	90%	97%
Researching	15	18	17	17
Planning	32	38	33	41
Implementing	39	38	29	32
Evaluating	39	38	29	32

TABLE 4.1 Continued

Public Relations Activities	Traditional (Low Scope, Low Complex) (n = 10)	Mechanical (High Scope, Low Complex) (n = 11)	Organic (Low Scope, High Complex) (n = 10)	Mixed Mech/Organic (High Scope, High Complex) (n = 34) SD[b]
Fund raising	70%	27%	70%	50%
Researching	14	10	19	19
Planning	24	20	33	17
Implementing	31	15	33	25
Evaluating	32	26	18	21
Meetings and conferences	80%	55%	90%	97%*
Researching	12	21	14	7
Planning	31	29	35	39
Implementing	40	11	35	42 *
Evaluating	18	13	16	7 *
Print advertisements	60%	73%	50%	68%
Researching	12	17	18	19
Planning	30	24	33	25
Implementing	36	49	37	25
Evaluating	23	10	13	15
Broadcast ads and PSAs	60%	64%	60%	62%
Researching	13	8	14	23
Planning	23	22	29	29
Implementing	30	24	33	25
Evaluating	36	49	37	25
Government relations	60%	73%	70%	85%
Researching	22	15	17	24
Planning	24	30	29	26
Implementing	38	18	29	27
Evaluating	16	13	10	12
Investor relations	30%	46%	30%	47%
Researching	20	5	31	16
Planning	18	20	11	24
Implementing	45	20	12	30
Evaluating	18	5	6	15
Issues management	60%	46%	90%	68%*
Researching	22	17	34	25
Planning	32	20	33	28
Implementing	15	3	14	11
Evaluating	18	15	25	22
Consumer affairs	50%	28%	40%	65%*
Researching	15	35	30	23
Planning	30	45	37	30
Implementing	17	N5	7	19
Evaluating	16	24	15	19

TABLE 4.1 Continued

Public Relations Activities	Traditional (Low Scope, Low Complex) (n = 10)	Mechanical (High Scope, Low Complex) (n = 11)	Organic (Low Scope, High Complex) (n = 10)	Mixed Mech/Organic (High Scope, High Complex) (n = 34) SD[b]
Sales promotion	70%	64%	50%	65%
Researching	16	24	15	19
Planning	28	31	30	26
Implementing	40	40	35	34
Evaluating	18	5	15	10

(a) Percent engaging in public relations activities based on respondents indicating either "very frequently" or "sometimes" to four-point scaled question that included "rarely" and "never." Percent of staff time is based on response to the following question: "Textbooks in this field often emphasize four stages in the public relations process: research, planning, implementation and evaluation. What percentage of your organization's staff time is normally devoted to these stages for each of the following activities? [Note: the total for each activity should equal 100 percent.]"

(b) Significance of difference determined by F-test; reported is the probability of difference due to chance: * = .05; ** = .01.

Most respondents, across all four types of decision-making structures, indicated between 40 and 50 percent of staff time was devoted to research and planning activities; approximately 40 percent of staff time was devoted to implementing campaigns; and between 10 and 20 percent of staff time was devoted to evaluating public relations activities.

A higher percentage of staff time was devoted to evaluating public relations campaigns designed for nonroutine events than for campaigns designed for routine events. For example, more staff time was devoted to evaluating special events, fund raising, and crisis communication, than for such routine activities as press releases, publications or meetings and conferences.

The implication for public relations managers is that the nature of the event being planned for—whether it is routine or nonroutine—is a significant factor to consider when allocating staff time to researching, planning, implementing and evaluating public relations campaigns. The nature of the event and its significance to the organization may be more powerful predictors of public relations management strategies than the decision-making structure of the organization itself.

The public relations professionals who participated in the survey also were asked how frequently public relations professionals within their organization were included in the dominant coalition, and how frequently their organizations engaged in certain public relations activities.

Table 4.2 indicates that public relations staffs which experienced more frequent contact with members of the dominant coalition were more involved in preparing press releases than were staffs with less contact with the dominant coalition. Those public relations staffs which experienced infrequent contact with members of top management were more often involved in sales promotion activities.

When the public relations staffs who had frequent contact with members of the dominant coalition were compared to those staffs with less frequent contact, no significant differences were found in the percent of staff time spent planning. However, significant differences were found in the amount of staff time devoted to evaluating press releases, press conferences, community relations, publications, special events, meetings and conferences. The implication of these survey results is that frequent contact by the public relations staff with members of the dominant coalition does not impact so much on planning as it does on evaluating public relations activities.

THE PLAN BOOK: PART II

By including Gantt, PERT and project management charts in The Plan Book, the document becomes a management tool that can be used not only to develop consensus but also to monitor and control activities and resources being used on a public relations program or campaign. At a minimum, most plan books have timelines specifying when various activities will be completed.

Sometimes, two versions of The Plan Book are developed: one containing detailed lists, diagrams, and charts that can be used by staff working on the program or campaign; and, the other version containing more streamlined information for senior management, the client, and others, who do not need to know as many specifics but would appreciate knowing basic information about milestones, due dates, and completion schedules.

AN ALTERNATIVE—PESSIMISTIC—THEORY OF PLANNING

An alternative theory of planning is implied in the research of Charles Perrow, who investigated why apparently sophisticated organizations cannot plan their activities so as to avoid serious industrial accidents and similar crises which some organizations appear to bring on themselves.[1]

His theory is that complex organizations institutionalize the potential for crises by establishing and maintaining cultures which become cognitive constraints for employees during crises, inhibiting and re-

TABLE 4.2:

Frequency of Contact with Members of the Dominant Coalition by Percent Staff Time Devoted to Researching, Planning, Implementing and Evaluating Public Relations Activities.[a]

Public Relations Activity	Frequent Contact (n = 41)	Infrequent Contact (n = 17)	SD[b]
Press release	1.27	1.58	*
Researching	25%	25%	
Planning	22	18	
Implementing	39	46	
Evaluating	14	9	*
Press conference	2.46	2.70	
Researching	21%	22%	
Planning	36	35	
Implementing	30	34	
Evaluating	13	9	*
Press interviews	1.68	1.94	
Researching	22%	21%	
Planning	25	21	
Implementing	41	47	
Evaluating	12	12	
Community relations	1.36	1.47	
Researching	18%	21%	
Planning	33	33	
Implementing	32	36	
Evaluating	14	11	*
Publications	1.14	1.29	
Researching	29%	27%	
Planning	22	27	
Implementing	36	38	
Evaluating	12	7	*
Employee relations	1.73	1.70	
Researching	14%	19%	
Planning	21	27	
Implementing	45	49	
Evaluating	15	14	
Crisis communication	2.17	2.05	
Researching	18%	15%	
Planning	25	26	
Implementing	38	36	
Evaluating	15	13	
Special events	1.53	1.47	
Researching	16%	19%	
Planning	36	36	
Implementing	31	35	
Evaluating	14	9	*
Fund raising	2.43	2.52	
Researching	18%	24%	
Planning	28	33	
Implementing	25	32	
Evaluating	12.	12	
Meetings and conferences	1.63	1.76	
Researching	14%	14%	
Planning	38	38	
Implementing	36	40	
Evaluating	14	8	*

TABLE 4.2 Continued

Public Relations Activity	Frequent Contact (n = 41)	Infrequent Contact (n = 17)	SD[b]
Print advertisements	2.14	2.11	
Researching	14%	21%	
Planning	28	34	
Implementing	33	32	
Evaluating	12	13	
Broadcast ads and PSAs	2.34	2.35	
Researching	18%	18%	
Planning	28	24	
Implementing	40	38	
Evaluating	13	13	
Government relations	1.87	1.76	
Researching	21%	25%	
Planning	23	28	
Implementing	31	32	
Evaluating	16	15	
Investor relations	3.12	2.93	
Researching	15%	16%	
Planning	21	19	
Implementing	22	28	
Evaluating	9	10	
Issues management	2.19	2.37	
Researching	22%	22%	
Planning	30	24	
Implementing	38	42	
Evaluating	14	13	
Consumer affairs	2.51	2.18	
Researching	23%	22%	
Planning	23	27	
Implementing	30	37	
Evaluating	14	17	
Sales promotion	2.34	1.65	*
Researching	15%	18%	
Planning	28	35	
Implementing	33	39	
Evaluating	10	9	

(a) Frequency of engaging in public relations activities based on four-point scaled question that frequently, sometimes, rarely and never. Percent of staff time is based on response to the following question: "Textbooks in this field often emphasize four stages in the public relations process: research, planning, implementation and evaluation. What percentage of your organization's staff time is normally devoted to these stages for each of the following activities? [Note: the total for each activity should equal 100 percent.]"

(b) Significance of difference determined by t-test; reported is the probability of difference due to chance: * = .05.

stricting flexible decision-making. Corporate cultures, Perrow argues, emerge from the nexus of an organization's technology and its environment. He argues that complex organizations have built into them, somewhere, like ticking time bombs, accidents waiting to happen. Perrow believes that even with the best of planning, Murphy's Law inevitably operates just enough to create some degree of confusion, which at some point in time will be compounded by more confusion and exacerbated by key decision-makers who refuse to consider alternatives—and, all hell breaks loose.

His theory is that complex organizations face conflicting pressures that naturally generate these troubles. On the one hand, to be flexible and innovative, an organization needs to be decentralized. On the other hand, to prevent errors and improve coordination, it needs to be centralized. Based on how "tightly coupled" or centralized it is, and on how important dynamic interactions are to its technology, each organization has a different potential for what Perrow calls "normal accidents."[2] He argues that while accidents will happen, they will happen at different frequencies and will have qualitatively different results depending on the degree of coupling among the organization's principal operating units, and on the degree of interaction required by the organization's technology and its external environment. For example, nuclear power plants are very complex and tightly coupled, whereas single-purpose government agencies (such as post offices and motor vehicle administrations) are loosely coupled and have relatively routine technologies. While both types of organizations will have their fair share of accidents, the accidents will differ dramatically in frequency and severity. Perrow points out that the responsibility of managers to plan for potential accidents also will vary dramatically from organization to organization.

IN SUMMARY . . .

The basic planning characteristics—recognizing the problem, getting a mandate from management, dividing and clarifying the problem into manageable components, determining goals and objectives, developing and coordinating an action plan—vary in how they are implemented, depending on a number of factors. One of the most important factors—the perceived routineness of the event that is prompting the public relations program or campaign—is, by definition, within the eye of the beholder, and varies not only from organization to organization, but also from one set of decision-makers to another. Consequently, the public relations manager, if she or he is to be effective, must know how to vary planning strategies from situation to situation. The best way to plan public relations programs and campaigns depends not only upon senior management's perception of the situation necessitating the public relations response, and the experience of staff and others in dealing with the situation, but also upon the consensus-building and resource management skills of the public relations practitioner.

Study Questions

1. What is the difference between planning for routine events and planning for nonroutine events?
2. What are the basic steps in the planning process?
3. Describe the steps required to produce a Gantt chart. Illustrate these steps by producing a Gantt chart for one of the following activities: holding a press conference, publishing an annual report, or writing a speech for a chief executive officer and evaluating its impact.
4. What are the steps for producing a PERT diagram? Illustrate these steps by drawing a PERT diagram for the production of a monthly employee magazine over a three-month period.
5. What are characteristics of planning for nonroutine events?
6. What is the difference between long-range strategic planning and planning for a crisis? Illustrate your answer with specific cases.
7. Discuss differences in the basic steps in the planning process for routine and nonroutine events by giving examples of specific public relations programs and campaigns.
8. True or false: there is a remarkable consistency in the percent of staff time spent researching, planning, implementing and evaluating public relations activities across a wide range of organizations. What are reasonable estimates of percent of staff time spent in these activities? When might you expect these percentages to vary most dramatically?
9. True or false: the nature of the event, especially as perceived by members of the dominant coalition, is a significant factor to consider when allocating staff time to researching, planning, implementing, and evaluating public relations activities. Defend your answer.
10. What factors might explain or predict why some apparently sophisticated organizations are unable to plan their activities so as to avoid serious accidents and crises?

Endnotes

1. Perrow, Charles. *Complex organizations: A critical essay* (New York, Random House, 1986) pp. 146–154.
2. Perrow, Charles. *Normal Accidents* (New York: Basic Books, 1984).

CHAPTER FIVE

How to Budget and Perform Cost-Benefit Analyses

. . . . . .

*A*round the oak conference table sat the managers of media relations, advertising, employee relations, community relations, government affairs, and their boss, the vice president of corporate affairs, plus three assistants who were attending the annual budget meeting this day to present specific details about separate public relations activities being conducted by the electric utility. Elsewhere in the building this week and next, other budget meetings would be occurring in all operations areas, including allied areas in public relations, such as customer billing and services, and investor relations, each with separate sets of managers and vice presidents. This was the third day of the infamous "two-weeks-that-was" that occurred each year during the budgeting cycle.

The community relations manager was explaining what would happen if certain proposed community relations activities were not funded: "While each of these functions—the speakers' bureau, the neighborhood safety program, and corporate sponsorships—is vital, we can assign priorities to them, based on the number of requests we receive and on the number of customers served. The speakers' bureau is our top priority; next, corporate sponsorships; then, the neighborhood safety program. Let me discuss the speakers' bureau first.

"We received almost 300 requests last year from community groups and others for speakers, all of which we responded to. Because of scheduling conflicts or because groups withdrew their requests, we had speakers at 280 functions last year. Five groups of managers, of about a half a dozen each, were rotated throughout the year to handle this speaking load. The major costs of this program are the speakers' training workshops, the new videotapes, slide productions, information kits, and administrative time. The benefits are not so much the number of people satisfied. We figured more than 8,000 people attended these events (which is what: less than one half of one percent of our customer base?). Anyway, what is important is: What would happen if these 8,000 people did not get their questions answered? Many of these people are community activists; that's why they come to these events. If we didn't meet them more than halfway by sending speakers to their groups, they would find other ways, I'm sure, to voice their concerns—other ways that would be more costly for us to respond to."

The vice president interrupted: "I don't have any problems with this, expect for the cost of the videotapes and the training program. The training I know is essential. But, don't you think we could do more of this training ourselves and not rely so much on the outside consultants? And what about the videotapes? What's wrong with the old ones?"

"The old ones are rarely used because they don't show our current operations, particularly our new generating plant, and our new customer service centers," the community relations manager explained. "I think our speakers would be more effective if they had current tapes with them. I think they would give more balanced presentations and not be sidetracked so often."

The vice president asked, "Have the community groups—or the speakers—complained about the lack of tapes in any way?"

"No, not really. You know, I have our people audiotape their speeches, so we can listen to them back here. I think some of them do get off the subject sometimes. I do think the videotapes, played before the speech, would keep them more on track, and the audience would receive a more balanced presentation," the community relations manager said.

The vice president said what everyone in the room knew but had not mentioned. "Something out of your budget is going to have to go. Or, someone else sitting around this table is going to have to give up something if you're going to be able to do all this. Would you agree that these videotapes are a low priority?"

There was a pause. "Yes," responded the community relations manager, "but at some point in time, we are going to have to update the tapes."

The vice president turned his attention to another manager at the table. "What about your videotape budget?" he asked the manager of employee relations. "Can't we kill two birds with one stone and produce that new employee orientation tape so that some or all of it could be used by the speakers bureau?"

Before the employee manager could respond, the manager of government affairs commented. "Two sets of objectives, two target audiences. I don't know."

"Yes, I think we could," said the employee relations manager, "if we scripted it correctly, so we could edit it quickly into two separate pieces. It could be done."

"Good," said the vice president. "Then let's try it that way. Scratch this item out of the community relations budget—except for staff time, obviously—and you two work together, producing it through employee relations. Okay?"

"I still think we're mixing apples and oranges," the government affairs manager said. "I mean the two groups are so different. With employees, you'd want to be specific about people and places and internal policies.

You'd want to be general with the general public. Mix these two, and we could end up with something that satisfies neither group."

"I agree," said the community relations manager.

"Okay," the vice president said, curtly. "Then I want you two to come up with a way to measure the reactions of these publics to the tapes. Figure out a way to measure reactions to the tapes you are currently using; then do the same for storyboards of the new tapes. Let's see some data that show the old tapes do what you think they do, and that the new tapes will do what you want them to, before we invest in them heavily. Can you do that?"

Both managers nodded in agreement.

"Okay, let's go on. What about the training? Why the hell do we need to have all these outside consultants?" the vice president asked in his abrupt way. He knew that if he didn't press his people to justify every expenditure, he would regret it next week when he, in turn, went before his superiors in the senior management group to negotiate for next year's budget.

. . .

BUDGETING: NEGOTIATING ABOUT ORGANIZATIONAL RESOURCES

A public relations manager is concerned—as are all managers—with directing, monitoring, and controlling organizational resources. Practitioners who do not concern themselves with how resources are used in public relations programs and campaigns are not managers; they may be skilled, creative technicians, but they are not managers. If public relations technicians wish to advance to middle management and senior management positions, they must learn how to budget. They also must learn, as was demonstrated in the vignette above, how to negotiate with others about the use of organizational resources. Effective public relations managers know how to use the budgeting process to their advantage.

A budget is a plan for coordinating resources and expenses over a period of time by assigning costs (either estimates or actual costs) to goals and objectives for specific activities. Budgets can be calculated for a single activity or set of activities, such as a public relations program or campaign, or for work units, such as departments, divisions, and organizations. The building blocks of budgets are costs. A "cost" is what it takes to achieve something, and it usually is calculated in terms of money and time.

As the vignette would indicate, an important set of questions to answer during the budgeting process is: Are public relations goals and objectives distinct and in line with the goals and objectives of the organization (or client)? And, can they be observed or measured? If public relations costs and benefits cannot be associated with organizational goals and objectives, then the public relations budget will represent a closed system serving a limited function within the organization. A budget cannot become an effective management tool unless it has a coherent structure and appropriate data that allow it to be compared to other budgets and be linked to significant organizational goals and objectives.

A typical public relations budget includes salaries and benefits, in-house production costs and equipment, contracts to vendors, media costs, travel, special project costs, contingencies, overhead, and profit. There are two basic types of public relations budgets: those prepared by in-house specialists and public relations departments, and those prepared by "outside" public relations firms and counselors. Each type of public relations budget can be viewed differently. If the budget reflects in-house costs, these costs can be viewed as overhead, billed to the business units requesting the public relations services, or considered part of a separate profit center within the organization. If the budget reflects the cost of work performed by an "outside" agency, then these costs can be viewed in two ways: from the client's perspective (as an "out of pocket" vendor expense), or from the agency's perspective. From any vantage point, budgets are vitally important to public relations managers.

UNSOPHISTICATED BUDGETS ARE COMMON IN PUBLIC RELATIONS

Professor William P. Ehling, former chair of the public relations department at Syracuse University, has identified five reasons why most public relations budgets are not very sophisticated:[1]

1. Public relations is often not seen as strategic management, but as technical production. Public relations is not seen as a problem-solving activity focused on serious management issues but rather as a peripheral support service producing publicity and media materials. Consequently, costs for these technical services are considered part of overhead: they are placed on the debit side of the corporate ledger. To raise the question about the size of the public relations budget, using this rationale, is to ask: What can we afford to write off? When public relations costs are considered part of overhead and a debit, there are few if any expectations for a return on the organization's investment.
2. Outcome goals for public relations programs and campaigns are considered intangible. When asked to document the value of public relations, a practitioner using this argument would counter with questions, such as: "How do you measure goodwill? How do you

assign a value to a positive image? How do you quantify the public's trust?" When outcome goals are declared intangible, senior management is expected to accept on faith the fact that public relations activities are worthwhile.

3. The current public relations budget is based on the previous one. The rationale is that the organization has a history of budgeting for public relations. It's part of the corporate culture; it's tradition. This approach does not expect any more accountability than was demonstrated the last time the budget was reviewed. It is not a zero-based budget that builds and justifies anew each year's set of public relations activities; rather, it is an incremental budget based on past experience. A likely comment from a practitioner using this rationale would be, "Given inflation and other increases, what we need is ten percent more funding than we received last year."

4. A variation on the incremental approach to public relations budgeting is justifying the budget because it will allow the organization to keep up with the competition. Sometimes objective, quantitative information is gathered about the competitions' public relations activities, but more often than not, subjective, anecdotal information about the competition is used to justify the public relations budget. The rationale is that matching or increasing the amount of money and resources spent on public relations by others may provide to the organization (or client) the competitive edge needed to win in the marketplace.

5. Public relations costs are subsumed under other operating budgets, such as marketing, advertising, or human resources. When this happens, public relations is looked upon as a "logistical support service."[2] This means that public relations goals are displaced by, or embedded within, other goals of the organization. It occurs most often when public relations is integrated into marketing communications—when most public relations activities are expected to contribute to product promotion. Some consider this type of public relations goal displacement a form of encroachment and "marketing imperialism."[3] Others, however, acknowledge that some public relations practitioners willingly engage in what Ehling calls "functional subservience" because it makes public relations appear more relevant to important organizational goals.[4] When public relations is not viewed as a separately budgeted function, then monitoring and controlling public relations resources are often not considered part of the job description of public relations staff. Instead, the responsibilities fall on someone else's shoulders, and public relations practitioners are viewed as technicians.

STANDARD APPROACHES TO PUBLIC RELATIONS BUDGETING

The most common approach to budgeting in public relations is imposed from the top down: senior management determines, with very little input from others, the amount of resources that can be devoted to a public relations program or campaign.[5] Then, the public relations manager directs, monitors, and controls this predetermined amount of resources. A bottom-up approach has the public relations specialists and technicians responsible for performing various tasks estimate, with very little input from top management, the amount of resources that will be required. Then, these estimates are passed up the chain of command. Eventually, using this bottom-up approach, senior management receives a fairly accurate estimate of what specific activities will cost and can decide at what level to fund the full set of public relations activities.

The advantage of the top-down approach is that it is easier for senior managers to have insight into the "bigger picture" and to see all the various activities that need to be performed; specialists and technicians often do not know about all of the necessary components of a multi-faceted program or campaign. Obviously, the top-down approach leaves control and power at the top. The disadvantage of the top-down approach is that it tends to underestimate costs, and lower-level participants may not understand, and may resist, budget constraints. In addition to generating more accurate estimates, the bottom-up approach empowers lower participants and increases their support and cooperation. The major disadvantage of bottom-up budgeting is that lower-level participants tend to inflate their estimates, assuming (correctly, in most cases) that their initial budget estimates will be reduced by top management.[6]

Very few organizations depend entirely on the bottom-up approach. Using management-by-objective principles, most organizations mix the two approaches by having senior management issue a directive to lower-level participants asking them to submit budget requests.[7] The directive explains current fiscal constraints, guidelines for submitting budget requests, and other matters related to the budgeting process. Then, with all its strengths and weaknesses, bottom-up budgeting begins. Only this time, the initial budget estimates are more realistic and more closely linked to organizational goals and objectives.

Standard Categories within Budgets

The typical public relations budget includes two basic categories of expenditures: administrative costs and program costs. Administrative costs are salaries and fringe benefits for full- and part-time employees.

Program costs include everything else: contracted services from outside vendors and consultants, production materials, equipment, media time and space charges, special project costs, distribution and mailing expenses, office communication such as telephones and facsimile transmission, office space, travel, entertainment, and contingency reserves.

Overhead and profit are two items handled in a variety of ways, depending on the organization. Most often, overhead is a percentage of program costs; sometimes, it is a percentage of administrative costs; rarely, it is an across-the-board percentage of total costs. Some public relations agencies calculate one overhead charge based on a small percentage of administrative costs and another overhead charge based on a larger percentage of program costs. As business professors Meredith and Mantel state, "The matter of what overhead costs are to be added and in what amounts is unique to the firm . . . and generally a source of annoyance and frustration to one and all."[8] Because of its arbitrary nature, overhead charges cover not only the miscellaneous and hidden costs of maintaining an organization but also profit.

Profits can be incorporated into budgets for public relations programs and campaigns in several places: as a percentage of overhead; as a percentage of purchased media; as a percentage of hourly rates for professional services; and, as a separate percentage of administrative, program or total costs. The allocation of profit is often unique to the organization. The one consistent aspect of profit in public relations is the commission earned by advertising and public relations agencies when they purchase media time and space. In the United States, most media outlets give commissions of 15–18 percent to certified media buyers, including public relations agencies.

Standard Budgets in Public Relations

Two types of standard budgets are used in public relations: one presents an income statement for a significant business unit (SBU); the other describes resources allocated to and used by a specific set of public relations activities.

See Figure 5.1 for an example of a budget for a significant business unit: a public relations agency. The income statement is divided into two sections: revenue and operating expenses. Income-generating revenue items include professional fees, technical service fees, media buying commissions, overhead, and other income sources. Income-reducing operating expenses include administrative costs (wages), program costs (equipment and "out-of-pocket" expenses, such as postage and printing), media space (advertising) costs, overhead, and miscellaneous costs, such as travel, food, and lodging. Notice that both actual and budgeted figures are listed, with the variance calculated and presented as a percent of the original budgeted figure.

FIGURE 5.1

Budget by significant business unit: a public relations agency

	Current			
	Actual	Budget	Variance	Pct
Income statement				
Revenue:				
Professional fees				
Account #1	$2,000	$2,000	$0	0%
Account #2	10,000	9,100	900	10%
Technical services fees				
Account #1	450	500	−50	−10%
Account #2	1,300	1,500	−200	−14
Media buying fees				
Account #1	23,400	23,400	0	0
Account #2	34,515	34,281	+234	+1
Overhead charges				
Account #1	1,000	1,000	0	0
Account #2	5,000	5,000	0	0
Other income				
Source #1	0	0	0	0
Source #2	500	400	+100	20
Total revenue =	$78,165	$77,181	+$984	1%
Operating expenses:				
Administrative costs				
Account #1	$500	$500	$0	0%
Account #2	2,200	2,200	0	0
Program costs				
Account #1	300	300	0	0
Account #2	800	1,000	−200	−20
Media space costs				
Account #1	20,000	20,000	0	0
Account #2	29,500	29,700	+200	1
Overhead costs				
Account #1	500	500	0	0
Account #2	2,500	2,500	0	0
Miscellaneous costs				
Account #1	200	300	−100	−34
Account #2	800	1,200	−400	−34
Total operating expenses	$57,300	$57,800	−$500	−1%
Income statement balance =	$20,865	$19,381	$1,484	+7%

Figure 5.2 presents a budget for a public relations department within an organization. The format of this budget is much the same as it is for the public relations agency. The only difference in the two budget formats is that income-generating revenue is referred to in the department's budget as "allocations." The function of the budget for both types of business units remains the same: to document cash flow into and out of the unit.

To document cash flow and resource allocations for a public relations program or campaign, a public relations manager needs to prepare a budget similar to Figure 5.3—a budget by activities. In this budget, costs are divided into program costs and administrative costs. Actual and budgeted expenditures are shown in Figure 5.3. In addition to total costs, budget variances can be calculated from these figures.

For many managers, the mark of excellence is not to bring the project in under budget but to accurately estimate costs in the beginning and to "bring in" specific line items in the budget with zero variance.

Narrative Budgets Are the Workhorses in the Field

One of the most useful budgets for managing public relations programs and campaigns is the narrative budget (see Figure 5.4). It's called a narrative budget not because elegant prose is associated with it, but because line item calculations are explained (most often, parathetically) in the terse, truncated language of mathematical formula. With a narrative budget, decision-makers can see the bases on which various costs were determined. The narrative budget is the basic budget for most public relations managers. Most other budgets are built upon the information from the narrative budget developed for a specific set of activities. This is the budget that explains the greatest amount of detail about a public relations program or campaign. Like a solid, dependable workhorse, the narrative budget is the key to getting the job done. Effective public relations managers are masters at developing and using narrative budgets.

Figure 5.5 presents a form that can be used to estimate costs and develop a narrative budget for a specific set of activities. There are no simple, accurate ways of estimating costs. Monitoring previous expenditures for similar activities and projecting these to future costs is time-consuming but often very useful. Obtaining several bids from independent sources is the most commonly used technique to estimate costs, and one of the most reliable.

FIGURE 5.2

Budget by significant business unit: a public relations department within an organization

	Current			
	Actual	Budget	Variance	Pct
Income statement				
Budget allocations:				
Professional staff				
Person #1	$45,000	$45,000	$0	0%
Person #2	25,000	25,000	0	0
Technical staff				
Person #1	15,000	15,000	0	0
Person #2	14,000	14,000	0	0
Temporary staff				
Person #1	7,200	6,000	1,200	+20
Person #2	2,000	3,000	−1,000	−34
Office maintenance				
Account #1	3,200	4,000	−800	−20
Account #2	5,800	6,000	−200	−3
Vender services				
Account #1	1,500	2,000	−500	−25
Account #2	250	250	0	0
Additional allocations				
Item #1	1,000	1,000	0	0
Item #2	800	500	+300	60
Total allocations =	$120,750	$121,750	−$1,000	−1%
Operating expenses:				
Administrative costs				
Professional staff	$70,000	$70,000	$0	0%
Technical staff	29,000	29,000	0	0
Temporary staff	9,200	9,000	200	2
Program costs				
Vendor services				
Account #1	1,500	2,000	−500	−25
Account #2	250	250	0	0
Other expenses				
Account #1	3,200	4,000	−800	−20
Account #2	5,800	6,000	−200	4
Additional costs				
Item #1	1,000	1,000	0	0
Item #2	800	500	+300	60
Total operating expenses	$120,750	$121,750	−$1,000	−1%
Income statement balance =	0	0		

FIGURE 5.3

Budget by activities

	Program Costs		Administrative Costs		Total Costs	
	Actual	Budget	Actual	Budget	Actual	Budget
Program A: Activity						
#1	$ 500		$ 2,000		$ 2,500	
#2	1,200		4,000		5,200	
#3	2,500		3,600		6,100	
#4	500		1,000		1,500	
#5	1,000		1,000		2,000	
Total =	$5,700		$11,600		$17,300	
Program B: Activity						
#1	$ 3,200		$ 2,000		$ 5,200	
#2	4,800		500		5,300	
#3	15,000		2,000		17,000	
#4	5,000		800		5,800	
#5	10,000		1,800		11,800	
Total =	$38,000		$ 7,100		$45,100	
Campaign A: Activity						
#1	$10,500		$ 2,000		$12,500	
#2	18,000		3,000		21,000	
#3	12,000		3,000		15,000	
Total =	$40,500		$ 8,000		$48,500	
Campaign B: Activity						
#1	$ 5,500		$ 1,500		$ 7,000	
#2	9,000		1,500		10,500	
#3	6,000		1,000		7,000	
#4	11,000		2,000		13,000	
#5	9,500		2,000		11,500	
Total =	$41,000		$ 8,000		$49,000	

	Program Costs		Administrative Costs		Total Costs	
	Actual	Budget	Actual	Budget	Actual	Budget
Significant Business Unit Total =	$125,200		$34,700		$159,900	

FIGURE 5.4

Narrative budget by activities

	Program Costs (how determined)	Administrative Costs (how determined)	Total Costs
Program A:			
Activity			
#1	$21,000 ($300 x 70)		$21,000
#2		$4,000 ($100/hr x 40 hrs)	$4,000
#3	$10,000 (20,000 @ $.50 each)	$1,000 (20/hr x 50 hrs)	$11,000
#4	$500 (vendor fee)	$200 ($100/hr x 2 hrs)	$700
#5	$1,300 (vendor fee)	$100 ($10/hr x 10 hrs)	$1,400
	Program Costs	**Administrative Costs**	**Total Costs**
Total Program A =	$32,800	$ 5,300	$38,100

Program A	Goals and objectives: x x x x x x x x x x x x x x x x x x x x x x x x x x x x x x x x x x x x x x x x x x x x x x x x x x x x
Activity #1	x x x x x x x x x x x x x x x x x x x x x x x x x x x
Activity #2	x x x x x x x x x x x x x x x x x x x x x x x x x x x
Activity #3	x x x x x x x x x x x x x x x x x x x x x x x x x x x
Activity #4	x x x x x x x x x x x x x x x x x x x x x x x x x x x
Activity #5	x x x x x x x x x x x x x x x x x x x x x x x x x x x

FIGURE 5.5

Form for estimating costs of public relations activities

Program A: Brief description:

Activity #1 Brief description:

What specifically is needed:

When is it needed:

Resource persons to contact:

	Estimate of Program Costs (how determined)	**Estimate of Administrative Costs (how determined)**	**Estimate of Total Costs**
1st estimate			
2nd estimate			
3rd estimate			

Activity #2 Brief description:

What specifically is needed:

When is it needed:

Resource persons to contact:

	Estimate of Program Costs (how determined)	**Estimate of Administrative Costs (how determined)**	**Estimate of Total Costs**
1st estimate			
2nd estimate			
3rd estimate			

THREE CASE STUDIES

The following three case studies illustrate how a corporation incorporated parts of a public relations budget within other functional units, and how two public relations agencies prepared budgets for clients with different needs and expectations.

An Example of Corporate Public Relations Budgeting

. . .

CASE 5.1:

Blue Cross and Blue Shield Communication Plan for Corporate Clients

Blue Cross and Blue Shield (BCBS) is one of the world's largest health insurance companies. Its Custom Benefit Services Department is a business unit within the company that specializes in packaging employee benefit programs to fit the needs of specific corporate clients. One function of the department is to prepare communication plans to help BCBS corporate clients explain to their employees the various aspects of the BCBS insurance program. Each communication plan is designed to help the client persuade, recruit, and enroll employees into the benefit program the client has purchased from BCBS. The communication plan, which corporate clients purchase as an add-on to the benefits program, "offers a custom-designed communication program for pre-enrollment and enrollment materials, plus planning and evaluation services . . . also, employee education, training, and enrollment meetings . . . (and) experts (who) will train meeting leaders and serve as a resource for an employee hotline." Here are the steps the director of the Custom Benefit Services Department went through as she prepared the communication plan and its budget:

1. Contracts for BCBS benefit programs with corporate clients stated that there would be a start-up fee to include the cost of communication services. Specific client fees were determined after the BCBS marketing staff requested and received from the client a description of the organization, its employees, and current enrollments in existing benefit programs.
2. After BCBS received the necessary information, the client was invited for a presentation at BCBS corporate headquarters, in what staffers call their "marketing theater," a multi-media auditorium. It was not unusual for a client to come to this presentation with their own human resource specialists and employee communication consultants.
3. To prepare the proposal for the communication plan, which included the costs of various options to be charged to the client, the director and her staff conducted in-house brainstorming sessions with experts and circulated drafts of the proposal for review.

4. The director and her staff also rehearsed their presentation in the marketing theater, with BCBS employees playing the role of clients.
5. The client was offered three increasingly comprehensive options of communication materials and services, and three corresponding budgets. If the client wanted additional materials and services, an additional budget for those items was prepared. Each option included a set of meetings with the client to fine-tune the communication plan. A fee-per-day was charged for the planning meetings, with the client expected to pay for travel, lodging and related expenses.
6. Using a bottom-up approach to budgeting, the staff collected several estimates from outside vendors and calculated staff time and resources needed to develop the client's communication program. Then, they determined overhead and profit for each of the three optional communication plans. The total cost of each option was included in the final proposal to the client, supported by a narrative section of the report comparing potential values and costs of the three options. Also included with the proposal was a letter of agreement for the client to indicate the option selected and to sign before services would be provided.
7. For her own management records, the director constructed detailed narrative budgets that allowed her to compare estimated versus actual expenditures. She prepared these budgets on a monthly, quarterly, and annual basis. While developing and implementing the communication program, the staff tracked the cost of additional services and production rush charges not factored into the original budget, and these additional costs were billed to the client.
8. Within any fiscal period, total sales and profit were not broken out by client at the departmental level, so it was impossible for the director of Custom Benefit Services to compare the profitability of various communication plans used for different clients. Also, revenue generated by the communication plans was not credited to the department; rather, it was considered general revenue for Blue Cross Blue Shield. Consequently, the specific contribution that a single communication plan made to corporate profits could not be determined.

Two Examples of Budgeting by Public Relations Agencies

. . .

CASE 5.2:

Media Relations for the Roman Catholic Pope's Tour of the United States

In the late 1980s, one year before Pope John Paul was to tour the United States, the U.S. Conference of Catholic Bishops contacted several major public relations agencies in the United States and asked them to bid for a contract to provide media relations during the papal visit. (See Case 7.4 for more information about the winning campaign.) The public relations agency of Manning, Selvage and Lee/Washington (MS&L) won the contract. The agency's two major assignments were to recommend strategies for positioning and presenting issues important to the Pope, and to tour with the Pope and coordinate press pools and media coverage for the nine-city Papal visit. The U.S. Conference of Catholic Bishops established and monitored budgets for all aspects of the visit, including costs of building stages, renting stadiums, traveling, lodging and food arrangements—plus, the work of MS&L. Estimates of the overall budget for the Pope's ten-day visit exceeded two million dollars. The U.S. Conference of Catholic Bishops expected and received detailed budgets from MS&L, but the criteria for selecting the public relations agency were not based on costs so much as they were on the ability of the agency to provide sophisticated media relations. Here is how MS&L prepared its budget for the media relations campaign:

1. The senior account executive prepared separate budgets for each task in the media relations campaign. These were compiled into separate budgets for each city on the tour and a comprehensive budget for the entire nine-city tour. For example, one of the tasks was to provide an escort service for the press. This involved agency personnel staffing press pools and making sure media arrangements went smoothly at each event. There were 10 to 15 media events per day; the number of events varied from city to city. Consequently, the budget for this task varied from day to day and from city to city.
2. To determine administrative costs, the account executive originally estimated three staff per pool of 40 media representatives. Then, he revised this estimate to two staff persons per pool of approximately 35 media people. He determined the number of events and the number of staff people required and calculated the total number of billable hours. Junior agency people from affiliated agencies in each of the major cities were used to staff the pools. The local affiliates were told the total amount budgeted for them and the number of staff required.
3. To determine part of the program costs, the account executive estimated the cost of travel, lodging, and food for the members of the agency who toured with the Pope's entourage. Initially, a full complement of approximately ten professional staff from the agency's main office was considered. Then, in discussions with MS&L staff and the U.S. Conference of Catholic Bishops, it was determined that local public relations personnel from affiliates and from local Catholic church offices could be trained to perform the duties of press pool escorts.
4. Numerous meetings were held to work out logistics and to fine-tune estimates of staff time and the amount of time required to train personnel.
5. Potential public relations benefits were not spelled out, per se, in either the original proposal or in later reports. The account executive attributed this to working with "a very sophisticated client" who understood the benefits of smooth media relations. The client realized the consequence of not properly staffing press pools. The negative consequences of poorly managed press pools would have been media coverage about the media's problems in covering the Pope, and the public's attention to the Pope's serious messages would have been diverted to relatively trivial matters.

6. To monitor costs, budgets of estimated and actual billable hours and program costs were reviewed every two weeks. If needed, adjustments were made prior to the preparation of the client's monthly report and budget. Overhead costs were presented as a line item in the budget. Profit was incorporated into professional billable hours.
7. Because circumstances changed for certain events, the agency had to bill the client for additional services. In the original proposal and final contract, it was stipulated that costs for additional authorized services would be billed to the client. The U.S. Conference of Catholic Bishops paid the additional charges and praised the professional services they received from the agency.

CASE 5.3:

Porter/Novelli and the International Apple Institute

Following media reports of possible health risks from the chemical Alar, which were generated by a public relations campaign sponsored by a group of food safety activists, there was a public outcry about the safety of apples. Apple sales dropped dramatically, and government agencies moved to ban the use of the chemical, which was used to control ripening and to maintain the quality of apples while they were in storage. Reacting to public pressures, the International Apple Institute circulated an RFP to a number of public relations agencies. They wanted a public relations campaign that supported their members' efforts to market apples.

1. An executive with Porter/Novelli met with officials of the Institute to discuss details of the proposed campaign. During initial discussions, the annual budget for public relations by the Institute was discussed in general terms, so the agency knew an appropriate budget range to propose for the campaign.
2. The executive formed an account team that included the directors of research and creative services. This team prepared a document that included a description of the situation, a strategy statement, and a specific set of objectives.
3. The team circulated the preliminary document and invited a dozen agency colleagues to participate in a brainstorming session to identify practical, creative tactics to meet the proposed objectives. The session lasted about two hours.
4. Considering these suggestions, the account supervisor prepared the final proposal which included a detailed budget that listed six separate tasks, each with several activities, for a total of eighteen separately budgeted activities. Sets of activities were linked to specific goals. Estimates of the costs were based on the experience of the account supervisor plus current prices the executive received from the various vendors he called. For the initial proposal, only total costs per activity were presented to the client.
5. From the several proposals submitted, the Institute invited three agencies to make presentations.

6. The Porter/Novelli account team rehearsed their presentation, which did not precisely follow the formal proposal but, instead, dramatically described the proposed campaign, using graphics and visuals. The 30-minute presentation concluded by detailing the six tasks and all eighteen activities, emphasizing the flexibility of the campaign and the options available to the client.
7. The agency won the account. The client selected an option that consisted of fifteen activities that were part of the following six tasks: a consumer brochure, media relations for Apple Month, year-round media relations, reaching opinion leaders and intermediaries, media relations for Applesauce Month, and account management.
8. A letter of understanding was sent to the client, along with the client-approved public relations plan, which included a detailed budget. The letter—a legal contract—contained paragraphs explaining each of the following: basic purpose of the campaign; specific set of tasks; timetable; total costs; monthly billing procedure; a service fee based on total administrative costs; direct (program) costs, such as printing and production expenses; overhead, based on direct costs; media placement costs; and, an industry-standard commission for purchasing products and services on behalf of the client. Profits were incorporated into professional billable hours. The letter said it was expected that, as the campaign progressed, client-approved changes would be made and billed accordingly. The letter also contained a statement of indemnification, specifying conditions protecting the agency against loss should the client terminate the contract before its completion. The letter also identified specific aspects of the campaign that would either become the intellectual property of the client or remain the property of the agency.
9. The Institute was billed monthly with a fifteen-item narrative budget. The format of the bill remained the same each month. For those months when no charges were incurred for a specific activity, zero costs were reported on that line in the budget.
10. Part of the campaign included an ongoing evaluation of the publicity generated, which was reported regularly to the client. The agency knew the client was satisfied when the contract was renewed and the scope of the public relations campaign increased.

Similarities

The most obvious similarity among these three cases was that they all used relatively simple procedures to estimate administrative and program costs. Also common among the cases was that, in order to build consensus during the budgeting process, numerous staff meetings and negotiating sessions occurred, resulting in several revisions of the budgets. No cost-benefit analysis was employed in any of the cases, primarily because there was little or no expectation on the part of management or client of a precise monitoring of cost and benefits.

Differences

Because the Blue Cross and Blue Shield communication plan and the Apple Institute promotional campaign were packaged as sets of deliverables, the budgets were more inflexible and dramatically different than the budget used to monitor and control resources spent on the Pope's tour. The campaigns that contained tangible products and quantifiable services had budgets that were relatively inflexible, and additional costs were not passed on to the clients (except for rush production charges requested by the client). The papal media-relations campaign needed to respond to unforeseen market conditions, so its budget was flexible and unanticipated costs were passed on to the client.

ADDITIONAL BUDGETING STRATEGIES

In addition to the traditional comprehensive and task-oriented budgets described above, there are other budgeting strategies that can help a practitioner manage public relations programs and campaigns. We will describe five additional strategies: what-if-not-funded scenarios, benefit shadow pricing, cost-benefit compensation estimations, expected value analysis, and cost/benefit ratios. The first four can help a manager fine-tune a campaign during the planning and initial implementation stages. The last one, using cost/benefit ratios, is helpful when the total impact of a program or campaign needs to be assessed.

What-If-Not-Funded Scenarios

This strategy will force public relations practitioners, if they have not already done so, to acknowledge the set of assumptions and theories underlying the public relations program or campaign. The strategy is to play a mental game: What would happen if there were no public relations activities as planned? Obviously, the problem, or opportunity, would continue, but how would it manifest itself? How do you measure the continuing impact of the problem, or opportunity, should there be no public relations program or campaign? Planners probably have already answered this question when they make the initial decision to go ahead with the planning efforts, so this broad question in the what-if-not-funded scenarios is fairly simple to answer. But, the mental game becomes more complex when these questions are asked: What if one particular activity out of the full set of planned activities was not performed? For example, what would happen if everything was funded except for one activity? Would the problem, or opportunity, change? How? Why? In other words, what contribution does each activity make to the total impact of the public relations program or campaign? One by one, a manager can predict the likely consequence of each activity's not being funded, assuming that all others are funded. See Figure 5.6 for an example of a budget using a what-if-not-funded scenario.

FIGURE 5.6

What-if-not-funded scenarios for a hypothetical public relations program.

Program A
Brief description: Quality Hotline, a special voice message system for employees to use to call in problems they may hear about from customers, friends, family, and others about the quality of service provided by the company.

Corporate goal Program A is designed to help meet:

To constantly improve the quality of service delivered to our customers.

Program A total costs = $12,500 for initial six-month period

Activity	Priority	Cost	What-if-not-funded scenario
Referral service	1	$5,000	Without one professional staff devoting four hours per week to reviewing and referring problems to appropriate departments and personnel, the program cannot be implemented without the potential for inappropriate referrals, confusion, and more problems.
Employee hotline	2	$1,000	This is electronic heart of system. Without the special phone line, written memos from employees would have to be used, which would be slower and likely lead to lower employee participation.
Weekly updates via staff memos	3	$500	Would need to rely on supervisors passing on word, probably inconsistently, to all employees.
Six articles in employee magazine	4	$6,000	Alternative (more expensive) ways of acknowledging employee participation would need to be found; employee participation would probably not increase as rapidly.

In Case 5.1, a multi-media communication program targeted to employees included brochures announcing the new benefit options, workbook materials, workshops, and workshop-instructor training sessions. To illustrate the technique of what-if-not-funded scenarios, imagine what would happen if employees did not receive the brochures. Some other way of informing the employees would have to be found—probably memos or word-of-mouth—which might not be less expensive and might generate more confusion or contain less precise information. If no other ways of announcing the new benefit options were used in

FIGURE 5.7

What-if-not-funded scenarios for Case 5.1: Blue Cross Blue Shield's Communication Plan.

The goal of the Communication Plan is designed to help clients enroll as many eligible employees as possible in appropriate health care benefit programs.

Activity	Priority	What-if-not-funded scenario
Brochures	1	Some other way of informing the employees would have to be found—probably memos or word-of-mouth—which might not be less expensive and might generate more confusion or contain less precise information. Employees would arrive at workshops with more questions, and they would have to rely on less effective ways of explaining benefits to family members and others.
Workshop materials	3	More instructor time would be spent answering basic questions, and employees would spend too much time taking notes and not asking questions. Less effective learning would occur.
Workshops	2	These are essential. Without the workshops, all employee questions would need to be answered via printed material and could not be tailored to individuals; fewer employees would enroll.
Workshop instructors' training	4	Instructors would need to learn everything from printed material and videotapes, which would not be as effective; consequently, clients attending workshops led by these instructors would receive less information, and fewer employees would enroll.

place of the now missing brochures, employees would arrive at the workshop with little or no information about the program; consequently, more time would have to be spent by workshop instructors and others to explain the new benefit options. Furthermore, employees who wished to take the brochures home to discuss options with their families would have to rely on other potentially less effective ways to communicate this information. This scenario highlights the role of the brochure in facilitating the workshops and in helping employees discuss the matter with their families. How this scenario might be expressed in a budget format is presented in Figure 5.7.

In Case 5.2, one aspect of media relations for the Papal visit was using press pools and assigning two public relations staff members to

FIGURE 5.8

What-if-not-funded scenarios for Case 5.2: Papal Tour of the United States

---

The goal of the media relations program is to facilitate accurate media coverage of the Pope's message.

Activity	Priority	What-if-not-funded scenario
Staff media pools	1	Two staff per pool of 35 media representatives, if not funded, would mean more responsibility for fewer staff, a greater potential for dissatisfied, frustrated media reps, and potentially less accurate coverage of the Papal visit.
Media pool transportation	4	Alternative modes of transportation would have to be found by the media at their expense, and we would have a greater need to coordinate directions to specific locations, with the potential for some confusion and "no shows" among interested media. Also, an alternative way to distribute media advisories and other information to the media would need to be found.
Prepare and distribute media advisories	2	Media would not know time schedule, etc., of the papal visit, and there would be less media coverage.
Advance work by agency staff in each city visited	3	The agency would have to depend on the client's local coordinators who may not be as skilled in establishing and maintaining professional relationships with local media or in estimating the local needs of visiting international media representatives.

---

each pool of about 35 media representatives. Because it was not likely that press pools would be eliminated from the campaign, a more realistic what-if-not-funded scenario would be: What would happen if they could only staff each press pool with one public relations specialist? Would one staff person be able to handle all the requests and special needs of 35 journalists? Would there be more complaints from those in the press pools? Would their coverage of the Pope's tour shift from what the Pope was saying and focus more on how the media were being treated? What would happen if no public relations staff were assigned to the pools, and reporters simply were put on buses, taken to "press only" areas of events, and left on their own to cover the event and get back on the buses in time to make it to the next event? See Figure 5.8.

FIGURE 5.9

What-if-not-funded scenarios for Case 5.3: The International Apple Institute

The goal of the campaign was to support the marketing efforts of the members of the International Apple Institute by impoving the media's and consuming public's perception of the nutritional quality of apples.

Activity	Priority	What-if-not-funded scenario
Media campaign for Apple Month	1	This is the heart of the year-long campaign, the one with the greatest tradition; an alternative set of celebrations would need to be initiated and would not have the immediate public recognition as the established Apple-Month celebration.
Media campaign for Applesauce month	2	An alternative set of celebrations would need to be found, or more emphasis could be placed within Apple Month.
Year-long media relations targeting media intermediaries	3	Without the direct and often personal contact proposed here, media relations would continue to be dependent on press kits and media advisories, and the same low level of placement and media coverage of apple stories would continue.
Consumer brochures	4	More reliance would have to be placed on advertising, which would be more expensive; alternative means of quickly and efficiently distributing this information would need to be found for press kits, membership materials, and schools' packages.

In Case 5.3, the International Apple Institute authorized a promotional campaign that included media materials and special events for an Apple Month and an Applesauce Month, during which the agency would stage appropriate events and generate special publicity about apples. A what-if-not-funded scenario would ask questions, such as: What if neither one of those special months in the campaign was funded? What if both month-long sets of activities were not funded? To generate the same level of public exposure, other aspects of the campaign would have to be highlighted, but more than likely, certain publics would not be reached at all. See Figure 5.9.

The advantages of what-if-not-funded scenarios are: 1) they force planners to think out the practical consequences of planned activities; 2) they enable others who review such a budget to see the rationale for including each item in the budget, which is especially important if the reviewers are in a position to affect budget allocations; and 3) if, for whatever reason, certain activities need to be cut, they facilitate elimination of those with the least defensible justifications. Concerning this last point, as Figure 5.6 indicates, budget items can be assigned priorities based on what-if-not-funded scenarios, thus facilitating budget discussions and negotiations.

Benefit Shadow Pricing

Shadow pricing is a procedure for assigning values to goods and services which do not have a market. Like a center stage with all its bright lights, a marketplace is where the values of goods and services—most often with an exchange of money—are clearly seen. Shadow pricing takes place off stage—in the shadow of the marketplace. There, someone is asked how much she would be willing to pay for a good or service *as if it were something that could be purchased in the marketplace.* The assumption of shadow pricing is that individual estimates of an appropriate price for something can be aggregated to represent a fair market value.

Benefit shadow pricing public relations programs and campaigns involve calculating the price that members of target publics would be willing to pay to receive the program or campaign *as if it were something that could be purchased in the marketplace.* For example, in all three cases in this chapter, a monetary value was assigned to each public relations campaign when the client paid for it. The question is: Was the price paid by the clients a fair market value? Shadow pricing could answer that question. In Case 5.1, the corporate client of Blue Cross and Blue Shield could have asked its employees to hypothetically estimate how much they would be willing to pay to receive the brochures, lectures, and other materials included in the communication plan. Multiplying an average of this hypothetical price by the number of employees would yield an estimate of how much the plan was worth to the employees. See Figure 5.10.

In Case 5.2, a sample of the general population could have been asked how much they would be willing to pay to receive via the media, one of two types of news accounts about the U.S. tour of the Roman Catholic Pope: 1) a relatively straightforward news account of the Pope's views; or 2) the same length feature article focusing less on the Pope's views and more on the excitement surrounding the Papal visit. Subtracting the price paid for option #2 from option #1 would yield an estimate, per individual, of the value of the type of reportage and media relations desired by the U.S. Conference of Catholic Bishops. Individuals who valued the feature article about the excitement more than the straight-news account would be eliminated from the calculations, because they would not be considered members of the target audience. Multiplying the average difference in price by the total number of

FIGURE 5.10

Hypothetical benefit shadow pricing based on Case 5.1: Blue Cross Blue Shield's Communication Plan*

Communication Plan for Corporate Clients
    Corporate goal Communication Plan is designed to help meet:
        To help clients enroll as many eligible employees as possible in appropriate health care benefit programs.

Activity	Shadow price plus cost company willing to pay	
Brochures	$ .10	Average price willing to pay
	8,000	Number of employee interested
	$800	Shadow price for 4,000 brochures
Workshop materials	$1.00	Average price willing to pay
	4,000	Number of employees interested
	$4,000	Shadow price for workshop materials
Workshops	$3.00	Average price employees willing to pay to attend workshop
	$10	Average salary of 4,000 employees company is willing to pay while employees attend one-hour workshop
	$13	Subtotal: Shadow price + cost of an employee attending workshop
	4,000	Number of employees interested
	$52,000	Subtotal: Shadow price + cost
	10	Number of instructors
	20	Number of workshops per instructor
	$20	Average hourly salary of instructors
	$4,000	Subtotal: cost of instructors
	$56,000	Shadow price + cost of workshops
Workshop instructors' training	$20	Average hourly salary of instructors
	4	Hours of training
	$80	Subtotal: cost company willing to pay while instructor attends
	$300	Price company willing to pay for comparable workshop training
	$380	Subtotal
	10	Number of instructors
	$3,800	Shadow price for instructor training
Total	$64,600	Shadow price + cost**

* These figures are hypothetical and are for instructional purposes only.
** Cost excludes value of work not performed while at training.

FIGURE 5.11

Hypothetical benefit shadow pricing based on Case 5.2: The Papal Visit to the United States.*

One goal of the media relations program for the papal visit was to increase the amount of accurate coverage by the media of the Pope's message and decrease the amount of media coverage focused on the logistics of the Pope's visit.

Public	Type of media coverage	Shadow price willing to pay	Differential
Prefers focus on Pope's message	10-column-inch news story on Pope's message	$ .10	
	10-column-inch news story on logistics	$ .05	$ .05
	1-minute TV report on Pope's message	$ .25	
	1-minute TV report on logistics	$ .10	$ .15

Type of media coverage	Estimated number	Shadow price differential	No. in public	Shadow price
10-column-inch news stories generated during papal visit	20,000	$ .05	2 mil.	$100,000
1-minute TV reports about papal visit	5,000	$ .15	5 mil.	$750,000
			Value of media relations =	$850,000

Note: Shadow price does not include other forms of media coverage, such as by magazines or radio stations.

* These figures are hypothetical and are for instructional purposes only.

people willing to pay more for the balanced news account would yield an estimate of the value of effective media relations during the Pope's tour. See Figure 5.11.

In Case 5.3, all members of the International Apple Institute, which represents hundreds of apple growers and distributers, could have been asked how much they would be willing to pay for the promotional campaign planned by the public relations agency. This price, which would vary from member to member, depending on each member's investment and commitment to the apple industry, could be totalled to yield an estimate of the value of the campaign—not to the general public, but to Institute members. See Figure 5.12.

FIGURE 5.12

Hypothetical benefit shadow pricing based on Case 5.3: The International Apple Institute*

The goal of the campaign was to support the marketing efforts of the members of the International Apple Institute by improving the media's and consuming public's perception of the nutritional quality of apples.

Membership categories (based on annual sales)	Average price member willing to pay	Number of members in category	Shadow price
Group 1	$50,000	20	$1,000,000
Group 2	40,000	30	1,200,000
Group 3	30,000	40	1,200,000
Group 4	20,000	50	1,000,000
Group 5	10,000	100	1,000,000

Total shadow price = $5,400,000

* These figures are hypothetical and are for instructional purposes only.

As these examples illustrate, one difficulty in benefit shadow pricing is determining how best to include stakeholders—primary, secondary or more distant target publics. Of course, all stakeholders should be included in the calculations, but this becomes a cumbersome technical problem. Furthermore, it is difficult to determine the various estimates from members of publics who have varying degrees of interests, problem recognition, and involvements. Despite these technical difficulties, the advantage of benefit shadow pricing—especially, for federal- and state-funded social action programs—is that it helps administrators determine and justify appropriate levels of funding.[9]

Another approach to benefit shadow pricing is to identify a comparable product or service that has a market value and to equate it to a product or service that has no market. A good example of this approach in public relations would be equating media space generated by publicity with paid advertising space: column inches (or air time) generated by "free" publicity is translated into advertising dollars that would be charged for a similar amount of space (or time). As this example illustrates, the difficulty inherent in this approach lies in finding equally comparable products or services. For instance, in any particular medium, the impact of information presented in paid advertising space would not be equal to the impact of the same information presented within the "news hole." For an example of a public relations budget that incorporates this type of benefit shadow pricing, see Case 6.7. Regardless of the limitations, the advantage of this approach, and of all approaches, to benefit shadow pricing is that it allows decision-makers to make judgments based on analogies.

Cost-Benefit Compensation Estimation

Unlike benefit shadow pricing, cost-benefit compensation estimation does not focus on components of the public relations program or campaign. Rather, it asks people affected by a problem (or opportunity) to give a value to their *not* being affected *by the situation*: What is it worth to them—in dollars and cents—to be left feeling unaffected by the situation? If the person perceives the situation and public relations activities positively, then the question is similar to one asked in benefit shadow pricing: What kind of payment would that person think appropriate for having received this benefit? If the situation and public relations activities are perceived as a "dis-benefit," or cost, then: What kind of compensation would be required to make the person feel indifferent to the situation and its perceived dis-benefit, or cost? The assumption of cost-benefit compensation estimation is that a price tag can be attached to a situation by people who consider themselves "gainers" or "losers."[10] The argument is that the sum of the individual cost-benefit compensation estimations is equal to the value of the public relations program or campaign that solves the problem (or takes advantage of the opportunity).

For example, in Case 5.1, the Blue Cross and Blue Shield case, only a certain percentage of employees would be "on the market" for new benefit options. See Figure 5.13. Some employees might like their current benefits and, being disinclined to change, might consider the communication program a waste of their time. Other employees might appreciate what Blue Cross and Blue Shield had to offer; if they are dissatisfied with their current plan, they might consider the communication plan to be a good thing. Still other employees might want changes to their benefits but not be interested in what was being offered. Although on the market for new benefits and initially appreciative of information about the proposed new benefits, they still might not be persuaded by the communication program and would remain dissatisfied with their situation. For each group of individuals, separate cost-benefit compensation estimations would need to be made. The question is: What amount of money would compensate each employee so that he or she would feel neutral about the situation? Unlike benefit shadow pricing, the question does not focus directly on how much value is placed on the public relations program or campaign; rather, the question focuses on the situation—the problem (or opportunity)—and what it would take to make the individual feel unaffected by it. In this case, only a few dollars or cents might make those already satisfied

FIGURE 5.13

Hypothetical cost-benefit compensation estimation based on Case 5.1: Blue Cross Blue Shield's Communication Plan*

The goal of the Communication Plan is to help clients enroll as many eligible employees as possible in appropriate health care benefit programs.

Publics	Value to employees of NOT being affected by comparison of health benefits, which, in this situation, is the value of being satisfied with current health plan.	
Employees currently satisfied	Benefit compensation (annual premium)	$200
	Number of employees in this public	7,000
	Subtotal	$1,400,000
Dissatisfied with current plan and appreciative of what new plan offers	Cost compensation	$400
	Number of employees in this public	800
	Subtotal for this public	-$320,000
Dissatisfied with current plan but not appreciative of what new plan offers	Cost compensation	$1,000
	Number of employees in this public	200
	Subtotal for this public	-$200,000
	Subtotal benefit compensation	$1,400,000
	Subtotal cost compensation	-520,000
Total cost-benefit compensation estimation for health care program and Communication Plan		$880,000
Cost of administering health care program 8,000 employees @ $100/year		$800,000
Value of the Communication Plan		$80,000

* These figures are hypothetical and are for instructional purposes only.

with their health benefits feel unaffected and compensated for time "wasted" spent participating in the communication program. On the other hand, the two types of employees on the market for new benefits would want to be paid tens, if not hundreds, of dollars on an annual basis to feel neutral and disinterested about the situation. Totalling the individual cost-benefit compensation estimations yields a value for the solution to the situation. In this case, this solution includes the cost of the new benefit program, plus the communication program. If it is assumed that the complete program of new benefits and communication

FIGURE 5.14

Hypothetical cost-benefit compensation estimation based on Case 5.2: The Papal Visit to the United States*

One goal of the media relations program for the papal visit was to increase the amount of accurate coverage by the media of the Pope's message and decrease the amount of media coverage focused on the logistics of the Pope's visit.

Factors used to calculate amount of money it takes to make affected publics feel neutral about situation.

Publics	Percent of total population exposed	Number of exposures	Average amount willing to pay or required to compensate
People who liked media coverage and considered it balanced and appropriate	80%	8 million	$ .15/exposure
People who disliked media coverage	5%	.5 million	$ .50/exposure
People who felt neutral about media coverage	15%	1.5 million	$ .00

Benefit compensation = (8,000,000 x $ .15) = $1,200,000
Cost compensation = (500,000 x $ .50) = 250,000
Value of media relations = $ 950,000

* These figures are hypothetical and are for instructional purposes only.

plan "solves" the problem, then subtracting the cost of the benefit program from the total cost-benefit compensation estimations leaves, as a remainder, the value of the communication plan.

As another example, consider the media relations campaign conducted for the Papal visit (Case 5.2). See Figure 5.14. If the situation that needed to be "solved" for the U.S. Conference of Catholic Bishops was the potential miscommunication of the Pope's views, should media relations for the Papal visit be mishandled and become a focal point of press coverage, then the question would be: What amount of money would compensate an individual receiving information from the media so that he or she would feel neutral about the media's coverage of the Pope's visit? If an individual thought the media's coverage distorted the views of the Pope, then: What kind of compensation would be required to make the individual feel indifferent about the media's coverage? If the person liked the press coverage of the Pope's views, then: What kind of payment would that person think appropriate for having received this kind of information? In addition to estimating the answers for each of the preceding questions, using cost-benefit compensation estimations in this case requires that estimates be made of the percent of the total target audience who fit into each of two categories: those who liked the coverage, and those who didn't. The number of individuals in each category can be calculated and multiplied by the appropriate average compensation value to arrive at an estimate of the value of the media relations campaign for each of the two groups. Adding these two values together yields an overall estimate of the value of the media relations campaign.

From the point of view of members of the International Apple Institute in Case 5.3, the situation that needed to be "solved" was a major crisis: people were dramatically cutting back on their consumption of apples. During this crisis, probably no member of the Institute thought the situation was positive. Consequently, the critical question for cost-benefit compensation estimation in this case was similar to the one asked for benefit shadow pricing: What amount of money would Institute members be willing to pay for a promotional campaign that would make them feel neutral about the current situation? See Figure 5.15.

The two major difficulties in making cost-benefit compensation estimations are: reaching consensus on the definition of the situation, and accurately estimating how stakeholders in the situation need either to pay or be paid so that with an exchange of money they feel neutral and unaffected by the situation. Delphi studies (see Chapter 8) and survey research (see Chapter 6) involving experts and/or members of target publics are appropriate techniques for making these estimations. The major advantage of cost-benefit compensation estimation is that it focuses on the situation and its "solution" and not on the components of the public relations program or campaign. It forces decision-makers to see a broad view and not just the technical aspects of public relations.

Benefit-Cost Remainders (Net Value) and Benefit-Cost Ratios

Cost-benefit compensation estimates, and other measures of relative costs and benefits, can be used in two other types of calculations: 1) the cost estimate can be subtracted from the benefit estimate to yield a remainder that represents the net value of the program or campaign; and 2) the benefit estimate (the dividend) can be divided by the cost estimate (the divisor) to yield a quotient that is the benefit-cost ratio. For

FIGURE 5.15

Hypothetical cost-benefit compensation estimation based on Case 5.3: The International Apple Institute*

The goal of the campaign was to support the marketing efforts of the members of the International Apple Institute by improving the media's and consuming public's perception of the nutritional quality of apples.

Membership categories (based on annual sales)	Average loss in sales	Members in category	Total loss/cost compensation
Group 1	$100,000	20	$2,000,000
Group 2	80,000	30	2,400,000
Group 3	60,000	40	2,400,000
Group 4	40,000	50	2,000,000
Group 5	20,000	100	2,000,000

Value of media campaign = $10,800,000

* These figures are hypothetical and are for instructional purposes only.

example, if the total compensations for dis-benefits (costs) were subtracted from the total of benefit shadow prices (benefits), the remainder would be net benefits. If these costs were divided into the total benefits, this would yield a benefit-cost ratio.

When to use which calculation depends upon the situation.[11] If the decision will result in a summative judgment about the overall merit of a single activity, program, or campaign, either net values or benefit-cost ratios is appropriate. If the decision is between two or more mutually exclusive options—for example, either buying media (broadcast and print advertisements), or sponsoring a special sporting event—net value is best because it identifies the "option" which gives the better return for the single investment. On the other hand, if there are several options which are not mutually exclusive—such as having a fixed media budget and needing to determine which of hundreds of media to buy—benefit-cost ratios are best because they allow each option to be ranked from best to worst, thus identifying the best set of options. In this last example, the set of media buys at the top of the list which could be purchased within the limits of the fixed budget would be the best choice, because it would be the option returning the most benefit for a fixed investment.

Expected-Value Analysis

A budgeting strategy that can focus on the components of public relations programs and campaigns is expected-value analysis. It is a procedure for calculating the expected value of specific public relations activities. Two sets of estimations are required: 1) the values of various outcome goals; and 2) the probabilities of different activities achieving these various outcome goals. Expected-value analysis forces managers to recognize the linkages between process goals and outcome goals. Process goals are the desired ways by which planners want to get the job done; they are the planned activities, completed on time, as promised. Outcome goals are desired end states that effectively "solve the problem" that prompted the public relations program or campaign. The assumption of expected-value analysis is that each of the various activities contributes in some way to achieving each of the goals set for the program or campaign.

To conduct an expected-value analysis, the following steps, need to be followed:

1. List outcome goals in priority order. Most programs and campaigns have multiple goals, some of which are more important than others. If there are a dozen goals, there may be a dozen individual ranks. But, if some goals are of equal importance, these should be tied in priority rankings. For an expected-value analysis, the value assigned to each goal will be its *reversed* rank order. This means if there are ten rank orders (including ties), those goals ranked #1 get a value of 10; those ranked #2 get a value of 9; those ranked #3 get a value of 8, etc.; and, those ranked #10 get a value of 1.

2. For each activity, answer this question: What is the probability that this activity will achieve this stated goal? To do this, link each activity to each of the stated goals, and assign a probability to each linkage. (Note: not all activities will have a direct, logical linkage to all goals; yet, they will contribute indirectly, in some slight way, to achieving each goal. Consequently, some activities will have very low probabilities of achieving certain goals and moderate to high probabilities of achieving others.)

3. For each activity, multiply the probability that the activity will achieve a particular goal by the value of that goal. Do this for each goal to which the activity is linked, then sum the products. The sum of the products is the expected value of this activity. This expected value represents the relative contribution the activity is expected to make toward the achievement of all outcome goals—in other words, to the success of the complete public relations program or campaign.

The advantage of an expected-value analysis is that it allows comparisons to be made between planned activities, so that decision-makers can make judgments about which activities to monitor closely and which to reduce or eliminate, if necessary. For example, consider the outcome goals and specific activities in the communication plan of Blue Cross and Blue Shield (Case 5.1). To keep the example simple, let us assume there were two goals, listed here in priority order: 1) to enroll employees in the new health benefit options, and 2) to increase awareness of all employees about their health benefit options. Also, to keep matters simple, let us assume there were only three activities: 1) brochures, 2) workshops for employees, and 3) training programs for workshop leaders. Through staff discussions, previous experience, or original research, the probabilities of each of these activities achieving each of the two goals could be determined. See Figure 5.16 for the calculations. The expected values for each of the activities indicated that, among the three activities, the workshop for employees was most important; brochures were next in importance; and least important was the training for workshop leaders.

For another example, consider the goals and activities of the media relations campaign conducted for the Papal visit (Case 5.2). Let us assume there were two primary goals and two activities. The goals, in priority order, were: 1) to increase the public's awareness of the Pope's views on critical issues, and 2) to make the media's coverage of the Pope's visit as unobtrusive as possible. Two media relations activities were: 1) making follow-up calls to reporters, when requested, and 2) providing escort services to press pools. Neither of these activities would have a major direct effect on the public's awareness of the Pope's views, but both would impact significantly the media's coverage, which in turn would impact the public's awareness of the Pope's views. See Figure 5.17 for estimates of probabilities and calculations. The expected-value analysis in this case indicated that the escort service was more important than the follow-up calls to reporters.

In Case 5.3, the public relations campaign for the International Apple Institute had two major goals; in priority order, they were: 1) to increase consumption of apples, and 2) to increase public awareness of the nutritional value of apples. To illustrate expected-value analysis, we will focus on two of several activities in the campaign: 1) media events surrounding Apple Month, and 2) press kits containing brochures, press releases about planned events, and news items about apples. See Figure 5.18 for probability estimates and calculations. The expected-value analysis indicated that planned media events were more important than were the press kits.

In all of these examples, the expected-value analyses highlighted the relative contributions of different components of programs and campaigns. However, the analyses did not indicate how decision-makers could use this information. In the International Apple Institute case, for example, the results of the expected-value analysis could not be used to eliminate either activity, for both were found to be very important; but, the expected-value analysis could be used to underscore the importance of properly planned and supervised media events, which were shown by the analysis as being crucial to the success of the

FIGURE 5.16

Hypothetical expected-value analysis based on Case 5.1: Blue Cross Blue Shield's Communication Plan.*

Corporate goal the Communication Plan is designed to help meet:

> To help clients enroll as many eligible employees as possible in appropriate health care benefit programs.
>
> Specific outcome goals:

Rank		Reverse Weight
1.	To increase sales of the benefit package to corporate clients.	6
2.	To increase the number of eligible employees who sign up for the new benefit package.	5
3.	To make more employees aware of the new benefit package.	4
4.	To decrease the number of questions employees have about the new benefit package.	3
5.	To increase the speed with which the workshop training can occur.	2
6.	To increase the confidence of company workshop trainers in their ability to present the new information.	1

Activity	Goal	Probability of achieving	Weight of goal	Product
Brochures	1 (sales)	.01	6	.06
	2 (numbers)	.05	5	.2
	3 (aware)	.90	4	3.6
	4 (questions)	.75	3	2.25
	5 (speed)	.75	2	1.5
	6 (confidence)	.80	1	.8
			Expected value of this activity =	8.41
Workshop materials	1 (sales)	.01	6	.06
	2 (numbers)	.20	5	1.0
	3 (aware)	.80	4	3.2
	4 (questions)	.75	3	2.25
	5 (speed)	.90	2	1.8
	6 (confidence)	.95	1	.95
			Expected value of this activity =	9.26
Workshop	1 (sales)	.50	6	3.0
	2 (numbers)	.80	5	4.0
	3 (aware)	.80	4	3.2
	4 (questions)	.75	3	2.25
	5 (speed)	1.0	2	2.0
	6 (confidence)	1.0	1	1.0
			Expected value of this activity =	15.45
Instructors' training	1 (sales)	.75	6	4.5
	2 (numbers)	.75	5	4.0
	3 (aware)	.01	4	.04
	4 (questions)	.75	3	2.25
	5 (speed)	1.0	2	2.0
	6 (confidence)	1.0	1	1.0
			Expected value of this activity =	13.79

*These figures are hypothetical and are for instructional purposes only.

FIGURE 5.17

Hypothetical expected-value analysis based on Case 5.2: The Papal Visit to the United States*

The goal of the media relations program is to facilitate accurate media coverage of the Pope's message.

Rank	Specific outcome goals:	Reverse Weight
1.	Obtain maximum local coverage of the Pope's message	6
2.	Obtain maximum national and international coverage.	5
3.	Get the press pool to media events on time with a minimum of hassle.	4
4.	Decrease the number of questions from media representatives about the Pope's itinerary and message.	3
5.	Handle unexpected situations that demand media coverage and generate additional requests from media.	2
6.	Increase the access of the media to the Pope.	1

Activity	Goal	Probability of achieving	Weight of goal	Product
Staff media pools	1 (local)	.50	6	3.0
	2 (national)	.75	5	1.5
	3 (pool)	.90	4	3.6
	4 (questions)	.75	3	2.25
	5 (unexpected)	.75	2	1.5
	6 (access)	.80	1	.8
			Expected value of this activity =	12.65
Media pool transportation	1 (local)	.50	6	3.0
	2 (national)	.75	5	1.5
	3 (pool)	.90	4	3.6
	4 (questions)	.10	3	.3
	5 (unexpected)	.10	2	.2
	6 (access)	.80	1	.8
			Expected value of this activity =	9.4
Prepare and distribute media advisories	1 (local)	.75	6	4.5
	2 (national)	.75	5	1.5
	3 (pool)	.90	4	3.6
	4 (questions)	.90	3	2.7
	5 (unexpected)	.75	2	1.5
	6 (access)	.10	1	.1
			Expected value of this activity =	13.9
Advance work by agency staff in each city visited	1 (local)	.90	6	5.4
	2 (national)	.75	5	3.75
	3 (pool)	.50	4	2.0
	4 (questions)	.50	3	1.5
	5 (unexpected)	.75	2	1.5
	6 (access)	.80	1	.8
			Expected value of this activity =	14.95

* These figures are hypothetical and are for instructional purposes only.

FIGURE 5.18

Hypothetical expected-value analysis based on Case 5.3: The International Apple Institute.*

The goal of the campaign was to support the marketing efforts of the members of the International Apple Institute by improving the media's and consuming public's perception of the nutritional quality of apples.

Specific outcome goals:

Rank		Reverse Weight
1.	To increase the placement of apple-related stories in the media.	5
2.	To increase media gatekeepers' awareness of apple-related food safety and nutrition issues.	4
3.	To increase the public's awareness of apples as a nutritious, safe food.	3
4.	To give information to members that they can include in their own marketing and public relations efforts.	2
5.	To increase the use of apple-related educational materials in public schools.	1

Activity	Goal	Probability of achieving	Weight of goal	Product
Consumer brochures	1 (placement)	.10	5	.5
	2 (gatekeepers')	.20	4	.8
	3 (public's)	.50	3	1.5
	4 (members)	.50	2	1.
	5 (educational)	.90	1	.9
		Expected value of this activity =		4.7
Media campaign for Apple Month	1 (placement)	.80	5	4.
	2 (gatekeepers')	.80	4	3.2
	3 (public's)	.80	3	2.4
	4 (members)	.80	2	1.6
	5 (educational)	.50	1	.5
		Expected value of this activity =		11.7
Media campaign for Applesause Month	1 (placement)	.80	5	4.
	2 (gatekeepers')	.80	4	3.2
	3 (public's)	.80	3	2.4
	4 (members)	.80	2	1.6
	5 (educational)	.50	1	.5
		Expected value of this activity =		11.7
Year-long media relations targeting media intermediaries	1 (placement)	.90	5	4.5
	2 (gatekeepers')	.90	4	3.6
	3 (public's)	.70	3	2.1
	4 (members)	.10	2	.2
	5 (educational)	.10	1	.1
		Expected value of this activity =		10.5

* These figures are hypothetical and are for instructional purposes only.

campaign. In both the media relations case and the employee health benefits' case, the obvious conclusions generated by the expected-value analyses were a function of simplified examples, using very few goals and activities, and were not a reflection of the weakness of the analytic technique. The power of an expected-value analysis is demonstrated most clearly when it is used to sort out the relative contributions of dozens of different public relations activities designed to achieve numerous goals.

FACTORS ASSOCIATED WITH PUBLIC RELATIONS BUDGETING

Research results based on a mail survey of more than 100 public relations practitioners, described in Chapter 1 and elsewhere, indicate that budgeting for public relations programs and campaigns is positively associated with strategic planning and research.

Correlations presented in Table 5.1 indicate that budgeting for new activities in public relations is positively and significantly associated with:

Developing long-range strategic plans.

Developing short-range tactical plans.

Forming a committee to coordinate a new public relations activity or campaign.

Preparing timelines and milestones for activities.

Conducting research before implementing a public relations activity or campaign.

Informally evaluating public relations activities.

Conducting formal research after implementing a public relations activity to evaluate that activity.

While long-range and short-range planning activities, and research activities, are significantly associated with public relations professionals being included within the dominant coalition, budgeting for new public relations activities, as a separate activity, is not. Yet, public relations budgeting and both long- and short-range planning activities are strongly associated together. The implication is that by integrating budgeting and planning activities, public relations professionals become more closely associated with senior management.

TABLE 5.1

Correlation Matrix for Factors Associated with Public Relations Budgeting.[a]

Factors	1	2	3	4	5	6	7	8	9
1. Preparing public relations budgets									
2. Developing long-range plans	.34***								
3. Developing short-term plans	.16	.54***							
4. Forming an oversight committee	.29**	.31***	.15						
5. Preparing timelines and milestones for activities	.34***	.24*	.30***	.30***					
6. Informally evaluating activities	.25**	.32***	.39***	.31***	.31***				
7. Conducting research before implementation	.26**	.27**	.07	.24**	.09	.29**			
8. Conducting formal research after implementation	.37***	.36***	.21*	.43***	.16	.35***	.66***		
9. Frequency of public relations professionals being included in the dominant coalition	.07	.29**	.22*	.12	.09	.17	.24*	.22*	

(a) N = 103; probability of Pearson's product moment correlation caused by chance: < .000 = ***; < .01 = **; < .05 = *

THE PLAN BOOK: PART III

The type of budget included in The Plan Book depends on the purpose of the document. If the purpose is to present a client or senior management with a non-negotiable price for a public relations service, then a brief budget, possibly a streamlined narrative budget, would be most appropriate. If the purpose is to negotiate about priorities and commitments of resources, then a detailed narrative budget with cost-benefit analyses would be more appropriate.

If planning for a public relations program or campaign has developed to a point where a detailed budget has been prepared, it is unlikely that budget negotiations would focus on whether or not to go forward with the entire project; rather, the issue would be how to go forward, who would do what, when, to whom, with what effect, and at what costs.[12]

During such negotiations, there are four sets of guidelines that public relations managers should keep in mind:

1. Do not focus on personalities, especially of the people involved in the budget negotiations. Do focus on substantive issues that can be described objectively.

2. Do not set the agenda by exchanging wish lists or statements that describe the immediate wants of the negotiating parties. Do identify both short-term and long-term mutual interests.
3. Before reaching a final agreement, try to identify and explore additional, creative options that might not have been considered at the beginning of negotiations, but may (now that the parties better understand each other) be seriously considered and just might increase the win-win possibilities for all those involved.
4. Incorporate criticisms, doubts, and objections into objective measures of both process and outcome goals and objectives.[13]

IN SUMMARY...

Knowing how to budget successfully separates the managers from the technicians in public relations. Budgeting is more than keeping track of expenses: it is a means of negotiating, monitoring and controlling organizational resources. There are a variety of budgeting styles. While each organization, and client, often has unique differences in budgeting procedures and formats, this chapter has presented basic concepts found in most public relations budgets. In addition, it has introduced a few more sophisticated techniques for estimating costs and benefits, although these are not widely used in public relations, primarily because practitioners have not been instructed in how to use them. The key to selecting an appropriate budgeting technique is to anticipate the requirements of principal decision-makers in the budgeting process, and to negotiate and work with these individuals to develop consensus about appropriate budgeting procedures.

Study Questions

1. True or false: practitioners who do not concern themselves with how resources are used in public relations programs and campaigns are not managers; they may be skilled, creative technicians, but they are not managers. Defend your answer.
2. What is a cost, and how is it calculated? What is a budget? What are typical items in a public relations budget?
3. Give five reasons why most pubic relations budgets are so unsophisticated.
4. What are "top down" and "bottom up" budgeting techniques? Give specific examples. Which is more common? Why?
5. How can profits be incorporated into a public relations budget?
6. What is a narrative budget? In your explanation, give examples of both administrative and program costs.
7. Demonstrate how you would use a what-if-not-funded scenario to justify a budget for a shopping mall's multi-media community relations program using radio and television public-service announcements. Display ads and

articles in the shopping mall's free, home-delivered newspaper; in mass transit display ads; and in feature stories, media advisories and press releases about community groups staging special events in the mall.
8. What is shadow pricing? Demonstrate how to use shadow pricing to justify the cost of a specific public relations campaign.
9. Discuss how you would use the cost-benefit compensation estimation technique to justify a specific public relations campaign.
10. Discuss the uses of net value and benefit-cost ratios.
11. Explain how you could use an expected-value analysis to determine the best way to reduce a budget. For example, demonstrate how you would know which activity to reduce or eliminate from a budget should you have to cut the budget by 25 percent.
12. True or false: budgeting, long-range planning, and short-range planning are closely associated activities. Defend your answer.
13. What are appropriate guidelines to follow when negotiating a budget?

Endnotes

1. Ehling, William P., "Public relations economics: Application of benefit-cost analysis to evaluation of public relations programs," paper presented to the Educator Academy of the International Association of Business Communicators, June, 1988.

2. Dilenschneider, Robert L., "Corporate accountability, with constituent publics," paper presented to the Corporate Section, Public Relations Society of America, Nov., 1987.

3. Dozier, David M., and Martha M. Lauzen, "Antecedents and consequences of marketing imperialism on the public relations function"; and, Lauzen, Martha M., "Losing control: An examination of the management function in public relations"; papers presented to the Public Relations Division of the Association for Education in Journalism and Mass Communication, August, 1990.

4. Ehling, *op.cit.*

5. Meredith, Jack R., and Samuel J. Mantel, Jr. *Project Management,* 2nd edition (New York: John Wiley & Sons, 1989); see especially the chapter on budgeting, pp. 235–257.

6. Gagnon, R. J., "An exploratory analysis of the relevant cost structure of internal and external engineering consulting," Ph.D. dissertation, University of Cincinnati, 1982.

7. Nager, Norman, and T. Harrell Allen, *Public Relations Management by Objectives* (New York: Longman, 1984).

8. Meredith and Mantel, *op.cit.,* p. 244.

9. Haveman, Robert H., and Julius Margolis, *Public Expenditures and Policy Analysis* (Chicago: Markham Publishing, 1970), especially Chapter 12, "Shadow prices for incorrect or nonexistent market values."

10. Ehling, *op.cit.*

11. Ehling, *op.cit.,* p. 190.

12. Meredith, Jack R., and Samuel J. Mantel, Jr., *Project Management,* 2nd edition (New York: John Wiley, 1989) p. 215.

13. Fisher, R., and W. Ury, *Getting to Yes* (New York: Penguin Books, 1983).

CHAPTER SIX

How to Select a Research Design and Conduct Research to Help Plan and Evaluate Public Relations

. . . . .

*T*he walk-in closet of the public relations office had floor-to-ceiling shelves of three-ring binders filled with press clippings generated by the public relations department over many years. It also contained file cabinets full of correspondence and written testimonials about various public relations campaigns. Some of the shelves were filled with video and audio tapes of selected public relations activities.

"This is just one way we document what we do here," the manager of public relations said to her visitor, who was looking at the press clippings in one of the binders. "Once, about ten years ago, before we pasted the clippings into the binder, we arranged them on a scroll of paper that stretched out more than thirty yards. I presented the scroll to management to indicate what the department had accomplished. Back then, it made a point I wanted to make. But, that was ten years ago.

"Today, we have our clipping service electronically scan publications of interest to us. They correlate column inches of publicity we know we generated with specific objectives we have set for each of our product lines. Then, when we get the results, if we achieve certain publicity goals, we reassign staff and move on to other goals.

"But that's only one way we do research. We do lots of electronic searches of databases to track trends and prepare material for speeches and things like that. We do quantitative research—surveys and things like that—but, frankly, I find the qualitative information more compelling than the big, elaborate studies. Many times, I think it is easier to convince others of the value of public relations with soft, qualitative research than it is with hard, quantitative research. But, when it comes to playing hardball, nothing wins like a bunch of solid numbers."

This opinion is typical of many public relations managers. Her comments reflect the dramatic shift over the past ten years in the level of sophistication in public relations research. Her candor acknowledges the persuasive power of both qualitative and quantitative research. As a savvy manager, she clearly understands the importance of research to her career in public relations.

. . .

WHAT IS RESEARCH?

Research involves systematically investigating something to discover facts and theories. Systematic research means that it is done in an orderly, predictable way. Facts are accurate statements about reality. Theories are statements of relationship between two or more concepts. Scientific research means conducting an investigation that can help explain or predict phenomena that occur in the observable world.

There are two basic types of scientific research: exploratory research and confirmatory research. Exploratory research is designed to identify basic facts, patterns of relationships, and trends; it is descriptive research. According to Kerlinger, exploratory research has three basic purposes: to discover and describe significant variables in the field, to discover relationships among these variables, and to lay the groundwork for more systematic and rigorous testing of hypotheses.[1] In the field of public relations, exploratory research is the most common form of research. Almost all campaigns begin by conducting research; rarely is this research used to test hypotheses or predictions about the effect of the campaign. Most research in public relations is descriptive, providing basic information from which campaigns can be planned and evaluated.[2]

Confirmatory research is designed to test specific relationships—to confirm predictions and expectations. Confirmatory, predictive research is theory-based because it examines specific relationships that are assumed to be operating in the field situation. In public relations, confirmatory research most often examines relationships between components of the public relations campaign and the public's reaction to the campaign. A public relations manager predicts that the campaign will have a particular impact and collects data to document, or refute, this prediction.

Exploratory and confirmatory research may be qualitative or quantitative. Qualitative research is primarily descriptive research that often involves the researcher's being a participant in the situation being analyzed, with the primary data being in-depth observations and self-reports by people involved in the situation. The assumption made in qualitative research is that it is impossible for the research not to interact with and affect whatever is being observed.[3] Although qualitative research can involve analysis of secondary sources, traditional library research, it often involves collection of original data. Properly conducted qualitative research can be very systematic, precise, and extremely practical. Qualitative research can be used to examine relationships and confirm expectations; most often it is used in exploratory research.

Scientific research may range from informal to formal. The more formal it is, the more likely the research can be replicated. Formal and informal research can be either qualitative or quantitative. All types of research—formal and informal, qualitative and quantitative—have the potential to yield scientific results, because all types of research can yield insights into relationships which help explain or predict natural phenomena. It is wrong to associate qualitative research with nonscientific research. One insightful revelation from one focus group can be as telling as the key result from a massive public opinion poll.

An effective public relations manager knows the strengths and weaknesses of all types of research. While it is true that much of the research that is done in public relations can be described as informal, qualitative research, there is an increasing amount of formal, quantitative research being conducted.[4] Knowing how to conduct these types of research—especially more formal, quantitative research—is vital to career growth and success in this field, especially for women.[5] As with any public relations activity, research requires a plan of action, and an effective public relations manager knows how to plan, implement and evaluate research.

WHAT IS A RESEARCH DESIGN?

A research design is the overall plan and set of activities necessary to conduct research. It is a plan of action that helps the public relations manager "control for" various alternative explanations for campaign results. A research design establishes guidelines for collecting and analyzing data. It tells you whom or what to measure and when to make your measurements, and to a certain extent, it tells you how to analyze the data.

A research design is required for basic and applied research. Basic research is often called "pure" research because the research results do not necessarily have any immediate practical use; it is conducted to add to the body of knowledge in the field. Applied research is designed to help decision-makers make practical decisions; the results are applied to a practical problem.

BASIC STEPS IN THE RESEARCH PROCESS

Although there are distinctions between basic and evaluative research, between exploratory and confirmatory research, and between qualitative and quantitative research, they all follow the same essential steps:

1. Defining the problem and, consequently, the purpose of the research.

    Questions at this step: Are we doing preliminary, baseline research only—collection data we will use only during the planning stages—or do we intend to follow-up and analyze the data not only before but also after implementation? Are we examining relationships and trying to confirm assumptions we are making about this situation or the public relations campaign?

2. Subdividing the problem into manageable components.

   Most often in public relations research, only certain aspects of the situation and only certain aspects of the public relations campaign will be examined. Subdividing the problem (or opportunity) means requiring members of management to articulate theories about what they think is going on in the situation. These theories most often will involve relationships between the public relations campaign and its impact on target publics.

   Questions at this step: What are the goals and objectives of the program or campaign? What is the budget? How much time do we have? What assumptions are being made if we assume this campaign is going to be a success? What is expected to happen at each of the anticipated stages in the communication process if this campaign is to be successful? Why is this particular public relations "solution" expected to solve this particular problem (or take advantage of this particular opportunity)?

3. Selecting a research design by answering three major questions:

   Why do you want to conduct the research?

   ___ To help plan the campaign, but not to evaluate its overall impact.
   ___ Both to help plan and evaluate the campaign.
   ___ Only to evaluate the campaign after implementation: not to help plan it, but to document its impact and to make recommendations about future campaign activities.

   What public(s) do you intend to measure?

   ___ One public or one set of publics fully exposed to the same campaign.
   ___ Two or more publics, each exposed to different versions of the same campaign.

   When do you intend to make these measurements?

   ___ Before only
   ___ Before and after
   ___ After only
   ___ Before, during and after

   A decision-tree (Figure 6.4), presented later in this chapter, indicates the practical consequences of answering these questions.

4. Making observations and measurements, and collecting data.

   Two major questions to ask at this step: Are our research measurements valid? Are they reliable? Kerlinger has suggested that these two questions can be answered by answering two other questions.[6] Are we measuring what we think we are measuring? If we were to repeat this or a similar measurement procedure again and again, would we end up with the same or similar results?

5. Analyzing the data.

   Questions at this step focus on "cleaning" the data, making sure there are as few data compiling and processing errors as possible. Also, there are questions that need to be asked about the appropriateness of various "number crunching" techniques and statistical procedures. For example: Are the data legible and properly recorded? Are there any duplicate entries or typos? Should we use computer analysis or hand tabulations? Do we use the mean, the median or the mode? Are we using the proper statistical procedure?

6. Reporting the results.

   Questions at this step focus on issues common in science writing: Are all the research questions which were initially asked answered in this report, and if not, why not? Is the methodology explained in sufficient detail so the reader can determine the validity and reliability of the research findings? Are the findings presented clearly and understandably?

The first six steps in the research procedure apply to both basic and applied research. The next step applies only to applied research. Properly addressing the issues in the next step will affect, often in very fundamental ways, how the first set of steps are accomplished.

7. Making a judgment based on results.

   This means the public relations person conducting this research should involve key decision-makers in the initial problem definition and research design stages, because they will be making final decisions based on the research. If these key decision-makers are not comfortable with the research design, they will not be confident in the research results. These questions need to be answered at the very beginning of the research: Who will be making judgments based on this research? Are they comfortable with the proposed research? How will they be involved in the research process? How and when do they want the results presented?

FIGURE 6.1

Variables in public relations research designs

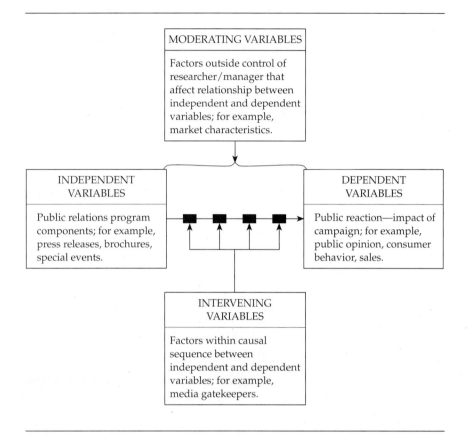

WHAT GETS MEASURED?

Aspects of the problem or opportunity are the first things measured in most public relations research. Basic facts are needed to describe the situation so an appropriate campaign can be planned. Savvy public relations managers recognize this initial planning data can be compared to data which is collected later to document the effectiveness of the campaign; consequently, they collect the data systematically so the before-after comparison can be made.

There are four aspects of any public relations program which may be considered in any research or evaluation effort (see Figure 6.1):

1. Dependent variables: components or dimensions of the problem or opportunity which prompted the campaign. These "target" variables may be considered similar to certain aspects of the target audiences or intended publics; they are what the campaign is

designed to impact. They are called dependent variables because, when measured, their value is assumed to be influenced by—dependent upon—the actions of other variables. For example, improving public goodwill is often considered a goal of many campaigns. It can be measured by logging incoming phone calls and correspondence, analyzing media coverage of certain events, or surveying public opinion.
2. Moderating variables: conditions outside the control of the manager but which definitely influence the campaign. For example, identical public relations campaigns run in different markets may yield different results because certain aspects of the market (for instance, the number or sophistication of media) vary significantly, consequently affecting the dependent variable, the impact of the public relations campaign.
3. Intervening variables: factors which may be either inside or outside the control of the public relations manager and which are in a causal sequence between the independent and dependent variable. For example, writing and distributing press releases are traditional public relations activities; having people receive and act upon the information would be considered appropriate goals for these activities. An intervening variable in this sequence would be getting editors to accept and publish the press releases, which is often outside the direct control of the public relations manager. If the campaign included purchasing media space, this intervening variable of getting the media to publish the information would be inside the control of the public relations manager.
4. Independent variables: program components of the campaign. For example, not only the media mix used in the campaign but also the planning and production activities involved in producing the campaign are factors which are under the direct control of the public relations manager. These are the factors which can be manipulated and changed by the public relations manager to find the right combination of resources and personnel to create the best possible campaign. These are the factors that can be independently varied by the public relations manager to create a different impact on the public, the dependent variable.

WHO GETS MEASURED?

Important distinctions have been made in earlier chapters about the differences between publics, markets and target audiences. Publics are groups which are aware of themselves and share certain concerns, and they are not synonymous with markets. Most markets are composed of both latent and active publics. Campaigns aimed at certain target audiences may reach intended and unintended publics. Only on rare occasions would all members of the target audience include all members of an intended public, primarily because media and campaign activities which can reach a target audience do not reach all individuals considered members of a public. For example, a campaign aimed at all pregnant women may use a purchased list of readers of a popular baby magazine—a very precisely defined target audience; yet, not all pregnant women are included on the list, and some women—and men!—on the mailing list (for instance, doctors, educators, nurses, day care managers) may not be pregnant. Employees would be an example of a public which could be considered synonymous with a target audience, depending on the accuracy of the employee list and penetration of the media (for instance, paycheck envelopes).

To evaluate a public relations campaign, publics are defined in yet another way—as either fully exposed publics, or as partially or unexposed publics. In evaluative research, there are two basic groups: treatment groups which receive the full "treatment" (a term derived from medical research), and control groups which do not receive the complete treatment. Comparisons are made between these two groups, and judgments are made about the treatment and its effectiveness. For public relations specialists, treatment groups are synonymous with publics which are exposed fully to a public relations campaign (the "treatment"), and control groups are synonymous with publics which are not exposed or only partially exposed to the public relations campaign.

There are two basic purposes for conducting evaluative research: 1) to better formulate campaign plans and activities, and 2) to summarize the results of the campaign. The former is called formative evaluative research, and the latter is called summative evaluative research. Data collected for formative evaluations can be used with data collected after the campaign has been implemented to yield a data set useful for summative evaluations.

An all-too-frequent approach to evaluating public relations campaigns, and one of the least effective, is to observe and measure the reaction of publics only after they have been fully exposed to the campaign. Evaluating a campaign by measuring fully exposed publics immediately after exposure raises a number of serious questions. For example, even if the desired public reaction is observed, how would the manager know it was the public relations campaign and not something else that caused the reaction? Could it be that the public, even though it was exposed to the campaign, reacted to something else—a special TV show, a major news event, a sudden shift in the economy—and it just appears as if the public relations campaign was a success? What if the public, for whatever reason, was not exposed to the campaign, and yet is observed reacting in an appropriate and predicted way because they were influenced by something else; would it be right to say the campaign was a success?

In most cases, questions like these cannot be answered if the public relations manager only evaluates fully exposed publics. With comparative data from either different publics (exposed vs. partially exposed or unexposed) or from the same publics over time (before vs. after), these questions can be answered with confidence.

Control groups are crucial to conducting convincing evaluations. Ideally, control groups are identical in every respect to the treatment groups except for one factor: the control groups receive less or none of the treatment. Both groups share the same characteristics—educational level, age range, interests, involvements, etc.—and most often, they are as similar as possible. Yet there are differences. Just as no two individuals are exactly alike, so too, no two publics are exactly alike.

Fortunately, with randomization, it is possible to eliminate many systematic differences when forming two similar groups. Randomization does not mean assigning people to groups arbitrarily. It means selecting people for different groups by using a table of random numbers which may be computer generated or found in appropriate books about statistics.

When creating treatment and control groups, randomization equalizes built-in biases by randomly scattering such traits throughout the various groups being formed. For example, if a mailing list was divided into two groups arbitrarily—say those on the first half of the list vs. those on the second half—there may be built-in biases within each group that might make them at the outset quite different. If the mailing list was arranged by Zip Codes, people from certain geographic regions may be put in one group and not in another; one half could live on one side of the tracks and the other half could live quite differently. If a table of random numbers is used to randomly pick names from the mailing list, the Zip Code bias would most likely be eliminated. There would still be two groups, each with some differences, to be sure, but the built-in Zip Code bias would have been randomly scattered between the two groups. If other geodemographic traits—such as age, sex, or income level—are assumed to have been equally scattered between the two groups, then the groups are, technically, equivalent.

In evaluative research, there are two ways to divide people into groups. One way randomly assigns people; the other way doesn't. There are equivalent groups, formed with randomization, and there are nonequivalent groups. See Figure 6.2. Equivalent publics are publics which have been formed in some way by random assignment. Nonequivalent publics are publics which have been formed by some method other than randomization.

In public relations, most publics are nonequivalent. Practitioners, however, can use their administrative controls to create equivalent publics. Equivalent publics are extremely useful for making convincing comparisons. When equivalent publics are exposed to two versions of a public relations campaign, most likely any differences found later between the publics are due to the differences between the two versions

FIGURE 6.2

Equivalent and nonequivalent publics in research design

		EXPOSURE TO PROGRAM/CAMPAIGN	
		Full exposure	Partial exposure
EQUIVALENT PUBLICS			
TARGET AUDIENCE random assignment → "Treatment" publics		Receives complete program/ campaign	
TARGET AUDIENCE random assignment → "Control" publics			Receives partial program/ campaign
NONEQUIVALENT PUBLICS			
TARGET AUDIENCE nonrandom assignment → "Treatment" publics		Receives complete program/ campaign	
TARGET AUDIENCE nonrandom assignment → "Control" publics			Receives partial program/ campaign

of the campaign. With nonequivalent publics, there will be lingering suspicions that any differences seen after the public relations campaign are a reflection of pre-existing differences between the publics.

Practitioners have several ways to build randomization into their administration of a public relations campaign. Most public relations involves the dissemination of some kind of information through some kind of distribution procedure—a mailing list, a series of media buys or timed media placements, a schedule of special events, etc. By randomly selecting certain people from such distribution "lists"—some to be fully exposed and some to be partially exposed to the public relations campaign—the practitioner can create equivalent publics so that clear-cut comparisons can be made, and the public relations activity can be accurately assessed.

When equivalent publics cannot be formed, the practitioner should try to use nonequivalent publics which are as similar as possible. Geo-demographic and other types of data should be collected so that the traits of members of the two groups can be compared.

A control public could receive none of a public relations campaign, though often this is unnecessary, if not unrealistic. It is practically impossible for a true public, one made up of individuals living and working in society, not to actively seek out and passively experience a wide range of influences. In practice, most control publics in public relations research receive a modified version of a public relations campaign. For example, the fully exposed treatment public gets all media materials, while the partially exposed control public receives only some of the media materials. If the two publics are equivalent, then any differences should be due to the two versions of the public relations campaign.

WHEN TO MEASURE?

When research about public relations campaigns is conducted before the campaign is implemented, this is called a before-only research design. An after-only research design occurs when the research is conducted after the campaign begins, or sometimes even during it. When before and after data sets are compared to evaluate the campaign, this is known as a before-after research design. When systematic research is collected before, during and after the campaign, and is used to identify trends among the data sets, this is called a time-series research design.

Most research in public relations occurs before the campaign is implemented, and it is used to plan the campaign; sometimes this initial research is used to evaluate the campaign by comparing it to data collected after the campaign is implemented. Exploratory research often is conducted before a campaign begins so that problem dimensions can be identified and public attitudes and behaviors can be assessed.

Research techniques may be nonobtrusive or obtrusive: people being observed or measured can be aware of what is going on, or not. For example, filling out a questionnaire makes an individual aware that research is being conducted. On the other hand, an electronic surveillance of a drug store, in addition to recording any crimes, can also be used for tracking traffic flow through the store without anyone being aware that such research is underway. In many instances, obtrusive before-only measurements influence how people respond to after-only measurements, because people learn from the research instruments what might be expected of them later. Fortunately, in public relations, this "testing effect" can work to the advantage of the public relations campaign, because the underlying message of most research efforts is that the organization sponsoring the campaign and the research genuinely appreciates the ideas and suggestions of the people participating in the research: conducting research helps spread the word. In practical terms, observing and measuring public relations campaigns can be viewed as initial publicity. With an appropriate evaluation design, to be described later, the confounding influence of conducting before-only measurements can be isolated and the unique contribution of the public relations campaign identified.

During a public relations campaign, research can be conducted to assist in the formation and fine-tuning of the campaign. Data collected during a campaign can be used to evaluate the effects of the campaign. Many public relations campaigns last for weeks, months, sometimes years. Once a campaign is underway, dozens of measurements and observations may be made to help the public relations manager make decisions about various components of the campaign.

Sometimes it pays off to make the same measurements a number of times over a period of time: before, during and after a campaign. Such measurements are called a time-series. Trends are identified with a set of time-series measurements. For example, a public relations manager can plot the trendline for a particular public relations problem (for instance, public opinion, sales, morale) and see whether or not the public relations campaign has altered that trendline.

Observations and measurements made after a campaign is complete are called posttests. Again, such measurements can be obtrusive or nonobtrusive. In most instances, it makes sense to be as obvious as possible about your after-only measurements, for the act of evaluating a public relations program reinforces an important point—that you care about what people think. However, there may be times when the after-only measurements should not be obvious and should be discreet—for example, when evaluating certain lobbying efforts.

Whatever the technique, public relations managers should measure and track campaign results, for without such documentation, it is practically impossible to accomplish two very important management tasks: to know how to adjust and fine-tune the campaign so that it can be more effective, and to demonstrate the effectiveness of the campaign when it is completed.

HOW TO SELECT AN APPROPRIATE RESEARCH DESIGN

To select an appropriate research design, a public relations manager should answer the set of questions presented in the Figures 6.3 and 6.4, which are based on years of work by a number of evaluative research specialists.[7] The first question in Figure 6.4 is:

Why do you want to conduct research? (CHECK ONE)

___ Only to help plan the program or campaign, not to evaluate its overall effectiveness.

FIGURE 6.3

Selected research designs in public relations

	What public(s) do you intend to measure?		
	____ One public or one set of publics, fully exposed to the campaign	____ Two or more publics, each exposed to different versions of the same campaign	
		Equivalent publics ____	Nonequivalent publics ____
When do you intend to make these measurements?			
____ Before only*			
____ Before and after	Design A	Design B	Design C
____ After only	Design D	Design E	Design F
____ Before, during and after	Design G	Design H	Design I

Brief description of each research design:

* A before-only research design: used to plan a program or campaign, not to evaluate it; no attention paid to equivalent or nonequivalent publics; however, publics may be segmented and background research conducted to help managers precisely target specific audiences.

Design A   A before-and-after design with no control publics; assumes the publics are not affected by anything else beside the public relations program (which is not very realistic); alternative explanations abound for positive or negative results.

Design B   A true control public; before-after design; one of the best designs.

Design C   A nonequivalent control public, before-after design; all the strengths of before-after; all the weaknesses of nonequivalent publics.

Design D   After-only design—not recommended because after-only results could be caused by almost anything, and there are very few ways to eliminate alternative explanations.

Design E   A true control public, after-only design that has merit; all the advantages of equivalent publics; may be preferred when time or budget constraints limit the amount of measurement possibilities.

Design F   After-only designs; see Design D criticisms; only slightly improved with nonequivalent publics.

Design G   A single public (or set of publics) time-series design: useful trend data, yet alternative explanations abound.

Design H   A true control public, time-series design; one of the best; however, not very practical because it is both expensive and difficult to administer because of the requirements for randomization.

Design I   A nonequivalent control public, time-series design: very useful and relatively easy to administer.

___ Both to help plan and evaluate the effectiveness of the program or campaign.
___ Only to evaluate the campaign after implementation; not to help plan it, but to document its impact and to make recommendations about future activities.

If the purpose of the research is only to help plan the campaign—the data will not be used to evaluate the overall impact of the campaign—then the appropriate research design is called a before-only design. For example, the following are examples of before-only research activities: initial fact-finding efforts used to document the problem or opportunity; journalistic investigations and news reporting; and information collected for use in the production of media materials. It is also possible that relevant research may be conducted and completed prior to a mandate to develop the public relations campaign. For example, a client may have conducted research prior to contracting for a campaign from a public relations agency; or, a government research report may be used by a national association as the basis for a public relations campaign. The before-only research design may be appropriate if the purpose of the research is only to help plan the campaign. But, it is important for the public relations manager to recognize the limitations of a before-only research design: it cannot be used by itself to evaluate the effectiveness of the program or campaign. See Cases 6.1, 6.5, and 6.8.

If the purpose of the research is not only to plan but also to evaluate the campaign, or if the purpose is only to evaluate the program or campaign, then more sophisticated research designs are possible. Refer to Figure 6.3 to see how a variety of evaluative research options are generated by answering the following two basic sets of questions:

What public(s) do you intend to measure? (CHECK ONE)
___ One public or one set of publics, fully exposed to the same campaign.
___ One or more publics exposed to different versions of the same campaign. (CHECK ONE)
   ___ Equivalent publics
   ___ Nonequivalent publics

When do you intend to make these measurements? (CHECK ONE)
___ Before and after
___ After only
___ Before, during and after (a time series)

Use Figure 6.4 to select an appropriate research design, basing your answers on specific campaign conditions. A public relations manager should temper the ideal selection with the reality of time constraints, budgets, cooperative arrangements and other field conditions. It is best

FIGURE 6.4

Decision-tree checklist for selecting public relations research design

1. Why do you want to conduct research? (CHECK ONE)

    ____ Only to help plan the program or campaign, not to evaluate its overall effectiveness. GO TO 1A.

            ____ Both to help plan and evaluate the effectiveness of the program or campaign. GO TO 2.

                    ____ Only to evaluate the campaign after implementation; not to help plan it (there is no time or resources to do that) but to document its impact and to make recommendations about future activities. GO TO 2.

1A. Use before-only research design

    O   PR

2. Whom do you intend to measure? (CHECK ONE)

    ____ One public or one set of publics, all fully exposed to the same campaign. GO TO 3A.

    ____ One or more publics exposed to different versions of the same campaign. If so, specify type of publics. (CHECK ONE)

            ____ Equivalent publics GO TO 3B.

            ____ Nonequivalent publics GO TO 3C.

3A. When do you intend to make these measurements? (CHECK ONE)

    ____ Before and after ⟶ Use Design A

$$\begin{array}{ccc} O & PR & O \end{array}$$

    ____ After only ⟶ Use Design D

$$\begin{array}{cc} PR & O \end{array}$$

    ____ Before, during, and after ⟶ Use Design G

$$\begin{array}{ccccc} O & O & PR & O & O \end{array}$$

3B. When do you intend to make these measurements? (CHECK ONE)

    ____ Before and after ⟶ Use Design B

$$\begin{array}{ccc} & O & PR & O \\ R & & & \\ & O & & O \end{array}$$

    ____ After only ⟶ Use Design E

$$\begin{array}{cc} & PR & O \\ R & & \\ & & O \end{array}$$

    ____ Before, during, and after ⟶ Use Design G

$$\begin{array}{ccccc} & O\;O & PR & O\;O \\ R & & & \\ & O\;O & & O\;O \end{array}$$

3C. When do you intend to make these measurements? (CHECK ONE)

    ____ Before and after ⟶ Use Design B

$$\begin{array}{ccc} & O & PR & O \\ NR & & & \\ & O & & O \end{array}$$

    ____ After only ⟶ Use Design E

$$\begin{array}{cc} & PR & O \\ NR & & \\ & & O \end{array}$$

    ____ Before, during, and after ⟶ Use Design G

$$\begin{array}{ccccc} & O\;O & PR & O\;O \\ NR & & & \\ & O\;O & & O\;O \end{array}$$

to use those designs with true control publics. Second best are the time-series designs. Last are the designs without control publics. Least preferred of the nine evaluative research design options is the after-only design; any manager using it, should be aware of its many limitations.

NINE EVALUATIVE RESEARCH DESIGNS

Special notations will be used to describe the nine possible evaluate research designs.

R means random assignment using tables of random numbers, either computer-generated or from appropriate books about statistics.

NR means nonrandom assignment.

O1 means some kind of observation or measurement is made at this time. (Separate observations would be O2 . . . O3 . . . O4 . . . etc.)

T1 means the time at which observations are made. (Also . . . T2 . . . T3 . . . T4 . . . etc.)

X means experimental treatment program (a term derived from medical research); here it refers to some form of the public relations campaign.

CPR means the complete public relations campaign.

PPR means a partial or modified version of the public relations campaign.

(blank space) means no treatment or exposure to any aspect of the public relations campaign.

The notation will be used in special diagrams that will have the general appearance of the following one, which illustrates a before-after design with randomly assigned treatment and control publics:

			Time	
	Publics	**T1**	**X**	**T2**
R	Fully Exposed Publics	O1	CPR	O2
	Control Publics	O3		O4

The above diagram indicates that the control publics would receive none of the public relations campaign. An example here would be a direct mail campaign that involved randomly dividing a mailing list, sending one half of the list all the campaign materials, and not sending anything to the other half of the list. Pretest and posttest would be conducted of all the people on the lists—both treatment and control publics. The prediction would be that, if the campaign were effective, there would be a significant difference between measures of change over time between the treatment and control publics. Expressed mathematically, this difference would be: $(O2 - O1) > (O4 - O3)$.

If costs were a factor and reaching everyone on the list was important, then a more realistic example would be sending one half the list a partial or modified set of direct mail materials and sending the other half of the list a complete set of direct mail materials. This way, basic information would reach all members of the target audience, yet certain members would receive more information than others. An example would be mailing a letter without a brochure, and mailing a letter with a brochure. Not only is this more realistic, it is more efficient. If it can be determined that the letter without the brochure is just as effective, then the cost of the brochure can be reduced or eliminated. Here is what the diagram would look like for that type of research design:

	Publics	T1	Time X	T2
R	Fully Exposed Publics	O1	CPR	O2
	Control Publics	O3	PPR	O4

More information about these two designs is given below under the description of Design B. Refer to Figure 6.3 for a brief description of each of the following designs.

Design A: Before-After with No Control Publics

Publics	T1	Time X	T2
Fully Exposed Publics	O1	CPR	O2

Because no control groups are involved, it is difficult if not impossible to prove why observations at T2 might be different than observations at T1; nevertheless, this design is widely used, if for no other reason than because it is straight-forward. Observing and measuring the publics—the before measure—often is performed as part of the initial fact-finding stage of any campaign. If comparable data are collected as an after measure, then it is fairly easy to compare the before and after measures to see if there are any differences. Alternative explanations for campaign results (positive or negative) abound primarily because outside influences have not been controlled; yet, this design is useful and much better than conducting an after-only design (Design D). A useful analysis of data generated by this research design

FIGURE 6.5

Example of data from before-after design

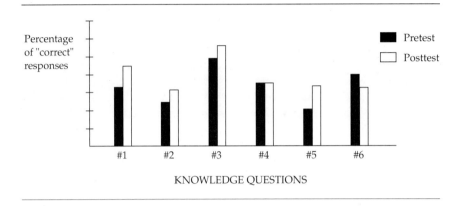

is to compare different subpublics to see if they were affected differently by the campaign. For an example of how parallel bar graphs can be used to show Design A before-and-after measurements, see Figure 6.5. See also Cases 6.2, 6.3, and 6.9.

Design B: Before-After with True Control Publics

	Publics	T1	Time X	T2
R	Fully Exposed Publics	O1	CPR	O2
	Control Publics	O3		O4

The key to this design is the random assignment of individuals to treatment and control publics. Not disseminating public relations materials to a randomly selected group may be one way to reduce costs; but, using obtrusive measurements to collect before and after data while not sending them anything else may raise questions in the minds of the recipients about what is going on and may generate problems for the campaign. However, if the measurements are nonobtrusive, this can be a very good design. The key comparison is between observations made at T2: if they are different, then the chances are these differences were caused by the public relations campaign. True control publics probably have the same ongoing life experiences as the fully exposed publics (both receiving outside influences, getting older, wiser, etc.), so many alternative explanations can be eliminated. What is left is the influence of the public relations campaign. A graph illustrating how to display data collected using Design B is presented in Figure 6.6.

FIGURE 6.6

Example of data from before-after with true control publics design

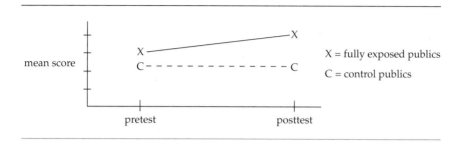

Design C: Before-After with Nonequivalent Control Publics

	Publics	Time		
		T1	X	T2
NR	Fully Exposed Publics	O1	CPR	O2
	Control Publics	O3	PPR	O4

This design uses similar publics and treatment and control publics, with the fully exposed publics receiving the complete public relations campaign and the control publics receiving only part of the campaign. If the two publics are very similar, differences observed at T2 should be due only to the differences between the complete and partial public relations campaign. But, because the nonequivalent publics may have built-in biases that somehow interact with the public relations campaign and yield differences in after-only measurements, the unique contribution of the public relations campaign to the final observations cannot be determined. The key to this design is fully describing similarities and differences between the two publics at T1, so that when T2 results are known, these qualifications can be carefully considered. Also, the differences between the complete and partial public relations campaigns need to be fully explained and related to campaign results. See also Case 6.10.

Design D: After-Only

Publics	Time		
	T1	X	T2
Fully Exposed Publics		CPR	O1

This is one of the worst designs possible; yet, it is one of the most frequently used in public relations. It is disarmingly simple: after a public relations campaign is implemented, its impact is documented. Unfortunately, in most cases, it is difficult, if not impossible, to prove that the public relations campaign actually caused the observed results, particularly if what is being measured is human behavior or opinions. There are so many alternative explanations for what is observed at T2 that one particular explanation can be easily countered with another. If the campaign is unique, then it may be possible to logically link the campaign to certain observed results. However, most public relations campaigns are not unique; they exist in a sea of other sources of information and influence. This is not a recommended design, but sometimes it is all that can be done. See Case 6.7.

Design E: After-Only with True Control Publics

	Publics	T1	Time X	T2
R	Fully Exposed Publics		CPR	O1
	Control Publics		PPR	O2

The control publics in this design receive some part of the public relations campaign. Assuming that random assignments to control and treatment publics equally scatter individual differences between both publics, then any differences observed at T2 may be attributed to the differences between the partial and complete public relations programs. The key to this design is accurately describing the two versions of the public relations program and explaining how these program differences might account for differences observed with the after-only measure.

Design F: After-Only with Nonequivalent Publics

	Publics	T1	Time X	T2
NR	Fully Exposed Publics		CPR	O1
	Control Publics		PPR	O2

This design, similar to Design D, is frequently used by practitioners because it is temptingly easy: two difference publics are exposed to two different yet related public relations campaigns and the differences are observed at T2. The trouble with this approach is that there are so many alternative explanations that unless the two publics are extremely similar, differences can be accounted for by a variety of factors. Even if the publics are very similar, unexplained, possibly unnoticed, differences between publics may account for some, if not all, of the differences observed at T2. If this design is used, the nonequivalency of the publics must be documented, and public relations practitioners need to be prepared to have the evaluation discounted. See Case 6.6.

Design G: A Single Time-Series

Publics	Time
	T1 T2 T3 T4 X T5 T6 T7 T8
Fully Exposed Publics	O1 O2 O3 O4 CPR O5 O6 O7 O8

There are two problems with this design: 1) avoiding the "testing" effect of using one measurement technique over and over again, and 2) identifying possible "outside" influences that might confound any of the measurements. If outside events and possible sources of influence are adequately documented and taken into account, this can be a very good design. Fortunately, one problem is not that big: the testing effect, so often a bother in other forms of evaluative research, can work to the public relations practitioner's advantage—just as the Hawthorne effect in various business and educational research designs often facilitates movement toward certain program goals. Repeatedly evaluating a public relations campaign, which is what creates the testing effect, reinforces a certain message of most public relations practitioners because it shows genuine interest in feedback. The purpose of this design is to compare trendlines before and after a public relations campaign, so there should be at least three measurements at regular intervals before the campaign and three after the campaign. The data might look like the trendline for Design G presented in Figure 6.7. See also Case 6.4.

Design H: A Time-Series with True Control Publics

	Publics	Time
		T1 T2 T3 T4 X T5 T6 T7 T8
R	Fully Exposed Publics	O1 O2 O3 O4 CPR O5 O6 O7 O8
	Control Publics	O9 O10 O11 O12 PPR O13 O14 O15 O16

This design, while apparently one of the best possible, is rarely used because it is not practical: randomization is not an easy task. Over a great length of time, this design becomes fairly hard to administer. If measurements are made frequently over a short period of time, then

FIGURE 6.7

Example of data from a single time-series design

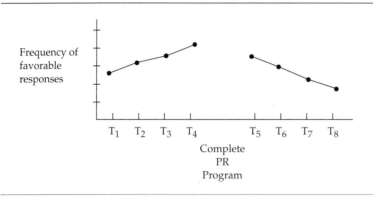

this can be an excellent design. As with all time-series designs, the purpose is to compare trendlines before and after the public relations campaign. In this design, there is a significant advantage in monitoring over a period of time equivalent publics receiving slightly different public relations campaigns: any differences between trendlines after exposure to the campaigns should be attributed to the differences between the two campaigns. Trendlines generated from Design H are presented in Figure 6.8.

Design I: A Time-Series with Nonequivalent Control Publics

	Publics	T_1	T_2	T_3	T_4	Time X	T_5	T_6	T_7	T_8
NR	Fully Exposed Publics	O1	O2	O3	O4	CPR	O5	O6	O7	O8
	Control Publics	O9	O10	O11	O12	PPR	O13	O14	O15	O16

This design has all the advantages of Design G, plus it has data from nonequivalent publics that can be used to eliminate some alternative explanations for differences found in the trendlines before and after the public relations campaign. Because publics are not randomly assigned, this is an easier design to execute than Design H. However, administrative care must be taken to fully describe similarities and differences between the publics, for these and other differences may account for apparent differences in the trendlines that might otherwise be attributed to differences in the public relations campaign. The data from this design could be displayed similarly to that for Design H, presented in Figure 6.8.

FIGURE 6.8

Example of data from a time-series with true control publics design

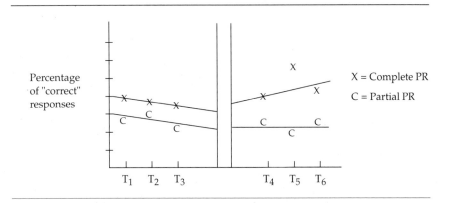

THE "GARBAGE CAN" THEORY OF RESEARCH DESIGN

The decision tree presented in this chapter suggests that designing research is a rational process that follows certain logical steps. Scientific research, in the ideal world, is rational and follows very specific procedures. However, rarely is research in the social sciences, especially public relations, practiced in such an ideal world. Most often, the final research design selected by public relations managers is determined by a confusing mix of economic, organizational, and political factors. For example, the eagerness of decision-makers (the client) to have the research results, the amount of money and time available, the professional strengths of the public relations staff, and unknown and unpredictable characteristics of the target audiences strongly influence the final research design.

Organizational decision-making is rarely as logical as we would like; to an uninformed observer, many decisions in an organization appear to be irrational. One reason, according to March's "garbage can" theory of organizational decision-making, referred to in Chapter 2, is that decision-makers throw so many different solutions at problems that it is difficult to sort out how the interacting jumble of possible solutions generate a specific decision.

In designing public relations research, a number of solution components are tossed into the mix:

> theories, ideas and assumptions about the public relations program or campaign being investigated;

human and material resources, including time, money, and knowledge of research methodologies; plus,

anticipated and actual consequences of the research results.[8]

Effective public relations managers, stirring this mix of solutions together, know how difficult and yet important it is to be flexible in designing research. Effective public relations managers know how to be creative and how to foster and encourage serendipity as they go about the process of designing research appropriate to a specific public relations situation.

WIDE RANGE OF RESEARCH METHODOLOGIES AVAILABLE

A wide range of research methodologies can be used in any of the above ten research designs. No one research technique is necessarily associated with any one design. Often a public relations manager will use a combination of qualitative, quantitative, exploratory and confirmatory techniques in research designed specifically for one campaign. In many instances, qualitative, exploratory research is conducted to help plan a campaign, and quantitative, confirmatory research is conducted to help evaluate a campaign.

Through traditional library resources and computerized databases, a public relations manager can analyze media content both qualitatively and quantitatively. Four case studies will be presented in this chapter to illustrate media content analyses.

In addition to media content analyses, other qualitative and research methods used in public relations include in-depth interviews, subjective analyses of stakeholder relationships, participant observations, testimonials, case studies, and corporate communication archives.

To both plan and evaluate campaigns, public relations practitioners conduct in-depth interviews with key opinion leaders within target publics and summarize these interviews in narrative reports.

Systematically recording incoming phone calls and correspondence can be helpful to ascertain demands for information and services by a public relations department.

Reports from public relations staff who are involved in designing and implementing campaigns also is a qualitative research technique that can assist a public relations manager.

An excellent source of qualitative information about a campaign is written and verbal testimonials from satisfied members of the target audience.

When public relations managers summarize and prepare campaign materials for submission to professional awards' contests, the resulting document is a case study and constitutes qualitative research. And, when they win an award, it constitutes a very important testimonial to the campaign's effectiveness.

Establishing and maintaining a record of all communication activities, including planning documents and research reports, is an important activity for many public relations departments, for this becomes an archive for the corporation (or client) and a significant resource for the development of corporate histories and the continuation of corporate cultures.

One of the most widely used qualitative research techniques in public relations is the focus group, which consists of a small group of 8 to 12 individuals who participate in a focused group discussion led by a trained researcher. Two case studies will be presented in this chapter to illustrate how to conduct focus groups in public relations.

In addition to the analysis of media content presented in the following case studies, there are other quantitative methodologies that are used in public relations research, particularly survey research and public opinion polling. The last three cases in this chapter will present more information about these quantitative research techniques.

FOUR CASE STUDIES ABOUT MEDIA CONTENT ANALYSIS

Four case studies based on the research services of Porter/Novelli illustrate a variety of ways that media content analyses can be used to plan and evaluate public relations campaigns. Porter/Novelli is one of the world's largest public relations agencies, employing hundreds of public relations professionals. In its Washington, D.C. offices, it has a separate research department and ten account executives, many with advanced degrees in the social sciences, who specialize in research. These cases illustrate one set of research techniques—analyzing media content and media gatekeepers—which can be considered a combination of qualitative and quantitative techniques. These cases serve as examples of before-only, before-after, and time-series research designs.

CASE 6.1:

Porter/Novelli's Background Review Service

A national pharmaceutical trade association became involved in a major effort to mount support for tort law reform in state legislatures. They contracted with Porter/Novelli (then known as Doremus Porter Novelli) to provide a range of services, including what the agency called their Background Review Service. The association wanted the agency to gather information that would help them plan a national public education and lobbying campaign. The agency went through the following steps to prepare a Background Review for their client:

1. Agency account executives met with the client and determined that the key issues to be researched were product and drug liability, the need for tort law reform and proposed reform measures.
2. They refined these issues and topics into a list of search terms to be used with computerized databases.
3. They searched the databases to obtain:
    past coverage of the issues and topics in newspapers, trade journals and consumer magazines;
    national public opinion polls and consumer surveys;
    demographic, economic and industry trends;
    technical/professional journal articles;
    wire services stories; and,
    corporate communications and newsletters.
4. Account executives summarized this information in a report that included copies of supporting documents, tables and annotated bibliographies.
5. The information was used to develop a national campaign that included a brochure on product and drug liability designed to inform lobbyists and state legislators about the need for tort law reform.

This case is an example of a before-only research design. The information collected for the Background Review was used only to plan the campaign; it was not used afterwards to evaluate the campaign. The research data was used extensively in developing informational materials. To help the association evaluate its campaign, the agency provided other research services that not only tracked issues but also monitored legislation in the various states.

CASE 6.2:

Gatekeeper Audit and Publicity Evaluation

A federal health organization conducting a national public education campaign about the control of high blood pressure asked the public relations agency to investigate why the airings of their TV public service announcements (PSAs) were declining in certain markets. In addition to the public relations agency tracking PSA placements and broadcasts (which they accomplished, in part, with a subcontract to another company that specialized in monitoring electronic media), the agency conducted what they called a Gatekeeper Audit. While the target audience for the PSAs was the TV viewing public, the agency knew that the campaign had to work through intermediaries, such as editors, reporters, producers and managers of media organizations. To conduct their audit of these gatekeepers, the agency went through the following steps:

1. Account executives used the distribution list of TV stations that had been sent the PSAs, plus a report from a broadcast monitoring service, to determine which stations were airing, however frequently, the PSAs.
2. Account executives, with the client and TV specialists, developed questions to ask media gatekeepers about the PSAs.
3. In-depth telephone interviews with public service directors representing high- and low-play TV stations were conducted by the public relations agency. Those interviewed were promised: 1) the information they shared would remain confidential, 2) the purpose of the interview was not to "pitch" a feature story or specific PSA placement, rather 3) the purpose was to help the client evaluate the effectiveness of the PSA, because they were preparing to update and revise the PSAs. Those contacted were asked questions regarding:
    their awareness of the blood pressure PSAs and factors that affected their decision to air the PSAs;
    their personal interests in the topic;
    their perceptions of their local audience's awareness, knowledge and attitudes about high blood-pressure control.
4. The results of the Gatekeeper Audit and PSA broadcast monitoring were prepared as a summary report that could be described as more qualitative than quantitative and that included a set of recommendations for the client. The recommendations focused on PSA distribution, schedule and formatting.
5. Based on the report's recommendations, a number of changes were made in a new set of PSAs, which were distributed nationwide.
6. A broadcast monitoring service was used to measure the use of the new PSAs. Usage significantly increased, particularly among previously low-play stations.

This case is an example of a before-after research design. Data about media placement and airing of TV PSAs from two sources (broadcast monitors and telephone interviews) were collected before and after changes were made in the campaign, and the data sets were compared to see if significant changes had occurred. The case also is an excellent example of research focused on an important set of intervening variables—media gatekeepers.

CASE 6.3:

Publicity Evaluation and Tracking Service

A state lottery requested that the public relations agency measure and evaluate media coverage of its statewide public relations campaign, particularly those activities introducing a new computer feature called Quick Pick. Lottery officials were particularly interested in analyzing publicity generated by a statewide tour of Lotto officials and local personalities announcing Quick Pick. The public relations agency used its Publicity Evaluation and Tracking Service, which included proprietary measurement procedures, to conduct the requested evaluation. They followed these steps:

1. Account executives met with the client and developed measurable campaign objectives, including specifics about the target audience, communications strategy, desired publicity copy points, and targeted media.
2. They did a number of calculations to assess the current volume of media placement efforts:
    they counted the number of press releases and publicity materials distributed;
    they counted the number of media releases placed, the number of articles generated by publicity efforts, and the circulation of each media outlet;
    they measured the quality of each media placement by assigning weights to message location, media outlet's target audience penetration,
    number and position of key message points; and,
    they calculated total gross impressions for the specific target audience—adults 21 and over—by summing the number of target audience members per media outlet.
3. By intensive analysis of the media content, using the above statistics but also simply reading and understanding what was published, they established whether placement messages were on target, and they identified areas of confusion and negative coverage.
4. They prepared a report that provided a summary of the publicity efforts and a series of graphs presenting:
    placement volume,
    message content,
    target audience impressions, and
    quality measures.

The final report also discussed implications for future placement activities. The evaluation showed that compared to past Lotto coverage, the media tour generated significantly more coverage on Quick Pick. The findings from the evaluation also were used later as baseline information for an evaluation of campaign activities announcing other new lottery games. Because data from before the campaign were compared to that collected after the campaign, this case is an example of a before-after research design.

· · ·

CASE 6.4:

Issues and Market Monitoring

A major trade coalition engaged in a national public relations campaign needed regular reports of issues and trends that might affect their campaign. They asked the public relations agency to provide that information on a monthly basis. These are the steps the agency followed:

1. Account executives met with the client to determine specific strategies and objectives for the campaign, and the range of issues and trends that needed to be monitored.
2. Based on this list of issues and topics, agency staff prepared a list of search terms to use with computerized databases.
3. In addition to databases, information was collected from staff specialists about perspectives of thought leaders and realignments in legislative and interest groups.
4. The agency prepared the first of a series of reports that included summaries of issues and trends, supporting documents, and bibliographies.
5. On an as-needed basis, special reports were presented personally and in writing to the client, especially for fast-breaking events of importance.

The coalition used this systematic analysis of current events to make strategic adjustments in their campaign. This is an example of a time-series research design.

TWO CASE STUDIES ABOUT FOCUS GROUPS

The following two cases illustrate how focus groups can be used in before-only and after-only research designs.

· · ·

CASE 6.5:

Focus Groups Used for a Formative Evaluation

Seven automobile dealerships were acquired by one family over a number of years, and the owner allowed each to maintain its separate identity; only one of the dealerships carried the name of the owner. An account executive with Rolle Communications, Inc., a public relations agency based in Bethesda, Maryland, which handled the owner's advertising and public relations, suggested that a single name for all dealerships might aid advertising, allowing larger combined ads, and improve customer awareness and recall. The client was reluctant to change, for business was good, but gave the go-ahead for the agency to investigate how customers felt about such a name change. The agency decided to conduct a series of three focus groups with current and potential customers. To conduct the focus groups, the following steps were taken:

1. The account executive prepared a list of potential names and discussed them with the client. The list was narrowed down to three potential new names.
2. The agency subcontracted with research consultants, specialists in conducting focus groups, who were to develop the research instruments, select and invite the group participants, conduct the group sessions, and prepare audio tapes, a written summary of each group session, and an overall summary and set of recommendations.
3. The agency's account executive secured a list of customers from each of the dealerships, which was given to the researchers. From this list, the researchers randomly selected 25 customers from each of the seven dealerships.
4. The researchers also selected a random sample of 25 households within five miles of each dealership, using criss-cross directories to identify each occupant's name, address and phone number.
5. Each member of each sample of current customers and potential customers received a personal letter from the owner of the dealership explaining that someone from an independent research firm would be calling soon to ask a few questions about current and future plans for the auto dealership.
6. The research firm called the individuals and invited them to one of three "special meetings of customers" at one of the dealerships "to discuss your reactions to proposed new advertising." They were told that the purpose of the meeting was not to sell them anything but to hear their ideas and suggestions about current and future plans for the dealership. They also were informed that the meeting would last two hours, that there would be free food and beverages, and that each participant would receive $25. When 15 individuals accepted the invitation for each of the three scheduled meetings, for a total of 45 participants, all others who were interviewed were asked a short sequence of questions dealing with the proposed name changes, but they were not invited to participate in a focus group.
7. Reminder letters were sent to the participants one week before the scheduled focus group session.
8. On the day of the focus group session, the conference room at the dealership was prepared with coffee, soft drinks and donuts for everyone; pencils and note pads for the participants; and, for the researchers, blank flip charts, large felt-tip pins and blank index cards.
9. Using the Nominal Group Technique, the participants were asked to identify strengths and weaknesses of each of the current and proposed names of the dealerships. See Figure 6.9 for an explanation about how to conduct a focus group using the Nominal Group Technique. At the end of the group session, each individual was given a letter of thanks from the owner and a check for $25.
10. Reports for each focus group session and a summary report and set of recommendations were prepared by the research firm and presented to the

FIGURE 6.9

How to use the Nominal Group Technique to conduct a focus group

1. Prior to convening the focus group, determine the best set of questions for the group to focus upon. Be precise. Do not ask double-barreled questions. Do not ask questions that can be answered with a simple "yes" or "no."

2. Pose one question in writing to the group and ask them to *consider it in silence*. The leader should explain that each member of the group will work in silence for at least 20–30 minutes, answering in writing, on pads of paper provided, *what the individual thinks is the best way to answer the question.*

3. The leader most likely will need to admonish—politely—individuals who whisper or talk. Explain to the group—not neccessarily looking at the talkative individual(s)—that there will be an opportunity to discuss ideas later and that silence now ensures a richer array of ideas to discuss later.

4. After all in the group have stopped writing, begin listing ideas. The leader goes from individual to individual in round-robin fashion asking each person to suggest *one* idea. Each person should suggest only new ideas and not repeat ideas similar to those already on the list. This step also occurs in relative silence—only the group leader and the person suggesting the idea should talk: no group discussion should be allowed.

5. After all ideas are listed on pages from a flip chart and taped around the room like wallpaper, the group leader reads the entire list slowly, asking the group members to consider the merits of each. This process, too, occurs with an absolute minimum of group discussion. If questions about the meaning of certain ideas are raised, the group leader should refer to the person who originally suggested the idea. Do not collapse or combine different listed ideas at this time: explain that the next step—voting for top choices—will identify best ideas.

6. Each individual should look over the entire list and select the top choices. Selecting the top 5 or 10 seems to work best. It is recommended that each choice (its number and a brief phrase to describe it) be written on separate index cards, to make assigning weights and voting easier.

7. After all individuals have made their choices—and still with no group discussion—ask the group members to "reverse weight" their choices. For example, if the top five have been selected, then the first choice gets a value of five; the second choice gets a value of four; the third choice, a value of three; the fourth choice, a value of two; and, the fifth choice, a value of one. Individuals should record this reverse weight next to each choice prior to the next step.

8. The group leader should go from individual to individual and get each person's complete set of choices and each choice's reverse weight. For example, a person might say, "My first choice was #22, so it gets a value of five." The group leader records the votes and tallies the scores.

9. The group leader should highlight the groups' top choices, based on the total scores. Then, the leader can open up the meeting to a general discussion of the top choices, or discuss one item at a time.

10. Careful notes should be taken of the group discussion at this point. Later the ideas listed on the flip chart, the priority rankings, and the notes from the group discussion can be typed and analyzed in a formal report. Audio and video tapes of the entire process can augment the written report.

*For more information, see McElreath, Mark P. "Using the Nominal Group Technique to teach ethics in public relations," in *Ethical Trends and Issues in Public Relations Education*, proceedings of/IABC District 3, (San Francisco, CA, 1986); and, "Appendix C: How to conduct a four group study," in *Using Research in Public Relations: Applications in Program Management*, by Broom, Glen M., and David M. Dozier (Englewood Cliffs, NJ: Prentice-Hall, 1990) pp. 325-330.

agency. The reports included audio tapes and priority listings of verbatim statements of strengths and weaknesses for each name. The major recommendation was to prepare sample advertising of the most popular new name and to conduct additional research.
11. The account executive presented the results to the client, who decided not to change the name of the dealerships. This decision was based not on the research results but rather on legalities pertaining to negotiations underway to purchase and sell certain dealerships.

This case is an example of research designed to be before-after, yet it ended up being before-only. The case is an excellent example of how appropriate research may be conducted but not acted on because decision-makers take into consideration other matters when making their final decision.

. . .

CASE 6.6:

Focus Groups Used for a Summative Evaluation

Potomac Electric Power Company, the electric utility in the nation's capital, had scheduled with their advertising and public relations agency for two concept-testing focus groups to be conducted to determine customer reactions to proposed advertising. One week before the scheduled focus group sessions, however, one of the region's worst summer storms in this century roared through the Washington, D.C., area, leaving several communities without power and electrical service for days. Immediately, the company activated its Crisis Communication Plan, which included a range of public relations and advertising activities designed specifically to deal with the storm and its aftermath. Because the focus group facilities and research specialists were already scheduled, the manager of public relations went ahead with the research but changed the focus of the groups from the topic of proposed new advertising to the performance of the company dealing with the storm. The company took these steps:

1. The manager of public relations for the company contacted the account executive at the advertising and public relations agency and instructed him not only to refocus the groups so that they discussed the company's performance during and after the storm but also to invite two different groups of people to participate in the research: residents whose home was in the path of the storm and who had experienced property damage and outages; and, residents whose home was outside the storm's path but who were, of course, well aware of the devastating storm and its aftermath.
2. The company's customer service group telephoned and invited the homeowners in these two publics to participate in a "small group meeting with other customers." The homeowners were told the meeting would last approximately an hour and a half, that it would be conducted by an independent research firm, and that each participant would receive $25.

Utility company's response to storm damage was the focus of its research. Reprinted with permission of Potomac Electric Power Company.

3. Confirmation letters were mailed to the 10 to 15 individuals who agreed to participate in each of the two meetings. (It was assumed that 20 percent of those agreeing to attend would be unable, at the last moment, to attend, which meant that 8 to 12 people were expected to participate in each group.)
4. The focus group sessions took place in a conference room designed specifically for this purpose. On one wall there was a one-way mirror, and on the other side of this mirror was space for video equipment and observers to watch the focus group in session.
5. A trained focus group leader led the discussion that covered the following topics: reactions to the performance by the company and other institutions in the community to the storm; recall of safety warnings, crisis messages and other storm-related communication and community relations activities of the company; and, awareness of economic and technological issues affecting the electric company.
6. A five-page summary report was prepared by the agency and presented to the manager of public relations. A videotape of the two sessions was available but was not presented with the report. The report included the following statement:

> Methodology involved the collection and analysis of qualitative data only. Focus group participants were not necessarily representative of any known or projectible segment of the generic population and, thus, data derived from this technique are not quantifiable. Individual panelists' opinions, likes, and dislikes should be ignored as representing no more than personal idiosyncracies. The significant qualitative appraisal is a function of the group dynamics of the panel, the consensus that forms through discussion, and some debate.

As a result of the suggestions from the focus groups, the company incorporated new activities into the crisis communication plans: assigning employees to specific neighborhoods to provide ongoing assistance and information, and using the postal service to distribute information to directly affected customers.

This case is an example of a concept-testing before-only design being changed to an after-only research design. It illustrates two major strengths of focus group research: how quickly it can be conducted, and how flexible the agenda can be for group discussion. In the hands of an effective public relations manager, focus group research can be a very powerful decision-making tool.

SYSTEMATIC USE OF PRESS CLIPPINGS

Some public relations managers clip out articles from newspapers and magazines that have been generated by a media relations campaign, put the clips into a file folder or scrapbook (or, tape them together into an impressively long scroll, as one practitioner did), and brag about the amount of press coverage. Other managers use more sophisticated techniques to analyze press clippings, as the next case illustrates.

. . .

CASE 6.7:

Content Analysis Using an After-Only Research Design

A small firm specializing in computer applications created a new product, a form of music software. The firm's marketing department hired The Right Brain, Inc., a public relations firm in Minneapolis, Minnesota, to conduct a product promotion campaign that involved preparing a press kit, press releases, feature stories, and distributing this information to trade, industry and general interest media—primarily to print media, but also to broadcast outlets. The firm's marketing department also hired an advertising agency to create and place appropriate advertisements. The product manager said she was concerned that senior management would not approve a larger promotion budget for next year unless the current campaign was evaluated to show "the company's dollars were being spent effectively." In order to track and evaluate the impact of the public relations component of the promotion campaign, the public relations agency used a special computer program, a relational database, called NewsTrack. (Developed by the president of the agency initially to track the progress of various clients' campaigns, NewsTrack now is sold by his firm, The Right Brain, Inc., as off-the-shelf public relations software.)[9] For the music software client, these are the steps the agency took to conduct a content analysis that assessed the effectiveness of the public relations campaign:

1. Working with sales materials provided by the client, the public relations agency prepared and distributed a press kit containing releases, feature stories, photographs, and illustrations to scores of national and specialized media.
2. From a clipping service and a broadcast monitoring service, the agency received clips of print placements and transcripts of broadcast placements documenting more than 260 media placements.

An example of software used to track publicity. Reprinted with permission of the Right Brain, Inc., Minneapolis, MN. Copyright © 1990 by the Right Brain, Inc.

3. Using circulation figures for each publication, the agency calculated the total gross impressions to be in excess of 33 million.
4. For each publication, the agency estimated a percentage of the circulation which could be considered part of the campaign's target audience. With these estimates, they calculated the total effective impressions to be in excess of 2 million.
5. More than 95 percent of media placements were in print. The agency measured the number of column inches of each of the 255 print placements and added them to arrive at a total of 3,448 column inches, an average of 13.5 column-inches per placement.
6. Using the following scale, they assigned a value for the position of each print placement in the publication:
   10 = Front page or front cover of publication
   9 = Front page or important section appropriate to topic or product
   8 = Front page of less important section
   7 = Prominent page position inside a section
   6 = Neutral position (not immediately obvious to the reader)
   5 = Relatively short copy, in rear of publication or otherwise "buried"
   4 = One paragraph of copy, or less, definitely "buried"
7. They calculated an average position value by adding individual placement values and dividing that total by the total number of placements. In this case, they calculated an average position value of 7.24, meaning the average print placement was positioned on an inside prominent page.
8. They assigned a content value for each print placement by using the following scale:
   10 = All three key copy points covered; good photo or illustration; bold, positive headline
   9 = Three key copy points covered, without photo or illustration
   8 = Two key copy points covered, with photo or illustration
   7 = Two key copy points covered, without photo or illustration
   6 = One key copy point covered, with photo or illustration
   5 = One key copy point covered, without photo or illustration
   4 = Regardless of copy point coverage, negative slant
9. They calculated an average content value by adding individual content values and dividing that total by the total number of placements. In this

case, they calculated an average content value of 7.99, meaning the average placement contained two key copy points and was accompanied by a photo or illustration.
10. They used similar scales for the 12 broadcast placements to calculate an average "time of day" value and an average content value. Also, for broadcast placements, they calculated the average number of minutes of air time by dividing the total minutes of air time by the total number of broadcast placements.
11. Based on advertising rates for each media outlet, the agency was prepared to calculate for their client, if asked, a total equivalent advertising value. For each medium, they would have multiplied the ad rate by the amount of space or time given to the placement; then, they would have summed the individual advertising values to reach a total equivalent advertising value, a figure that represented what it would have cost the client had the equivalent amount of advertising space been purchased as was generated by the "free" publicity. The client in this case did not request this value be calculated. (The equivalent advertising value is based on the questionable assumption that editorial "news hole" space has an equivalent impact on readers and viewers as does advertising space.)
12. The agency also calculated a gross cost per impression by dividing total cost of the public relations campaign by total gross impressions. And, they calculated an effective cost per impression by dividing total cost of the public relations campaign by total effective impressions.

This case study is an excellent example of an after-only research design without the use of controls. The evaluation occurred after the campaign was implemented, and the results were not used to fine-tune the campaign but to assess its overall impact. The product manager was impressed; she said later that the agency's reports proved to top management "in black and white terms that public relations is effective."[10] Much of the time required to conduct the content analysis was involved in collecting the data (primarily by the clipping and broadcast monitoring services), coding the placements, and entering the facts and numbers into the computer program. An advantage of a relational database program such as NewsTrack is that once the basic facts about the media are entered into the system, they can be called up at any time, in a variety of different combinations, for additional analyses—for example, tracking publicity by markets or by billing period.

QUANTITATIVE RESEARCH MEANS USING STATISTICS AND SAMPLES

Most often quantitative public relations research involves a scientific survey, which can be defined as an extensive appraisal of something observable. Surveys involve the use of research instruments, most often questionnaires, that spell out in detail how data are to be collected.

Quantitative research involves observations that are summarized, somehow, using numbers—statistics. When probability samples are drawn from the population of all possible observations, and research

Publicity for a single event (a news conference), analyzed by NewsTrack software. Reprinted with permission of the Right Brain, Inc., Minneapolis, MN. Copyright © 1990 by the Right Brain, Inc.

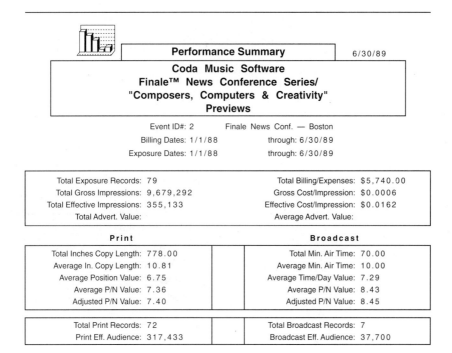

Comments:

Position Value is evaluated on this basis (similar equivalent for Broadcast Exposures):
10 = Front Page or front cover of publication
 9 = Front page of important section appropriate to topic or product
 8 = Front page of inappropriate, or less-important, section
 7 = Prominent page position inside a section
 6 = Neutral position (not immediately obvious to reader)
 5 = Relatively short copy, in rear of publication or otherwise "buried"
 4 = One paragraph of copy or less, "buried"

Positive/Negative Value is evaluated on this basis (similar equiv. for Broadcast Exposures):
10 = All three key copy points covered; good photo or illustration; bold, positive headline
 9 = Three key copy points covered, without photo or illus.
 8 = Two key copy points covered, with photo or illus.
 7 = Two key copy points covered, without photo or illus.
 6 = One key copy point covered, with photo or illus.
 5 = One key copy point covered, without photo or illus.
 4 = Regardless of copy point coverage, negative slant

Overall publicity analyzed by NewsTrack software. Reprinted with permission of the Right Brain, Inc., Minneapolis, MN. Copyright © 1990 by the Right Brain, Inc.

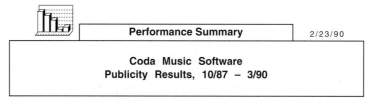

Performance Summary	2/23/90
Coda Music Software **Publicity Results, 10/87 – 3/90**	

Client ID#: 1   Coda Music Software
Billing Dates: 10/1/87   through: 2/23/90
Exposure Dates: 10/1/87   through: 2/23/90

Total Exposure Records: 267	Total Billing/Expenses: $87,966.77
Total Gross Impressions: 33,240,758	Gross Cost/Impression: $0.0026
Total Effective Impressions: 2,576,678	Effective Cost/Impression: $0.0341
Total Advert. Value:	Average Advert. Value:

Print	Broadcast
Total Inches Copy Length: 3,448.00	Total Min. Air Time: 165.00
Average In. Copy Length: 13.52	Average Min. Air Time: 13.75
Average Position Value: 7.24	Average Time/Day Value: 7.25
Average P/N Value: 7.99	Average P/N Value: 8.50
Adjusted P/N Value: 8.12	Adjusted P/N Value: 8.55

Total Print Records: 255	Total Broadcast Records: 12
Print Eff. Audience: 2,528,978	Broadcast Eff. Audience: 47,700

Comments:

Position Value is evaluated on this basis (similar equivalent for Broadcast Exposures):
10 = Front Page or front cover of publication
 9 = Front page of important section appropriate to topic or product
 8 = Front page of inappropriate, or less-important, section
 7 = Prominent page position inside a section
 6 = Neutral position (not immediately obvious to reader)
 5 = Relatively short copy, in rear of publication or otherwise "buried"
 4 = One paragraph of copy or less, "buried"

Positive/Negative Value is evaluated on this basis (similar equiv. for Broadcast Exposures):
10 = All three key copy points covered; good photo or illustration; bold, positive headline
 9 = Three key copy points covered, without photo or illus.
 8 = Two key copy points covered, with photo or illus.
 7 = Two key copy points covered, without photo or illus.
 6 = One key copy point covered, with photo or illus.
 5 = One key copy point covered, without photo or illus.
 4 = Regardless of copy point coverage, negative slant

is conducted on this limited set of observations, generalizations are possible not only to the specific set of observations (the sample) but also to the population from which the sample was drawn. This potential for generalizing to a larger population is one of the compelling reasons for conducting quantitative research.

There are two types of samples: probability and judgmental samples. The key to being able to generalize is selecting a probability sample. Probability samples are selected in such a way that the probability for being part of the sample can be calculated. Imagine there are ten people waiting in a room nearby, and you want to randomly sample half of them. You could go into the room and assign numbers to each person (1 through 10). Then, you could turn to a table of random numbers and scan down a column until you see the first number between 1 and 10. You then could ask that person to complete the first questionnaire, and you could ask every other person, beginning with that person, to complete a similar questionnaire. Using this procedure, you could calculate the chance or probability of each person being in the sample: because five of ten people were selected, there is a fifty-fifty chance, or .5 probability, of being selected into the sample. Because every member of the population had an equal chance of being selected (because a table of random numbers was used when you selected the first person to receive the questionnaire), it would be a random sample. The random sample is a special type of probability sample. It is the one that is used most often in quantitative public relations research.

Judgmental samples are not probability samples. Members of judgmental samples are selected based on subjective criteria—judgments—made by those conducting the research. It is impossible to calculate the probability of being selected into a judgmental sample. Consequently, it is impossible to generalize the results of research based on a judgmental sample to the larger population from which the sample was selected. Results based on a judgmental sample apply only to the specific members of the judgmental sample. It is possible to hypothesize from the results of the judgmental sample to a larger population, but such hypotheses would need to be tested in future research.

The assumption made about the statistics generated from probability samples is that, if an infinite number of similar size samples were selected, they would yield a statistical average that would vary plus or minus a certain margin of error from what the true population statistic would be if it were possible to conduct a census of every member of the population. In other words, if you were to go back into the room with ten people in it and follow the same procedure as before (asking every other person to complete the questionnaire), and you were to do this dozens of times—going from the room, coming back in, randomly selecting the first person to complete the questionnaire, distributing it to every other person, etc.—and you were to do this over and over, then you would generate scores of similar survey results. The average of all of these surveys would be a fairly accurate estimate of how everyone in the population would complete the questionnaire—which you could determine easily enough in this example by asking all ten people to complete the questionnaire. The assumption is that a statistic based on an infinite number of samples drawn from a population would vary plus or minus a certain margin of error, and that a graph of these dozens and dozens of sample estimates would take on the shape of a bell-shaped curve. See Figure 6.10.

Random Samples Reduce Sources of Error

The sources of error in survey sample statistics are many. They can be the result of differences in how people perceive different questions on the questionnaire, how tired or anxious they are when they fill out the questionnaire, or how the data are processed, or they can be the result of unusual things that happen while the survey is going on, such as people talking about their answers among friends before they complete the questionnaire. Often the assumption is made that these sources of error are randomly distributed among an infinite number of samples. If a random sample is used, the rationale is that the sources of error are reduced, but not eliminated.

Another assumption is that the larger the sample is, the smaller the margin of error will be; there will be less variance in the sample statistic. In other words, the larger the sample is, the tighter and more symmetrical the bell-shaped curve will be. Selecting a sample of two from the room of ten people will yield a statistic with lots of variance; the bell-shaped curve will vary widely from the true population statistic.

On the other hand, selecting a sample of nine from the room of ten people will yield a statistic with very little variance from the true population statistic. A sample of nine from a population of ten, however, would not be used in the field. When the population being studied has fewer than 100 members, a census, not a sample, is the preferred procedure.

Most samples need to be of a certain size to be able to generate stable bell-shaped curves. Samples of 30 or more generate statistics with relatively predictable variances. In practice, most samples in quantitative public relations research are much larger.

As sample size increases, the margin of error decreases. This is especially true as the sample size goes from 1 to 600. Above 600, as the sample size increases, the relative decrease in the margin of error becomes less and less. Figure 6.11 contains the margin of error based on increasing sample sizes for surveys yielding different percentages.

FIGURE 6.10

Distribution of many sample percentages about true population percentage. Reprinted with permission. Copyright © 1991 by Prentice-Hall Publishers. From *Using Public Relations Research* by Glen Broom and David Dozier.

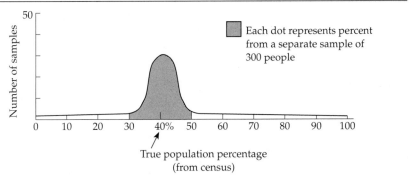

The percentages provided by many samples of the same size drawn from the same population will form a bell-shaped curve around the true population parameter.

Adapted from Earl Babbie, *The Practice of Social Research*, 5th ed. (Belmont, Calif., Wadsworth, 1986), p. A.32.

Selecting the right sample size is neither simple nor mysterious. It is a function of the cost of collecting the data plus the margin of error that can be tolerated by decision-makers. If money is no object, a public relations manager should consider conducting a census, a survey of all members of the population. More often than not, however, money is a definite factor in public relations research. Consequently, the manager needs to consider the advantages of conducting less expensive surveys using relatively small samples with larger margins of error, versus conducting more costly large-sample surveys which have much smaller margins of error. The deciding factor should be whether or not key decision-makers who will use the data need very small margins of error (plus or minus 3–4 percentage points, for example) or need simple approximations (plus or minus 10–15 percentage points). The answer to the constantly asked question in public relations research about sample size cannot be answered without considering the needs of specific decision-makers.

THREE CASE STUDIES INVOLVING QUANTITATIVE RESEARCH

The following case studies illustrate the use of quantitative research in public relations. The first case uses a before-only research design. The second case uses a before-after design. The third case uses a before-after quasi-experimental design with controls.

FIGURE 6.11

Margin of Error Chart for different sample sizes and different survey outcomes to compute the 95 percent confidence interval. Reprinted with permission. Copyright © 1991 by Prentice-Hall Publishers. From *Using Public Relations Research* by Glen Broom and David Dozier.

SIZE OF SAMPLE	SAMPLE OUTCOME (PERCENTAGES NEAR...)								
	10%	20%	30%	40%	50%	60%	70%	80%	90%
100	6	8	9	10	10	10	9	8	6
200	4	6	7	7	7	7	7	6	4
300	4	5	5	6	6	6	5	5	4
400	3	4	5	5	5	5	5	4	3
500	3	4	4	4	5	4	4	4	3
600	2	3	4	4	4	4	4	3	2
700	2	3	4	4	4	4	4	3	2
800	2	3	3	4	4	4	3	3	2
900	2	3	3	3	3	3	3	3	2
1000	2	3	3	3	3	3	3	3	2
1500	2	2	2	3	3	3	2	2	2
3000	2	2	2	3	3	3	2	2	2

Adapted from Earl Babbie, *The Practice of Social Research,* 5th ed. (Belmont, Calif., Wadsworth, 1986), p. A.32.

. . .

CASE 6.8:

Black and Decker Campaign: A Before-Only Design

One of the world's largest manufacturers of power tools and related products, Black and Decker, was interested in conducting an economic education campaign for its employees. Senior management was concerned that employees fully understand the economic constraints within which the company operated worldwide. The campaign primarily would involve placement of articles in company publications, distribution of bulletin board material, special contests, and an award program for employees.

Prior to designing the campaign, the director of public relations authorized that a study be conducted by an outside consulting group. The study was to be focused on employee sources of information and employee opinions about a wide range of economic issues, such as government regulation of profits, the impact of automation, and economic productivity in the United States. The survey also was to ask questions about certain economic facts, such as the corporation's net sales for the previous year, the definition for net profits, and the average U.S.-based manufacturer's annual net profit after taxes (the question was: is it 5 cents, 10 cents, 20 cents or 30 cents on the dollar of sales?). The public relations consulting firm subcontracted the technical aspects of the survey to a university-based research group. Here are the steps the research firm took to conduct the study:

1. The corporation's computerized personnel records were used to generate a random selection (based on every nth employee) that provided a

representative start sample of employees within the United States. The corporation gave the researchers three sets of pressure-sensitive mailing labels of a random sample of more than 600 employees from eight U.S. locations. The first set of labels was for the initial mailing; the second for the reminder postcard; and the third for recording returned questionnaires.

2. The consulting group and researchers designed the questionnaire and pretested it on a judgmental sample of 30 employees at the corporation's largest location. The pretest sample of employees was participating in a week-long training seminar, and, the director of public relations was able to have the seminar leaders devote a small portion of the workshop to having the employees complete the pretest. The analysis of the pretest indicated no major problems either in question wording or questionnaire flow patterns or later in processing the data and generating appropriate tables and graphs using the data.

3. Approximately 600 employees were mailed questionnaires, along with a cover letter from the corporate president. The cover letter explained the purpose of the study and that participation in the study was voluntary. The letter also explained that responses to the survey would be treated confidentially: only researchers associated with an independent research firm would see their individual responses, and none of their answers would be associated with their names or places of work. The letter stressed that they had been scientifically selected as part of a representative sample of all corporate employees and that their participation in the survey was very important to the overall success of the study. They were given postage-paid envelopes and two weeks in which to respond. One reminder postcard was mailed one week after the respondents received the questionnaire and cover letter.

4. Sixty percent of those surveyed responded in time with completed, useable questionnaires. Based on the following rough approximation, the margin of error was calculated to be plus or minus five percentage points: Margin of error = Square root of (1/sample size)*

5. To see if there were differences between the 40 percent who did not respond to the survey and the 60 percent who did, the proportion of

---

*The margin-of-error rule of thumb is based on the assumption that for a particular question, 50% will respond one way, and 50% will respond another way. If the assumption is that the survey will generate different statistics—for example, that the responses to a particular question will be 80% vs. 20%; or 90% vs. 10%; or, 99% vs. 1%—then, this rule of thumb, admittedly a crude estimate, would yield an even less accurate estimate of the margin of error. This rule of thumb is based on the assumption that 95 times out of 100, if the survey were repeated, the resulting sample statistic would be so close to the true population figure that it would be within the estimated margin of error.

A variation of this rule of thumb can be used to calculate sample size. The sample-size rule of thumb is:

$$\text{Sample size} = \text{Square root of } \frac{1}{\text{margin of error}}$$

management and nonmanagement employees in the return sample was compared to the proportion in the start sample. It turned out that slightly more managers responded than nonmanagers. In the final report, the researchers stated:

The facts that 1) the survey was designed to test interest in an economic education program and that 2) 40 percent of the employees did not respond would indicate that the results reported here represent the responses of employees with some minimum level of interest in the topic (only two percent of those who responded said they had no interest in such a program).

6. The final report included: an executive summary, background information on the situation leading up to the research, description of the methodology, discussion of the results, conclusions and recommendations. In the appendix was the questionnaire and response frequencies for each question. Some of the findings from the study were:
   a. The primary source of economic information for employees was "the grapevine," fellow employees. The employee's supervisor was the second major source, and company bulletin boards were the third most popular source of information.
   b. Relatively new employees and nonmanagers were more likely to report that the company did not keep them well informed; whereas, managers and senior employees said the company did keep them informed.
   c. For each of the four "fact" questions about economics, most who answered each question knew the right answer, except for the one about the average net profit of U.S. manufacturers (only 29 percent knew it to be approximately 5 cents on the sales dollar). Senior employees were more likely to know the correct net profit answer than junior employees.
   d. Each employee's "Economic I.Q." was calculated by giving a weight to correct responses to the four economic questions and summing the weights given to the four questions. Employees who correctly answered only one or two economic questions were classified as having a low Economic I.Q. Employees who answered three correctly were classified as having a moderately high Economic I.Q. And, employees who answered all four correctly were classified as having a high Economic I.Q. The employee's Economic I.Q. was cross-tabulated with other factors, which resulted in the following conclusions:
      1) The higher an employee's Economic I.Q., the more likely the employee was to reject the notion that big business doesn't care about "the effect of its actions on the individual," and the more favorable the employee's description was of the company's effort to disseminate information to employees.
      2) Managers had higher Economic I.Q.s than nonmanagers.
   e. Managers expressed more interest in the proposed economic education program than did nonmanagers.
7. The research report concluded by recommending that focus groups be conducted with samples of specific target audiences (such as nonmanagers

and new employees) to test various messages, and that similar mail surveys be conducted on a regular basis, which would allow trends about the impact of the campaign as it progressed to be tracked.
8. Because of budget constraints, but primarily because the public relations staff was confident it understood the kinds of economic information the employees wanted, the corporation implemented the economic education campaign without conducting focus groups. The public relations staff received very positive, informal feedback from both managers and nonmanagers about the campaign; consequently, they decided not to conduct any immediate follow-up surveys. Rather, they included questions measuring employee opinions and knowledge of economic issues in the corporation's periodic communication audits. The measures also indicated the campaign was effective.

This case is a good example of how a survey of employees can be used to help plan a communication program. The research had the potential, using a before-and-after design, to evaluate the impact of the economic education program. However, because decision-makers determined on their own that the program was a success, no follow-up survey was conducted. There was no need for additional quantitative information if senior decision-makers, using qualitative feedback from their peers and subordinates, already had made the decision to continue the program.

. . .

CASE 6.9:

D.C. Statehood Campaign by David Apter & Associates: A Before-After Design

Eighteen months before the 1988 presidential elections, a public relations firm was hired by the D.C. Statehood Commission to target the 1,600 delegates to the Democratic National Convention with the purpose of having the delegates, and the presidential candidates of both parties, seriously discuss the prospects for the District of Columbia to become the 51st state and be called the State of New Columbia. To prepare their winning proposal, and campaign, the agency took the following steps:

1. The agency conducted informal research by discussing with professional political advisors and others what kind of public relations campaign would persuade the delegates to pay attention to and react favorably to the notion of D.C. statehood. The key, they were told, was to demonstrate public support for the issue within each delegate's local area. The agency's winning proposal included funds for conducting two national public opinion polls: one, more than a year before, and the other, two months before, the Democratic National Convention.

2. The agency knew they would need to subcontract the technical aspects of conducting the survey. They could have solicited bids from various research firms; instead, they deliberately asked for the survey to be conducted by the research firm owned by the pollster used by then-President Reagan, Richard Wirthlin. The agency knew that if D.C. statehood were to occur, it most likely would yield two new Democratic senators and new Democratic members of the House of Representatives. Therefore, the issue was seen as one favoring the Democratic Party. The agency wanted its poll about the D.C. statehood issues conducted by a Republican pollster so the cynical media and doubting delegates might be persuaded the survey methodology was not biased and, therefore, might accept more readily the research findings. (Because project managers at Decision/Making/Information, which Wirthlin founded, initially looked upon the agency's proposal as a standard request for research services, a design for two surveys was discussed and a contract to conduct the first survey was signed without Wirthlin's direct knowledge.)
3. The president of the public relations agency, in cooperation with specialists from the research firm, developed five basic questions, plus a few about party affiliation and demographics. The basic questions were:
    a. Is Washington, D.C., a state?
    b. Did you know that even though Washington, D.C., has a greater population than four states, there are certain rights Washington, D.C., citizens do not have because it is not a state? For example, Washington, D.C., citizens pay taxes every year, serve in the military, and yet they have no representation in the Senate and only one non-voting delegate in Congress.
    c. Do you think the citizens of the District of Columbia should have the same rights as the citizens of the 50 states?
    d. As you may know, there is a bill before Congress that would allow Washington, D.C., to become a state. Do you agree or disagree with this bill?
    e. [If respondent disagreed with the statement in Q4:] What objections do you have to statehood for the District of Columbia?
4. The research firm used a random digit dialing procedure (with a quota on sex) to complete telephone interviews with approximately 500 men and 500 women. The firm generated thousands of random four-digit numbers, matched these with known area codes and prefixes throughout the continental United States, and placed more than 2,000 calls, in order to complete 1,000 interviews over a three-day period. There were many reasons for unuseable numbers and nonresponses: not-assigned phone numbers, non-residential numbers, no answers, busy signals, and no available adult 18 years of age or older. The interviews lasted less than ten minutes and were conducted by trained interviewers, in a central location, supervised by a telephone research specialist. Only one interview was conducted per household. The sample size of 1,000 yielded a margin of error of plus or minus three percentage points.
5. The results were:
    a. Approximately one of every four adults surveyed (23%) believed that the District of Columbia was a state.

b. Three out of five adults surveyed (60%) assumed that the citizens of the District of Columbia have the same rights as other citizens of the United States.
c. The majority of those surveyed (78%) believed the citizens of D.C. should have the same rights as the citizens of all 50 states.
d. Approximately half of those surveyed (52%) supported legislation to make "New Columbia" the 51st state.
e. The most frequently reported objection by respondents who disagreed with the notion of D.C. statehood was that it was "not a state now, so why make it one?"

6. While the national statistics were of interest to the agency because they could use them in press releases to the major news organizations and national media, the most important data from the survey were the breakout analyses provided for 11 key states: California, Florida, Illinois, Michigan, New Jersey, New York, Ohio, Texas, Pennsylvania, Georgia and North Carolina. The agency could use this information to localize the press releases in states that advocates for D.C. statehood said would be pivotal to the success of the campaign.
7. The public relations agency was under no obligation to release the data to the public: the research results were proprietary. The president of the agency said later that had the data not put the D.C. statehood issue in a favorable light, the survey results probably would not have been released but would have been used only for internal planning purposes. As a result of the first survey, particularly the large proportion of people who were undecided about the D.C. statehood issue, the campaign planners decided their best strategy was to use emotion-laden symbols and to stress patriotism, fairness and justice.
8. The agency generated a tremendous amount of press coverage when they released the first survey results, not only nationally but most importantly in the pivotal states. (After the initial surge of publicity about the survey, Wirthlin called the agency and informed them that his research firm was not interested in bidding on the second survey.)
9. After the success of the first survey, a range of additional publicity activities and special events (described in detail in Chapter 2), were conducted as part of the campaign.
10. More than a year after the first survey and two months prior to the Democratic National Convention, the second survey was conducted, this time by Opinion Research Corporation (ORC), one of the nation's largest public opinion polling organizations. While the identical questions were asked in both surveys, some of the methodology was different. Instead of customizing the survey by making a specific set of calls just to collect answers to five specific questions, as was done in the first survey, the second survey was integrated into a much larger Telephone Caravan Survey that ORC conducted for a large number of clients. One result of piggybacking the five questions onto the larger caravan survey was that it was less expensive to conduct the second survey. This is what ORC did for its caravan survey:
    a. As they did on a regular basis, they conducted a telephone survey of a national probability sample of approximately 500 men and 500 women 18 years of age and older living in private households in the United

States, excluding Alaska and Hawaii. The exact number of questions and number of clients involved in each caravan varied, but for each caravan, ORC made sure the questions flowed properly from one set to the next and that the entire survey took approximately 20 minutes to complete.

b. They protected the confidentiality of the respondents: none of their clients had access to the original data; ORC clients only received summary statistics for the specific set of questions they paid to have included in the survey.

c. All interviews were conducted in a central location under direct supervision of telephone research specialists.

d. A random digit dialing procedure was used to generate and match four random numbers with a selected set of area codes and prefixes. Screening procedures were used to eliminate nonresidential numbers. The research firm estimated the percentage of unuseable numbers and nonresponses, then prepared a start sample that would meet the stated goal of 1,000 completed interviews.

e. The start sample was divided randomly into subsets or replicates; each replicate was itself a national probability sample. The individual replicates were released one at a time to the pool of telephone interviewers. When the quota of approximately 500 men and 500 women was reached, the telephone interviewing was stopped.

11. When the two surveys were compared, there were statistically significant differences in all four quantitative measures, indicating more awareness of the D.C. statehood issues and more favorable opinions about D.C. becoming New Columbia. For example, the second survey indicated that approximately 40%—compared to 60% in the first survey—of those surveyed assumed that the citizens of the District of Columbia have the same rights as other citizens of the United States.

12. Breakout analyses of the second survey also allowed localized press releases to be prepared and distributed in targeted markets where key delegates to the Democratic National Convention lived. The survey results generated lots of publicity and sparked discussions among delegates and political candidates.

13. Beyond the publicity the surveys generated and the statistically significant differences "before" and "after," the success of the campaign was indicated by the Democratic Party voting to put a favorable statement about D.C. statehood in its official party platform, and in the serious discussions about the D.C. statehood that were engaged in by both the Republican and Democratic presidential candidates.

This case is an excellent example of the multiple uses of a before-after research design. The research results were used primarily to generate publicity for the campaign. Secondarily, the results were used to document the impact of the campaign, particularly within different regions of the country, so that planners could make appropriate adjustments in the campaign. The case is also an excellent example of how public relations managers use professional research firms. One implication of this case is that public relations practitioners do not need to know the technical side of research as much as they need to know how to design and administer research, and they need to know how to use the research results.

CASE 6.10:

"McGruff" Crime Prevention Campaign: A Before-After Quasi-Experimental Design with Controls

In 1979, in the wake of national concern over increasing crime, the National Crime Prevention Coalition initiated the "Take a bite out of crime" campaign, with its trench-coated "spokesdog," McGruff. In cooperation with the Advertising Council and the Dancer Fitzgerald Sample Advertising Agency (now DFS Dorland), the coalition sponsored a multi-media campaign that included:

1. Television and radio public service announcements;
2. Newspaper ads;
3. Publicity that highlighted a wide range of locally supported collateral activities, sponsored by law enforcement agencies, community groups, PTAs and other school organizations, and businesses:
    a. speaker's bureaus,
    b. community workshops,
    c. school programs, and
    d. neighborhood-watch programs.

Here are the steps the coalition took to plan and evaluate their campaign:

1. Qualitative research was conducted to test concepts and messages, and to determine appropriate media channels. The advertising agency conducted a series of focus groups with small judgmental samples of target audiences, including children 6 to 12 years of age, teenagers, adults, and the elderly. These formative studies found audiences perceived the McGruff character as non-threatening and humorous, yet authoritative. One of the recommendations from the formative research was to keep the crime prevention strategies positive and simple—for example, "don't forget to lock up at night," and "turn on the porch light"—and not to put messages in the campaign that might arouse fear.
2. To evaluate the implementation of the campaign, two special studies were conducted:
    a. A quasi-experimental panel survey of 426 adults in three representative cities were interviewed by phone just prior to the beginning of the campaign, and two years later, they were interviewed again.
    b. At the same time that the panel was interviewed the second time, two years into the campaign, a national probability sample of 1,200 adults was interviewed by phone.
    c. Both studies measured effectiveness by relating exposure to the campaign with:
        1) awareness of appropriate prevention techniques,
        2) positive attitudes toward citizen prevention actions,
        3) feeling personally efficacious about preventing crime,
        4) personal concern about crime, and
        5) taking various crime prevention actions.[13]

d. The result from all samples surveyed was that the majority had been exposed to the campaign; of those exposed, almost half said they had been reminded by the campaign of useful crime-prevention techniques, and a fourth indicated they had learned something new. The panel studies indicated significant differences between exposed and nonexposed citizens, particularly with regard to taking campaign-recommended actions to prevent crime. The national sample indicated almost one fourth of those exposed took the recommended actions.[12]

This case is an excellent example of a quasi-experimental research design used to test the impact of public relations programs. The costs in time and money to design and administer such a series of studies is significant, so there must be a compelling need for the research before such an undertaking occurs. Most often, the primary reason for conducting such elaborate research is that public funds are involved, and the public, through its representatives and various government agencies, insists that the expenditure of these funds be closely monitored. Conducting successful quasi-experimental public relations research, as was done in this case, requires a major commitment and an official mandate from members of the dominant coalition.

CHECKLIST FOR CONDUCTING RESEARCH

Here are appropriate steps for conducting public relations research:

1. Develop a precise statement of the problem to be investigated.
2. Spell out assumptions and explain theoretical relationships.
3. Determine the amount of money and time available.
4. Decide how best to collect and analyze the data:
    a. Define the population.
    b. Identify the sampling frame.
    c. Determine the appropriate sample size.
    d. Select the sample.
    e. Construct the measurement instrument.
    f. Pretest the instrument; pretest the design.
    g. Reduce or eliminate threats to validity.
    h. Make measurement procedures as reliable as possible.
    i. Know how to process and analyze the data—before it is collected. Hint: process and analyze fictitious "dummy" data.
    j. Prepare a timeline (Gantt or PERT chart).
    k. Prepare a budget and have it approved.
5. Collect the data:
    a. Prepare final version of instrument; make appropriate number of copies.
    b. Prepare office copies of distribution lists.
    c. Distribute instrument.

d. Monitor data collection procedures.
   e. Keep records of incoming instruments.
6. Process and analyze the data.
   a. Scan incoming instruments for glaring errors or omissions; establish a policy for dealing with these exceptional cases.
   b. Enter the data into the system (either hand tabulations or computers) and double-check to make sure there are no typographic or clerical errors.
   c. Prepare calculations, write computer software program, and "crunch" a sample of the data. Debug calculation procedures and/or computer programs.
   d. Initially calculate basic frequencies and double-check to make sure summary statistics internally agree with each other and with original input records.
   e. Then, run data through all calculations and prepare all appropriate tables, charts and graphs.
7. Present the results.
   a. Be direct. Write clearly. Stick to the facts.
   b. Prepare an executive summary in a style most acceptable to the decision-makers. If using an inverted pyramid style, first mention the major findings and recommendations, then essentials of the research methodology, then more findings, then more details about the research methodology, particularly strengths and weaknesses.
   c. Disclose the following information:
      1) Who sponsored the research, and who conducted it.
      2) The exact wording of questions asked, including the text of any instructions or explanations to researchers or respondents that might reasonably be expected to have affected the results.
      3) A definition of the population studied, including a description of the sampling frame (for example, the master list of names of potential respondents) used to identify this population.
      4) A description of the sample, for both probability and judgmental samples, that clearly indicates the method by which respondents were selected.
      5) The size of the sample and, if applicable, completion rates, eligibility criteria and screening procedures.
      6) A discussion of the precision of the findings that includes, if appropriate, an explanation of sources of sampling errors (for example, the margin of error, weighting techniques, and

other sample estimating procedures) and nonsampling errors (for example, nonresponses, inconsistent responses, biased responses, and data processing problems).
7) Which results were based on parts of a sample, rather than on the total sample.
8) Method, location, and dates of data collection.[13]
d. Include as many graphs and charts as possible.
e. Include testimonials and appropriate quotes from those involved in the research.
f. Make a preliminary report to a small group of elite decision-makers and include their comments and suggestions in the final version of the report.
g. Tailor research reports to specific target audiences. Hint: prepare several versions of the final report, and pretest them before they are distributed.
h. Prepare collateral material such as videotapes, slide presentations, workshop materials, feature articles, etc., including multi-media presentations.
8. Make judgments based on the research results.
a. Involve as many decision-makers as possible.
b. Recognize factors that work to "freeze and unfreeze" organizational change processes, the forces that work for and against innovation.[15]

SURVEY RESULTS

Table 6.1 presents the results of an analysis of survey data from more than 100 public relations professionals who participated in the mail survey described in Chapter 1 and elsewhere. The respondents were asked to indicate the probability that their organizations would engage in a variety of public relations research activities. They also were asked to indicate how frequently public relations professionals within their organizations were included in the dominant coalition. Several significant correlations are seen in Table 6.1:

1. Informally evaluating public relations is associated with analyzing clips and news reports, informal surveys of employees, and library research. Informal research is used both before and after a public relations program or campaign has been implemented.

2. Formally evaluating public relations is associated with before-after research designs, using focus groups, opinion polls of both internal and external publics, plus library research and other informal evaluation activities.

TABLE 6.1:

Correlation Matrix among Measures of Conducting Research Activities and the Frequency with Which Public Relations Professionals Are Included Within the Dominant Coalition. (n = 103)

	1	2	3	4	5	6	7	8	9	10	11
1. Conducting research before implementing a public relations activity or campaign											
2. Formally tracking legislation	.05										
3. Analyzing clips and news reports	.29**	.38***									
4. Conducting a focus group	.39***	.18	.19*								
5. Conducting a public opinion poll	.46***	.26**	.21*	.39***							
6. Conducting a formal survey of employees	.38***	.25**	.15	.35***	.59***						
7. Conducting an informal survey of employees	.31***	.23**	.38***	.18	.29**	.56***					
8. Doing library research	.18	.29**	.34***	.15	.12	.22*	.32***				
9. Informally evaluating public relations activities	.29***	.16	.46***	.08	.17	.11	.31***	.41***			
10. Conducting formal research after implementing a public relations activity to evaluate that activity	.66***	.19*	.29**	.43***	.56***	.47***	.29**	.32***	.35***		
11. Frequency of public relations professionals within organization being included in the dominant coalition	.24*	.19	.26**	.20*	.21*	.13	.06	.09	.17	.22*	

"Probability that Pearson's product-moment correlation coefficient is the result of chance: < .000 = ***; < .01 = **; < .05 = *.

Measures of conducting research activities based on 9-point scale of the "probability that your organization will engage in any of the following public relations activities in the next month."

Frequency of public relations professionals within organization being included in the dominant coalition based on 5-point scale from "very infrequently" to "very frequently."

3. The more frequently public relations professionals are included in the dominant coalition, the greater the probability that the organization will:
    * conduct research before implementing a public relations activity or campaign,
    * analyze press clippings and news reports,
    * conduct focus group research,
    * conduct public opinion polls, and
    * conduct formal research after implementing a public relations activity to evaluate that activity.

THE PLAN BOOK: PART IV

When presenting research data in The Plan Book, the rule is: Keep it simple. You should not assume research specialists are the principal audience of any planning document. Most decision-makers reading The Plan Book will not be technical specialists. Consequently, all technical data, complicated formulae, involved tables, charts, and graphs—if they are essential to the document—should be placed in an appendix. Only easy-to-understand (this does not mean simplistic) tables, charts, and graphs should be placed in the body of the document.[14]

Humanize impersonal research data in The Plan Book, and in presentations, as much as possible. For example, the public relations agency described in Case 4.6 conducted baseline research about the client's community that resulted in lots of data. But, when they made their presentation of this data to the client, they illustrated it with slides of the community, using only one or two key facts per slide.

The public relations agency of Porter/Novelli once conducted research that allowed them to develop a profile of the typical traveler to the client's resort island community. Instead of presenting impersonal statistics at the client presentation, the agency wrote a special day-in-the-life-of script, hired an actress and, at the right moment in the presentation, introduced her as a living model of the target audience profile. The actress not only explained her lifestyle and her travel plans but also answered questions from her unique perspective.

ALTERNATIVE REASONS FOR CONDUCTING RESEARCH

We have presented a number of solid, good reasons for conducting research: primarily to help plan, implement, and evaluate public relations programs and campaigns. Here are some not-so-obvious and not-so-ethical reasons for conducting research:

1. To document decisions that have already been reached.

   Sometimes a public relations manager will have too little time initially to conduct research and will have to make a series of decisions about launching a program or campaign based on "soft data," hunches, and professional experience. Later, to convince others (such as clients and members of senior management) and to bolster current opinions and attitudes among key decision-makers, the public relations manager will conduct research to document these earlier decisions.

2. To go along with a corporate culture that supports lots of research, but with little or no intention of using the results directly in planning or evaluating a program or campaign.

Some organizations have a tradition of conducting communication audits, readership surveys, opinion polls, and content analyses of press clippings and trade publications. Yet, some managers in these organizations do not use the results of the research to the degree that they could because the results are not produced in a timely fashion. Managers find the results interesting but out of sync with when they need to make decisions.

3. To keep staff busy.

   Routine, institutionalized research, such as that cited above, while it may not meet the specific needs of certain decision-makers, does keep support staff busy with what appears to be meaningful work.

4. To sabotage this or another activity.

   Sometimes research is authorized by certain members of a dominant coalition because they anticipate results that can be used to stop or curtail a disputed program or campaign. This tactic most often occurs when there are disputes among members of management about goals and objectives, particularly between departments with overlapping functions, such as marketing, advertising, and public relations.

5. To make a greater profit from a client's campaign.

   Some types of research, particularly before-after and time-series designs, can be very profitable for an agency to conduct. So, sometimes research is recommended to the client not so much to aid decision-making but to increase the agency's profit on the account.

ETHICS IN PUBLIC RELATIONS RESEARCH

As the examples above illustrate, research in public relations can be conducted for both ethical and unethical reasons. As Dozier and Broom point out, public relations research is an organizational change process that has implications not only for decision-makers but also for members of target audiences for public relations programs and campaigns.[16] Because research can force people to think and act differently, it is important that it be conducted ethically, that participants and decision-makers not be used in a coercive, dishonest, or hurtful manner.

The American Association for Public Opinion Research (AAPOR) has established ethical standards which apply to public relations research:

1. Give full disclosure of research procedures.
2. Make sure results are accurately reported and distributed as freely and as widely as possible.
3. Keep respondent information confidential (or anonymous), as promised.

4. Do not overpromise clients and sponsors by promising what cannot be delivered.
5. Do no harm.

As it is with most professional and personal behavior, the key to ethical public relations research is honesty, honesty with oneself and with others. Ethical public relations managers acknowledge to themselves and to others both the obvious and not-so-obvious reasons they have for conducting research. Ethical public relations managers explain to potential respondents what the research is about, and in enough detail so that the respondents understand its purpose and can make an intelligent decision about participation. At the same time, they do not give information which might bias the participants' responses, should they choose to participate. Ethical public relations managers explain to potential respondents who is sponsoring the research and why the respondents' participation is valued by the sponsor.

Ethical researchers do what they say they are going to do: they deliver research data to decision-makers, as promised; and they protect the confidentiality and anonymity of respondents. Promising confidentiality means protecting the identity of respondents from others who are not members of the research team. Promising anonymity means setting up procedures so that even the research team does not know the identity of the respondents.

Doing no harm in public relations research means giving potential respondents a comfortable, graceful way to decline participation, not asking questions that put the persons at risk or that might exacerbate or cause psychological problems, and protecting the respondents' right to privacy.

IN SUMMARY . . .

Systematic public relations research may be exploratory, confirmatory, informal, formal, qualitative or quantitative. The key set of questions to answer when designing public relations research is: What to measure? Whom to measure? And, when to measure? A decision-tree, based on the answers to these three questions, was presented to help select an appropriate research design. Common steps occur in the research process; these steps were illustrated in numerous cases in this chapter, and a checklist for conducting public relations research was presented.

Survey results indicate that formal research in public relations is associated with organizations that have close relationships between the public relations staff and members of the dominant coalition, and with complex organizations faced with a great deal of uncertainty. The survey also found that most public relations managers engage in informal research as a normal part of their job.

The ethical issues of public relations research primarily concern fully disclosing methodologies, protecting respondents' right to privacy, and doing no harm. Public relations managers who are honest with themselves and others about the reasons for doing the research will be in the best position to conduct ethical public relations research.

Study Questions

1. What is research? What is a research design? What three questions are important to answer when designing research?
2. What are the basic steps in the research process? Give examples of the kinds of issues that should be addressed at each step.
3. Describe a public relations campaign of your own choosing that includes independent, moderating, intervening, and dependent variables. Be sure to specify conceptual and operational definitions of each set of variables.
4. Give examples of each and explain the advantages and disadvantages of the following research designs: before-after with no control publics; before-after with true control publics; and before-after with nonequivalent publics.
5. What is the "garbage can" theory of research?
6. Describe how you would go about designing and executing media content analysis to help plan and implement a public relations campaign.
7. Describe how you would conduct a series of at least four focus groups to help plan and evaluate a public relations campaign.
8. What are the advantages and disadvantages of random and judgmental samples?
9. Write a brief checklist for conducting a mail survey of readers of a company publication. What size sample would you use, and why?
10. True or false: the more frequently public relations professionals are included in the dominant coalition, the more frequently they will conduct focus groups, public opinion polls, and media content analyses. Explain your answer.
11. What are unethical reasons for conducting public relations research? What can you do to offset or eliminate such unethical research strategies?
12. What are some of the ethical standards of the American Association for Public Opinion Research?

Endnotes

1. Kerlinger, Fred, *Foundations of Behavior Research,* 2nd edition (New York, NY: Holt, Rinehart and Winston, 1973) p. 406.
2. Lindenmann, Walter, "Research, evaluation and measurement: A national perspective," *Public Relations Review,* Summer, 1990, pp. 3–16.
3. Marshall, Catherine, and Gretchen Rossman, *Designing Qualitative Research* (Newbury Park, CA: Sage, 1989).
4. Ibid.
5. Dozier, David M., "Breaking public relations glass ceiling," *Public Relations Review,* Vol. 14, No. 3, Fall, 1988, pp. 6–14.
6. Kerlinger, *op.cit.*

7. Fitz-Gibbon, Carol Taylor, and Lynn Lyons Morris, *How to Design a Program Evaluation*, one of a series of books in the *Program Evaluation Kit*, edited by these two specialists from the Center for the Study of Evaluation at the University of California-Los Angeles (Beverly Hills, CA: Sage, 1978).

8. Martin, Joanne, "A garbage can model of the research process," in *Judgment Calls in Research*, by Joseph McGrath, Joanne Martin, and Richard Kalka (Beverly Hills, CA: Sage, 1982) pp. 17–39.

9. The Right Brain, Inc., 970 Ford Centre, 420 N. Fifth Street, Minneapolis, MN 55401, (612) 334-5620.

10. Quoted in a column by Tom Eisenhart, "Proof that PR works," in *Business Marketing*, March, 1989.

11. O'Keefe, Garrett J., "Taking a bite out of crime: The impact of a public information campaign," *Communication Research*, Vol. 12, 1985, pp. 147–178.

12. O'Keefe, Garrett J., "The 'McGruff' national media campaign: Its public impact and future implications," in D. Rosenbaum (ed.), *Community Crime Prevention: Does it Work?* (Beverly Hills, CA: Sage, 1986), pp. 252–268.

13. Based on the March 1986 Code of Professional Ethics and Practices of the American Association for Public Opinion Research, Princeton, New Jersey, by permission.

14. Tufte, Edward R., *The Visual Display of Quantitative Information* (Cheshire, CN: Graphics Press, 1983).

15. Broom, Glen, and David Dozier, *Using Research in Public Relations: Applications to Program Management* (Englewood Cliffs, NJ: Prentice Hall, 1990).

16. Ibid, especially Chapter 14, pp. 294–313.

CHAPTER SEVEN

How to Analyze and Evaluate Public Relations Using Systems Concepts—and a Special Checklist

. . . . .

*B*rian, who had been recently promoted to the position of director of community relations, pulled from his office bookshelf a copy of one of his favorite professional books, Manager's Public Relations Handbook, by Nathaniel Sperber and Otto Lerbinger.[1] It contained a series of checklists for managing different types of public relations activities, from crises and contingency plans to financial relations and special events. He asked his secretary to make a photocopy of one of the checklists.

Later, Brian edited the checklist so that it fit the public relations program he was planning. He had his secretary type a finished version of the revised checklist, and she made multiple copies so that Brian could hand them out at a planning meeting he was scheduling for later that week.

Brian liked using checklists because he found that even though they were constantly being revised and updated, they were useful devices for building consensus and getting commitments from staff for performing various public relations tasks.

Before writing a memo that afternoon to the staff about the planning meeting's agenda, Brian scanned another checklist he had; this one was about conducting effective meetings.

. . . .

STRENGTHS AND WEAKNESSES OF CHECKLISTS

As a relatively new manager, Brian used checklists not only to make sure that his staff considered all options, but also to make sure he did not forget or overlook any aspects of managing his department.

Checklists help remind people of their options. They can give a new perspective on a program or campaign. Because they are often based on the hard-earned experience of others, they also can provide a sense of security, especially for new managers.

But, checklists have their disadvantages. They are rarely definitive; they always seem to leave something out, which is why they constantly need to be revised. Unless they are revised, they do not focus on the unique aspects of a situation.

Checklists need to be used with caution. They are useful management tools for prompting discussions, building consensus, and reminding others of tasks that need to be done.

THE MASTER CHECKLIST

Because all the questions in the checklist are not appropriate for all programs and campaigns, a unique set of questions should be prepared for any specific program or campaign. The master checklist is presented only as a starting point—not as the final word—in a discussion about how to analyze and evaluate a specific program or campaign. A more specific checklist can be prepared by checking off those questions from the master checklist that are most relevant, revising others, and adding new questions.

The questions in the following master checklist focus on the major topics covered in the first six chapters: 1) identifying problems, 2) setting goals and objectives, 3) defining publics and relationships, 4) planning, 5) budgeting, and 6) conducting public relations research and evaluations.

Identifying problems:

_____ 1. What is the background on the situation the public relations program or campaign is designed to address? Is it a problem or an opportunity? What are the factors that have caused the current situation?

_____ 2. Has there been a formal inquiry into the need for this public relations program or campaign? If so, what is it? If not, is there any documentation available that would justify planning and launching an appropriate public relations effort? What kind of documentation would be appropriate? Where would you go to get it?

_____ 3. Who has a stake in maintaining the status quo? Who wants to change the status quo? Who else is interested in the situation? What are the values, loyalties, and principles of the stakeholders? How do they define the problem (or opportunity)? Is there consensus on the definition of the situation? What can you do to help facilitate this consensus?

____ 4. How have the issues involved in this situation been "framed"—that is to say, what is the picture that is being presented to others about this situation? What kind of "spin" or viewpoint is being given to the facts in the situation, and who is involved in framing and spinning the issues?

Setting goals and objectives:

____ 5. What are the goals of the public relations program or campaign? What are the outcome goals: specifically, what kinds of impact will the campaign or program have on targeted publics? What are the process goals: specifically, what kinds of "internal" management goals (such as meeting deadlines, exceeding minimum quality standards) are necessary in order to achieve the desired outcome goals? Is there consensus on both outcome and process goals? Who has been or needs to be involved in reaching consensus on the goals?

____ 6. What are the objectives of the public relations program or campaign? For each process and outcome goal, what are specific objectives, concrete actions, that are designed to achieve the stated goal?

____ 7. What is the theory behind this public relations program or campaign? What is the rationale or set of assumptions that logically connects the process goals and objectives to the desired outcome goals and objectives? What is supposed to happen? What causes what? What sequence of events is assumed to occur if the program or campaign is to be considered successful? What is the timetable for this sequence of events?

Defining publics and relationships:

____ 8. What publics are involved? What are the existing attitudes and behaviors of these various publics?

____ 9. Who specifically is to be exposed to the public relations program or campaign? When do you plan to expose these publics to the program or campaign? How will you know if and when people have been exposed?

Planning, including research and evaluation efforts before implementation:

____ 10. What resources are required to implement this public relations program or campaign—people, supplies, equipment, outside consultants, professional services, etc.?

____ 11. Who is responsible for seeing that various activities occur?

____ 12. What are the limitations of this campaign or program? What alternative activities are not being engaged in, for whatever

Chapter 7 How to Analyze and Evaluate Public Relations   261

reason, that could help make this public relations effort more successful? Why are these alternatives not being included at this time?

____ 13. Who is concerned about the outcome of this program or campaign? Who might or should be interested in the outcome, and why? How have these concerned individuals been involved in the planning of the campaign? If some of these concerned individuals have not been involved in planning activities, why not?

____ 14. What is the purpose of any evaluation of this program or campaign: to help improve the program or campaign (formative evaluation); to assess the overall impact of the program or campaign (summative evaluation); or, some combination of the two?

____ 15. What kinds of decisions are expected to be based on the results of this evaluation? Who are these decision-makers? What kind of information about the program or campaign do they require, and when do they require it?

____ 16. How is "success" or "effectiveness" for this program or campaign to be defined? Is it to be determined by an internal group of managers—the organization's dominant coalition? Or, is it to be determined by external publics and groups—criteria of success (or failure) that will be imposed by others outside the immediate control of the organization? Is there consensus on this definition? How can you facilitate consensus?

____ 17. What are the limitations to the evaluation you have planned? Are certain aspects of the public relations program or campaign not being considered in this evaluation? How generalizable will the results of your evaluation be?

____ 18. What kind of research design should be used to evaluate the activity? What factors should be taken into account and controlled? What factors should be manipulated? What steps should be taken to avoid confounding factors?

____ 19. What factors, events, or situations prevent you from using a more rigorous research design? What are these factors? How will they limit the results of your evaluation?

____ 20. How do you propose to measure in concrete terms the results of the public relations program or campaign? How valid and reliable are these measurement instruments and procedures? How are these measures related to the outcome goals? Are they an exact measure of what the program or campaign is designed to accomplish, or are they approximations?

____ 21. How are data to be collected? How often? By whom? Do you anticipate any problems in collecting the data? What are these problems?

____ 22. What crucial aspects of the activity are to be observed, recorded, or otherwise measured? Why did you choose to measure these aspects of the program or campaign and not others?

____ 23. What limitations or deficiencies are there in the procedure you plan to use to evaluate the program or campaign? What other factors that might influence expected results need to be considered?

____ 24. How can you present the research results: how many people were influenced by the problem (or opportunity); how do target publics think and behave; what activities were implemented as planned; how many people were exposed; what impact was observed; etc.? How will "before" and "after" data be compared: parallel bar graphs; trendlines? What descriptive statistics and other forms of empirical analysis will you use? What kinds of tables and graphs will you use?

____ 25. What kinds of soft data can you present: informal observations, testimonials, anecdotes, etc.?

____ 26. How certain will you be that the activity caused the results you observe? Are there alternative explanations for anticipated results? What are these alternative explanations?

____ 27. How would you measure public attitudes and behavior if there were to be no public relations program or campaign as is currently planned? How can you measure characteristics of those not exposed to the public relations program or campaign?

____ 28. If a control group is to be used, how can you tell if the treatment group performed differently? How will you know if this difference between control and treatment groups is statistically significant? How will you know if this is a meaningful difference?

____ 29. Will you be able to tell if certain aspects of the program are more effective than others? How will you know this?

Budgeting:

____ 30. What method can you use to compute costs and benefits? Is there some formula you can use? How can you arrive at these estimates informally? How have others calculated similar costs and benefits? How confident can you be of these cost/benefit estimates? How much confidence will others place in the estimates?

____ 31. What are costs associated with the program or campaign? How much money for supplies, equipment, professional services, staff time, media time, etc., is expected to be spent on the activity? How might this money have been used if it had not been earmarked for this public relations effort? What portion of the monies spent accounts for start-up costs (pretesting, initial construction and production costs, demonstration work, etc.), and what portion might be considered on-going if the program or campaign were to be continued?

____ 32. What are the non-dollar costs of the program or campaign? How might the program adversely affect either those who work on it with you, or those who are exposed to it? Will those who work on the program or campaign be missing other career opportunities which they value? What opportunities might not be taken by those who are likely to be exposed to and participate in the public relations program or campaign? Will any harm be done by any aspect of the public relations program or campaign?

____ 33. What are the dollar benefits? Will people directly contribute or spend money that immediately will go to sponsoring organizations? How will you know that they made this dollar contribution as a direct result of being exposed to the public relations program or campaign?

____ 34. What are the non-dollar benefits? How much progress do you anticipate toward the achievement of the public relations goals? How big a difference in the problem (and in the cost of this problem to the sponsoring organization) do you expect if the activity is a success? How might your expected results from this public relations activity compare to its cost to the organization, if there had been no such program and the status quo were maintained? Might there not be some unanticipated benefits, such as reactions of unintended publics, or extremely favorable responses by secondary publics?

Evaluating, after implementation:

____ 35. What judgments can be made about the program or campaign based on your evaluation? What judgments should be deferred until a more comprehensive evaluation can be conducted? Did this evaluation overlook anything that should be investigated later?

____ 36. What recommendations can you make, based on this evaluation? What kind of predictions about probable sequences of events for similar types of public relations programs or campaigns can you make after analyzing the results of this evaluation?

___ 37. What questions remain about the effectiveness of this public relations effort? How might the evaluation of this or a similar program or campaign be improved in the future?

___ 38. How can you best summarize the effectiveness of this public relations program or campaign, and how might it be improved in the future?

TWO CASE STUDIES COMPARED

The master checklist can be modified to fit all types of campaigns and programs. The following pair of case studies illustrates how organizational publications and media relations can be analyzed and evaluated using the checklist. The cases also illustrate how systems concepts can be used to help explain and predict public relations.

. . .

CASE 7.1:

Towson State University's Publications

With reduced funds from the state, the problem facing the director of university relations for Maryland's second largest public university was to eliminate one of his publications and still keep the campus and key publics informed of the hundreds of diverse activities occurring on campus each semester. His office published a popular weekly newsletter for faculty and staff. The handsome alumni magazine was one of the university's most important publications. A relatively new publication, a once-a-semester calendar of events for the neighborhood community, would have to be reconsidered.

. . .

CASE 7.2:

Giant Food's Publications

The challenge facing the vice president of public affairs for the region's largest grocery store chain was to revise and expand his publications so that more in-depth articles could be published. Giant Foods Inc. was faced with increasingly complex issues that needed more extensive coverage in the company publications. The employee newspaper was, in many ways, the corporation's flagship publication. Making changes in this publication would require careful consideration. Someone without the experience and skills of the vice president of public affairs might have approached this challenge differently.

Key Factors

In these two case studies, the amount of pre-publication planning and post-publication evaluation varied from organization to organization. One organization was faced with problems of budget reductions; the other was experiencing economic growth. While these environmental factors affected decisions about the organizations' publications, the pressures were not as important as other factors. The two most important factors affecting the planning and evaluation of the publications were the different technologies of the two organizations, and the relationships between the public relations practitioners and the dominant management coalitions.

The technology of the university was nonroutine. This meant there was a wide variety of relatively well-educated publics which, because they were so numerous, often had to be ranked in importance. It also meant the university needed to publish a style manual to guide editing decisions concerning the dozens of departmental brochures and program publications.

The technology of the grocery store chain was routine. This meant there were relatively few key internal publics, each of which was vitally important to the corporation. As the market share and number of stores and employees increased, the complexity of the issues affecting the organization increased, which was reflected often in the contents of the organizational publications.

The close relationship of the vice president of public affairs with the dominant management coalition of the grocery store chain facilitated his making significant decisions about the flagship publication. He held many informal meetings with his colleagues and used his close relationships to help guide his decisions about the redesign of the publication.

The Similarities

Both large organizations—one, a diversified state institution of higher education, and the other, a publicly owned, profit-oriented company—used a variety of publications to meet the informational needs of their key publics. There were strong similarities in how the two sets of publications were established, edited, and managed.

The organizations were similar in terms of capital assets, number of employees and geographic regions of influence. Both were very large institutions with distinct corporate cultures. The two organizations also were similar in the size and professional qualifications of their editorial staffs. Both had one person write, edit and manage the publications and report to one supervisor, who served as a managing editor. Both editors were women with solid journalism credentials and fewer than ten years seniority with their organizations; both supervisors were men with extensive experience managing public affairs.

The Differences

A significant difference between the two organizations was the relationship between the senior public relations practitioner and top management. The senior public relations practitioner for the grocery store chain had been with the company for more than two decades and was a vice president and member of the senior executive staff. The senior public relations practitioner for the university had been with the university for fewer than five years. He did not have as close a relationship to the central administration of the university as the grocery store public relations executive did with his top management.

The most significant difference between these two organizations was their core technologies: the essential work of each organization influenced not only decision-making, but also the number and kind of target audiences and, consequently, the content of their publications.

The core technology of the grocery store chain was fairly routine: vast quantities of consumable goods were moved through the stores. Decision-making was highly centralized. The primary goal of the grocery store chain, which was one of the nation's first to use optical scanners at checkout counters and to fully computerize inventory control and accounting systems, was to make a profit by processing and distributing quality consumables as efficiently as possible.

The core technology of the state university was nonroutine: a great variety of students, faculty, and staff lived and worked on the sprawling, suburban campus. The primary purpose of the university, with its numerous academic programs and research facilities, was to generate and disseminate knowledge. Decision-making was decentralized. There were scores of different academic disciplines, each with its own set of goals and objectives, and some with quasi-independent sources of revenue through federal, state, regional, and private funding agencies. Academic freedom was encouraged. As a state institution, it was subject to financial constraints. But, as a major university, its goal was not to process as many students as efficiently as possible; its primary goal was to provide quality education.

The technologies of the two organizations generated different types of internal and external publics. The two organizations had different kinds of target audiences. The university had a more educated and diversified set of key publics than the grocery store chain, which had more homogeneous and less well-educated publics. Consequently, the contents of the publications were different for the two organizations. The publications for the grocery store chain, targeted to broadly defined publics, emphasized quality customer service and teamwork. The university publications, targeted to narrowly defined publics, presented information that showed the diversity of activities and talents of individuals at the university.

Public Relations at the University

The Office of University Relations published a weekly calendar/newsletter, primarily for internal publics; an alumni magazine three times a year; an annual recruiting magazine for prospective students; and, an annual state-of-the-university report for state legislators and others. The university relations staff also collected and distributed current press clippings for senior administrators, and they assisted the university's development and fund-raising activities, alumni relations, and student recruitment. Each of these activities was a line item in the annual budget of the Office of University Relations.

Staff within the Office of University Relations regularly wrote and distributed news releases, and they coordinated community and media relations for the university. Several university departments and academic programs, at different times, with various sources of funds, produced their own publications. Consequently, the university relations staff published a campus-specific style manual to be used when writing copy for department brochures and other publications.

For several semesters, the Office of University Relations published a calendar of events distributed once a semester to nearby neighbors of the suburban university. The calendar was an "experiment" by the director of public relations, who produced several issues with funds from his general operating budget; the calendar was not a line item in his annual budget.

Public Relations at the Grocery Store Chain

The grocery store chain published a 24–page, two-color bimonthly tabloid and a 32–page quarterly magazine for employees. To encourage a spirit of family as part of the corporate culture, the public affairs office established a policy of always referring to employees as "staffers" or "associates."

The public affairs staff also published an annual financial report for employees, which augmented the separately published stockholders' annual report. In addition, they published periodic internal news bulletins which were sent to key personnel, called "communicators." They subscribed to press clipping and media scanning services and regularly sent copies of appropriate articles and transcripts of TV and radio coverage of interest to key members of management. Occasionally, the Public Affairs Office helped different departments publish special brochures by coordinating the production of copy, art, pictures, layout and design elements.

In addition to publications, the Public Affairs Office for the grocery store chain also helped to produce short videotapes about current corporate activities, which were viewed in "break rooms" by staffers at individual grocery stores. They helped coordinate both annual award ceremonies for employees and corporate donations to local charities and others in the community. The Public Affairs Office also was responsible for government and community affairs, and for media relations.

Planning and Production Schedules

To provide timely news to internal publics, the university published a weekly calendar that was filled with department news, grant deadlines, cultural activities, and other information supplied primarily by administrators, department secretaries, and individual faculty members. The grocery store chain published internal news releases, called "news bulletins," for those key personnel designated by their departments or stores as "communicators." The communicators then determined if these news bulletins should be disseminated to others within their departments or stores.

For both organizations, the network of "correspondents," who supplied information for the publications and the relatively inexpensive and quick methods of production, combined to make planning and production schedules for these publications minimal and fairly routine. In contrast, planning and production schedules for the grocery store chain's 2–color, 24–page bimonthly employee newspaper, and for the university's 2–color, 32–page quarterly alumni magazine were more sophisticated.

How the Grocery Store Chain Published Its Employee Newspaper

These are the steps the grocery store chain's editor took to publish the employee tabloid newspaper:

1. She discussed story ideas and picture possibilities with the vice president of public affairs and others and reached a consensus about copy for a particular issue two months in advance of the publication date. The organization was so large and predictable in its set of activities (community activities, employee awards, store awards, new stores, waste reduction efforts, consumer relations programs, etc.) that the annual content of the six tabloids was fairly predictable. Although the layout and design, the precise set of stories, the way the stories were written, and the emphasis a writer would give to the stories would vary, but the publication's overall content was predictable.
2. She wrote a memo to the vice president confirming specific stories, pictures, and art for a specific issue. Often, she would prepare thumbnail sketches of page layouts for a specific issue.

3. She wrote memos to the people involved in publishing the newsletter, informing them about the production schedule. This is what the production schedule memo looked like:

Number of work days allowed

	Photos due to editor	date
	All copy to editor	date
5	In-position type/proof due editor	date
2	Proofing complete	date
3	Mechanical complete	date
2	Final proof/type corrections made	date
3	Printing	date

4. She supervised the production of the publication, making sure activities were performed on time, and if they were not, she made adjustments in the schedule.
5. She had the printed newspaper delivered to a private mailing firm which mailed the publications directly to employees.

How the State University Published Its Alumni Magazine

The university relations office established fairly formal planning procedures and detailed production schedules for its three-times-a-year alumni publication. These are the steps the university's editor took to publish the alumni magazine:

1. She discussed story ideas and picture possibilities with the director of university relations and others, and reached a consensus about copy for a particular issue at least two months in advance of the publication date. The organization was so diversified, with so many story possibilities, that there was never a problem identifying possible articles.
2. She wrote memos to the people involved in publishing the newsletter, informing them about the production schedule. She often would prepare thumbnail sketches of page layouts, which would accompany these memos. This is what the editor's production schedule looked like:

Alumni magazine planning

    Issue date _____

    Copy deadline _____

    To Design Department _____

    To printer _____

    In the mail _____

    Production schedule out _____

Memos to
- Deans, Vice Presidents _____
- Institutional Advancement _____
- Bookstore _____
- President _____
- University Club _____
- Student Government _____
- Continuing Studies _____

Meetings
- Alumni/Development _____
- University Relations and the Design Department _____
- Copy deadline meeting _____
- Pre-pasteup meeting _____
- Post-issue meeting _____

3. She supervised the production of the publication, making sure activities were performed on time, and if they were not, she made adjustments in the schedule.
4. She had a private firm mail the magazines to alumni.

Common Steps in Publishing

These are some of the common steps both public relations staffs took as they originally developed their organization's publications:

1. Determined the need for the publications through informal discussions with senior management, department heads, and others. The Office of University Relations rarely conducted formal research to help plan or evaluate its publications. The Public Affairs Office of the grocery store chain would, at critical times, conduct formal employee surveys and communication audits.
2. Established goals and objectives for the publications by developing within the staff an appropriate document and circulating it for approval by senior members of management.
3. Identified types of stories, pictures, and art requirements. To do this, both wrote and circulated regular memos regarding story ideas and picture possibilities to key executives for their comments and suggestions.
4. Set up a network of news sources and established standard operating procedures for supplying editors with stories and picture possibilities.
5. Made arrangements with photographers, design artists, and printers that were within budget constraints.
6. Established copy-approval and production schedules for each publication.

7. Oversaw the production and distribution of the publications.
8. Evaluated the effectiveness of the publications on a continuing basis. Both staffs considered the need for the publications to be justified so long as there was an abundant and timely supply of information to the editors.

How the Grocery Store Chain Evaluated Its Publications

Periodically, the Public Affairs Office conducted formal surveys and communication audits to help evaluate the impact of employee communication activities. For one study, all employees received a questionnaire on the job and mailed their responses to an independent researcher, who also conducted a focus group with a judgmental sample of employees who discussed their reactions to the publications.

Recently, in response to senior management's desire to cover in greater depth some of the more complex issues facing the corporation, the vice president for public affairs conducted a series of informal meetings with key employees to discuss design options for the publications. Following this series of meetings, the staff decided to reduce the frequency of some publications and to redesign and expand others.

After the decision was made to redesign and reduce the frequency of the employee monthly publication, the design artists developed several different mock-up issues for evaluation by the staff. After the public relations staff shared some of the design possibilities with a limited number of key publics, the vice president for public affairs selected what he considered to be the best new design. An announcement of the redesign decision was made in the next issue of the "old" monthly publication, and then the redesigned employee newspaper was published once every two months.

The most frequently used method of evaluating the publications at the grocery store chain was informal: listening to what others said; being aware of complaints, comments, and suggestions; and conducting special meetings. Occasionally, however, when major decisions were to be made about the communication programs, the Public Affairs Office contracted an outside research consultant to design and conduct formal evaluation studies.

How the State University Evaluated Its Publications

The only form of evaluation done by the Office of University Relations of its alumni magazine and other publications was informal. In response to an expected reduction in funds from the state, the director of university relations reviewed his set of publications and decided to eliminate the biannual calendar sent to nearby community residents. He based his decision upon informal feedback and upon his judgment that this reduction would cause the university the least difficulty. When there were no major complaints from the residents who no longer received the publication, the director assumed that he had made the correct decision.

Common Evaluation Criteria

Both organizations evaluated their publications. For the university, the public relations director evaluated the publications informally through discussions with key members of the staff. For the grocery store chain, some key questions about the publications were answered more formally at special meetings and by specially commissioned surveys.

For both organizations, these are the major questions the public relations staff asked when they evaluated their publications:

1. Is there a steady supply of story ideas and picture possibilities?
2. Is proposed copy approved on time?
3. Are copy, pictures, and art ready on time?
4. Is the design ready on time?
5. Is typesetting completed on time?
6. Are galleys ready and corrected on time?
7. Is the "blueline" from the printer okayed on time?
8. Is the publication printed per specifications, and on time?
9. Is the publication distributed on time?
10. Was the publication received as planned?
11. Was there any negative feedback?
12. Were there any direct compliments?
13. How favorable or unfavorable were any overheard conversations or other observations of readers?
14. Were there any requests for additional copies?
15. How favorable or unfavorable were comments made at specific meetings?
16. What were the results of informal and formal surveys of readers?

Two Unique Yet Predictable Solutions

With state funding reductions in effect, the problem facing the director of university relations for the state university was solved by eliminating the biannual community calendar. The rationale was that while this publication was on target and effective, its absence would have the least impact on university relations. The community calendar also had been an experiment. It had not been designated an official publication within the director's annual budget; rather, it was being produced with funds from his general operating budget. Eliminating this publication required the least amount of administrative approval. No one formally asked community residents if they missed the publication, and no informal negative feedback was received.

The problem facing the vice president of public affairs for the grocery store chain—to provide more coverage of increasingly complex issues—was solved by redesigning the employee newspaper. Because the publication affected so many people, and the potential impact of the publication was so significant, the vice president of public affairs held a number of informal meetings with his colleagues before changing the design of the employee newspaper. The final decision was made by the vice president. The redesign resulted in a new look for the publication that employees liked; informal feedback was very positive.

Major differences in how the publications were managed are partially accounted for by the differences between the organizations' technologies and the organizations' target audiences. Also, the closeness of the public relations director to the dominant coalition accounted for differences in how the publications were managed.

The amount of pre-publication planning—for example, the number of meetings with department heads and the use of in-house style manuals—was more extensive for the diversified university than it was for the centralized grocery store chain. The neighborhood community was only one of many target audiences of concern to the university, and compared to faculty, staff, and alumni, the community target audience was not as central to the on-going operation and technology of the university. Because the importance of the employee target audience of the grocery store chain was more central to the organization's technology than the neighborhood-community target audience was for the university, the vice president for the grocery store chain used more consensus-building, decision-making strategies than did the director of university relations. A major factor affecting the publications' operations was the close relationship of the vice president of public affairs with the dominant coalition of senior management because it facilitated informal decision-making about the important redesign of the employee publication.

The quantity and quality of evaluation and emphasis on costs and benefits were more extensive within the profit-oriented grocery store chain than within the state university. The budget for the university relations office was prepared and reviewed annually. Twice a year, the public affairs office of the grocery store chain would prepare current and projected budgets for their operations, each time using zero-based budgeting principles that questioned the continuing need for each activity. When major reductions were required in the publications budget of the university, informal research was used to determine the best way to make the cost reductions. When similar cost reductions were required with the grocery store's publications, a series of focus groups, surveys, and more formal feedback procedures were used.

The public relations staffs for both organizations had extensive professional experience in writing, editing, and producing effective publications. In many ways, how they went about planning, implementing, and evaluating their publications were the same, but there were distinct differences. The question is why.

The economic conditions of each organization affected basic decisions about the publications. In one, the decision was to cut the budget by eliminating a publication, and in the other, the decision was to increase the "news hole" by redesigning the publication. The technology of each organization affected the number and kinds of target audiences, the network of news sources, the content of publications, the need for style manuals, and the number of individuals "in the loop" who suggested and approved copy. The closeness of the relationship between one of the senior public relations managers and the dominant management coalition made it possible to make significant changes in a flagship publication by using informal planning and evaluation procedures.

A REVISED CHECKLIST FOR PUBLICATIONS

The following questions for analyzing and evaluating publications are derived from the master checklist. All of the following questions need not be asked; which questions are most relevant depends on the publication.

Identifying the problem:

    ____ 1. What was the origin of the publication? What problems or needs were being addressed when the publication was first established? What was the corporate rationale for establishing the publication? Have any of the initial problems or needs that served as justification for the publication changed? If so, how?

    ____ 2. Who has a stake in maintaining the status quo? Who wants to change the status quo? Who else is interested in the situation? What are the values, loyalties, and principles of the stakeholders? How do they define the problem (or opportunity)? Is there consensus on the definition of the situation? What can you do to help facilitate this consensus?

    ____ 3. How have the justification and purpose of the publication(s) been "framed" as issues? What is the picture being presented to others about the role played by the publication(s) in the life of the organization?

    ____ 4. What kind of "spin" is being given to the facts and content of the publication(s), and who is involved in framing and spinning these facts and issues as they appear in the publication(s)?

Setting goals and objectives:

___ 5. What are process and outcome goals and objectives for the publication? What is the order of priority for these goals and objectives?

___ 6. What is supposed to happen if the publication is effective? Which communication theories help explain and/or predict the manner in which the publication will be produced or how the reader will use and be gratified by the publication? What sequence of events is assumed to occur if the publication is to be produced on time and have the desired impact? What is a reasonable timetable for this expected chain of events?

Defining publics and relationships:

___ 7. What is the best way to classify the various groups of readers? What is the profile of the typical reader within each of these groups? Which reader attitudes and behaviors can be influenced by the publication? How do these readers react to the publication?

___ 8. Who specifically is to be exposed to the publication(s)? When do you plan to expose these publics to the publication(s)? How will you know if and when people have been exposed? What reactions do you expect them to have to the publication(s)?

Planning, including research and evaluation efforts before implementation:

___ 9. What resources are required to produce the publication—people, supplies and equipment, outside consultants, professional services, etc.? Who are the people responsible for each of the various publishing activities?

___ 10. Who has asked that the publication be evaluated? Who might be interested in the results of the evaluation? Are these decision-makers involved in the design of the evaluation? What kind of information would these decision-makers like to have about the publication, and when do they want it? What criteria do these decision-makers have for defining the effectiveness of the publication? To what extent is there consensus on the goals and objectives for the publication? How can you facilitate consensus on the goals and objectives?

___ 11. What are the size, quality, quantity, format, frequency, and distribution system for the publication?

___ 12. Which set of goals and objectives and what aspects of the publication will be the focus of the evaluation, and why?

What aspects of the publication will not be focused on, and why? What specific set of questions about the publication needs to be answered? How do the questions and research procedures relate to the specific goals and objectives of the publication?

Budgeting:

____ 13. What are the costs associated with the publication? How might this money have been used if it had not been spent for the publication?

____ 14. How might you assign a dollar value to both negative and positive reader reactions to the publication? What is a breakdown of the various costs and benefits of the publication?

____ 15. In terms of lost opportunity or real and perceived harm, how might the publication adversely affect either those who work on it with you, or those who are exposed to it?

Evaluating, after implementation:

____ 16. How are the data to be collected—for example, informally, by holding special meetings and listening to what others say, or more formally, by telephone survey, mail questionnaires, or focus groups? What are the problems in collecting the data, and what are feasible solutions to these problems?

____ 17. How valid and reliable are the data? How certain are you that the publication caused specific results? Are there alternative explanations for the observed results?

____ 18. What other types of data might be helpful in evaluating the publication? How can testimonials, previous surveys, informal observations, expert judgments, and other data be used to augment the current information?

____ 19. Who wants to see the results of the evaluation? What kinds of tables and charts, if any, would they like to see? When do they want to see the results, and how do they want them presented?

____ 20. What judgments can be made about the publication, based upon the evaluation? Is there consensus about these judgments? Does there need to be consensus? What judgments could or should be deferred, and why?

____ 21. Did this evaluation overlook anything that should be investigated later? What questions remain about the effectiveness of the publication? How might the evaluation be improved the next time?

TWO ADDITIONAL CASE STUDIES COMPARED

Manning, Selvage and Lee, one of the world's largest public relations firms, provides a full range of professional services for its clients. The following cases describe situations involving two of their clients, each of whom wanted the agency to provide media relations services.

. . .

CASE 7.3:

The National Coffee Association

An advocacy group of food nutritionists sponsored research that indicated coffee was potentially unhealthful, particularly for certain individuals. On a Friday, they distributed an invitation to national and local media in New York City, announcing that the group was going to release the research results at a special news conference on Thursday of the following week. The announcement said the results would be a major indictment against coffee and that they hoped people would reduce their consumption after learning about the research findings. Friday afternoon, after hearing about the planned press conference, the director of public affairs for the National Coffee Association called an executive with Manning, Selvage and Lee, with whom he had worked on other coffee-related campaigns. He wanted the public relations agency to help the association respond to the potential crisis being generated by the food nutritionists at next week's press conference.

. . .

CASE 7.4:

The Papal Visit

In the late 1980s, the Roman Catholic Church planned for the Pope to visit several cities in the United States. One year before the Pope's visit, the U.S. Conference of Catholic Bishops, through whom the tour would be coordinated, contacted a number of major public relations agencies in the United States and requested proposals for handling media relations during the Papal visit. Manning, Selvage and Lee/Washington was one of the agencies to receive this Request For Proposal (RFP). The RFP, and discussions with senior officials of the U.S. Conference of Catholic Bishops, made it clear that the Pope did not want to avoid controversy on the tour, but rather wanted to deal directly with a complex set of religious issues. What Catholic Church officials did not want was a disrespectful "media circus" atmosphere surrounding the Papal visit. The U.S. Conference of Catholic Bishops said their organization would handle most of the logistics—press credentialing, hotel arrangements, and transportation. What they wanted from the winning public relations agency would be counseling about how best to communicate complex issues, dignified, substantive publicity, and sophisticated media relations.

Key Factors

When a full-service agency engages in public relations activities, the purpose and scope of those activities is based not so much on the characteristics of the agency but on the needs and expectations of the client. In both of these cases, only certain professional services, media relations, were requested by the clients; the total expertise and skills of the agency was not required. Consequently, the major factors which best explained and predicted the public relations activities in both cases were within the clients' domain and outside the immediate control of the public relations agency.

The key to successful media relations is not the relationship between the public relations agency and the media, but between the client and the media. If the public relations agency is successful, its role in the relationship is unobtrusive—transparent—with the media focused not on the mechanics of press conferences, interviews, and releases, but on the client's message. To make this possible, the agency must second-guess the needs and expectations of the media and provide whatever is needed to make the media's job of reporting the client's message as easy as possible. In the two cases, a common ingredient was the agency's extensive experience in working with the media. They knew deadlines, format requirements, and personalities; they were media savvy.

A key characteristic of the agency-client relationship was the long-term view the agency's dominant coalition of senior executives took toward both clients' situations. Each client had a threatening "fire" that needed to be put out: one was worried about the news from the anti-coffee press conference; the other was concerned about intensive media attention getting out of hand during the Pope's tour. While these fires were dealt with promptly and professionally, the agency's senior management conducted their business with a view toward additional long-range public relations work after the immediate situation had been handled successfully. The agency confidently expected to find itself working professionally with the media and with the two clients long after the rush of the current campaigns had passed.

The Similarities

The major similarity between these cases is that the same agency is involved. Different personnel and agency resources were involved, but the same level of expertise and professionalism was brought to bear in both cases. Manning, Selvage and Lee has offices located worldwide. For any one client, they are able to assemble an account team of professional and support staff who are best suited to meet the client's needs and expectations.

Both clients in these two cases had similar goals: smooth, transparent media relations so that the client's message was clearly received, first by the media, and then by target publics. Also common to both cases was the fact that the message the client wanted delivered to the media, and to the public, was not simple: the religious issues of the Pope and the health issues of the National Coffee Association were complex topics, subject to debate.

The Differences

Several dramatic differences are apparent in these two cases. The first is that the Coffee Association was "under the gun" and working against a rapidly approaching deadline, maybe even a crisis. The U.S. Catholic Bishops, on the other hand, had allocated an adequate amount of time to plan for the Pope's visit. Once the Pope's visit got underway, the media pressures would be quick-paced and demanding, but there was sufficient time to plan an appropriate campaign. With the Coffee Association, there was barely enough time; later, after they had "put out the fire," there would be more time to plan a more deliberately paced media campaign.

Another major difference was the number of "players" involved in the two cases. The National Coffee Association's director of public affairs, the leaders for the advocacy group, and New York-based media representatives were the principal players in one case—a total of less than fifty individuals. In the other case, the major players were the Pope and his entourage, including an international pool of journalists, the U.S. Catholic bishops, local church leaders, national journalists, local media representatives from each city visited, local law enforcement agencies and, wielding a great deal of power over the structure and implementation of the entire campaign, the U.S. Secret Service. Hundreds, if not thousands, of individuals were actively involved in the campaign.

Another obvious difference between the two media relations efforts was the scope of the campaign. The coffee campaign was relatively small, compared to the Pope's multi-city tour, and the two clients' budgets differed dramatically. In addition to the differences in the total cost of the two campaigns, one of the critical differences in the two cases was the amount of reserves or slack resources that were available to the clients, and, hence, to the public relations agency. The coffee campaign was conducted on a very restricted budget. While expenses of the media relations component for the Pope's visit were monitored closely by campaign planners, the cost of the campaign was not the central concern of the U.S. Conference of Catholic Bishops. First, they wanted excellent media relations; cost was secondary.

Two significant differences between these two cases were media sophistication and marketplace resources. The location of the press conference for the Coffee Association was New York City, one of the world's most sophisticated cities, with hundreds of media organizations. It is a city with a great deal of experience hosting press conferences. During peak periods on a regular news day, there may be more than a dozen press conferences underway at the same time in different locations, each trying to attract as many reporters to it as possible. The Pope's tour involved three major and six mid-size cities, each with a different array of media outlets and community resources. Staging a press conference in New York City was dramatically different than doing media relations for a world leader visiting more than a half dozen communities, each with its own media, and each with different resources, such as police protection, medical facilities, telephone connections, and electric power capabilities.

Media Relations for the Coffee Association

After receiving the call from the director of public affairs for the Coffee Institute, the account executive conferred briefly with his superiors. He called the client back and told him the agency would handle the situation. Here is what they did:

1. Within hours, the account executive had developed a list of coffee nutrition specialists by getting specific names of experts from the client and by reviewing articles and scientific reports wired ("faxed") by the client to the agency.
2. By making a few calls to key editors and reporters and by talking with his colleagues in the office, he also gathered information about issues of concern to the media and other media events which would take place within the New York City market during the next week, particularly during the announced time of the health group's press conference.
3. During these first few hours, the account executive held quick meetings with staff members to identify appropriate goals and objectives. As a result of these rapid-fire meetings (some of which took place in the account executive's office, some of which occurred in the hallway between offices, and some of which included telephone conference calls with the client), they decided to preempt the health group's press conference by holding an earlier press conference that week, on Tuesday, to release scientific information from the coffee association. That way, the media's agenda would be partially set by the coffee association by the time the health group held their press conference. It was decided to put out the fire first; later, they would consider more creative, long-range solutions to the positioning of the coffee issues. First, they had to deal with a week full of press conferences, and a weekend full of getting ready for Tuesday's press conference.

4. Within these first few hours, the account executive developed an informal action plan. He had no time to write a formal proposal. He only had time for handwritten notes about objectives and media strategies, which he discussed with his colleagues and with the client over the phone.
5. A facsimile of a standard contract was wired to the client, who approved it. It included a preliminary cost estimate for one week's worth of consultation and professional services, and it included procedures for making budget adjustments, if needed.
6. Before "the end of business" Friday afternoon, a press conference site was selected, experts were contacted, and media representatives were invited to Tuesday's press conference.
7. Over the weekend and on Monday, the agency professionals coordinated the production of media kits, which included a series of press releases. They continued calling and discussing the press conference with targeted media. And, they made last-minute arrangements for the conference, including catering services and room reservations.
8. On Tuesday, they held the press conference, where they distributed press releases and press kits. The expert on coffee reviewed current research and explained the strengths and weaknesses of various approaches to assessing the nutritional value of coffee. The agency staff made a list of media representatives attending the conference—mostly reporters specializing in health and food issues, including those working for industry and trade publications, but also reporters for wire services, the area's major newspapers, and one local TV station.
9. Agency staff members made follow-up calls to selected reporters, providing more specific information about coffee issues.
10. The agency collected and analyzed the press coverage of the Tuesday conference. It was considered more than adequate, given the short lead time, with most coverage mentioning the desired "copy points." More coverage was expected following Thursday's press conference.
11. Agency staff attended the health group's press conference on Thursday and noted that many of the same reporters attended both conferences and asked questions based on the earlier information provided by the Coffee Association.
12. The agency continued to collect and analyze press coverage. One trend was apparent: the facts presented at the Tuesday press conference were used by many reporters to frame the issues raised at the Thursday conference.
13. The account executive discussed with the client a possible retainer, so that the agency could build on the hard-won research and media relations work they had just performed and reposition coffee issues

nationally by engaging in a long-range public relations campaign. The client agreed, and an appropriate proposal was developed. It included:
   a. Situation statement.
   b. Goals and objectives.
   c. Media strategy:
      1) Feature stories in major media.
      2) Experts on radio and TV talk shows.
      3) Press releases and press kits.
      4) Regular contact with media.
      5) Content analysis of press coverage and public reactions, with regular reports of this information to the client.
      6) Procedures for evaluating and adjusting the media strategies, when appropriate.
   d. Timeline.
   e. Budget.
   f. Benefit statement.
14. The agency considered the one-week media relations work a success because they were able to frame the potentially hostile press conference in a way that suited their client. They put the anti-coffee group on the defensive; they generated lots of favorable publicity; and most importantly, their client agreed to a new contract for a long-range public relations campaign.

Media Relations for the Papal Visit

The Request For Proposals (RFP) from the U.S. Conference of Catholic Bishops generated a number of written proposals; these were narrowed to five agencies which, in turn, were asked to make formal presentations. Here is what senior executives of Manning, Selvage and Lee did to respond to the RFP and to win the contract:

1. A team of three professionals was assembled, with a senior officer serving as the account executive.
2. The team conducted background research by immersing itself in press coverage of previous Papal visits. None of the previous tours by the Pope had employed professional public relations firms, so there were no records or planning documents which could help the public relations firm develop its proposal.
3. Team members spoke to people who had handled other "state visits" by dignitaries, particularly members of their own agency. One member of the agency's professional staff who was called upon to advise the team had been responsible for protocol for then-Vice President George Bush. Other public relations professionals on the agency's staff who gave useful advice to the team were former public affairs specialists and diplomats with The White House and the U.S. Department of State.

4. The account executive wrote a working draft of the proposal for review by staff within the agency. It included the following media relations strategies: to provide as much unrestricted media coverage as possible, to rely on media pools for close coverage, and to use the standard protocols established for The White House press corps when organizing press pools and other news gathering procedures concerning the Pope's visit.
5. The team modified their proposal based not only on comments from their colleagues within the agency and others, but also on suggestions from members of the U.S. Secret Service which had overall responsibility for the safety of the Pope during the U.S. visit.
6. The team included in the final proposal a media relations plan for each city on the tour. It also included suggestions about how to stage certain events and how to present certain issues so that the Pope's message was reinforced by the media's coverage. The final proposal consisted of: a brief situational analysis, goals and objectives for media relations, media strategies, planning activities, a timetable, agency staffing requirements, agency qualifications and professional experience handling media relations for other heads of state, evaluation and management control procedures, and a detailed budget.
7. Four other agencies vied for the account by making formal presentations to the U.S. Catholic Bishops. The team from Manning, Selvage and Lee rehearsed their presentation by presenting it to senior executives and others on their staff. During their formal presentation, the team emphasized not only their current plans but also their previous experience in handling media relations for dignitaries and world leaders. They won the account.
8. The team visited the first two cities on the Pope's ten-city tour (Miami, Florida, and Columbia, South Carolina), where they talked to local church leaders, agency affiliates and media representatives.
9. The agency coordinated media relations activities by developing a massive plan book that the team affectionately called "the bible." Eventually, this planning document was contained in a five-inch thick three-ring binder. For each city on the tour, it listed hour-by-hour (and in some instances, minute-by-minute) details of the Pope's visit. It described specific tasks, indicated beginning and completion dates for each task, and designated the people involved and the person responsible for performing each task. Updating and maintaining the plan book was a major task in and of itself; it was the responsibility of the account executive.
10. In addition to other "advance work," the agency published periodically a four-page newsletter about planning activities surrounding the Pope's visit, which was distributed to agency staff, local and national members of the Catholic Church, and others, such as community leaders.

11. The agency initially expected almost a dozen public relations professionals from their agency to accompany the Pope. Their assignment was to: coordinate press pools; make follow-up calls to media representatives, providing them with additional information when requested; double-check arrangements with local church officials, security and law enforcement agencies; and go to the next city on the tour to make sure advance preparations were in place and ready for the Pope's arrival.
12. While formal rehearsals were impossible (estimates were that more than a quarter of a million people would attend each public ceremony, and for certain cities, more than half a million people were expected), the team "walked through" the media relations activities with as many of the principals as could be assembled in each of the cities involved in the Pope's visit. They conducted these walk-throughs several times in each city.
13. The team cut back on the number of staff members from the agency's headquarters who would accompany the Pope throughout the tour. Instead, they made arrangements with affiliated public relations agencies in the specific cities to handle certain aspects of the media relations. The agency established separate contracts with fixed budgets with each of these affiliates.
14. Just before the Pope's arrival in the United States, the agency purchased scores of dress shirts for the six men and women on the staff who would be making the nine-city tour; they knew that once the tour "took off," they would not have any slack time to launder their clothes. The team members put in 18–hour days during the Pope's visit and ate lots of fast food while standing up.
15. No major media problems occurred during the Pope's visit, despite the steady downpour of rain at one ceremony and the spectacular collapse of a massive stage backdrop at another event. Millions of people attended the Pope's public ceremonies in nine U.S. cities. Millions more witnessed the events on television. Media coverage was extensive and focused on the Pope's messages, with very little press attention given to the hubbub surrounding the Papal visit. The U.S. Catholic Bishops expressed great satisfaction with how the media relations campaign for the Pope's visit was handled, and they indicated they would use U.S.-based public relations professionals in planning future Papal visits to the United States.

Crucial Steps in Conducting Media Relations

Four steps in conducting media relations were common, and crucial, in both these cases: researching the situation, establishing realistic goals and objectives, generating ideas and alternatives, and developing a flexible action plan. The first step in both campaigns was to conduct informal, qualitative research that identified the needs and expectations not only of the client but also the media. Pre-campaign research in both cases also identified marketplace resources and media characteristics.

The second step in both campaigns was to establish achievable goals with specific objectives, such as properly positioning the client's issues, generating lots of favorable publicity, and establishing and maintaining a long-term relationship not only with the client but also the media.

The third step was to generate ideas and alternatives for conducting effective media relations. In both cases, they did this by conducting numerous brainstorming sessions with staff and others. In the process of generating ideas and clarifying strategies, the agency helped educate the clients to the realities of professional media relations.

The fourth crucial step was developing a flexible action plan. In both cases, the initial plans were developed after informal research and intense discussions with the client. The account executive in charge of both cases was responsible for adjusting the media relations plans as events unfolded and as client needs and expectations changed.

A REVISED CHECKLIST FOR MEDIA RELATIONS

The following questions for analyzing and evaluating media relations are derived from the master checklist. All of the questions do not necessarily apply to all media relations campaigns. Which questions are most relevant depends on the issues, the marketplace, and the needs and expectations of both the client and the media.

Identifying the problem:

    ____ 1. What is the background on the situation the media relations campaign is designed to address? Is it a problem or an opportunity? What factors have caused the current situation?

    ____ 2. What are the issues that need to be communicated? How have various publics presented these issues in the past? What is the origin of the problem (or opportunity) that has generated these issues? How are the various issues presented now? What are the ramifications of these issues?

    ____ 3. What facts are known about the client's needs and expectations, the media's needs and expectations, the issues, the characteristics of the marketplace? What research has been conducted? If research has not been conducted, what kind of documentation would be appropriate? Where would you go to get it?

    ____ 4. Who has a stake in maintaining the status quo? Who wants to change the status quo? Who else is interested in the situation? What are the values, loyalties and principles of these stakeholders? How do they define the issues?

___ 5. How have the issues involved in this situation been "framed"—what is the picture that is being presented to others about this situation? What kind of "spin" is being given to the facts in the situation, and who is involved in framing and spinning the issues?

Setting goals and objectives:

___ 6. What are the goals of the media relations campaign? What are the outcome goals? Specifically, what kinds of impact will the campaign have on media gatekeepers and targeted publics? What are the process goals? Specifically, what kinds of "internal" management goals (such as meeting deadlines, always making requested follow-up calls) are necessary in order to achieve the desired outcome goals? Is there consensus on both outcome and process goals? Who has been or needs to be involved in reaching consensus on the goals?

___ 7. What are the objectives of the media relations campaign? For each process and outcome goal, what are specific objectives, concrete actions, that are designed to achieve the stated goal?

___ 8. What is the theory behind the media relations campaign? What aspects of the agenda-setting model of mass communication apply to this situation? What is the rationale or set of assumptions that logically connects the process goals and objectives to the desired outcome goals and objectives? What is supposed to happen? What causes what? What sequence of events is assumed to occur if the media relations campaign is to be considered successful? What is the timetable for this sequence of events?

Defining publics and relationships:

___ 9. What publics are involved? What are existing attitudes and behaviors of these various publics? Which media are best suited for reaching each of these publics?

___ 10. Which media gatekeepers need to be considered in this situation? What are their attitudes and behaviors concerning the client's situation? What constraints are the media gatekeepers working under that can affect this situation? What else is going on in the marketplace that has the attention of the media gatekeepers?

___ 11. Who specifically (both media gatekeepers and target audiences) will be exposed to the media relations campaign? When do you plan to begin the media relations campaign? How will you know if and when people have been exposed? How are they likely to react to the campaign?

Chapter 7 How to Analyze and Evaluate Public Relations 287

Planning, including research and evaluation efforts before implementation:

____ 12. What resources are required to implement this media relations campaign—people, supplies, equipment, outside consultants, professional services, etc.?

____ 13. Who is responsible for seeing that various activities occur?

____ 14. What are the limitations of this media relations campaign? What alternative activities are not being engaged in, for whatever reason, that could help make this media relations effort more successful? Why are these alternatives not being included at this time?

____ 15. Who is concerned about the outcome of this campaign? Who might or should be interested in the outcome, and why? How have these concerned individuals been involved in the planning of the media relations? If some of these concerned individuals have not been involved in planning activities, why not?

____ 16. What is the purpose of evaluating the campaign: to help improve it (formative evaluation) or to assess the overall impact of the media relations (summative evaluation), or some combination?

____ 17. What kinds of decisions are expected to be made based on the results of this evaluation? Who are these decision-makers? What kinds of information about the media relations campaign do they require, and when do they require it?

____ 18. How is "success" or "effectiveness" for this media relations campaign to be defined? Is it to be determined by an internal group of managers, the organization's dominant coalition? Or, is it to be determined by external publics and groups, criteria of success (or failure) that will be imposed by others outside the immediate control of the organization? Is there consensus on this definition? How can you facilitate consensus?

____ 19. What are the limitations to the evaluation you have planned? Are certain aspects of the media relations campaign not being considered in this evaluation? How generalizable will the results of your evaluation be?

____ 20. What kind of research design should be used to evaluate the media relations? What factors should be taken into account and controlled? What factors should be manipulated? What steps should be taken to avoid confounding factors?

____ 21. What factors, events or situations prevent you from using a more rigorous research design? How will these factors limit the results of your evaluation?

___ 22. How do you propose to measure in concrete terms the results of the media relations campaign? How valid and reliable are these measurement instruments and procedures? How are these measures related to the outcome goals? Are they an exact measure of what the program or campaign is designed to accomplish, or are they approximations?

___ 23. How are data to be collected? How often? By whom? Do you anticipate any problems in collecting this data? What are these problems?

___ 24. What crucial aspects of the media relations campaign are to be observed, recorded or otherwise measured? Why did you choose to measure these aspects of the campaign and not others?

___ 25. What limitations or deficiencies are there in the procedure you plan to use to evaluate the campaign? What other factors that might influence expected results need to be considered?

___ 26. How can you present the research results: the number of people influenced, how target publics reacted, what actions were taken as planned, the number of people exposed, what impact was observed, etc.? How will "before" and "after" data be compared (parallel bar graphs, trendlines)? What descriptive statistics and other forms of empirical analysis will you use? What kinds of tables and graphs will you use?

___ 27. What kinds of soft data can you present: informal observations, testimonials, anecdotes, etc.?

___ 28. How certain will you be that the media relations campaign caused the results you observe? Are there alternative explanations for anticipated results? What are these alternative explanations?

___ 29. How would you measure public attitudes and behavior if there were to be no such media relations campaign as is currently planned? How can you measure characteristics of those not exposed to the campaign?

___ 30. If a control group (made up of either media gatekeepers or target publics) is to be used, how will you know if the treatment group performed differently than the control group? How will you know if this difference was statistically significant? How will you know if there was a meaningful difference?

___ 31. Will you be able to tell if certain aspects of the media relations campaign were more effective than others? How will you know this?

Budgeting:

____ 32. What method can you use to compute costs and benefits? Is there some formula you can use? How can you arrive at these estimates informally? How have others calculated similar costs and benefits? How confident can you be in these cost/benefit estimates? How much confidence will others place in the estimates?

____ 33. What are costs associated with the campaign? How much money for supplies, equipment, professional services, staff time, media time, etc., is expected to be spent on the activity? How might this money have been used if it had not been earmarked for this media relations effort? What portion of the monies spent accounts for start-up costs (pretesting, initial construction and production costs, demonstration work, etc.), and what portion might be considered on-going, if the media relations campaign were to be continued?

____ 34. What are the non-dollar costs of the campaign? How might the campaign adversely affect either those who work on it with you, or those who are exposed to it? Will those who work on the media relations campaign be missing other career opportunities which they value? What opportunities might not be taken by those who are likely to be exposed to and participate in the campaign? Will any harm be done by any aspect of the media relations campaign?

____ 35. What are the dollar benefits? Will people directly contribute or spend money that immediately will go to sponsoring organizations? How will you know that they made this dollar contribution as a direct result of being exposed to the media relations campaign?

____ 36. What are the non-dollar benefits? How much progress do you anticipate making toward the achievement of the media relations goals? How big a difference in the problem (and in the cost of this problem to the sponsoring organization) do you expect if the media relations campaign is a success? How might you expect results from this campaign to compare to the cost that the organization would have paid had there been no such media relations campaign and the status quo was maintained? Would there have been some unanticipated benefits, reactions by unintended publics or extremely favorable responses by secondary publics?

Evaluating, after implementation:

____ 37. What judgments can be made about the campaign based on your evaluation? What judgments should be deferred until a more comprehensive evaluation can be conducted? Did this evaluation overlook anything that should be investigated later?

___ 38. What recommendations can you make based on this evaluation? What kind of predictions about probable sequences of events for similar types of media relations campaigns can you make after analyzing the results of this evaluation?

___ 39. What questions remain about the effectiveness of this media relations campaign? How might the evaluation of this or a similar campaign be improved in the future?

___ 40. How can you best summarize the effectiveness of this media relations campaign, and how might it be improved in the future?

SIMILARITIES AND DIFFERENCES IN REVISED CHECKLISTS

The basic similarity between different versions of the checklists is the set of topics addressed: identifying problems, setting goals and objectives, defining publics and relationships, planning, including research, budgeting, and evaluating after implementation. These are the basic steps in designing and conducting any public relations program or campaign.

The major differences between the revised checklists were due to system differences between sponsoring organizations and the types of public relations activities. For example, the two publication case studies described internal communication activities. The two media relations case studies described external communication activities. Consequently, different theories or rationales would be used to explain and predict outcomes from these different campaigns. Also, differences in the expectations of clients and senior management, which would be based on system differences, would account for the use of different versions of the checklists.

THE PLAN BOOK: PART V

The checklists presented in this chapter would be appropriate to include in The Plan Book, if the primary purpose of the planning document was to develop consensus and commitments from staff specialists and principal decision-makers. The checklists would be appropriate for the section of The Plan Book containing timelines, Gantt and PERT charts, and similar project diagrams.

One of the advantages of The Plan Book is that it can be used to document the early stages of the program or campaign. Sometimes, certain information from The Plan Book—such as problem statements, goals, and objectives—can be incorporated almost verbatim into the final report. As the planning process unfolds, changes will be made in the design and execution of the program or campaign; this is an inevitable part of public relations planning. The Plan Book, when it is kept up-to-date, can be useful in preparing the final report to the client, because the various revised versions of The Plan Book will reflect the history of the program or campaign. Some public relations managers write monthly updates of The Plan Book, even when only minor events or changes have occurred, so that at the end of the program or campaign, it is relatively easy to write the history from the monthly updates.

Most final reports are not truly final because they make recommendations for the future, based on the assumption that certain aspects of the public relations problem (or opportunity) still need to be addressed. Consequently, one of the functions of a final report is to set the stage for the next phase or the next approach to the problem (or opportunity). Based on a plan book, the final report has the potential to become The Plan Book for the next phase. This means the final report needs to address topics discussed in any plan book: problem definition, publics, goals, objectives, strategies, timetables, budgets, and evaluation methods.

If the final report is written with the knowledge that there most likely will be a next phase, then it should emphasize the results of formative research and evaluation. If it is prepared with an expectation that it really will be the final report, then it should emphasize the results of summative research and evaluation. As with The Plan Book, the final report should only use easy-to-understand tables, charts, and graphs in the body of the report, with all technical matter placed in an appendix. All final reports should begin with an executive summary or abstract.

ALTERNATIVE APPROACHES TO EVALUATIONS

Evaluative research in public relations is a form of applied, administrative research. It is designed to provide decision-makers with information they can use to monitor and control organizational resources; it is a management tool. There are, however, alternative approaches to evaluating public relations.

Research in the social sciences can be described along a continuum from subjective to objective measurement, and along a continuum from support for decision-makers interested in maintaining the status quo to support for decision-makers interested in making radical changes.[2]

Most evaluative research in public relations tries to be objective and supports decision-makers interested in maintaining the current social order. While most public relations programs and campaigns are designed to change attitudes and behaviors, they are not designed to make radical changes in how people live. Rather, most campaigns are designed to make incremental changes that are socially acceptable.

Historians and social scientists using critical theories might use more subjective measures and focus on the role of public relations in social movements and radical changes in society. Historian Marvin Olasky's critique of public relations' role in maintaining U.S.-based business cartels is an example of an evaluation of public relations that was not designed for on-line decision-makers; yet, it provides useful insights that can be used to predict and explain public relations.[3]

IN SUMMARY . . .

System concepts such as organizational mission, size, complexity, technology, and environmental uncertainty are useful for analyzing and evaluating public relations programs and campaigns. Checklists based on the fundamental steps in the public relations process—research, planning, implementation, and evaluation—are useful management tools. There are, however, other ways to research and evaluate public relations. Some of these additional research strategies, and more than 100 priority research questions, will be discussed in the next chapter.

Study Questions

1. What are the strengths and weaknesses of checklists?
2. What are appropriate questions to ask when evaluating the following aspects of a public relations campaign or program: 1) identifying the problem, 2) setting goals and objectives, 3) defining publics and relationships, 4) planning, including research and evaluation efforts before implementation, 5) budgeting, and 6) evaluating, after implementation.
3. How would you evaluate a set of corporate publications? Be as specific as possible by describing a particular corporation and its set of publications.
4. How would you evaluate a corporation's media relations?
5. What is evaluative research? How does it compare to basic and applied research?
6. True or false: most evaluative research in public relations supports the status quo. Defend your answer.
7. How are concepts such as organizational mission, size, complexity, technology, and environmental uncertainty useful for analyzing and evaluating public relations? Give examples of how each concept might help account for the performance of a public relations campaign or program.

Endnotes

1. Sperber, Nathaniel H., and Otto Lerbinger, *Manager's Public Relations Handbook* (Reading, Mass.: Addison-Wesley, 1982).

2. Burrell, G., and G. Morgan, *Sociological Paradigms and Organizational Analysis* (London: Heinemann, 1979).

3. Olasky, M., *Corporate Public Relations: A New Historical Perspective* (Hillsdale, N.J.: Lawrence Erlbaum Associates, 1987).

PART TWO

Using Research Priorities and Ethical Theories to Guide Professional Development in Public Relations

. . . . . .

CHAPTER EIGHT

How to Identify and Investigate Priority Research Questions in Public Relations

*F*rank *knew that if the next corporate-wide meeting of public relations managers, representing all the significant business units from various parts of the world, was to be a success, he needed to facilitate some sort of consensus among the managers prior to when they arrived at the conference. Otherwise, the discussions would go off in a thousand directions and nothing of substance would be accomplished. At their last quarterly long-range planning meeting, the public relations managers had wrestled unsuccessfully with two major sets of questions:*

How does, and how should, our corporation address significant trends in society? There are trends such as the feminization of the workforce, the aging of the general population, and changes within minorities and ethnic groups that are potentially positive. There are also dysfunctional trends, such as terrorism, drug abuse, the spread of sexually transmitted diseases, and illiteracy. How can our corporation not be reactive but proactive to these trends?

What are the most effective techniques our corporation could use to monitor globally significant issues and events, such as those underway in Europe, Russia, China, Africa, and the Middle East? How do, and how should, public relations professionals present this information most effectively to top management?

Frank's task was to identify likely answers and potential solutions to these two sets of questions so that the managers at the conference would be able to use most efficiently their valuable time together. Frank decided to conduct a Delphi study. Initially, he would write to the managers and have each one, independently, write a detailed answer to each of the questions. Then, when he had received all the initial responses, he would compile and lightly edit them so that the uniqueness of each response was retained. At this point, he knew he might need to classify the various responses into categories, but he would need to wait until he had seen the initial responses to know the best way to classify them. Then, he would prepare a second mailing to his colleagues. He would send a complete, edited listing of everyone's set of answers. In this second mailing, he would ask his colleagues to rank order the various suggestions. When he got back this second mailing, he would tally the results and prepare a final document that would list the suggestions in priority order. With the results of the Delphi study in the hands of the managers when they arrived at the meeting, Frank felt confident there would be meat on the table; discussions would be of substance. Frank turned to his task; the meeting was in three months, just enough time to conduct a Delphi study.

. . .

TOP PRIORITY RESEARCH QUESTIONS IN PUBLIC RELATIONS

The body of knowledge in public relations is not static: there are many more questions than answers. Scholars in public relations recently identified the following sets of questions as the most important research questions in the field today:

> What criteria are used or would be appropriate to use to evaluate the contributions public relations makes toward the achievement of organizational goals and objectives?

> What are the concepts of public relations held by current, past and future members of top management? How do these perceptions of top management compare to those of public relations practitioners? How do attitudes of top management affect role expectations and performances of public relations practitioners?

> How, when, where, and why do (or why don't) the roles of public relations practitioners reflect the ethical codes of the profession?

> How and why do public relations roles and practices vary from one type of organization to another: private vs. public, profit vs. not-for-profit, retail vs. wholesale, routine vs. nonroutine technologies, highly regulated vs. unregulated?

> How do practitioners and others measure changes in attitudes, opinions and behavior of various publics? What are causal relationships among these factors? How do these factors influence relationships among individuals, groups and organizations?

> To what extent do public relations ethics reflect society's growing ethical concerns about financial relations, government affairs, religion?

What is the role of organizations and their public relations in influencing societal values, beliefs and morals?

It is a challenge to the public relations profession to find answers to these and other priority research questions. It bodes well for the public relations profession that important questions such as these are being raised, that there are researchers working on them, and that sources of information are available to help those who want to investigate possible answers.

HOW TO CONDUCT A DELPHI STUDY

The Delphi technique is a method of generating ideas and facilitating consensus among geographically separated individuals who have special knowledge to share. Most often, Delphi studies are conducted through the mails, by telephone, and sometimes by personal interviews. Initially, the panelists do not interact with each other; but, through the efforts of the researcher, who serves as a clearinghouse, the panelists see and react to each other's ideas and, through a series of surveys, share and generate new ideas based on an emerging consensus among the panel members. The Delphi technique is an innovative way to involve busy experts and specialists who may not be able to come together to brainstorm but who, nevertheless, need to interact with each other to generate new ideas.

The hallmark of Delphi studies is the series of surveys or "waves." If each wave of the Delphi study takes approximately three to six weeks to conduct, as it normally does when conducted through the mails, one complete Delphi study may take several months, depending on the number of survey waves. The initial wave asks each individual panelist to complete and return to the researcher a questionnaire, which often is composed of open-ended questions. The researcher then compiles the responses to the initial wave and prepares a new questionnaire containing all the ideas suggested by the Delphi panel members. This second survey instrument is sent to the panelists, who may be asked to rank order, to edit, to modify, or to add to the initial set of responses, based on the nature of the research. When the second wave of data is returned to the researcher, often a third survey instrument is prepared and sent to the panelists for yet more clarification and elaboration. These iterations of surveys make the panel members become increasingly aware of each other's ideas, and it facilitates a growing consensus among them.

Here are steps to follow when conducting a Delphi study:

1. Identify a panel of experts or specialists by soliciting nominations from specialists or individuals appropriate to serve on the Delphi panel. Cooperation and participation is improved significantly

when prospective panelists are told how they were nominated by their peers. The panelists' primary qualification should be their special knowledge. This knowledge can be gained through experience (for example, readers of a certain publication) or advanced education (for example, safety engineers). Another key qualification is that panelists be willing to share their information (for example, non-competitors).

2. Invite an appropriate number of panelists to participate. Thirty to fifty individuals should be members of the final panel; this is large enough to see patterns in responses but not so large as to overwhelm the researcher, who must sift through all the responses individually. The invitation should explain what is expected from each panel member in terms of time and effort to complete each wave of the Delphi study.

3. Prepare and distribute the initial survey instrument. The initial survey may contain open-ended probes or specific closed-ended questions, depending on the focus of the research.

4. Receive and analyze the initial wave of data. Compile the responses by question, with only minor editing as necessary for clarity and consistency. If open-ended questions were used extensively, then it may be necessary to analyze and present the first set of responses within an appropriate theoretical framework, typology or outline.

5. Prepare and distribute the second survey instrument. Most often panelists are asked with the second wave to clarify and rank order survey items suggested during the first wave. When the panelists receive the second survey instrument, it will be the first time they will have seen the responses of the other panel members. It is often appropriate at this time to ask for additional ideas, clarifications and elaborations based on the initial survey responses.

6. Receive and analyze the second wave of data. If the initial questions were open-ended and the second wave asked for clarifications and elaborations, the analysis of the second wave of data can be very challenging because it requires numerous subjective decisions about rewording and revising the initial responses. Care should be exerted to include all the new ideas and suggestions, for the main purpose of the Delphi study is to generate new ideas.

7. Prepare and distribute the third survey instrument. Most often, panelists are asked with the third wave to rank order and clarify the new set of revised survey items.

8. Receive and analyze the third wave of data. Often by this stage, the analysis is less subjective and judgmental and more quantitative and objective.

9. Repeat the process with additional waves, if necessary. For example, sometimes certain priority items are selected for more in-depth treatment by the Delphi panelists, who may be asked to propose answers to questions or short-range strategies for long-range goals, etc.

10. Prepare and distribute a final report to panel members. One of the motivations for participating in a Delphi panel, particularly for specialists, is to learn firsthand, before others, what the results of the Delphi study are.

TWO DELPHI STUDIES IDENTIFY PRIORITY RESEARCH QUESTIONS

In an attempt to encourage more systematic theory-building research in the field of public relations, the author conducted a Delphi study that identified priority research questions in public relations for the 1980s.[1] In that study, a judgmental sample of thirty public relations scholars and researchers was selected to participate in a Delphi panel. The 1980 panelists were specially nominated members of the Public Relations Division of the Association for Education in Journalism and Mass Communication (AEJMC) and members of the Public Relations Society of America. The first wave of the Delphi study asked panelists to suggest, independently, what they considered to be important research questions in the field. More than 100 questions were suggested. After being edited for clarity, they were classified into a theoretical framework based on a systems analysis of organizational behavior (to be explained later). Then the complete set of questions was mailed to the panelists. The second wave of the Delphi study asked the panelists to rank order the questions and indicate possible sources of information and appropriate citations that could be used to answer the research questions. The results of the study were published in 1980 by the Foundation for Public Relations Research and Education.

In 1989, the author conducted a follow-up Delphi study, based on the earlier study, to determine if there have been shifts in research priorities in public relations in the past ten years, to identify new research questions, and to forecast major research trends in the field of public relations during the 1990s.[2] This second Delphi study involved more than fifty members of the newly formed Commission on Public Relations of the Speech Communication Association (SCA), the Public Relations Division of AEJMC, and the Public Relations Special Interest Group of the International Communication Association (ICA), each of whom was nominated by active researchers and scholars in the field.

For both the 1980 and 1990 studies, the research questions generated by the panelists were clustered into six categories suggested by an "open systems" analysis of organizational behavior.[3] In this systems analysis, whether the public relations function is provided by staff or by outside counsel, public relations is considered to be one of the set of management activities engaged in by an organization to deal with its environment, both internal and external. See Figure 8.1.

FIGURE 8.1

A systems framework for classifying priority research questions in the field of public relations.*

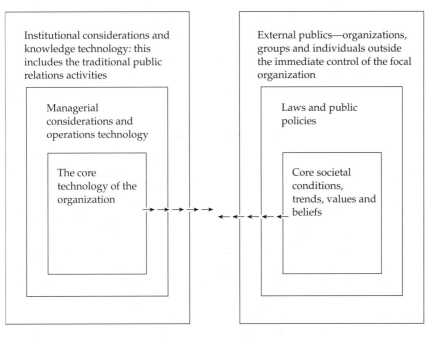

Three internal levels of concern affecting public relations

Three external levels of concern affecting public relations

* This framework is based on one developed by Lee Preston: see, Preston's "Corporate social performance and policy: A synthetic framework for research and analysis," in *Research in Corporate Social Performance and Policy,* edited by Lee Preston, Vol. 1, (Greenwich, Conn.: JAI Press, 1978) p. 16.

This systems analysis of organizational behavior highlights three internal levels of concern affecting public relations:

1. Institutional considerations and knowledge technology, which include the traditional public relations activities of research, planning, implementation, and evaluation;
2. Managerial considerations and operations technology, which focus on how public relations departments are managed and how they operate;
3. The core technology of the organization: where and how the essential work of the organization is performed—for example, in the classroom or research laboratory of a major university, the assembly line of an automotive plant, or places within a hospital where hands-on patient care is delivered.

The systems analysis identifies three external levels of concern affecting public relations:

4. External publics: organizations, groups, and individuals outside the immediate control of the focal organization;
5. Laws and public policies;
6. Core societal conditions, trends, values, and beliefs.

Results of 1980 Study Used in 1990 Study

For the 1980 Delphi study, there were two waves of data gathering. The initial wave was an open-ended questionnaire asking panelists to suggest independently what they considered to be important research questions. Their suggestions were edited and classified according to the systems framework described above. The second wave asked the panelists to rank order the more than 100 research questions and to suggest appropriate citations and sources of information that could be used to answer the questions.

For the 1990 Delphi study, the initial wave asked a new set of panelists to rank order the 1980 set of priority research questions. They also were asked to suggest new research questions and to identify major research trends in the field of public relations during the 1990s. For the second wave, panelists were asked to rank order the set of revised and new questions, and to suggest appropriate citations others could use to pursue answers to the top priority research questions. To counter any response bias due to the ordering of the questions, three versions of the second wave instrument were prepared and distributed, each with a different randomized listing of the questions. A third wave asked the panelists to clarify and suggest additional sources of information and strategies appropriate for answering the research questions.

Figures 8.2–8.7 present the rank orders given by the 1990 Delphi panelists to public relations research questions, classified according to the six levels in the systems framework. In the left-hand columns are the rank orders given to these questions by members of the 1990 Delphi panelists. Endnotes to each set of questions cite references recommended by the Delphi panelists. Figure 8.8 presents research trends in the field of public relations during the 1990s.

The Key Question: What Is the Best Way to Evaluate Public Relations?

One professional issue or research question that stands out from all the others, as it has for decades, is the importance of evaluating the effectiveness of public relations. Here are some of the Delphi panelists' predictions:

> "More research by public relations practitioners to measure the impact of their campaigns."

FIGURE 8.2

Questions and institutional considerations, including the public relations function.

Rank Order	Priority Questions from the 1990 Panel
1.	What criteria are used or would be appropriate to use to evaluate the contributions public relations makes toward the achievement of organizational goals and objectives?[4]
2.	To what degree and in what ways are public relations planning efforts coordinated with overall and divisional organizational planning efforts?[5]
3.	In an era of corporate mergers, massive reorganizations and workforce reductions, what is and should be the role of public relations? What messages, under what circumstances, will be both productive for management and believable/salient to employees?[6]
4.	When and to what extent are members of the dominant coalition changing policies based on input from public relations practitioners?[7]
5.	How can the relationship enhancing function of public relations and its contribution to organizational culture be evaluated?[8]
6.	How can employee information needs be identified and met? How and why do these needs vary? What is the relationship between meeting these needs and productivity?[9]
7.	How, and why and with what results are qualitative and quantitive research techniques used in public relations? What are good ways to evaluate the various research and evaluation techniques?[10]
8.	How can the effectiveness of public relations be communicated effectively to top management?[11]
9.	How can top management be persuaded to share information that employees seek?[12]
10.	What are agenda-setting functions of employee media? How is it decided what subjects and issues will be addressed in employee media? How do these media help further an organization's agenda? How do they affect an orgaization's climate?[13]

"More emphasis on evaluation techniques."

"More emphasis on evaluation of the effectiveness of public relations, especially campaigns, and especially in the public sector—for example, in health care and drug abuse."

"More emphasis on methods of assessing productivity of public relations efforts."

"Increased pressure on public relations to prove itself as a professional discipline—pressure from both academic purists and practitioners, for antithetical reasons."

FIGURE 8.3

Questions about internal factors specifically, managerial considerations

Rank Order	Priority Questions from the 1990 Panel
1.	What are the concepts of public relations held by current, past and future members of top management? How do these perceptions of top management compare to those of public relations practitioners? How do attitudes of top management affect role expectations and performances of public relations practitioners?[14]
2.	How, under what circumstances, and to what extent is public relations considered by members of the dominant coalition? What are typical—and ideal—working relationships between public relations practitioners and members of an organization's dominant coalition?[15]
3.	What are ideal and actual roles of public relations practitioners? What are gender, organizational and situational factors that predict role expectations and performances of public relations practitioners? What are professional and educational qualifications of practitioners that make them best suited to perform these roles?[16]
4.	What are the effects of the public relations deparment's position within the hierarchy upon departmental effectiveness? What factors help predict or explain the hierarchical position of the public relations department?[17]
5.	What are the ways public relations considerations can be employed or brought to bear in other departments of the organizations? How can other managers be trained and sensitized to public relations issues and techniques?[18]
6.	How, when, where, why do—and why don't the roles of public relations practitioners reflect the ethical codes of the profession?[19]
7.	How are departmental goals and objectives defined by public relations departments? What kinds of cooperative efforts are required to reach consensus about these goals and objectives? How and in what ways is management by objectives used in public relations?[20]
8.	To what extent are—or should—the functions of advertising, marketing and public relations be coordinated within an organization?[21]
9.	What are typical and the most effective management styles and decision-making structures within public relations departments?[22]
10.	How do relationship-enhancing roles of public relations practitioners compete with others roles, such as those of propaganda and publicity?[23]

This last comment does not suggest countervailing trends so much as it does a confluence of trends affecting today's public relations practitioners and scholars. On the one hand, practitioners are being pressured to be more accountable and cost-effective; consequently, there is a trend for practitioners to use more applied research strategies in their work to measure their effectiveness. On the other hand, scholars in the field are being pressured to conduct more systematic, theory-building

FIGURE 8.4

Questions about internal factors specifically, the technical core of the organization

Rank Order	Priority Questions from the 1990 Panel
1.	How and why do public relations roles and practices vary from one type of organization to another: private vs. public, profit vs. not-for-profit, retail vs. wholesale, routine vs. nonroutine technologies, highly regulated vs. unregulated?[24]
2.	What are the consequences of the new communication technologies or the practice of public relations? For example, how can new technologies be used to improve employee relations, or financial relations? What are the consequences of the new communication technologies on organizational structure and patterns of communication?[25]
3.	What are preconditions for and consequences of marketing, advertising and public relations units merging—either agencies or departments? What factors help explain or predict the growth of public relations agencies and departments?[26]
4.	How does the concept of organizational culture help explain or predict the function of public relations?[27]
5.	What organizational factors might account for the subordination of public relations to advertising, marketing—or, vice versa?[28]
6.	What are the relationships among various measures of organizational size and scope (such as assets, degree of slack resources, number of employees, domain and marketplace) and the sophistication of public relations practices across industries, technologies, and environments?[29]
7.	What changes have taken place in the reliance on internal public relations specialists vs. external agencies and counselors for organizations of different sizes and types?[30]
8.	What are the implications of the different locations where the public relations function is performed—for example, separate department, outside counsel or agency, subsidiary or corporate headquarters?[31]
9.	How can the process of day-to-day decision-making be shaped to reflect management's relationship-building responsibilities?[32]
10.	What has been the impact of advertising agency takeovers on the public relations function of these agencies?[33]

research; consequently, there is a trend for scholars to conduct fewer descriptive, applied studies, and to conduct more long-range, generalizable studies that test and develop specific theories.

These two trends—the drive for accountability among practitioners, and desire among scholars to conduct more scientific research—probably will merge in the 1990s as never before, because there are several major scientific theory-building research projects underway

FIGURE 8.5

Questions about external factors specifically, organizations, groups and individuals outside the immediate control of the local organization

Rank Order	Priority Questions from the 1990 Panel
1.	How do practitioners and others measure changes in attitudes, opinions and behavior of various publics? What are causal relationships among these factors? How do these factors influence relationships among individuals, groups and organizations?[34]
2.	How do organizations resolve conflicts of interest among their own internal publics on the one hand, and external publics and society on the other?[35]
3.	What makes a public relations campaign successful? Does it depend on the cause, the way audiences are defined and targeted, the media, or what, and under what conditions?[36]
4.	What roles do public relations practitioners play in setting media agendas and, as a result, the public's agenda?[37]
5.	What factors might account for any gap between the public's perception and the organization's self-perception? How do internal self-perceptions affect external perceptions of an organization? What are the relationships of these perceptions to "the facts"?[38]
6.	When are public relations practitioners perceived as credible advocates for "external" publics, such as consumers, by those publics and by management? What factors influence how these publics perceive and express needs that might be met by public relations practitioners?[39]
7.	What are effective ways to establish two-way communication among critical—even hostile publics? When and under what conditions do these techniques work?[40]
8.	In what ways are the shift from journalism training to communications management training and its emphasis or public relations theory affecting the practice of public relations?[41]
9.	Are employer expectations being met by the current nature of public relations education? To what extent are employer expectations in conflict with the goals of higher education and professionalism in public relations?[42]
10.	To what degree are society's needs to understand and apply public relations being met by public relations education at both the high school and university levels?[43]

that will generate a range of immediately practical applications for public relations practitioners. Properly applied, this new scientific knowledge about the influence of public relations on organizational performance and social responsibility will increase the power and influence of the practice of public relations. Practitioners will have better conceptual frameworks and better technical tools to conduct even more systematic public relations.

FIGURE 8.6

Questions about external factors specifically, laws and public policies

Rank Order	Priority Questions from the 1990 Panel
1.	To what extent do public relations ethics reflect society's growing ethical concerns about financial relations, government affairs, religion?[44]
2.	What are appropriate criteria for evaluating the ethics of public relations practitioners? What are and have been trends in social consensus about what constitutes right/wrong behavior for individuals, groups and organizations?[45]
3.	How effective are public relations efforts to impact public policy and laws on behalf of their organizations or clients?[46]
4.	What impact does the First Amendment have on the practice of public relations? For example: Is there really such a thing as commercial free speech? When and why does the First Amendment affect private and public policies that reguate public communication? What connections does the First Amendment make between public relations practitioners and the news media?[47]
5.	What are the latest developments in the law that apply to public relations?[48]
6.	What are public relations consequences of affirmative action legislation and environmental impact policies?[49]
7.	What roles do codes of ethics, such as those by IABC and PRSA, play in establishing professional standards? How often and why do practitioners violate these codes? What are the best ways of revising, monitoring and enforcing these codes?[50]
8.	In what ways does the potential for litigation influence public relations practices?[51]
9.	How does publicity and public relations affect the outcomes of legal cases?[52]
10.	What are the pros and cons of licensing, professional certification, and accreditation of public relations practitioners—and how should they be implemented?[53]

The confluence of these two trends also will generate even more systematic, theory-building research conducted in public relations. Although there was among the 1990 Delphi panelists a wide variety of scholarly approaches to the subject, there was remarkable agreement on the importance of the priority research questions. Scholarly forums and professional associations in the next few years will play an increasingly important role in the development of the public relations profession, because they will encourage more systematic, theory-building research focused on an increasingly well-defined set of research questions.

FIGURE 8.7

Questions about the external factors specifically, core societal conditions, trends, values and beliefs

Rank Order	Priority Questions from the 1990 Panel
1.	What is the role of organizations and their public relations in influencing societal values, beliefs and morals?[54]
2.	How does—and how should—public relations address significant trends in society; for example, the feminization of the workforce, the aging of America's population, changes within minorities and ethnic groups, terrorism, drug abuse, the spread of sexually transmitted diseases, and illiteracy?[55]
3.	What are the most effective techniques public relations practitioners are using to monitor globally significant issues and events, such as those underway in Russia, China, the United States, Africa and the Middle East? How do practitioners present this information most effectively to top management?[56]
4.	How do social and environmental changes affect the demands for public relations from various types of organizations? How do the characteristics of an organization affect its ability to adapt to these changes?[57]
5.	How can public relations help resolve conflict between social and economic values?[58]
6.	In what ways does the interdependence of a global economy impact upon organizational public relations?[59]
7.	What responsibilities do public relations practitioners have toward a public's perceived "right to know"? How does this right vary from culture to culture? Is it an inalienable right?[60]
8.	To what degree are public relations practitioners responsible—and what corrective actions are possible—for mass media misrepresentations and the proliferation of false perceptions of social values and needs within popular culture?[61]
9.	How do concepts of corporate social responsibility vary from society to society?[62]
10.	How and why are issues management programs effective?[63]

Another important set of trends suggested by the Delphi panelists is the need for more research about relationships. For example, these were some of the predictions:

> "More relational research; that is, relationships developed through public relations practice, such as agency/organization, public relations management/top management, public relations/marketing/advertising, etc."

FIGURE 8.8

Major research trends in the field of public relations during the 1990s

Rank Order	Research Trends
1.	More emphasis on evaluation and assessment.[64]
2.	Increased interest in tracking of trends/issues which impact upon organizations and the methods for analyzing these trends/issues.[65]
3.	Increased interest in corporate social responsibility and values analysis.[66]
4.	Emphasis on integration of public relations with business practices; for example, using decision analyses, marketing research methods, etc.[67]
5.	More research on relationships: research about not only source/sender/receiver but also about agency/organization, public relations management/top management, public relations/marketing, etc.[68]
6.	An increased emphasis on coorientational relationships and "reality construction" (cognitive linkages of evaluations and behaviors) as key thrusts. Coorientation among practitioners, employers, clients, specialized publics and lay publics lie at the heart of recent work by Ehling, Jeffers, the Grunigs, Culbertson and others; yet, these relationships have only begun to get substantial research attention.[69]
7.	More analysis and discussion of ethics in public relations.[70]
8.	More use of critical theories to analyze public relations and its influence on society.[71]
9.	More applications of theories in public relations research, planning and evaluation.[72]
10.	More theory development.[73]

"More emphasis on relationship perspectives: the relationship between sources and communicators, communicators and audiences."

"An increased emphasis on coorientational relationships and 'reality construction' (cognitive linkages of evaluations and behaviors) as key thrusts. Coorientation among practitioners, employers, clients, specialized publics and lay publics lies at the heart of recent work. . ."

IN SUMMARY . . .

The major conclusion from the Delphi studies is that there remains much to learn about some very basic questions. While public relations practitioners have been engaging in more research over the past ten years, the bulk of this research can be described as applied, descriptive research with limited generalizability.[72] In the past ten years, while there has been an increase in the amount of research reported in the two major journals in the field, the bulk of the research being conducted and reported continues to be descriptive research, case studies, and philosophical discussions about public relations techniques and professionalism. What is so promising is that progress is being made investigating these issues. Research questions are becoming more sophisticated and more scientific. Data-based knowledge is now available from which to build even stronger theories about the causes and effects of public relations. As the Institute for Public Relations Research and Education has indicated from basic and applied research activities in public relations, managers will find "news they can use" to help them make practical decisions about public relations programs and campaigns.[73]

Study Questions

1. What are some of the most important research questions in the field of public relations?
2. Write a brief checklist for conducting a Delphi study. Using an example of your own choosing, explain how you could use this technique to develop consensus among members of the dominant coalition within a certain organization.
3. What are some of the most significant trends in public relations research?
4. True or false: the bulk of the research being conducted and reported in public relations continues to be descriptive research, case studies, and philosophical discussions about public relations techniques and professionalism. Support your answer with examples.

Endnotes

1. McElreath, Mark P. "Priority research questions in public relations for the 1980s," (New York, NY: Foundation, Now Institute for Public Relations Research and Education, 1980).
2. McElreath, Mark P., "Priority research questions in the field of public relations for the 1990s: Trends over the past ten years and predictions for the future," paper presented to the Speech Communication Assn., November, 1989.
3. Preston, Lee, "Corporate social performance and policy: A synthetic framework for research and analysis," in *Research in Corporate Social Performance and Policy,* edited by Lee Preston, Vol. 1 (Greenwich, Conn.: JAI Press, 1978) pp. 1–26.
4. Berger, C. and S. Chaffe, *Handbook of Communication Science* (Newbury Park, CA: Sage Publications, 1987); Grunig and Grunig, "Models of public relations: A review and reconceptualization," paper presented to the Public Relations Division of the Association for Education in Journalism and Mass Communication, August, 1990.

5. Dozier, David M., "Planning and Evaluation in Public Relations Practice," *Public Relations Review*, Vol. 11, No. 2, Summer, 1985, pp. 17–25; and, Finn, David, "The Elements of Sound Public Relations Planning," *The Forum* New York, NY: Ruder and Finn, Summer, 1984.

6. Acharya, Lalit, "Public Relations Environments," *Journalism Quarterly*, Vol. 62, No. 3, Autumn, 1985, pp. 557–584; and Tomasko, Robert M., *Downsizing: Reshaping the Corporation for the Future* (New York: Amacom, 1989).

7. Rossi, Peter, and Howard Freeman, *Evaluation: A Systematic Approach* (Newbury Park, CA: Sage Publications, 1989).

8. Stamm, Keith, "Strategies for Evaluating Public Relations," *Public Relations Review*, Winter, 1977, pp. 120–128; and Kruckebert, Dean, and Kenneth Starck, *Public Relations and Community: A Reconstructed Theory* (Hillsdale, NJ: Lawrence Erlbaum Associates, 1989).

9. Reuss, Carol, and Donn Silvis, *Inside Organizational Communication* (New York: Longman, 1985); and Pincus, J. David, Janice E. Knipp, and Robert E. Rayfield, "Internal communication and job satisfaction revisited: The impact of organizational trust and influence on commercial bank supervisors," in *Public Relations Research Annual*, edited by L. A. and J. E. Grunig (Hillsdale, NJ: Lawrence Erlbaum Associates, 1990) pp. 173–192.

10. Broom, Glen M., and David M. Dozier, *Using Research in Public Relations: Applications to Program Management* (Englewood Cliffs, NJ: Prentice-Hall, 1990).

11. Grunig, James E., editor, *Excellence in Public Relations and Communication Management: Contributions to Effective Organizations*, (Hillsdale, NJ: Lawrence Erlbaum Associates, 1992).

12. Pincus, J. David, and Robert Rayfield, "The relationship between top management communication and organizational effectiveness," paper presented to the Public Relations Division of the Association for Education in Journalism and Mass Communication, Norman, Oklahoma, August, 1986.

13. Grunig, Larissa A., "Meeting the communication needs of employees," *Public Relations Review*, Vol. 11, No. 2, 1985, pp. 43–53; and Carrell, Robert, and Douglas Ann Newsom, *Public Relations Writing*, (Belmont, CA: Wadsworth, 1986).

14. Lapetina, Alison, and Walter Lindenmann, "Management's view of the future of public relations," *Public Relations Review*, Vol. 7, No. 3, Fall 1982, pp. 3–14; E. W. Brody, "Changing roles and requirements of public relations," *Public Relations Review*, Vol. 11, No. 4, Winter 1985, pp. 22–28; and Larissa A. Grunig, "Power in the public relations department," in *Public Relations Research Annual*, edited by L. A. Grunig and J. E. Grunig (Hillsdale, NJ: Lawrence Erlbaum Associates, 1990).

15. Grunig, J. E., and L. A. Grunig, "Toward a theory of the public relations behavior of organizations: Review of a program of research," in *Public Relations Research Annual* (Hillsdale, NJ: Lawrence Erlbaum Associates, 1989) pp. 27–63.

16. Broom, Glen M., "A comparison of sex roles in public relations," *Public Relations Review*, Vol. 8, No. 3, Fall 1982, pp. 17–22; Brody, E. W., "Changing roles and requirements of public relations," *Public Relations Review*, Vol. 11, No. 4, Winter 1985, pp. 22–28; and Broom, G. M., and D. M. Dozier, "Advancement for public relations role models," *Public Relations Review*, Vol. 12, No. 1, Spring 1986, pp. 37–56.

17. Grunig, L. A., "Power in the public relations department," *op.cit.*

18. Burger, Chester, "How management views public relations," *Public Relations Quarterly,* Vol. 27, No. 4, pp. 27–30; Goldman, Jordon, "Public relations in the marketing mix: Introducing vulnerability relations," paper presented to the Public Relations Division of the Association for Education in Journalism and Mass Communication, August, 1985; Lauzen, Martha M., "Losing control: An examination of the management function in public relations," paper presented to the Public Relations Division of the Association for Education in Journalism and Mass Communication, August, 1990.

19. Wright, Donald K., "Examining ethical and moral values of public relations people," *Public Relations Review,* Vol. 15, No. 2, Summer 1989, pp. 19–33.

20. Nager, Norman, and T. Harell Allen, *Public Relations Management by Objectives* (New York, NY: Longman, 1984).

21. See the entire issue of *Public Relations Review,* Vol. 17, No. 3, Fall, 1991, which is devoted to public relations and marketing.

22. Grunig, J. E., editor, *op. cit.,* 1992.

23. Acharya, Lalit, "Effect of perceived environmental uncertainty on public relations roles," paper presented to the Public Relations Division of the Association for Education in Journalism and Mass Communication, East Lansing, Michigan, August, 1981; Cottone, Laura, D. G. Wakefield, R. Rocco Cottone, and Willard North, "Public relations roles and functions by organization," *Public Relations Review,* Vol. 11, No. 4, Winter 1985, pp. 29–37.

24. Acharya, Lalit, "Public Relations Environments," *Journalism Quarterly,* Vol. 62, No. 3, Autumn 1985, pp. 557–584; Broom, Glen M., and David Dozier, "Advancement for public relations role models," *op.cit.,* 1986.

25. Funk, Janet, and Charles Steinfield, editors, *Organizations and Communication Technology* (Newbury Park, CA: Sage, 1990).

26. Bernstein, J. "Merge Advertising and Public Relations: Yes and No." *Advertising Age,* May 13, 1985, p. 70; Crespy, Charles T., "Global Marketing is the New Public Relations Challenge," *Public Relations Quarterly,* Summer 1986, pp. 5–8; VanLeuven, James, editor, special issue of *Public Relations Review* devoted to marketing and public relations, Vol. 17, No. 2, Summer 1991.

27. Everett, James L., "Organizational culture and ethnoecology in public relations theory and practice," in *Public Relations Research Annual,* edited by L. A. and J. E. Grunig, Vol. 2 (Hillsdale, NJ: Lawrence Erlbaum Associates, 1990) pp. 235–251.

28. Lauzen, Martha M., "Marketing imperialism: Encroachment of the public relations function," *Public Relations Review,* Vol. 17, No. 2, Summer 1991.

29. Grunig, J. E., editor, *op.cit.,* 1992.

30. Gitter, A. George, "Public relations roles: Press agent or counselor?" *Public Relations Review,* Vol. 7, No. 3, Fall 1981, pp. 7–22; and, Brody, E. W., "Changing roles and requirements of public relations," *Public Relations Review,* Vol. 11, No. 4, Winter 1985, pp. 22–28.

31. Jablin, Frederick, "Formal organizational structure," in Jablin, et. al., editors, *Handbook of Organizational Communication* (Newbury Park, CA: Sage, 1987); and Grunig, Larissa A., "Power in the public relations department," *op.cit.*

32. Ehling, William P. "PR administration, management science, and purposive systems," *Public Relations Review,* Vol. 1, No. 2, Fall 1975, pp. 15–54; Steel, Fritz, *The Role of the Internal Consultant: Effective Role Shaping for Staff*

Positions, (Boston, MA: CBI Publishing Company, Inc., 1982); Strenski, James B., "The Future of Consultancy," *Public Relations Quarterly,* Spring 1983, pp. 18–21; and Grunig, J. E., editor, *op.cit.,* 1992.

33. Wells, William, John Burnett, and Sandra Moriarty, *Advertising: Principles and Practice,* particularly chapter 19, "Public Relations," (Englewood Cliffs, NJ: Prentice-Hall, 1989), pp. 475–492.

34. Grunig, J. E., "Symmetrical presuppositions as a framework for public relations theory," in *Public Relations Theory,* edited by Carl H. Botan and Vincent Hazleton, Jr. (Hillsdale, N.J.: Lawrence Erlbaum Associates, 1989) pp. 17–44; and Miller, G. R., "Persuasion and public relations: Two p's in a pod," in *Public Relations Theory, ibid,* pp. 45–66.

35. Putnam, L. L., and M. Scott Poole, "Conflict and negotiation," in *Handbook of Organizational Communication,* edited by F. M. Jablin, L. L. Putnam, K. H. Roberts, and L. W. Porter (Newbury Park, CA: Sage, 1987) pp. 549–599.

36. Rice, Ronald E., and Charles K. Atkins, *Public Communication Campaigns,* (Beverly Hills, CA: Sage, 1989); and Salmon, Charles T., *Information Campaigns* (Newbury Park, CA: Sage, 1989).

37. Weaver, David, and Swanzy Nimley Elliott, "Who sets the agenda for the media? A study of local agenda-building," paper presented to the Association for Education in Journalism and Mass Communication, Gainesville, Florida, August, 1984; Broom, Glen M., and David M. Dozier, "Advancement for public relations role models," *Public Relations Review,* Vol. 12, No. 1, Spring 1986, pp. 37–56; VanSlyke Turk, Judy, "Public relations' influence on the news," in *Precision Public Relations,* edited by Ray Hiebert (New York: Longman, 1988) pp. 224–239; and McCombs, Max, and Sheldon Gilbert, "News influence on our pictures of the world," in *Perspectives on Media Effects,* edited by Jennings Bryant and Dolf Zillman (Hillsdale, NJ: Lawrence Erlbaum Associates, 1989).

38. Euske, Nancy A., and Karlene H. Roberts, "Evolving perspectives in organization theory: Communication implications," in *Handbook of Organizational Communication,* edited by Fredric M. Jablin, Linda L. Putnam, Karlene H. Roberts, and Lyman W. Porter (Beverly Hills, CA: Sage, 1987) pp. 41–69; and Cheney, George, and Steven L. Vibbert, "Corporate discourse: Public relations and issue management," *ibid,* pp. 165–194.

39. *Organizing a Company's Consumer Advisory Panel: A Guide to Establishing Face-To-Face Consumer Participation Programs,* and other literature, are available from the Society of Consumer Affairs Professionals in Business, 4900 Leesburg Pike, Suite 311, Alexandria, Virginia 22302. See also *Pathways—Customer Satisfaction,* and other publications, by the American Productivity and Quality Center, 123 North Post Oak Lane, Houston, Texas 77024.

40. Carlisle, John A., and Robert C. Parker, *Beyond Negotiation: Redeeming Customer-Supplier Relationships,* (New York, NY: John Wiley & Sons, 1988); Putnam, Linda L. and M. Scott Poole, "Conflict and negotiation," in *Handbook of Organizational Communication,* edited by Frederic M. Jablin, Linda L. Putnam, Karlene H. Roberts, and Lyman W. Porter (Beverly Hills, CA: Sage, 1987) pp. 549–599.

41. VanSlyke Turk, Judy, and Don Wright, "Issues facing public relations education," in *Learning to Teach: What You Need to Know to Develop a Successful Career as a Public Relations Educator,* edited by Judy VanSlyke Turk (New York, NY: Public Relations Society of America, 1991).

42. Anderson, James W., "Survey reveals practitioners and educators agree on content for public relations education," paper presented to the Public Relations Society of America, Detroit, Michigan, 1985; and Cotton, Laura Perkins, Gay Wakefield, and Rod Troester, "State of the art of international public relations education," paper presented to the Association for Education in Journalism and Mass Communication, August, 1985.

43. Wright, Don, and Judy VanSlyke Turk, "Public relations education—the unpleasant reality," (New York, NY: Institute for Public Relations Research and Education, 1990).

44. Pearson, Ron, "Business ethics as communication ethics: Public relations practice and the idea of dialogue," in *Public Relations Theory*, edited by Carl Boton and Vincent Hazelton, Jr. (Hillsdale, NJ: Lawrence Erlbaum Associates, 1989) pp. 135–158; *Ethics Policies and Programs in American Business*, report by The Ethics Resource Center, Washington, D.C., 1990.

45. Pearson, Ron, "Ethical values or strategic values? The two faces of systems theory in public relations," in *Public Relations Research Annual*, Vol. 2 (Hillsdale, NJ: Lawrence Erlbaum Associates, 1990) pp. 219–234; Johannesen, Richard L., *Ethics in Human Communication*, 3rd edition (Prospect Heights, IL: Waveland Press, 1990).

46. Heath, Robert L., and Richard Alan Nelson, *Issues Management: Corporate Public Policymaking in an Information Society* (Beverly Hills, CA: Sage, 1986); special issue on issues management, *Public Relations Review*, Vol. 19, No. 1, Winter, 1991.

47. Walsh, Frank, *Public Relations and the Law* (New York, NY: Foundation for Public Relations Research and Education, 1988); Pratt, Catherine A., "First Amendment protection for public relations expression: The applicability and limitations of the commercial and corporate speech models," in *Public Relations Research Annual*, edited by Larissa A. Grunig and James E. Grunig, Vol. 2 (Hillsdale, NJ: Lawrence Erlbaum Associates, 1990) pp. 205–218.

48. Use Lexus or Nexus databases to search for current articles about public relations and the law; see also, index of current articles about legal issues published in *Public Relations Review*.

49. Buchholz, R. A., W. D. Evans, and R. A. Wagley, *Management Response to Public Issues* (Englewood Cliffs, NJ: Prentice-Hall, 1985); special issue devoted to issues management, *Public Relations Review*, Vol. 16, No. 1, Spring 1990.

50. Wright, Don K., "Ethics research in public relations: An overview," *Public Relations Review*, Vol. 15, No. 2, Summer, 1989.

51. Walsh, Frank, "Legal considerations," in *Inside Organizational Communication*, edited by Carol Reuss and Donn Silvis (New York, NY: Longman, 1985) pp. 291–314.

52. Simon, Norton J., "Right of privacy, right to know: Which prevails?" *Public Relations Review*, Vol. 3, No. 1, Spring, 1977, pp. 5–18; Byrnes, Sondra J., "Privacy vs. publicity: Flip sides of the same coin," *Public Relations Review*, Vol. 16, No. 4, Winter, 1990, pp. 29–35.

53. See the section on "Accreditation, certification, and licensing" in "The Public Relations Body of Knowledge," report, in *Public Relations Review*, Vol. 14, No. 1, Spring, 1988.

54. Everett, James L., "Organizational culture and ethnoecology in public relations theory and practice," in *Public Relations Research Annual,* Vol. 2, (Hillsdale, NJ: Lawrence Erlbaum Associates, 1990).

55. Burger, Chester, "Public relations in the twenty-first century," in *Experts in Action,* 2nd edition, by Bill Cantor, edited by Chester Burger (New York, NY: Longman, 1989) pp. 479–483; special issue devoted to "What's ahead in the 1990s," *Public Relations Journal,* January, 1990.

56. Cattell, Mark E., "An assessment of public relations and issue management in relations to strategic planning in American business corporations," *Public Relations Review,* Vol. 12, No. 3, Fall, 1986; Krippendorf, Klaus, "Monitoring an organization's symbolic environment," *Public Relations Review,* Vol. 12, No. 3, Fall, 1986; and Heath, Robert L., "Corporate issues management: Theoretical underpinnings and research foundations," in *Public Relations Research Annual* (Hillsdale, NJ: Lawrence Erlbaum Associates, 1990) pp. 29–66.

57. Grunig, James E., editor, *op. cit.,* 1992.

58. McLeod, Jack M., and Jay G. Blumler, "The macrosocial level of communication science," in *Handbook of Communication Science,* edited by Charles R. Berger and Steven H. Chaffee (Newbury Park, CA: Sage, 1987) pp. 271–324.

59. Clegg, Stewart R., *Modern Organizations* (Newbury Park, CA: Sage, 1990); and Featherstone, Mike, *Global Culture: Nationalism, Globalization and Modernity* (Newbury Park, CA: Sage, 1990).

60. Barron, J., and C. T. Diens *Handbook of Free Speech and Free Press* (Boston, MA: Little, Brown, 1979); Schauer, F., *Free Speech: A Philosophical Inquiry* (Cambridge, MA: Cambridge University Press, 1982).

61. Deetz, Stanley A., and Astrid Kersten, "Critical models of interpretive research," in *Communication and Organizations: An Interpretive Approach,* (Newbury Park, CA: Sage, 1983) pp. 147–172; Berger, Arthur Asa, *Media Analysis Techniques* (Newbury Park, CA: Sage, 1991).

62. Featherstone, Mike, *Consumer Culture and Postmodernism* (Newbury Park, CA: Sage, 1991).

63. Heath, Robert L., "Corporate issues management: Theoretical underpinnings and research foundations," in *Public Relations Research Annual,* Vol. 2, edited by Larissa A. Grunig and James E. Grunig (Hillsdale, NJ: Lawrence Erlbaum Associates, 1990) pp. 29–66.

64. Lindenmann, Walter K., "Research, evaluation and measurement: A national perspective," *Public Relations Review* Vol. 16, No. 2, Summer, 1990, pp. 3–16.

65. Broom, Glen M., and David M. Dozier, *Using Public Relations Research: Applications in Program Management* (Englewood Cliffs, NJ: Prentice-Hall, 1990).

66. Pearson, Ron, "Ethical values or strategic values? The two faces of systems theory in public relations," in *Public Relations Research Annual,* Vol. 2, edited by Larissa A. Grunig and James E. Grunig (Hillsdale, NJ: Lawrence Erlbaum Associates, 1990) pp. 219–234.

67. *The Role of Public Relations in Quality-Improvement Programs* (New York, NY: Public Relations Society of America, 1990).

68. Lauzen, Martha M., "Losing control: An examination of the management function of public relations," paper presented to the Association for Education in Journalism and Mass Communication, August, 1990.

69. Ehling, William P., "Public relations management and marketing management: Different paradigms and different missions," paper presented to Public Relations Colloquium, San Diego, CA, 1990; Jeffers, Dennis W., "Using public relations theory to evaluate specialized magazines as communication channels," in *Public Relations Research Annual,* Vol. 1 (Hillsdale, NJ: Lawrence Erlbaum Associates, 1989) pp. 115–124; Grunig, James E. and Larissa A. Grunig, "Toward a theory of the public relations behavior of organizations: Review of a program of research," in *Public Relations Research, ibid.* pp. 27–66; Culbertson, Hugh M., "Breadth of perspective: An important concept for public relations," in *Public Relations Research Annual, ibid.,* pp. 3–26.

70. Pearson, Ron, "Beyond ethical relativism in public relations: Coorientation, rules, and the idea of communication symmetry," in *Public Relations Research Annual,* Vol. 1 (Hillsdale, NJ: Lawrence Erlbaum Associates, 1989) pp. 67–86.

71. Olasky, Marvin N. *Corporate Public Relations: A New Historical Perspective* (Hillsdale, NJ: Lawrence Erlbaum Associates, 1988).

72. Salmon, Charles R., editor, *Information Campaigns,* (Newbury Park, CA: Sage, 1989).

73. Botan, Carl H., and Vincent Hazleton, Jr., editors, *Public Relations Theory* (Hillsdale, NJ: Lawrence Erlbaum Associates, 1989).

CHAPTER NINE

How to Conduct Ethical Public Relations, Considering Intrapersonal, Interpersonal, Small Group, and Organizational Factors

. . . . . .

*B*ill *shifted gears and accelerated as he entered the stream of highway traffic. It was Monday morning, and the weatherman on the radio said the week's weather looked fine. This was Bill's daily 45–minute commute one-way from his suburban home to his office downtown, and despite the distance and time involved, he liked it because, unless someone called him on the car phone, it gave him some time alone to listen to music and think.*

This day he found himself thinking about the pressures building on him at work, where he was director of public relations. They were not overwhelming pressures. Some were big; some were small; all were just part of the job. He liked the company. He'd been with them ten years. It was a prosperous, regional real estate development firm with lots of good people to work with. He liked his job, and he was well paid.

One bit of pressure he had to deal with later this afternoon would be getting the feature story for the company newspaper cleared through the research lab manager who always spent too much time on stylistic issues. Bill always yielded to specialists when it came to the facts, but the writer in him resented anyone who capriciously edited his copy. He punched a button on the radio and thought about the editorial review board meeting later this week. Here was something he felt proud about because getting clearance on copy for the annual report had been a problem for his predecessor. The report used to be dull. Now it was packed with timely, even controversial issues. Bill had formed a small committee of top people, including the corporate lawyer and the chief financial officer. They were meeting this week to go over the table of contents he and his staff had prepared for next year's report. Bill knew the group's discussion would be lively and focus not only on what to include but also on what "spin" to give each bit of information.

He liked the group, primarily because someone always resolved "hot topics" by asking, "What do our most sophisticated stockholders want to know?" He jotted a note on a pad next to him. A car honked nearby.

What really bothered him this morning was the way the head of marketing had suggested in a recent meeting that the lack of sales in the new territory was the fault of a public relations campaign. It irritated him the way the marketing fellow always had to find someone to blame. Bill was going to have to sit down with the man today, if at all possible, and discuss the situation. There were more than a half dozen explanations for why the new service had not been received well in that one market. It made him angry to think about the petty backbiting ways of the other manager, but he knew what to do about it. First, they would meet one-on-one. Then, he would arrange for the two of them to sit down with their boss, the CEO, to discuss the matter; but later, not today.

He had bigger things to discuss with the CEO today. Corporate security told him last week they had a group of workers under surveillance in the warehouse and expected to bring in police and make arrests this week. They wanted no publicity on the matter, even though, according to corporate security, the stolen equipment ended up in the low-income housing projects that were being built by a well known business associate of the city's mayor. Bill didn't see how the arrests could possibly stay out of the press. He definitely didn't think it wise to downplay the situation. He thought they should do the opposite and take lots of pictures, maybe even invite the media to witness the arrests. He would take up the issue with the CEO at their regular weekly meeting this morning.

The biggest issue he had to talk about with the CEO was the proposal from the head of the architectural group to increase profits by cutting back on the cost of certain building supplies and on the time spent to install certain sections of homes. Bill thought the short-term profits would be offset by a decrease in long-term sales, especially when the poorer quality construction began to wear thin and home owners began to consider remodeling or moving. He wouldn't talk to the CEO about it this morning, though. There was a managers' meeting later this afternoon, and he thought it best to raise the issue there. He thought about the best way to frame the issue. What he wanted to say was that he knew damn well that they weren't in the business of building cheap homes. But, he also knew that a more productive way to get the answers he wanted was to ask, "Are these short-term strategies to save money consistent with our long-term goals? What are the consequences in five or ten years of our cutting a few corners today? What's the best way to estimate these long-term consequences?"

As he pulled into the office parking lot, he felt better about some of the ethical dilemmas he was facing because he had visualized how he would deal with them. As he parked his car, he remembered the prayer: "God grant me the serenity to accept the things I cannot change, the courage to change the things I can, and the wisdom to know the difference." Then, he made a mental note to call the corporate attorney.

. . .

DEFINING ETHICS

The pressures described in this vignette were created by ethical dilemmas typical for a public relations manager. The dilemmas range from relatively small, personal ones to large, corporate issues affecting thousands, sometimes millions of people. They are experienced as pressure because they are not easily solved. By definition, ethical dilemmas are not easy; they are perplexing situations involving decisions about what is right and wrong. Often they are situations requiring a choice between equally undesirable alternatives. They always have something to do with values, which means they evoke strong emotions.

Ethics can be defined as the set of criteria by which decisions are made about what is right and what is wrong. As management scientists have pointed out, one of the most important functions of a manager is to establish the criteria by which decisions are made within an organization.[1] By establishing these criteria—for example, to increase sales at all costs, to turn away unsavory clients if need be, to never question the decisions of superiors, to give women and minorities equal opportunities—managers establish guidelines which employees use to decide what is right and what is wrong.

What Is Right? What Is Good?

Ethics also can be defined as a branch of philosophy that is concerned not only with what is right and what is wrong, but also with what is good and what is bad. Public relations scholar and philosopher Don Wright has pointed out that ethics is not about being right; it's about being good. The key to ethical decision making in public relations, according to Wright, is determining what is a "good" action by an organization. Wright points out that Socrates and other Greek philosophers insisted that certain acts are essentially good, regardless of motives for doing them or their consequences: being honest, sincere, and truthful, for example. Contemporary philosophers have made the same point by arguing that being virtuous is the same, regardless of culture; it is knowing and practicing goodness.[2]

Wright says there is a problem when law becomes the primary standard for ethical action because the emphasis is placed upon what is right rather than on what is good, and upon society rather than on the individual. Law, Wright says, cannot solve the problems of ethics. Being ethical means more than being honest and obeying the law; being ethical means being good.[3]

In the official code of ethics of the Caterpillar Tractor Company, the same point is made:

"The law is a floor. Ethical business conduct should normally exist at a level well above the minimum required by law."[4]

While ethics and morals are often used synonymously, some distinctions can be made. Ethics can be defined narrowly as standards of personal integrity and honest dealings, especially between individuals within organizational settings. Morals can refer to principles considered important for acceptable behavior by individuals within families, communities and society at large. For example, white collar crimes often are described as violations of business ethics while other crimes, particularly violent and sex-related crimes, are referred to in terms of morals. On the other hand, ethics can be defined as broadly as morals. According to Morton Simon, "Ethics is concerned with clarifying what constitutes human welfare and the kind of conduct necessary to promote it."[5]

One management scientist has argued that the basic dimensions of any ethical situation can be identified by asking the following questions:[6]

What are the goals of the people involved in this situation? What do they want to achieve?

How do they intend to achieve these goals?

What are their motives for doing this?

What will be the consequences of their actions?

META-ETHICS: THE LOGIC OF ETHICS

There are two approaches to the study of ethics. One is to study ethics from a normative perspective, that is, to look upon ethics as guidelines or prescriptions that explain what ought to be done in a certain ethical situation. The other approach is to try to explain or predict scientifically why ethical decisions are made. This is a positive perspective, one that looks upon decision-making about what is right and what is wrong as a field of study. In this chapter, both approaches will be used.

There are two basic sources of authority for ethical decisions: one is intuitive; the other is naturalistic. An individual may use either or both when making ethical decisions. The intuitive approach acknowledges that certain actions, by themselves, are good; it assumes that a rational, abstract "good" exists and that there is a definitive, ultimate source of authority on ethical decisions. The other approach is naturalistic because it focuses on the causes and consequences of actions in a natural setting; it is situationally specific. It does not assume a single source of authority, but rather emphasizes factors leading up to and following a specific action. Technically, the intuitive approach is based on deontology, and the naturalistic approach is based on teleology. "Deontos" is Greek for "of the obligatory." Deontologists believe certain actions are "right" and "ought" to be done, regardless of the consequence. "Teleos" is Greek for "brought to its end." Teleologists believe the rightness of an action is determined by its causes and consequences.[7]

Applying Rules

An example of the intuitive approach is applying the Golden Rule: Do unto others what you would want others to do unto you. This is a rule for making ethical decisions which is common to most world religions. A similar single rule applied to an ethical situation is from 19th-century philosopher Immanuel Kant: Acts are ethical only if they are based on the assumption that if the decision-making principles were to become a universal law, all other individuals in the same category or set of circumstances would act the same.[8] A modern-day version of Kant's "categorical imperative" is called the TV rule: Do only those things you would feel comfortable explaining to a national TV audience.[9]

Intuitive rules do not focus on consequences; they focus on intentions, motives, and means. Here are other examples of intuitive rules:

> To be ethical, live Aristotle's Golden Mean: Take only those actions that represent moderation between extremes; avoid excessive actions.[10]

> Justice is blind: To be fair, those being judged should step away figuratively from their current status in life and step behind a "veil of ignorance" to be judged as equals, regardless of race, sex, class, or other real conditions.[11]

> Take only those actions which would be viewed as proper by a disinterested panel of professional colleagues.[12]

> To be ethical, never be coercive, because coercion is the suppression of someone's rights and freedoms.[13]

> The customer is always right: profits are maximized in the long run by satisfying customer needs.[14]

Sometimes, multiple intuitive rules are involved in one situation, and the dilemma is to select from among competing, and sometimes conflicting, obligations. For example, Ross has identified categories of "prima facie" duties or obligations that on first sight appear to govern what should be done in a situation, assuming all other factors are equal and there are no conflicting duties.[15] When factors are not equal and there are competing duties, an ethical dilemma results: choosing the dominant duty. For example, a business executive may say his first duty is to make a profit, but that duty may be in conflict with another: to do no harm to others. Ross identified six potentially conflicting categories of duties:

1. Duties of fidelity: not lying, being faithful, keeping promises.
2. Duties of gratitude: acknowledging services rendered, returning a favor, reciprocity.
3. Duties of justice: being fair, being equitable, being impartial.
4. Duties of beneficence: sharing good fortune, helping others to achieve happiness.
5. Duties of self-improvement: knowing and improving yourself.
6. Duties of noninjury: doing no harm to others.

Living with the Consequences of Your Actions

Another set of ethical judgments are made based on the consequences of actions. According to this naturalistic approach to ethical decision-making, if the consequences of an act are good, the act is ethical; if they are bad, the act is unethical. The key questions are: Should we consider only the consequences to oneself? Or, should we consider them with respect to everyone involved? Egoism asserts that actions which support an individual's best long-term interests are ethical. Utilitarianism asserts that actions which take into consideration the best interest of everyone are ethical. Act utilitarians contend that the right act is the one that produces the greatest ratio of good to evil for all concerned. Rule utilitarians state that if keeping a rule produces more total good than not using it, then it is an ethical rule.[16]

The "consequential" theories of ethics, egoism and utilitarianism, have two obvious weaknesses. One, they logically lead to the notion that the ends justify the means. They justify committing an unethical act, such as lying, if as a result good, such as saving someone from an injustice, is accomplished. Two, there can be conflicting duties. For example, the duty of producing the most good for the most people may be in conflict with other duties, such as the duty of beneficence. For example, members of the dominant coalition of an organization might argue against making significant philanthropic contributions on the grounds that the money could be spent better producing an improved product which would yield a greater good not only for society but also for the organization. A major weakness of egoism is that it simply does not address unethical actions taken by pairs, small groups, organizations or larger groups of individuals.

A number of philosophers have combined elements of intuitive and naturalistic ethics. For example, Rawl has suggested that what he calls a "difference principle" can be used in conjunction with a "justice principle" to account for inequalities in society.[17] His argument is that a just society is not necessarily a society without inequalities; rather, it is one in which inequalities are justifiable. The difference principle would spell out conditions for justifiable inequalities. Garrett has suggested that all ethical decisions are composed of motives, means, and consequences, and that combinations of intuitive principles and consequential theories are used in making judgments.[18]

ETHICAL RELATIVISM

Ethical relativism combines intuitive and naturalistic ethics by emphasizing the importance of values and the way in which those values are determined. The assumption of ethical relativism is that different social groups have different values and, consequently, different ethics. Another assumption of ethical relativism is that intuitive rules are based not on absolutes but on social values, which may vary from society to society.[19]

Conventionalistic relativism argues that concepts of right and wrong, good and bad, are based upon the accepted ways, habits, and traditions—the conventions—of society. This form of relativism appears, at first glance, to be a tolerant ethic because it acknowledges that each culture is different. But it also assumes, within one society, the dominance of mainstream social values; minority and individual values that differ from those of the majority are not considered, and the acts of dissidents often are called unethical or immoral. On the other hand, conventionalistic relativism assumes any act within a social system that incorporates the values of the system is an ethical act. Consequently, a social system dedicated to what outsiders might consider evil, immoral activities would not judge these actions unethical unless the insiders violated their own conventions; in other words, there is honor among thieves. Conventionalistic relativism assumes the moral infallibility of the larger social system.[20]

Individualistic relativism assumes the moral infallibility of the individual. It says if a person genuinely thinks an act is moral, it is. This egoistic view of ethics invites moral anarchy because it subordinates the views of others while, at the same time, asserting that all sincere individuals are right.

Taken to its logical extremes, ethical relativism becomes a useless guide for public relations managers because it seems to say that each ethical decision is unique. However, if a more moderate approach is taken—that situational factors should be analyzed and considered when making an ethical decision—then, ethical relativism offers useful insights.

Some people like to use ethical relativism because they don't like what they consider to be the intolerant, absolutist positions of nonrelativism. They chose ethical relativism because it is the lesser of two evils. According to communication scholars James Jaksa and Michael Pritchard, this is unfortunate, because nonrelativism, the intuitive approach to ethics, does not necessarily mean making black/white inflexible decisions. They identified three major misconceptions about nonrelativism:[21]

1. Nonrelativists are often suspected of intolerance toward those whose moral beliefs and values which differ from their own. No doubt some are intolerant in this way. But not all nonrelativists think that they have all (or even many of) the answers to moral questions. They can be open to being persuaded that they are mistaken. What they are committed to is the belief that some moral views are more acceptable than other views, even if they, or others, currently do not subscribe to the most acceptable views.

2. Nonrelativists are often accused of being absolutists who believe that exceptionless moral principles exist, such as "Never lie," "Never kill," or "Never be cruel." But nonrelativists don't necessarily believe in absolutes in this sense. They do believe that some general principles, criteria, or values are universally relevant in making determinations of what is right and wrong. For example, a nonrelativist could insist that the fact that something is a lie counts against it, even if other factors might be more decisive in a particular situation.

3. Nonrelativists are sometimes thought to have no respect for moral traditions, conventions, or practices. However, there is no reason nonrelativists cannot admit the relevance, and even the great importance, of moral traditions, conventions, and practices to questions of right and wrong. They simply refuse to accept the conventionalist view that these matters are necessarily decisive. Furthermore, even if nonrelativists think that some traditions, conventions, or practices are in some respect morally objectionable, it does not follow that they think it would be appropriate to intervene. Nonrelativists need not be any more interventionist than anyone else. In fact, they may often find it very difficult to justify imposing their values on other cultures. Respect for the integrity and ways of life of other cultures is itself a principle for which nonrelativist support can be given. Relativists cannot provide similar assurances.

A MODEL OF ETHICAL DECISION-MAKING

These various approaches can be summarized into a basic model of ethical decision-making (see Figure 9.1):

1. An individual is confronted with an ethical dilemma that is situationally specific; it occurs within a social system.

2. The individual is motivated to make a decision.

3. The individual considers the dilemma and the situation and applies one of the following sets of criteria:
    a. Intuitive rules, principles, or duties based on authoritative sources.
    b. Naturalistic predictions about causes and consequences of actions.
    c. A combination of both.

4. The individual makes a decision and acts.

THE POTTER BOX

Another model of ethical decision-making was proposed by Ralph Potter of the Harvard Divinity School. He suggested that there are four stages in ethical decision-making: 1) defining the situation, 2) identifying values, 3) selecting principles, and 4) choosing loyalties to stakeholders. (See Figure 9.2.) Potter and others have argued that individuals confronted with an ethical dilemma would make better decisions if they more deliberately considered issues that arise within each of the four areas of what has come to be called The Potter Box.[22]

To better understand how to use The Potter Box, consider the following example:

> The wife of the chief executive officer does not like the look of her husband's picture that appears in a series of new brochures about the company, 50,000 of which have been printed and are being readied for national distribution. She calls the public relations manager who hears the following request: "Could we do something about his picture? Replace it or something? I know he hates it. But he doesn't want to say anything. You know, people will think he's vain. Do us a favor, would you, and don't distribute the brochures. Could you reprint them with a new picture? I just know he'll appreciate it. And so will I." The public relations manager says he's not sure, that he will need to discuss it with others. It might not be possible, he tells her, but he will see what he can do.

The first set of issues in The Potter Box involves defining the situation. In this case, the corporation has paid for more than 50,000 brochures that are ready for distribution. The boss's wife, and presumably the boss, wants to reprint them. She says it's because he doesn't like the

FIGURE 9.1

Basic model of ethical decision-making

1. An individual is confronted with an ethical dilemma that is situationally specific; it occurs within a social system.
2. The individual is motivated to make a decision.
3. The individual considers the dilemma and the situation and applies one of the following sets of criteria:
   a. intuitive rules, principles, or duties based on authoritative sources;
   b. naturalistic predictions about causes and consequences of actions;
   c. a combination of both.
4. The individual makes a decision and acts.

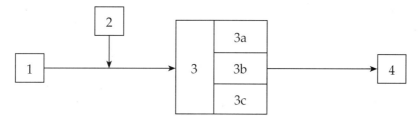

picture. Is there some other reason? What's her motive? What's the CEO's motive? Do you deny the boss's wife's request, possibly upsetting the boss? Do you reprint the brochures, absorbing the costs yet again? If you do, do you explain to others the real reason for the change, or do you develop an alternative justification for reprinting the brochures?

Identifying values in this case means recognizing the following: that the public relations manager wants to do a good job; that the wife wants the boss to look good; that the company doesn't want to pay for things twice; that the brochures are important and merit distribution; and, that the short-term loss may be recouped later in additional support from the CEO for other public relations projects which could generate more long-term benefits for the company and the public relations manager. With more analysis, more values could be identified. Going through The Potter Box several times enhances the analysis within each of the four areas.

A number of principles apply to this case. The dilemma is in selecting one or more of these principles over the others. Looking ahead to choosing loyalties may help this selection process. Here are some of the principles involved in this case:

1. A rational organization does not duplicate costs unnecessarily.
2. Spouses should not interfere in official business.
3. A favor for a superior will be returned.

FIGURE 9.2

The Potter Box

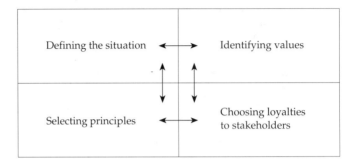

4. Give the greatest good to the greatest number of people.
5. Always look after #1—yourself.
6. Never make the boss look bad.
7. Do unto others as you would have them do unto you.
8. Never lie.
9. Do not waste the company's money.
10. When in doubt, don't do it.

Choosing loyalties in any ethical dilemma always is difficult. In this case, there are a number of loyalties to a variety of stakeholders: the boss, the boss's wife, the employees, the shareholders, the public relations manager's family, the manager himself, and his colleagues, including those in his profession.

What would be an ethical decision in this case? There are at least three options: 1) deny the wife's request, 2) honor her request, or 3) ignore the request and withdraw distribution of the brochures. Assuming the value of the brochures is substantial and that they warrant distribution, the third option is not ethical, nor is it good business sense. To honor her request can be defended on ethical grounds if an egoistic view is taken by the public relations manager that taking care of #1 is his most important job. To deny the wife's request can be defended on several ethical grounds: not wasting the company's money, and being loyal to the shareholders, employees, and others.

The key to using the Potter Box is to identify consistent sets of values, principles, and loyalties. A person holding inconsistent values, principles, and loyalties will experience psychic discomfort and will have difficulties rationalizing decisions based on such inconsistencies. Potter argues that relationships and negotiations are enhanced when all parties recognize not only differences but also similarities between and among the various sets of values, principles, and loyalties used by the people involved in the situation.

ETHICAL DECISIONS AT DIFFERENT LEVELS OF ANALYSIS

The factors that are considered important in an ethical situation depend upon the level of analysis. Within any communication system, there are five levels of analysis: intrapersonal, interpersonal, small group, organizational, and societal.[23] In this chapter, we will discuss the first four levels. The fifth level will be discussed in Chapter 10.

Intrapersonal Ethics

Within each individual there is a soul—the spiritual, emotional part of us that is full of thought about the world within us and about us. When an individual is confronted with an ethical dilemma, he or she feels it first deep within—sometimes physically becoming excited, nervous, or anxious—and at other times feeling it more abstractly, coming to grips intellectually with the conscience, that part of the self that is aware of what he or she is about. Hard ethical choices often are gut-wrenching, soul-shaking experiences.

Numerous individual characteristics influence a person's ethical decision-making. A laboratory experiment involving graduate business students suggested that four personality variables were associated with a person's unethical behavior: locus of control, economic orientation, political orientation, and dominant set of philosophical principles.[24] Unethical behavior was associated with a person's feelings that people and events outside the person's control were more powerful than the individual in directing the course of the person's life; with a strong drive to make money and be economically secure, at all costs; with an egocentric emphasis on individualism, versus egalitarianism; and, with a philosophical stance best described as Machiavellianism, the belief that political expediency is more important than morality.

One of the most common unethical acts is lying. At the "higher" levels of analysis—when pairs of individuals, small groups and organizations are considered—the act of lying is more accurately described with such words as duplicity, deception and fraud, concepts which suggest the coordination and cooperation of others in order to deceive, in other words, some kind of tacit or explicit conspiracy. At the "lowest" level, lying begins with an individual intentionally not telling the truth. Basic reasons people give for lying are the same as they give for telling the truth: they do it to acquire, maintain and protect valued resources.[25] However, the liar's intentions do affect how others judge the lies:[26]

> *Lies were considered more permissible if (1) lies saved others from shame or hurt, (2) lies protected people from punishment or disapproval for a minor failing that hurts no one, (3) lies were told to public officials, as long as no harm followed, and (4) lies were told to protect*

some gain the liar had previously acquired but to which the liar was not actually entitled. The least permissible lies were ones where liars could cause another to do something to bring about a benefit for the liar but a harm for the actor, and lies that hurt others for the liar's personal gain.[27]

Some individuals are better liars than others. With practice, liars cannot only mask nonverbal signals that might give away their lying behavior but also confuse the lie with the truth and behave as if the lie were the truth.[28] It takes focused concentration to tell a lie, however, so most liars give a number of consistent clues when they are lying: irrelevant statements, fewer hand gestures, increased pupil dilation, speech errors, and short, hesitant descriptions of the "facts." It is easier to tell the truth.[29]

Stages in Moral Development Kohlberg has hypothesized six stages of moral development in an individual:[30]

1. The stage of punishment and obedience—where right is the literal obedience to rules and authority.
2. The stage of individual instrument purpose and exchange—where right is serving one's own needs and making fair deals.
3. The stage of mutual interpersonal expectations, relationships and conformity—where right is being concerned about others, keeping loyalties and being motivated to follow rules.
4. The stage of social system and conscience maintenance—where right is doing one's duty to society.
5. The stage of prior rights and social contract or utility—where right is upholding the basic rights, values and legal contracts of society.
6. The stage of universal ethical principles—where right is determined by universal principles that all should follow.

At each of these stages, a person could experience cognitive dissonance—conflicting thoughts about what to do. When an individual acts unethically, what the person often feels is the discomfort of dissonance. Dissonance theory suggests that an individual will seek to reduce, if not eliminate, the displeasure caused by unharmonious thoughts by seeking out certain information and by rationalizing, "thinking away," the dilemma. The theory suggests that people want to avoid dissonance and will seek a balanced, harmonious set of thoughts; a healthy individual wants to be at-one-with-the-self.[31]

Differences Between Men and Women Kohlberg's stages of moral development have been criticized as being gender specific because the theory is based on research involving only males. Conducting research involving both women and men, Gilligan found significant differences between the sexes in moral values. Her explanation for the difference was not that one set of moral values was better than the other but that both sets of values were functional and consistent given the different expectations the two sexes experienced. According to Gilligan, it was only natural, given the differences in socialization, that men's and women's psychological and moral development would differ.[32]

While there are conflicting results, studies to date indicate some significant differences in ethical behaviors and predispositions between men and women. Based on surveys of more than 2,000 college students, two studies found that women are more sensitive than men to ethical issues.[33] Yet, two other studies indicated that, on the job, ethical perceptions of men and women are similar; but, in the workplace, men think that women—and women think that men—are less ethical than members of their own sex.[34] Wright also found mixed results when he measured moral values of public relations men and women: only on two of the six factors he identified were there slight statistical differences, with women being more severe in their judgments about socioeconomic and religious issues than men.[35]

Some feminist theories argue that significant differences exist between the ethics of men and women not only because of socialization but also because the two sexes are "hard wired" genetically to respond to relationships differently.[36] The argument is that from the moment of birth (which Judith Viorst called the first of "the necessary losses" in a person's lifetime), boys and girls respond differently to their initial separation from their mother and their increasing awareness of isolation and growing independence. Most boys deal with their isolation by becoming more aggressive and competitive, while most girls spend their time initiating and nurturing close relationships.[37] The essence of the argument is that, beyond whatever socialization may occur, women instinctively care more about relationships. The logic of this argument suggests that, with the increasing feminization of the public relations field, there will be more emphasis within the field on facilitating relationships, beyond that being caused by the spread of system-level interdependencies. For both men and women, it has been predicted that more emphasis will be given by professional associations to the ethic of caring.[38]

The Public Relations Society of America's Code of Professional Standards has been criticized as reflecting more male-oriented and fewer female-oriented ethical principles. Catherine Pratt of Ohio State University has argued that because the PRSA code emphasizes individual rights and responsibilities for protecting abstractions such as truth and accuracy, it reflects a male preference for rules and principles fostering individualism.[39] Women public relations managers, Pratt argued, "bring to the table" a different set of values than those of men, values that emphasize caring relationships, two-way communication, and empathy. While these principles of caring are not reflected in the PRSA code of ethics, Pratt pointed out, they are practiced daily by many public relations professionals, especially women.

Interpersonal Ethics

Analyzing ethical behavior between two individuals requires examining not only two sets of cognitions and perceptions but also the unique interaction, the chemistry, between two people.[40] Obviously, all factors at the individual level apply at this level also. At the interpersonal level of analysis, several factors affect ethical decision-making that are distinct from those considered at the individual level: bonding, power, loyalty, enabling behaviors, mutual exchange and communication.

Compared to being locked into a role relationship by contract—for example, between an employer and employee—bonding implies a certain degree of affection and trust between two people. To like and trust someone means to enjoy that person's company and to have confidence in their reliability and integrity. Unethical behavior erodes the trust and bonds that can develop between individuals.

Whenever two people are in a relationship, power exists; each person is able to influence the other. Power means influencing the behavior of another person in ways the affected person did not originally consider. To examine the ethical dimensions of a relationship means analyzing the ethical and unethical uses of power in that relationship. For example, coercion and brute force can be used to establish a relationship, though some would describe such a relationship as blatantly unethical because the freedom of one of the individuals has been restricted. Others would argue that there can be an ethical, unequal distribution of power in a relationship if the inequality can be justified, for example, restricting the rights of a prisoner in order to protect society or, taking the keys of a drunk friend and driving him home.

Sometimes the power of the dominant one in a relationship is based on expertise or seniority. At other times, the leader's ability to influence is based on the "power of the lower participant."[41] The enabling behaviors of partners in a relationship can foster trust and bonding, or they can generate and support unhealthy, unethical interactions. For example, two colleagues can actively help each other behave responsibly, or tacitly they can agree not to discuss certain behaviors, thereby silently endorsing these actions, even though the actions may be unethical.

Why do people sometimes enable each other to engage in unethical acts? Theories suggest that couples avoid costly exchanges and seek rewarding relationships.[42] If a person values the benefits of a relationship more than the cost of any one behavior by either partner, then undesirable or unethical actions may be overlooked, even encouraged. The value a couple gives to their relationship, and to each other, is determined, in part, by the rewards and costs of maintaining the relationship. In some instances, the partners may be more loyal to their relationship than to the unique selves in the relationship.

Loyalty most often refers to being faithful to a formal role or being committed to meeting an official obligation; so, it will be discussed in greater detail at the organizational level of analysis, specifically superior-subordinate relationships within hierarchies. However, friends and colleagues also exhibit loyalty to each other, and these loyalties may be more powerful than other role expectations and commitments. Personal loyalties are often used to justify lying. We want to protect from harm the person for whom we are loyal; we want to help that person; we want to maintain confidential information we have shared with that person; we want to meet that person's expectation of us—for example, respect that person's wish not to be told the truth.[43] Not keeping confidences, not volunteering to help in time of need and not avoiding public criticism of one another and the relationship are frequent causes of breakups in friendships.[44]

Healthy relationships between two individuals require honest, mutual exchanges and sharing of meanings; there must be good, ethical communication. Sadly, the more distressed the relationship, the more difficult it is for the partners to communicate and the more likely negative, unethical behaviors will be reciprocated.[45] Factors that cause stress in a couple's relationship may be identified at the individual, small group, organizational or societal levels of analysis.

Small Group Ethics

Public relations specialists are used to working with and for groups. Unique ethical issues occur within group settings that are distinct from what happens within a person or between two individuals. The hallmark of small groups is peer pressure, being forced by colleagues who are equal to each other in qualifications, abilities, maturity, etc., to consider an alternative point of view or set of actions. Sometimes, peer pressure can be positive, forcing groups to be innovative in their deliberations. At other times, peer pressure creates stagnating, predictable groupthink.

Peer pressure, actual and perceived, strongly influences ethical behavior. In a study of marketing managers in the United States, it was found that if a person perceived successful peers as behaving unethically or as having lots of opportunities to commit unethical acts, it was likely that that person also would behave unethically in comparable situations.[46] This study was later replicated with Israeli marketing managers, with the same results: the best predictor of ethical behavior is a person's perception of peer behavior.[47]

Perceived unethical behavior by peers can become a negative self-fulfilling prophecy. A survey of United States business executives found that most managers believed their colleagues to be far more unethical than they were themselves, giving the executives a rationale for unethical behavior.[48] This harmful, downward-spiralling tendency suggests its own antidote: training programs and communication campaigns that address ethics in the workplace may correct negative misperceptions about peer behaviors. We will discuss such training programs in greater detail in this chapter.

Sometimes loyalty to the group becomes so strong that opposing views are not solicited, critical thinking is threatened, and decisions are rationalized to meet peer pressure—groupthink occurs.[49] If independent thinking and freedom of choice are valued, then groupthink is unethical. If conformity and limited options are valued, then groupthink is ethical. There are a number of reasons why groupthink occurs:

1. The group, as a collective, thinks it is invulnerable and that it will protect its members from harm; consequently, group members will bolster each other and collectively take risks they would not take as individuals.
2. The group develops a we-versus-they mentality, with crude stereotypes of nongroup members.
3. The group defends, justifies and rationalizes its decisions to meet group expectations.
4. Group members operate on the assumption that they are moral and ethical, that whatever they're doing, it's the right thing to be doing.
5. To be a good group member means self-censorship: not saying what is not wanted. Even when the group encourages free-thinking—for example, in a brainstorming session—a lot of self-censorship occurs because group members want to save face and keep their colleagues from having to spend valuable time and energy discussing "inappropriate" issues.
6. The group most often perceives agreement and consent when there is silence, and there are many silent moments in most group meetings.
7. Direct pressure is applied when necessary to those who resist groupthink.[50]

Another reason groupthink is considered unethical in certain circumstances is because minority opinions are suppressed. "If some group members feel excluded, unappreciated, or powerless, it may indicate morally flawed group interactions," according to communication scholars Jaksa and Pritchard,[51] who based their argument on a principle of philosopher John Stuart Mill: "In order to find truth, we must hear all arguments in their most persuasive form." The 19th century philosopher gave four rules why minority opinions should be given a full hearing:

1. The minority might be right.
2. Even if the minority view is not wholly right, it might contain elements of truth.
3. Even if the minority opinion is not right, the majority opinion will be understood better if it can be defended against a dissenting opinion.
4. If majority opinions are not openly debated, they run the risk of becoming "dead dogmas."[52]

For many organizations, the solution to ethical problems in the workplace, including those generated by small groups, often involves another dose of small groups: in-house training programs to discuss and analyze corporate values and ethics. Most of these programs use peer pressure and small group dynamics in a positive way to facilitate a better understanding among employees of corporate values and ethics. A survey of 2,000 U.S.-based firms across eight industries indicated more than one-fourth had ethics training programs.[53] The purpose of the training is to create consensus on ethical issues.[54] Several organizations provide appropriate information and training materials.[55]

Organizational Ethics

An organization can be defined as a group of two or more people working together. While it is true that one person can operate as an organization (that's exactly what many independent public relations consultants do), most organizations are a collection of small groups operating together to achieve a common set of goals. Many people feel pressured to compromise their personal standards in order to achieve organizational goals.[56] At the organizational level of analysis, there are a number of factors that affect individual, small group and system-wide ethical behaviors: the size of the organization, its technology, rules and regulations, rewards and sanctions, hierarchy, roles, superior-subordinate relationships, boundary spanning relationships, and management strategies for dealing with the environment.

Size Measured in Terms of People and Money Two aspects of organizational size impact ethical behaviors. One is the number of employees. The greater the number of employees, the greater will be the diffusion of responsibilities. With more employees, there will be more finger-wagging and blame-ducking, and a lowering of the morale and morals.[57] The fewer the employees, the more easily ethical behaviors can be monitored. Consider two gas stations across the street from each other. One is owned and operated by an independent businessman who manages the station, buys his oil from a variety of places, and uses members of his family as employees. Across the street is a franchised dealership operated by one of the world's largest oil companies. One has very few employees; the other is linked to an organization employing hundreds of thousands of people worldwide. The prediction is that there will be more ethical problems—for example, employees' embezzling funds or stealing equipment and supplies—at the franchised gas station than at the mom-and-pop shop.

Another aspect of size is the amount of assets, often expressed as assets per employee. The greater the ratio of assets per employee, the more likely ethical behaviors will be monitored closely.[58] On the other hand, the greater the assets per employee, the greater the potential rewards for unethical behavior. Back at the franchised gas station, where the assets per employee are very high compared to the smaller station across the street, the potential rewards for unethical behavior are higher because the stakes are higher. Consequently, the behaviors of employees at the franchised gas station will be governed by more bureaucratic rules and regulations than at the family-owned station.

Technology In the above example, the technology, the essential work, of the two organizations was the same—pumping gas. Different technologies evoke different ethical behaviors. Sometimes the essential work of an organization is very routine; at other times, it is very nonroutine. If organizations strive to be rational and ethical, then we can assume that there will be more ethical dilemmas within nonroutine technologies because there are so many exceptions to the rules. The more complicated the technology is, the greater the uncertainty in doing the essential work of the organization will be. There also will be a greater number of ethical problems. For example, consider biogenetic research; not only is it difficult to manipulate genes, it also raises enormously difficult ethical issues. The manufacturer of car tires, a relatively routine technology, generates its fair share of ethical problems (for example, what to do with millions of nonbiodegradable used tires), but the ethical issues are less complex than those generated by nonroutine technologies.

Peripheral communication functions are often viewed as less ethical than centrally located technologies within an organization because these functions—such as marketing, advertising and public relations—are seen as dealing primarily with promotion and not so much with determining the actual form of the organization's products and services.[59] In many organizations, the concept of marketing communications has changed role expectations so that certain communication functions are seen as more central and, therefore, more ethical. For many organizations, however, public relations is not viewed as a core function that helps determine the final form of the product or service; consequently, the public relations function is viewed as less ethical than others.

Rules and Regulations Rules and regulations, red tape, are hallmarks of modern bureaucracies. While larger organizations do have more formal rules and regulations, they are common in all organizations, large and small.[60] An unorganized group of people is a bunch of people with nothing to do. To get this group of people to do some work, they need to get organized. To organize them means to establish certain procedures, rules and regulations which help to coordinate activities so tasks can be accomplished. Managers, including public relations managers, have the responsibility of establishing these rules and regulations, which become not only the criteria by which decisions are made within the organization, but also an outward manifestation of corporate ethics.

Rewards and Sanctions To enforce rules and regulations, managers use rewards and sanctions. Direct rewards include verbal praise, recognition, increased salary, promotion and other compensations. More indirect rewards are endorsements and support for projects, access to information, and inclusion in important decisions. Direct sanctions include verbal rebukes, disdain, no change or decrease in salary, demotion and other restrictions. More indirect sanctions are being ridiculed, having projects sabotaged, and being ostracized. Direct and indirect rewards and sanctions can be used to modify ethical behavior. Two laboratory studies involving business students indicate that rewarded unethical behavior increases; sanctioned ethical behavior decreases; and, visa versa—sanctioned unethical behavior decreases, and rewarded ethical behavior increases.[61]

Hierarchy One of the most important sets of rules within an organization establishes the hierarchy, or chain of command—who says what to whom with what effect. An organization's hierarchy dramatically affects ethical behavior because it defines superiors and subordinates and gives rise to invisible walls of accurate and inaccurate perceptions that are erected between "us" and "them." One study of business executives found that most members of lower management felt pressure from upper management to engage in unethical behavior. Furthermore, the study found, the lower the employee was on the chain of command, the more he or she perceived pressure to behave unethically.[62]

In a study that explored the ethical beliefs and behaviors of public relations professionals, Cornelius Pratt of Virginia Polytechnic Institute and State University found from self-reports that practitioners' beliefs are perceived as less ethical than those of management yet more ethical than those of their peers.[63]

Another study of business executives found the following factors influenced ethical decision-making: 1) personal codes of behavior, 2) behavior of superiors, 3) formal company policy, 4) industry ethical climate, and 5) the behavior of peers.[64] The majority of managers who participated anonymously in another study said that they felt pressure to compromise personal ethics to achieve corporate goals. The study of the U.S.-based international corporation found that more pressure was felt by managers who were under the age of thirty-five, earning under $30,000, and stationed at headquarters rather than in the field.[65]

Roles and Relationships The hierarchy defines roles and relationships. There are both formal role descriptions and informal role expectations.[66] In public relations, there are scores of possible job descriptions, but essentially two role expectations: to be a technician or to be a problem solver. These different role expectations will be explored in great detail in the last chapter which deals with career strategies in public relations. In terms of ethical behavior, the two role expectations for public relations practitioners have predictable results: technicians experience a limited array of ethical dilemmas, compared to those experienced by problem solvers. One reason why public relations practitioners, regardless of their personal role expectations, are often seen by others as less than ethical is because others see them as technicians responsible for the mechanics of communication and not the content.[67]

How public relations professionals relate to other professionals within their organization who have had formal training and adhere to independent standards of professional conduct raises a number of ethical issues:[68]

> Whose ethical code takes precedence over the others?
>
> What are the role expectations these different professions have for each other? Some define professionalism as having the ability, indeed, the responsibility, to work for any worthy client regardless of personal feelings and to perform competently. For example, lawyers and doctors will perform professional services for known criminals and unsavory persons. Should public relations practitioners provide professional services to similar types of despicable individuals who, nevertheless, should receive fair treatment?
>
> Where does the public relations professional turn for authoritative advice on how to handle such ethical conflicts brought on by different role descriptions and expectations—to the employer, the client, the self, or some "outside" authority?

Boundary Spanning Relationships Another set of relationships at the organizational level generates its own set of ethical questions. These relationships focus on public relations as it is practiced by independent agencies and by in-house specialists.

1. The practitioner-client relationship: Is all information shared by the client with the agency confidential? If so, how is it protected? If not, how is this determined? Is all of the client's information accurate? What if the client is shading the truth or not telling all the facts? What if the client is late in paying for services? When should an agency terminate a relationship with a client? When should a practitioner not take on a client? Should the agency bill clients for honest mistakes the agency makes? What if the client's request for market research borders on being industrial espionage?
2. The practitioner-as-agency-employee relationship: If the agency takes on a controversial client, or a client who is engaged in questionable, possibly illegal, practices, should the agency force all its employees to work on the account? (This is a hot question not only in public relations but also in advertising.)[69]

3. Practitioner-as-in-house-specialist relationship: To whom does the practitioner owe the greatest loyalty—immediate superior, members of the dominant coalition (which ones?), employees, or other stakeholders?
4. Practitioner-media-representative relationship: When do free passes, lunch, dinner, gifts, or junkets become bribes? When do awards for outstanding reporting from a client's industry become bribes for more good coverage? When can friends go off-the-record?
5. Practitioner-consumer relationship: Is puffery ethical? Is hype ethical? What is owed to the distant consumer in terms of truth in advertising and public relations?

Management Strategies for Dealing with the Environment In the next chapter, we will discuss in detail the impact of external publics, groups, other organizations, government agencies, institutions, and cultures on the ethical behavior of public relations practitioners; these are factors outside the immediate control of the focal organization. In this section, where the focus is on factors within an organization's control, we will discuss different management strategies for dealing with the environment. Often it is management's attitude, expressed as a strategy—more than the reality of what is going on in the environment—that affects the ethical performance of the organization and its employees, including public relations practitioners.[70] Depending on their perception of the environment, most managers adopt a combination of one or more of the following strategies: competition, co-optation, and/or coalition building. Each of these strategies has ethical implications.

Competition means considering publics, groups and organizations in the environment as striving to outdo one another for scarce resources. Competition is a win-lose proposition that assumes most players will not be winners. Competition encourages aggressive, ego-centered actions on the part of individuals and organizations. Competition does not require cooperation, although eliciting cooperation undoubtedly helps the aggressive competitor win.

Co-optation, on the other hand, is based on cooperation, and coercion. It uses subtle and, sometimes, not-so-subtle forms of coercion to bring together certain publics, groups and organizations into a temporary arrangement so that scarce resources can be used selfishly to the advantage of one party. Co-optation is a preemptive strategy used primarily to bring weak parties within the strong party's sphere of control. Even when the weak finesses the strong into compliance, co-optation has to use coercion to elicit cooperation because those being co-opted do not win as much out of the arrangement as the initiating party. Co-optation is a form of exploitation because it is a strategy for selfishly taking advantage of others, even though those being co-opted may benefit from the arrangement.

Coalition building also is based on cooperation, but without coercion. Building coalitions means forming alliances, often temporary, among various publics and organizations so that their collective power can be used to secure scarce resources and achieve common goals. But, unlike co-optation, coalition building is not necessarily exploitative; it is a negotiated arrangement based on a win-win assumption that all who cooperate will benefit.

Cooperation as a Strategy Cutting across all three strategies of competition, co-optation and coalition building is this question: Under what conditions will cooperation emerge? Robert Axelrod, a political scientist, developed a computerized version of the Prisoner's Dilemma to determine the answer to this question.[71] The essence of the dilemma is that two parties have been forced into a relationship where they have two choices: cooperate or not. The dilemma is that they are isolated from each other and can't communicate; they have to guess at what the other will do. If there is mutual cooperation, both win. If both choose not to cooperate, both lose big. If one chooses to cooperate and the other doesn't, then one ends up feeling like a sucker while the other gets some kind of benefit from fooling the other into cooperating, but neither gets exactly what he or she wants. The dilemma is that neither knows in advance what the other is going to do. As Axelrod explained:

> *The original story is that two accomplices to a crime are arrested and questioned separately. Either can defect against the other by confessing and hoping for a lighter sentence. But if both confess, their confessions are not as valuable. On the other hand, if both cooperate with each other by refusing to confess, the district attorney can only convict them on a minor charge. Assuming that neither player has moral qualms about, or fear of, squealing, the payoffs can form a Prisoner's Dilemma. From society's point of view, it is a good thing that the two accomplices have little likelihood of being caught in the same situation again soon, because that is precisely the reason why it is to each of their individual advantages to double-cross the other.*[72]

The Prisoner's Dilemma represents a situation where what is best for each person individually leads to less than desirable results, whereas everyone could receive exactly what they wanted if they would cooperate. The artificial aspects of the Prisoner's Dilemma are that the two participants are isolated from each other and that the payoffs are significantly different and ranked in order, with the least desirable payoff given for mutual lack of cooperation, modest payoffs given for suckering someone else into cooperating, and the highest payoff given for mutual cooperation.

An example of the Prisoner's Dilemma applied to a public relations situation would be two lobbying organizations finding out through mutual contacts that each is getting ready to make a presentation in a few days to an important legislative committee. They do not have time to meet to discuss the matter. Instead, they fax to each other the prepared discussion points of the experts who will be making the presentations to the committee. The dilemma is: Should they cooperate with each other by changing the discussion points of their respective experts or not? If they both cooperate and make copy changes, then a more persuasive presentation is possible. If one makes the changes but the other doesn't, the combined effect is not as great; and, the side that makes the changes will feel suckered, while the other side will get the benefit of having its discussion points reinforced. If both refuse to cooperate, then two separate and, possibly, disjointed presentations are made.

In the computerized version of the Prisoner's Dilemma, thousands of iterations of options were explored to identify conditions in which mutual cooperation would or would not emerge. Axelrod identified two general sets of conditions: 1) when the participants were locked into a situation they could not change, and 2) when the participants were able to change their options and environment, primarily because they were able to communicate with each other.

If the participants could not change the situation *and the relationships were short-term,* then not cooperating paid off best. If the participants could not change the situation *and the relationships were long-term,* then cooperation paid off best. The implication is that to facilitate cooperation in situations that cannot be readily changed, the participants should know for sure that they will see each other again and that they will, in time, have a long-term relationship. A facilitator should help them to see each other as colleagues.

Of course, the opposite implication is true if the purpose is to suppress cooperation. For example, public relations executives for the world's largest oil companies would not want to coordinate their public relations campaigns because this could be construed as restraint of trade. Consequently, the strategy should be not to meet frequently or to establish long-term relationships with each other.

When participants are able to communicate and change the environment in which they are operating, there are a number of actions that can be taken to improve the possibilities for cooperation:[73]

1. Enlarge each participant's view of the world so that they see lots of options and a long, prosperous future together.
2. Make the relationships among participants more durable and frequent.
3. Keep others from interfering in the relationships: establish a territory in which the participants feel safe.
4. Organize the relationship: establish a hierarchy so that participants have predictable roles.
5. Break down joint activities so that the cooperating parties can witness, as they progress from one small stage to the next, that each is cooperating as planned; this will establish a greater sense of confidence in their relationship.

6. Change the payoffs.
7. Teach participants to care about each other: explain the value of altruism.
8. Teach reciprocity by reminding the participants that being cooperative at all times leads to being exploited and that being uncooperative at all times is selfish and dysfunctional. Explain that reciprocity need not be coercive and unethical; it can be a mutual exchange of corresponding advantages and privileges.
9. Help participants see how they can verify that others are cooperating with them, so they will know, before it is too late, when they are being suckered.
10. Help others recognize cooperative possibilities by explaining how others have established cooperative arrangements and succeeded.

The combined effect of these actions is effective public relations—facilitating understanding and relationship between publics. The implication for public relations managers is that campaigns designed to foster cooperation can be more effective: 1) if they educate the publics about the value of cooperation, 2) if they explain the histories and successes of cooperative arrangements, particularly among participants, and 3) if they provide forums that facilitate the publics' getting to know each other and establishing long-term relationships.

Organizational Strategies for Improving Ethics Three strategies for institutionalizing corporate ethics have become increasingly common in the past decade: 1) establishing a corporate code of ethics, 2) designating an ethics committee on the board of directors, and 3) conducting ethics training programs.[74] A 1980 survey of U.S.-based firms found that 67% had ethics codes, 6% had ethics committees on boards, and 3% had management training programs that specifically dealt with ethics.[75] A 1987 survey of 2,000 American corporations found that 85% had codes of ethics, 9% had ethics committees on boards, and more than 28% had ethics training programs.[76]

According to the Ethics Resource Center, a comprehensive, enforceable code of ethics has four parts: 1) a credo, which is an overarching statement of corporate philosophy and values, 2) general guidelines for decision-making, 3) specific rules that prohibit certain actions and require others, and 4) definitions, rationales and illustrations.

The content of credos vary dramatically from company to company, but most link general guidelines and specific rules to higher ethical principles and statements of management philosophies. Here are sample statements from two credos:

> *We will conduct our business honestly and ethically wherever we operate in the world. To live up to this commitment, we will turn away from business, if getting the business means to operate illegally or*

unethically. We will not compromise our principles for short-term advantage. No illegal or unethical conduct is in the company's interest. No employee will ever be asked by a supervisor to compromise his or her own ethical standards. (Rexnord)

One of a company's most valuable assets is a reputation for integrity. If that is tarnished, customers, investors, suppliers, employees, and those who sell our products will seek affiliation with other, more attractive companies. We intend to hold to a single high standard of integrity everywhere. We will keep our word. We won't promise more than we can reasonably expect to deliver; nor will we make commitments we don't intend to keep. The ethical performance of the enterprise is the sum of the ethics of the men and women who work here. Thus, we are all expected to adhere to high standards of personal integrity. (Caterpillar Inc.)

Guidelines sometimes offer advice about specific situations—for example, explaining the prohibition against insider trading, or warning employees not to disclose confidential information. (See Table 9.1 for a list of topics most often addressed in corporate codes of ethics.) When specific advice is difficult to give for a certain situation, guidelines often offer basic principles, for example:

No "code of conduct" can hope to spell out the appropriate moral conduct and ethical behavior for every situation with which we will be confronted. In the last analysis we must rely on our own good judgment. Whenever we find ourselves with a hard decision to make, we must seek counsel—either from our colleagues, from our management, the Company Ethics Committee, and, most importantly, our own conscience. (Eastman Christensen)

The antitrust laws are general and in some respects vague; their exact interpretation is often uncertain. Therefore, legal advice should be obtained whenever there is any doubt as to the lawfulness of any contemplated course of action or of a proposed transaction. (Eli Lilly and Company)

Ethics guidelines also require certain behaviors in specific situations—for example, disclosure and approval of actions taken in particular areas, such as:

Conflict of interest

Any employee who feels that he or she may have a conflict situation, actual or potential, should report all pertinent details in a memorandum to his or her supervisor. The supervisor will be responsible for referring the matter to the legal department. (Martin Marietta Corporation)

TABLE 9.1:

Topics Most Often Addressed in Corporate Codes of Ethics*

1. Company philosophy and commitment to ethical conduct
2. Observance of laws and regulations
3. Conflict of interest
4. Bribes and kickbacks
5. Gifts, gratuities, and entertainment
6. Accuracy of books and records
7. Proper use of corporate assets
8. Anti-trust
9. Relations with competitors
10. Disparagement of competitors
11. Gathering competitor information
12. Protecting company confidential information
13. Protecting confidential information of suppliers, customers, and competitors
14. Insider information
15. Political contributions and activities
16. International activities
17. Truth in advertising
18. Customer relations
19. Product quality
20. Product safety
21. Employee relations
22. Equal employment opportunity
23. Worker safety
24. Use of agents, representatives, and consultants
25. Relations with suppliers
26. Relations with the community
27. Environmental protection
28. Relations with government representatives
29. Protecting shareholder rights

*Based on table of contents of *Creating a Workable Company Code of Ethics,* published by the Ethics Resource Center, (Washington, D.C., 1990). Reprinted with permission from the Ethics Resource Center.

Political contributions

When permitted by law, state and local political contributions may be made after approval by the company's government affairs, communications, and law departments. (FMC Corporation)

Guidelines may also present basic criteria for individuals to use when confronted with any ethical dilemma, for example:

If you have to make an immediate decision and have any doubts about what you're doing, don't do it. (Xerox)

Employees should not do anything—or be expected to take any action—that they would be ashamed to explain to their family or close friends (Eli Lilly and Company)

What questions should one ask in an ethical dilemma? Here are some suggestions:

What is company policy?

Who exactly will be helped and who will be hurt?

Would this violate someone's expectations?

How would this decision look on the front page of The Wall Street Journal?
(Citicorp)

Some codes of ethics stop with a comprehensive set of guidelines. Others go on to list specific rules which outlaw specific actions—such as price-fixing—or which require certain actions—such as blowing the whistle on code violators.

Some codes of ethics define terms, such as trade secrets, insider information, anti-trust, gifts and gratuities. Some provide rationales and illustrations of recommended ways of dealing with ethical situations, for example:

It has long been IBM's policy to sell products and services on merits, not by disparaging competitors, their products or their services. False or misleading statements and innuendos are improper. Don't make comparisons that unfairly cast the competitor in a bad light. Such conduct only invites disrespect from customers and complaints from competitors. (International Business Machines Corporation)

Reciprocal deals are understandings that one firm will buy another firm's products or services only if the favor is returned. Attempts to coerce a customer into reciprocal deals are usually illegal and certainly unethical. (Hewlett-Packard Company)

Whether you call them fees or commissions, kickbacks are morally wrong and legally criminal. The price for accepting kickbacks is high: your job, and even criminal prosecution. (Hughes Aircraft Company)

Imagine that you are required to submit a report and discover that one of the requirements you were supposed to have completed has not been done. However, it can be completed in a few days. The report is due immediately. Should you, out of loyalty, keep the company from looking bad by falsifying the report, since you should have the task completed prior to anyone having time to check it? No. Martin Marietta sincerely expects that all employees be completely honest, irrespective of the consequences. (Martin Marietta Corporation)

Steps in Preparing and Communicating Codes of Ethics Based on their survey of 2,000 firms, the Ethics Resource Center identified certain steps most organizations go through to develop and communicate a corporate code of ethics. Here, briefly, is what would happen:

1. Senior management initiated the process by establishing a high-level task force with representation from all significant business units.
2. The task force was charged with the responsibility of gathering statements from members of management and others about what they considered to be the organization's ethical principles.
3. The various statements were analyzed, edited and combined into a single set of principles, rules and guidelines, with definitions, etc.; and, a credo, or overarching set of principles, was written for the document. It normally took many months for this iterative process to generate consensus and a well-written document.
4. With senior management's approval, the document was published. Most were published as brochures, some as attractive, large posters, and a few as reports. About half of those surveyed distributed the code to all employees; the other half distributed it only to members of management.
5. Beyond the initial distribution of the basic document, many other communication activities were engaged in, such as preparing videotapes of corporate executives explaining the purpose of the code and its basic principles; placing articles in company magazines and trade publications; sending copies to suppliers, vendors and customers; writing speeches for executives to give to community groups, civic and trade associations; and, conducting training programs.

Two Approaches to Corporate Ethics Training To educate employees about the purpose and usefulness of its code of ethics, an increasing number of organizations (more than 25%) conduct training programs that range from intensive one- and two-day workshops to relatively short staff meetings, lectures and small group discussions. Two basic approaches are used in conducting most of these training programs:

1. Make employees more aware of ethics by helping them to recognize everyday ethical dilemmas and improve their ethical decision-making, giving them a framework (in particular, a corporate code of ethics) for dealing with ethical situations.
2. Make employees more aware of how and why they should comply with the law and other regulations governing such areas as antitrust, insider trading, and government contracting.

Compliance training is useful for many companies, specifically those in highly regulated industries. But, it has its weaknesses: it tends to equate compliance with ethical behavior; it assumes there are rules governing all situations; and it implies that if an action is not illegal, it must be ethical. According to the Ethics Resource Center,

> . . . the employee misconduct most harmful to a firm is usually not the result of ignorance of the laws or regulations, but is often driven by the company's own management style, aggressive goal-setting and incentive and reward systems. Most of the headline-making business scandals of the past decade have been caused not by employees who did not know the rules but by employees who chose to disregard the rules because the reward was so great, or because they felt that the company expected them to do whatever was necessary to meet budgets, schedules, sales quota, or the quarterly financial figures. Compliance training alone may neglect to address these pressures, which can lead ordinarily honest employees to behave unethically.

Monitoring and Enforcing Codes of Ethics Many codes included provisions requiring managers and supervisors to explain the code to their employees, for example:

> *All managers must annually take appropriate action to insure that persons reporting to them are fully informed of our ethics policy. (Xerox)*

> *Supervisors who fail to instruct their employees on the Code of Ethics may be subject to disciplinary action. (Learjet)*

Beyond "open door" policies and expecting managers to inform employees and make periodic reports about ethics, many organizations monitor and enforce their code of ethics by conducting audits that identify ethical problems, and by establishing whistle blowing mechanisms, such as hotlines for anonymous tips, ethics committees and designated individuals who serve as ethics advocates. For example:

> *The director of internal auditing of the company and the company's independent certified public accountants will report immediately any violations or suspected violations of this policy on business ethics which come to their attention as a result of conducting audits of the company. (The Kroger Company)*

> *In no event is action to be taken or threatened against you by the company as a reprisal for making a complaint or disclosing information in good faith. . . However, if you were involved in improper activity, you may be appropriately disciplined even if you are the one who discloses the matter to the company; but your voluntary act of disclosure will be given favorable consideration in any ensuing decisions. (McDonnell Douglas Corporation)*

> *Ethics Program Directors have been designated for each of the various company locations and are available for employee counseling and assistance . . . (they) may be reached by way of regular telephone, hotline, letter or personal visit. Inquiries will be treated with courtesy and discretion. (General Dynamics)*

Whether or not an organization is profit-oriented or not-for-profit apparently affects whether or not it will strictly monitor and enforce its code of ethics. Probably because they are anxious to avoid being accused of being overzealous by employees and of violating anti-trust regulations by competitors, less than half the profit-making corporations in a survey of U.S.-based organizations, and a significantly smaller percent of non-profit associations, reported that they rigorously monitored and enforced their codes of ethics.[77]

U.S. Defense Industry Initiatives on Business Ethics Since the late 1980s, scores of U.S. defense companies have signed pledges to promote ethical business conduct not only within their own organizations but also throughout the defense industry.[78] The written pledges were one of the recommendations of the Blue Ribbon Commission on Defense Management, appointed by President Ronald Reagan and chaired by David Packard, head of Hewlett-Packard Corporation. The recommendations, called the Defense Industry Initiatives (DII), stated that corporations signing the DII pledge were to adhere to the following six principles:

1. Each company will have and adhere to a written code of business ethics and conduct.
2. The company's code establishes the high values expected of its employees and the standard by which they must judge their own conduct and those of their organization; each company will train its employees concerning their personal responsibilities under the code.
3. Each company will create a free and open atmosphere that allows and encourages employees to report violations of its code to the company without fear of retribution for such reporting.
4. Each company has the obligation to self-govern by monitoring compliance with federal procurement laws and adopting procedures for voluntary disclosure of violations of federal procurement laws and corrective actions taken.
5. Each company has a responsibility to each of the other companies in the industry to live by standards of conduct that preserve the integrity of the defense industry.
6. Each company must have public accountability for its commitment to these principles.

The last principle means that participating organizations will pay for certified public accountants to conduct audits of their written responses to eighteen questions which are asked annually of all companies signing the DII pledge.[79] Some of the key points of the ethics audit are:

Is the code of ethics distributed to all employees?

Does the code assign responsibility to operating management and others for compliance with the code?

Is there a corporate review board, ombudsman, corporate compliance or ethics office or similar mechanism for employees to report suspected violations to someone other than their direct supervisor, if necessary?

Does the mechanism employed protect the confidentiality of employee reports?

Is there an appropriate mechanism for letting employees know the result of any follow-up into their reported charges?

Is there an ongoing program of communication to employees, spelling out and re-emphasizing their obligations under the code of conduct?

Call for Multinational Corporate Communicator Codes of Ethics Dean Kruckeberg of the University of Northern Iowa has called for all multinational corporations to regularly review and revise their corporate codes of ethics "as these relate specifically to professional communicators."[80] According to Kruckeberg:

> *". . . it would seem both instructive and beneficial to examine the feasibility of attempting to develop and apply a unified and comprehensive code of ethics for professional communicators representing transnational corporations. Ideally, this code would be capable of guiding behavior which attempts to resolve the inherent moral dilemmas of such widespread and diverse issues (as) . . . graft and corruption issues . . . consumer issues . . . environmental/human safety issues . . . and, political/humanitarian issues."*[81]

A Contingency Model of Ethical Decision-Making in Public Relations

The various factors discussed in this chapter have been incorporated into a contingency model of ethical decision-making in public relations.[82] (See Figure 9.3.) Individual, interpersonal, small group, and organizational factors are part of the initial set of factors operating in the model. Also, influences from other organizations, external publics, laws, public policies, cultural beliefs and values—which will be examined in greater detail in the next chapter—are part of the initial set of factors. These basic factors influence an individual's initial perception of an ethical problem and subsequent perceived alternatives and consequences. The initial set of factors also is the source of deontological (obligatory) and teleological (naturalistic) principles, the values assigned to perceived consequences of decisions, and the values assigned to loyalties owed various stakeholders.

FIGURE 9.3

A contingency model of ethical decision-making in public relations

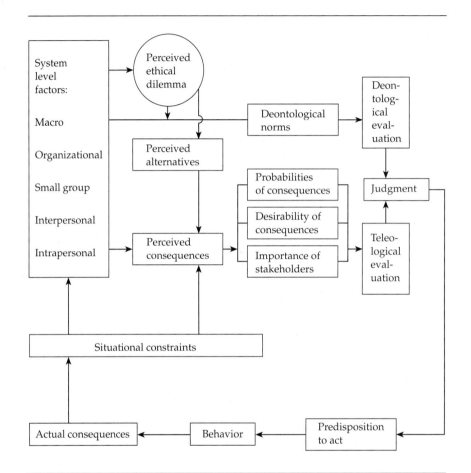

* This model is based on Scott J. Vitell's 1986 unpublished dissertation from Texas Tech University, "Marketing ethics: Conceptual and empirical foundations of a positive theory of decision making in marketing situations having ethical content," discussed by John Tsalikis and David Fritzsche in "Business ethics: A literature review with a focus on marketing ethics," Journal of Business Ethics, Vol. 8, No. 9, September 1989, p. 732.

When a person takes into consideration perceived alternatives and obligatory principles—such as, never tell a lie—this yields certain evaluations. When the person takes into consideration the values of perceived consequences, loyalties and naturalistic principles—such as, a cost-benefit analysis—this yields another set of evaluations. Considering both sets of evaluations, the obligatory and the naturalistic, an individual makes an ethical judgment.

This judgment is a predisposition to act, an intention. Given the right situational constraints, the person will act and real consequences will result. The actual consequences will feedback to the initial set of factors, most importantly to the individual, and learning will occur.

If factors in the model are conceptually defined in greater detail and operationally defined so that they can be measured, and if assumptions about relationships between the various factors are clearly expressed, then the model can be used not only to explain but also to predict ethical decision-making in public relations.

PERSONAL INTERVIEWS USED TO EXAMINE FACTORS IN MODEL

More than 25 personal interviews were conducted with public relations practitioners to examine various factors described in the contingency model of ethical decision-making in public relations. Almost all of those interviewed were members of the sample surveyed by the author and discussed elsewhere in other chapters. All those not part of the original sample were members of professional organizations in the field of public relations.

Each interview focused on ethical dilemmas the respondent knew about that occurred in the practice of public relations (not necessarily from the respondents own personal experience) and that involved common activities in public relations, such as media relations, employee relations, community relations, stockholder relations, and issues management. Interviewers probed to identify factors that affected the practitioner's ethical decision-making. The respondents also discussed the strengths and weaknesses of a sample ethics training program.

To protect the confidentiality of the respondents, the cases developed from the interviews were changed in minor ways to mask the identity of the organization and principal players in the scenario, without changing the essential characteristics of the ethical situation. Four cases will be presented in this chapter to illustrate individual, interpersonal, small group and organizational factors affecting ethical decision-making. More cases will be presented in Chapter 10.

. . .

CASE 9.1:

An Individual Is Affected by Not Having All the Facts to Answer Media Inquiries about a Crisis

The problem: **The director of public information for a state agency was left "out of the loop" and not informed about a planned police raid on a certain group of warehouse workers who allegedly were stealing government** supplies and equipment and selling them to local pawn shops. The director of public information was informed fifteen minutes before the raid and told to contact the media immediately and to give them the story.

The situation: The newly appointed head of the agency's Department of Security coordinated the police surveillance but did not want to inform the media until just moments before the raid. As the new head of security, he was eager to show his superiors he could handle this situation. He called the director of public affairs fifteen minutes before the raid and told her to alert the media to what was happening. Somehow, some of the information was miscommunicated, and the director reported to the media that the stolen material cost ten times more than it actually cost.

Values: The following values were identified as being important from the point of view of the public relations practitioner in this case; there are, undoubtedly, others.

- To be accurate in dealings with the media.
- To be "in the loop" and involved in key decisions.
- To be competent and successful on the job.
- To be helpful to others in getting their messages communicated.
- Not to be made to look like a fool.

Principles: The following principles were identified as being important from the point of view of the public relations practitioner in this case; there are, undoubtedly, others.

- Superiors should never be surprised, or embarrassed, by the actions of subordinates; superiors should always be informed in advance and, when necessary, their approval should be received before significant actions are taken.
- Never tell a lie.
- Misstatements are perceived as lies.
- When in doubt, don't do it.
- Obey orders.

Loyalties: The following loyalties were identified as being important from the point of view of the public relations practitioner in this case; there are, undoubtedly, others.

- To the media.
- To her superiors.
- To her peer managers and colleagues within the organization.
- To taxpayers and the general public.
- To #1: herself.

The solution: The director of public affairs assumed the facts told to her over the phone by the head of security were correct. She also assumed that the police raid had been authorized by the head of the agency. She called the media and alerted them to the raid. None of the media was able to send reporters in time to cover the raid "live." Most media covered the story by relying on their police reporters. Some of the initial facts released by the agency were not correct, particularly because the head of security overestimated the dollar amount of stolen items by a factor of ten. The senior administrator and elected officials of the agency had not been informed about the raid, so direct media inquiries of these individuals proved embarrassing. Days later, the director of public information called reporters who had covered the story and apologized for the earlier misstatement about the amount of stolen property. The senior administrator of the agency formally reprimanded the agency's new security chief for not keeping superiors and colleagues, including the director of public information, properly informed.

Analysis: The individual in this case rushed to judgment and made a major mistake: she did not double-check her facts before releasing them to the press. This was a large, government agency with all the classic characteristics of a bureaucracy, including internal politics, "turf wars," empire-building, and a lack of trust among different work units.[83] Better intra-departmental coordination and better, more timely reports to senior management of current projects and activities would have brought many more people "into the loop" of decision-makers. That way, fewer mistakes would have been made and better information would have been available about these various projects and activities. Had the individual questioned her peers about the facts and also about the senior-level approval of the action, the clumsy media relations and embarrassment of senior officials would have been avoided.

. . .

CASE 9.2:

Interpersonal Relationships Affect Press Interviews

The problem: How to keep untrained employees from making inappropriate comments to the media during press interviews without offending the employees, who are often members of senior management.

The situation: A reporter for a suburban daily newspaper requested an interview with the hospital's chaplain to get background information about the dedication of the hospital's new chapel. The newly appointed public relations manager made sure she was present during the interview. The interview, which took place in the chaplain's office, lasted three hours, instead of an anticipated thirty minutes. During this time the chaplain discussed a wide range of unrelated topics and made jokes with pejorative comments about certain classes of patients in the hospital, which he laughed about and asked to be kept "off the record." The reporter, who was from the same home state as the public relations manager, told her colleague, as a gesture of friendship, that she would not use the ill-chosen statements in the news feature story.

Values: The following values have been identified as being important from the point of view of the public relations practitioner in this case; there are, undoubtedly, others.

To be tactful.

To be forthcoming with the media.

Not to burden an old friend (the reporter) by asking for too many favors.

To be professional about media relations.

Not to offend superiors.

Principles: The following principles have been identified as being important to the public relations practitioner in this case; there are, undoubtedly, others.

Favors from important colleagues need to be saved for serious situations and not wasted on minor matters.

Don't tell the media anything off-the-record, unless you are prepared to see it published.

An observer in a room watching a conversation between two people will affect that conversation: the two people will be mindful that they are being observed.

A special room or a special setting can make a person think that something special is happening.

The organization's long-term interests are more important than any one employee's feelings.

Loyalties: The following loyalties have been identified as being important from the point of view of the public relations practitioner in this case; there are, undoubtedly, others.

To the organization.

To superiors and the chain-of-command.

To #1: herself.

To her friend, the reporter.

To the media.

The solution: The director of public relations thanked her friend, the reporter, for her professional courtesy. She then wrote a memo to the heads of all departments stating that, in the future, all media interviews were to be conducted in the conference room of the public relations office. Also, she explained in the memo, that a member of the public relations department needed to be present during all media interviews.

Analysis: Had the director of public relations not been present during the interview, the reporter might not have kept the ill-chosen words out of the feature story. The relationship between the public relations practitioner and the reporter affected how the story was published. In addition to endorsing the memo institutionalizing the presence of a public relations professional during all media interviews, management could have established a training program to make key staff members more sensitive to media inquiries and interviews. Staff should be told that "off the record" should rarely, if ever, be used, because a good reporter can repeat the comment to someone else, who might verify it or address it in some new way, and suddenly the off-the-record comment suddenly becomes on-the-record.

CASE 9.3:

A Small Group of Elite Decision-Makers Determines the Right Amount of Information to Release to Stockholders

The problem: The U.S. Securities and Exchange Commission (SEC) regulations are fairly specific: a publicly owned corporation should release all information which a sophisticated group of investors would consider material in their decisions to buy or sell the corporate stock. Yet, too much information can be overwhelming to readers and potentially counterproductive; important information may be overlooked in a sea full of relatively minor material facts. How do public relations managers determine the right amount of information to release to the investing public? What is the best way to present this information?

The situation: When the corporation was listed initially on the New York Stock Exchange, corporate attorneys, expert consultants and members of senior management prepared and released information in compliance with SEC regulations. They prepared annual reports and prospectuses that included an overview of corporate activities and all information required in the corporation's annual 10–K income tax statement. During the first few years when the corporation was publicly owned, the technical information presented in the back of the annual reports was prepared by the chief financial officer; the overview information in "the front of the book" was prepared by the director of public relations; and, the final report was approved by the CEO. As the corporate assets, profits, and scope of operation grew, more interest was shown by investors and the media. Yet, with this growth, the director of public relations found it increasingly difficult to produce interesting and readable reports; there was too much technical information. At the same time, she was receiving even more technical questions from media investment specialists that required the release of even more precise corporate information. Because she could not disclose inside information to one reporter without first making it widely available to all within the investing community, responding to these media inquiries required consensus and approval by senior management about what information could be released.

Values: The following values were identified as being important from the point of view of the public relations practitioner in this case; there are, undoubtedly, others.

To be legal and meet all the requirements of the SEC and stock exchanges.

To be accurate.

To be informative and interesting when presenting financial data.

To be a team member.

To be better than her predecessor at handling this situation.

Principles: The following principles were identified as being important from the point of view of the public relations practitioner in this case; there are, undoubtedly, others.

The stockholders' interests are paramount.

Never tell a lie.

Sophisticated investors want to know everything that can have a material impact on the price of stock.

Small groups of elite decision-makers, properly managed, can be innovative risk-takers.

Always comply with the law.

Loyalties: The following loyalties were identified as being important from the point of view of the public relations practitioner in this case; there are, undoubtedly, others.

To the stockholders.

To the financial media.

To senior management of the company.

To employees.

To #1: herself.

The solution: The director of public relations formed and chaired a committee of attorneys, financial specialists, and other members of senior management to meet quarterly, and on an as-needed basis, to determine what information should be disclosed to satisfy investors, government regulations, and the best interests of the corporation. She also contracted with a newswire delivery service for the electronic distribution of press releases and financial statements, which would allow her to respond in a more timely way to media inquiries.

Analysis: The success of this particular small group, as it is with many small groups, depended upon the right mix of people. Had the responsibility for chairing the committee been assigned to someone not as sensitive to the communication issues involved in financial disclosures, then the work of this committee might not have been as effective.

. . .

CASE 9.4:

Organizational Factors Affect Establishing an Independent Voice for the Company Newsletter

The problem: A new editor was hired for the ten-year-old company newsletter. He had just graduated from college where he majored in journalism and served on the editorial staff of the college's student-run newspaper. He viewed the current company newsletter as a "propaganda piece" for top management and wanted to change the situation so that the editor served as an employee-centered ombudsman for the corporation.

The situation: The head of personnel was the young journalist's boss and is quite content with the editorial content of the current publication. While his boss has said he was not opposed to changing the publication, the new editor senses that his boss would not support his efforts to make dramatic changes.

Values: The following values have been identified as being important from the point of view of the public relations practitioner in this case; there are, undoubtedly, others.

   To get what you want your way.

   To be successful.

   To be a champion for employees.

   To question all in authority.

   To be creative and innovative.

Principles: The following principles have been identified as being important from the point of view of the public relations practitioner in this case; there are, undoubtedly, others.

   Publish the truth and damn the consequences.

   Always look out for #1: yourself.

   Never trust anyone in a position of authority.

   Employees should have a greater voice in the management of the firm.

   The end justifies the means.

Loyalties: The following loyalties have been identified as being important from the point of view of the public relations practitioner in this case; there are, undoubtedly, others.

   To #1: the newsletter editor.

   To "us" (employees) versus "them" (management).

   To the organization.

   To professional journalists.

   To public relations professionals.

The solution: Without conferring with his boss, he approached the CEO and asked for authorization to conduct a readership survey. The CEO agreed, recommending that he work with the Research Department in preparing the questionnaire and conducting the survey. With his boss's permission, he conducted the survey and wrote a report that recommended a new design and set of topics for the publication. He also recommended that editorial clearances be limited to himself, his boss, and the CEO. The recommendations were accepted, and he began writing and publishing the new employee-centered newsletter.

Analysis: A more traditional or defensive management group might have resisted or refused the initial request to conduct the research and the final set of recommendations. His boss justifiably might have been upset about the young editor's going around him to the CEO, which could have affected the boss's decisions in the future about the work of the editor.

Conclusions from Personal Interviews

Two general conclusions can be drawn from these cases. One is that large, bureaucratic organizations generate a lot of ethical dilemmas that can be characterized as political infighting. For example, in Case 9.1, the public affairs director for the state agency released inaccurate information because one of his colleagues was "empire building" and not following standard procedures. In Case 9.4, the young editor was eager to buck authority and willing to break bureaucratic rules to get his way.

The other conclusion is that the more candid managers are, the more likely they will quickly and effectively resolve ethical problems. For example, in Case 9.2, the candor and rapport of the public relations director and the reporter helped solve an awkward situation. In Case 9.4, the openness of the CEO to suggestions and the willingness of the director of personnel to support the research indicated an open, flexible management philosophy which resulted in a new publication, and an enthusiastic editor.

TWO CONTROVERSIAL ALTERNATIVE EXPLANATIONS

The controversial field of sociobiology, first defined by Edward Wilson, helps explain and predict certain ethical behaviors when it argues that altruistic behaviors facilitate the development of strong gene pools—one of the basic purposes of life, according to Wilson.[84] Because extreme altruistic behaviors are self-sacrificing, they do not appear to be the types of actions that would contribute to the gene pool; whoever sacrificed himself or herself would not be able to reproduce and continue the species. However, sociobiologists argue that because most self-sacrificing behaviors are designed to help kin, and because those kin live on to contribute to the gene pool, altruistic behaviors are important to the survival of the species.

The sociobiologist's argument goes further; it asserts that human language developed tens of thousands of years ago as a result of altruistic utterances warning others of danger. The argument is that most communication and most cooperative actions, including altruistic behaviors, originally were prompted by and directed to kin and loved ones. These behaviors not only warned others of dangers, but also announced a source of food, and asked for, as one writer put it, "cooperation for the purpose of genetic recombination . . . sex."[85]

Unethical communication, lying, also is explained by sociobiologists because, the argument goes, in many instances deception helps contribute to the gene pool. For example, not telling an enemy about a danger, not disclosing a source of food, or exaggerating sexual prowess are behaviors which can facilitate kin selection and survival of the species.

The Evolution of Consciousness—and Conscience

An even more controversial theory than sociobiology is the radical notion of Princeton psychologist Julian Jaynes that the human brain has evolved, and continues to evolve, and with it, our conscience.[86] For thousands of years humans had very distinct left and right brain hemispheres which Jaynes describes as a bicameral mind. Within the past three to five thousand years, Jaynes states, humans physiologically have evolved to experience a more fluid interconnection between the two brain hemispheres. With what Jaynes calls the breakdown of the bicameral mind, consciousness, human self-awareness, emerged.

Jaynes argues that only with increasing self-awareness over time did humans develop a conscience, a sense of what is right and wrong in one's behavior. His provocative theory is that prior to the breakdown of the bicameral mind, ethical decisions were based on perceived external authorities heard as "voices" within the mind. (Jaynes contends that schizophrenics today hear similar internal voices "telling me what to do" because they suffer, for some reason, from an impeded breakdown of the bicameral mind.) During the bicameral period, humans behaved, according to Jaynes, in an unself-conscious, stimulus-response mode, reacting from moment to moment, with little or no sense of time or history. With the evolution of a more fluid interconnection between the two brain hemispheres, Jaynes argues, humans began to use both authoritative (deontological) and naturalistic (teleological) criteria for making ethical decisions.

Jaynes uses prehistorical and historical evidence to support his theory. He notes that during the bicameral period writing began. During this time, religious writings reflected polytheism, the belief in a variety of gods. With the advent of the breakdown of the bicameral mind, Jaynes notes, monotheism emerged and most world religions began to focus on a single god. At the same historic time period, secular writings, such as the "Iliad" (written in about 800 B.C.), used the narrative "I" for the first time to describe an author's self-awareness. His argument is that the notion that we can decide for ourselves what is right and what is wrong is three to five thousand years old. Jaynes argues that the development of ethics is linked closely to the development of language and an evolving sense of self-awareness.

IN SUMMARY . . .

When a public relations practitioner is confronted with an ethical dilemma and wants to do something about the situation, there are three options: 1) use intuitive rules or principles based on authoritative sources; 2) predict the consequences of different actions and choose the best one; or, most likely, 3) decide what to do based on some combination of the first two options. Whatever choices are made, they will be influenced by intrapersonal, interpersonal, small group, and organizational factors. The public relations manager who is aware of all the various forces operating within any particular ethical dilemma will be in a better position to make the right choice.

Study Questions

1. Define ethics. Define meta-ethics. Give examples of both.
2. What is ethical relativism? What are common misconceptions about nonrelativism?
3. Give examples of intuitive (deontological) and naturalistic (teleological) rules for making ethical decisions.
4. What is the Potter Box? How can it be used to analyze an ethical dilemma in public relations?
5. Give examples of ethical issues operating at the following levels of analysis: intrapersonal, interpersonal, small group, and organizational.
6. True or false: men are more sensitive than women to ethical issues. Qualify and defend your answer.
7. What is cognitive dissonance? How might cognitive dissonance and moral development be experienced differently over a person's lifetime?
8. How can an organization's size, technology, bureaucratic rules, rewards, sanctions, and hierarchy affect ethical decision-making?
9. How do practitioner-client relationships affect ethical decision-making in public relations?
10. Under what conditions will cooperation emerge to resolve ethical dilemmas? What actions can be taken to improve the possibilities for cooperation?
11. Describe some specific strategies organizations can use to improve ethical decision-making. Be specific.
12. Describe a contingency model of ethical decision-making in public relations. Give examples of how it can be used.
13. Discuss the sociobiological argument that lying, deception, and exaggeration on the part of humans contribute to the survival of the species.
14. What is the difference between consciousness and conscience?

ADDITIONAL CASES

HOW THE PRACTITIONER'S RELATIONSHIP WITH THE SPONSORING ORGANIZATION(S) OR CLIENT(S) AFFECTS ETHICAL DECISION-MAKING IN PUBLIC RELATIONS

. . .

CASE 9.5:

The Right Location for a Press Conference

The problem: Deciding where to hold a press conference when there are multiple clients or sponsoring organizations. What's fair—what is the right thing to do—when several equally valued sponsors are involved?

The situation: The university-based research lab developed biomedical engineering devices, such as a small insulin pump. When these devices were introduced to the public, other organizations were involved, such as other divisions of the university and private manufacturers, which often helped pay for the cost of the research and shared royalties with the university. For this reason, it was important that the lab share whatever publicity was generated by the product-introduction press conferences. The dilemma was whether or not to hold the press conference on the lab site or to hold it someplace else. It would be wrong to cast the media's spotlight too much on one institution by hosting all press conferences at the university. Potential and current corporate sponsors of research might be put off by what appeared to be the university's self-aggrandizement.

Values: The following values have been identified as being important from the point of view of the public relations practitioner in this case.

    To be fair.

    To share good fortune.

    To be gracious.

    Not to appear too eager for the spotlight.

    To generate favorable publicity for the project.

Principles: The following principles have been identified as being important from the point of view of the public relations practitioner in this case.

    Give credit where credit is due.

    Reciprocate good deeds.

    Give the greatest good to the greatest number.

    Get the best possible media coverage.

    Do not play favorites.

Loyalties: The following loyalties have been identified as being important from the point of view of the public relations practitioner in this case.

To the sponsors.

To the research lab.

To the media.

To physicians and other health professionals who would use the products of the lab.

To the general public.

The solution: Depending on the wishes of the research team, press conferences were held either at a neutral site or at the site of one of the non-university-affiliated sponsors, and representatives of each sponsoring institution were present at the press conference.

HOW INTERPERSONAL AND SMALL GROUP FACTORS AFFECT ETHICAL DECISION-MAKING IN PUBLIC RELATIONS

CASE 9.6:

Assigning Responsibility for Last-Minute Changes in a Special Event

The problem: How to handle a last-minute change in plans for a special event that involved several cooperating organizations. What was the right way to settle the conflict over whose fault it was that a change had to be made? This was a problem of the left hand and the right hand having to work together, but one side made a mistake. Did both hands take equal share of the blame? How was blame assessed? Who should have been responsible for fixing the problem?

The situation: A state institution was planning to host a reception for the state legislature in celebration of the institution's sesquicentennial anniversary. The institution's government liaison person thought she had reserved the impressive reception room in the governor's mansion and told the director of development for the institution to print the invitations using this room. After the invitations were printed, the director of development called and read the invitation over the phone to confirm the information with the institution's government liaison person. Then, the invitations were sent to every member of the state legislature. One week before the event, while reviewing the final details, the director of development discovered that the room reserved for the event was the reception room in the State House, not the governor's mansion.

Values: The following values have been identified as being important to the public relations practitioner in this case.

> To be blameless.
>
> To be worthy of respect—and more funding.
>
> To look good in the eyes of the boss.
>
> To be gracious to guests.
>
> To be dignified.

Principles: The following principles have been identified as being important to the public relations practitioner in this case.

> When things go wrong, someone always gets blamed.
>
> Always look out for #1—yourself.
>
> Always protect your flanks; cover your tail.
>
> If you look inept, you won't get serious funding.
>
> Never admit you made a mistake.

Loyalties: The following loyalties have been identified as being important to the public relations practitioner in this case.

> To #1: the self.
>
> To the institution.
>
> To the legislators and their guests.
>
> To the state.
>
> To the taxpayers.

The solution: The institution informed the members of the legislature of the mistake by hand-delivered letters. They posted nicely dressed male and female guides at the governor's mansion who would be available to escort anyone to the nearby State House who didn't get word of the change, or who forgot and showed up at the mansion anyway. The institution also had to call the caterers and others involved in the special event to make sure they understood the change. No one was willing to accept the blame, but after discussing the situation, it was decided that the government liaison person would take responsibility, and that both her department and the development office would divide the tasks of fixing the problem. The liaison person handled the hand-delivered letters, and the director of development called all the vendors and arranged for the escort guides.

HOW INTRAPERSONAL FACTORS AFFECT ETHICAL DECISION-MAKING IN PUBLIC RELATIONS

. . .

CASE 9.7:

Disclosing Insider Information to Friends

The problem: The real estate investment corporation was preparing to file for bankruptcy protection under Chapter 11. Two friends of the corporation's public relations manager asked to know the truth behind the rumors. What should the public relations manager have told his friends, one of whom had a significant amount of stock in the company?

The situation: Established during a major growth period in the real estate market, the corporation made extensive investments in high-risk real estate properties. Then, the market collapsed. The corporation sold several properties in an attempt to restructure itself, but the market continued its decline. The partners of the firm agreed among themselves that if the situation did not improve within the next ten days, the next step would be file for bankruptcy; they told their lawyers to begin preparing the necessary papers. The public relations manager, who was not involved in making the decision, was informed of the tentative decision and began preparing press releases and other documents which would not be released until the partners made the final decision about declaring bankruptcy. One evening, after work, the public relations director met, as he often did, with two close friends at a nearby bar. Several years ago, one of his friends had invested in the real estate corporation, but now the friend was worried about his investment. The conversation turned to the rumors that the corporation was going to file for bankruptcy. The friend asked point-blank, "Are you guys filing for bankruptcy, or what?"

Values: The following values were relevant to the public relations practitioner in this case:

To be a good friend.

To be honest.

To be a good employee.

To be a competent public relations professional.

To be legal.

Principles: The following principles were considered by the public relations practitioner:

Never disclose insider information; it must first be widely disseminated to the public before insiders can discuss it with others.

Never tell a lie.

Friends protect each other from harm.

It is the responsibility of the professional public relations person to be thoroughly familiar with, and to comply with, all laws and regulations about corporate disclosure, and to act in accordance with both the letter and the spirit of such laws and regulations.

Saying one thing but meaning another is not a lie.

Loyalties: The following loyalties were important to the public relations practitioner:

To the corporation.

To the investing public.

To the Securities and Exchange Commission and other regulators.

To #1: himself.

To his friends.

The solution: "All I can tell you is what is in the papers," the public relations manager said. He then reiterated what had been published, which included the facts that negotiations were under way to sign a long-term lease at one of the firm's largest properties, and that these negotiations would be concluded within the next ten days. At one point, he looked squarely into the eyes of his friend and said, plaintively, "You're asking me questions I can't answer. Does that answer your question?"

Endnotes

1. Simon, Herbert, *Administrative Behavior*, 3rd ed. (New York, NY: Free Press, 1976).

2. Kohlberg, Lawrence, *Essays on Moral Development*, Vol.1, in the series *The Philosophy of Moral Development* (New York: Harper and Row, 1981) pp. 300–301.

3. Wright, Donald K., "The philosophy of ethical development in public relations," *IPRA Review*, April 1982, pp. 22–27.

4. Walton, C., ed., *The Ethics of Corporate Conduct,* (Englewood Cliffs, NJ: Prentice-Hall, 1977) p. 5.

5. Henderson, Verne E., "The ethical side of enterprise," *Sloan Management Review,* Spring 1982, pp. 37–47.

6. Ibid

7. *The New Encyclopedia Britannica,* 15th edition, essay on ethics, pp. 976–998.

8. Kant, Immanuel, *Foundations of the Metaphysics of Morals,* translated by Lewis White (New York, NY: Bobbs-Merril, 1959).

9. Laczniak, Gene R., "Business ethics: A manager's primer," *Business,* 33, pp. 23–29.

10. McKeon, Richard, ed., *Introduction to Aristotle* (New York: Modern Library, 1947) pp. 333–340.

11. Rawls, John, *A Theory of Justice* (Cambridge: Harvard University Belknap Press, 1971) pp. 3–53.

12. Laczniac, *op.cit.*

13. Fisk, Raymond P., "Toward a theoretical framework for marketing ethics," *Southern Marketing Association Proceedings,* 1982, pp. 255–259.

14. Fisk, *op.cit.*

15. Ross, William D., *The Right and the Good* (Oxford: The Clarion Press, 1930).

16. Tsalikis, John, and David J. Fritzsche, "Business ethics: A literature review," in *Journal of Business Ethics,* Vol. 8, No. 9, Sept 1989, pp. 695–743.

17. Rawls, John, *A Theory of Justice* (Cambridge, MA: Harvard University Press, 1971).

18. Garrett, Thomas, *Business Ethics* (Englewood Cliffs, NJ: Prentice-Hall, 1966).

19. Fletcher, Joseph, *Situation Ethics: The New Morality* (Philadelphia, PA: Westminister Press, 1966).

20. Jaksa, James A., and Michael S. Pritchard, *Communication Ethics: Methods of Analysis* (Belmont, CA: Wadsworth, 1988).

21. Jaksa and Pritchard, *op.cit.*

22. Christians, Clifford G., Kim B. Rotzoll, and Mark Facker, *Media Ethics: Cases and Moral Reasoning* (New York, NY: Longman, 1983).

23. Berger, Charles R., and Steven H. Chaffee, *Handbook of Communication Science* (Newbury Park, CA: Sage, 1987).

24. Hegarty, Harvey W., and Henry P. Sims, "Some determinants of unethical behavior: An experiment," *Journal of Applied Psychology,* 63, No. 4, 1979, pp. 451–457; same authors, "Organizational philosophy, policies and objectives related to unethical decision behavior: A laboratory experiment," *Journal of Applied Psychology,* 64, No. 3, 1979, pp. 331–338.

25. Camden, C., M. Motley, and A. Wilson, "White lies and interpersonal communication: A taxonomy and preliminary investigation of social motivation," *Western Journal of Speech Communication,* Vol. 48, pp. 309–325.

26. Lindskold, S., and P. Walters, "Categories for acceptability of lies," *Journal of Social Psychology,* Vol. 120, pp. 129–136.

27. Knapp, Cody, and Reardon, *op.cit.*

28. Corcoran, J., M. Lewis, and R. Garger, "Biofeedback—conditioned galvanic skin response and hypnotic suppression of arousal: A pilot study of their relation to deception," *Journal of Forensic Sciences,* Vol. 23, 1978, pp. 155–162.

29. Mark Knapp, et.al., *op.cit.*

30. Kohlberg, Lawrence, *The Meaning and Measurement of Moral Development,* (Worcester, MA: Clark University Press, 1981).

31. Sears, David O., and Jonathan L. Freedman, "Selective exposure to information: A critical review," *The Process and Effects of Mass Communication,* revised edition, edited by Wilbur Schramm and Donald Roberts (Urbana, IL: University of Illinois Press, 1972).

32. Gilligan, C., *In a Different Voice: Psychological Theory and Women's Development* (Cambridge, MA: Harvard University Press, 1982).

33. Beltramini, Richard F., Robert A. Person, and George Kozmetsky, "Concerns of college students regarding business ethics," *Journal of Business Ethics* Vol. 3, 1984, pp. 195–200; and, Thomas M. Jones and Frederick H. Gautschi, III, "Will the ethics of business change? A survey of future executives," *Journal of Business Ethics,* Vol. 7, 1989, pp. 231–248.

34. Kidwell, Jeaneen M., Robert E. Stevens, and Art L. Bethke, "Differences in ethical perceptions between male and female managers: Myth or reality?" *Journal of Business Ethics,* 6, 1988, pp. 487–493; and, Charles W. McNichols and Thomas W. Zimmerrer, "Situational ethics: An empirical study of differentiators of student attitudes," *Journal of Business Ethics,* 4, 1986, pp. 175–180.

35. Wright, Donald K., "Examining ethical and moral values of public relations people," in a special issue of *Public Relations Review* devoted to ethics, Vol. 15, No.2, Summer 1989, pp. 19–33.

36. Noddings, Nel, "Ethics from the standpoint of women," in *Theoretical Perspectives on Sex Differences,* edited by Deborah L. Rhode (New Haven: Yale University Press, 1990), pp. 160–173.

37. Viorst, Judith, *Necessary Losses,* (New York: Simon and Schuster, 1986).

38. Bebaau, Muriel J., and Mary M. Brabeck, "Integrating care and justice in professional moral development," *Journal of Moral Education,* Vol. 16, 1982, pp. 189–203.

39. Pratt, Catherine, "Gender implications in public relations ethics: Kohlberg, Gilligan, and the PRSA Code of Professional Standards," paper presented to the Association for Education in Journalism and Mass Communication, August, 1990.

40. Cappella, Joseph N., "Interpersonal communication: Definitions and fundamental questions," *Handbook of Communication Science,* edited by Charles Berger and Steven Chaffee (Newbury Park, CA: Sage, 1987) pp. 184–238.

41. Mechanic, David, "Sources of power of lower participants in complex organization," *Administrative Science Quarterly,* Vol. 7, December 1962, pp. 349–364.

42. Fitzpatrick, Mary Anne, "Marital interaction," *Handbook of Communication Science,* edited by Charles Berger and Steven Chaffee (Newbury Park, CA: Sage, 1987) pp. 564–618.

43. Jaksa, James A., and Michael S. Pritchard, *op.cit.,* p. 101.

44. Argyle, M., and M. Henderson, "The rules of friendship," *Journal of Social and Personal Relationships,* Vol. 1, 1984, pp. 211–237.

45. Jacobson, N. S., "A component analysis of behavior marital therapy: The relative effectiveness of behavior exchange and communication/problem-solving training," *Journal of Consulting and Clinical Psychology,* Vol. 52, 1984, pp. 295–305.

46. Zey-Ferrell, Mary K., Mark Weaver, and O. C. Ferrell, "Predicting unethical behavior among marketing practitioners," *Human Relations,* 32, No. 7, 1979, pp. 557–569.

47. Izraeli, Dove, "Ethical beliefs and behavior among managers: A cross-cultural perspective," *Journal of Business Ethics,* Vol. 7, 1988, pp. 263–271.

48. Newstrom, John W., and William A. Ruch, "The ethics of management and the management of ethics," *MSU Business Topics,* Vol. 23, Winter 1975, pp. 29–37.

49. Rotzoll and Christians, *op.cit.*

50. Janis, Irving, *Groupthink,* 2nd ed. (Boston, MA: Houghton Mifflin, 1982).

51. Jaksa and Pritchard, *op.cit.*

52. Mill, John Stuart, "On Liberty," in *The Six Great Humanistic Essays of John Stuart Mill* (New York: Washington Square Press, 1963) pp. 52–53.

53. *Creating A Workable Company Code of Ethics,* published by the Ethics Resource Center, Washington, D.C., 1990.

54. Saul, George K., "Business ethics: Where are we going?" *Academy of Management Review,* Vol 6., No. 2, April 1981, pp. 269–276.

55. American Society of Association Executives, Ethics Information Center, 1575 Eye Street, N.W., Washington, D.C., 20040; Ethics Resource Center, 600 New Hampshire Avenue, N.W., Washington, D.C. 20037; The

Public Relations Society of America, 33 Irving Place, New York, New York, 10003; and, the International Association of Business Communicators, One Hallidie Plaza, Sixth Floor, San Francisco, CA 94102.

56. Bowman, J. S., "Managerial ethics in business and government," *Business Horizons,* Vol. 19, 1976, pp. 48–54; and Archie B. Carroll, "Managerial ethics: A post-Watergate view," *Business Horizons,* April 1975, pp. 75–80.

57. DeGeorge, Richard T., and Joseph A Pichler, editors, *Ethics, Free Enterprise, and Public Policy* (New York: Oxford University Press, 1978).

58. Hage, Jerald, *Theories of Organizations: Form, Processes and Transformation* (New York: Wiley-Interscience, 1980).

59. Steiner, John F., "The prospect of ethical advisors for business corporations," *Business and Society,* Vol. 16, pp. 5–10.

60. Hage, Jerald T., "An axiomatic theory of organizations," *Administrative Science Quarterly,* Vol. 10, No. 3, December 1965, pp. 289–320.

61. Hegarty and Sims, *op.cit.,* 1978, 1979.

62. Carroll, Archie B., "Linking business ethics to behavior in organizations," *Advanced Management Journal,* Summer 1978, pp. 4–11.

63. Pratt, Cornelius B., "Ethical inclinations of public relations practitioners," paper presented to the Association for Education in Journalism and Mass Communication, Minneapolis, Minnesota, August, 1990.

64. Baumhart, Raymond S., "How ethical are businessmen?" *Harvard Business Review,* Vol. 39, 1961, pp. 6–31.

65. "The pressure to compromise personal ethics," *Business Week,* January 31, 1977, p. 107.

66. Katz, Daniel, and Robert Kahn, *The Social Psychology of Organizations,* 2nd edition, (New York: Wiley, 1978) p. 251.

67. Wilcox, Dennis, *Ethics and candor in public relations and organizational communication: A literature review* (San Francisco, CA: IABC Foundation, 1984).

68. Ibid

69. Rotzoll, Kim, and Clifford Christians, "Advertising agency practitioners' perceptions of ethical decisions," *Journalism Quarterly,* Aug, 1980, pp. 425–431.

70. Litschert, Robert J., and Edward A. Nicholson, *The Corporate Role and Ethical Behavior* (New York: Petrocelli/Charter, 1977).

71. Axelrod, Robert, *The Evolution of Cooperation* (New York: Basic Books, 1984).

72. Robert Axelrod, *op.cit.* p. 125.

73. Axelrod, *op.cit.,* pp. 124–141.

74. Carroll, *op.cit.*

75. Weber, James, "Institutionalizing ethics into the corporations," *MSU Business Topics,* Vol. 29, 1981, pp. 47–52.

76. *Creating a Workable Company Code of Ethics* (Washington, D.C.: Ethics Resource Center, 1990).

77. Walters, Jonathan, "Uphold a code of ethics in the eighties?" *Association Management,* October 1983, pp. 63–107.

78. *Annual Report to the Public and Defense Industry,* published in 1988 by the Ethics Resource Center, Washington, D.C.

79. "Attestation interpretation: Defense industry questionnaire on business ethics and conduct," Exhibit 4, Official Release, *Journal of Accountancy,* August, 1987.

80. Kruckeberg, Dean, "The need for an international code of ethics," *Public Relations Review,* Vol. 15, No. 2, Summer 1989, pp. 6–18.

81. *ibid.,* p. 12.

82. The model is based on one developed in marketing. See Scott Vitell, Jr., "Marketing ethics: Conceptual and empirical foundations of a positive theory of decision-making in marketing situations having ethical content," unpublished dissertation, Texas Tech University, 1986.

83. Wilensky, Harold L., *Organizational Intelligence* (New York: Basic Books, 1967)

84. Wilson, Edward O., *Sociobiology* (Cambridge, MA: Harvard University Press, 1975); and *On Human Nature* (Cambridge, MA: Harvard University Press, 1978).

85. Wright, Robert, *Three Scientists and their Gods* (New York: Harper and Row, 1988) p. 200.

86. Jaynes, Julian, *The Origin of Consciousness in the Breakdown of the Bicameral Mind* (Boston: Houghton Mifflin, 1976, 1990).

CHAPTER TEN

How to Conduct Ethical Public Relations Considering External Publics, Laws, Public Policies and Cultural Factors

. . . . .

*T*he chief of the local labor union was obviously anxious and under pressure when he called Ray late in the afternoon to ask for some advice. Ray had conducted a very successful public relations campaign for the union a couple of years previously, but he had not talked with the union chief in six months. The chief said he had a union member standing in his office who had just told him that he had been subpoenaed by the local grand jury investigating bribes and kickbacks in the construction industry—and that he was scheduled to appear the next morning! The chief said he didn't know much about the situation except that the union member said he had nothing to hide from the grand jury. "How should the union handle the media?" the union chief asked Ray. Ray told him it was more complicated than that; they would need to discuss not only short-term strategies for tomorrow morning, but also long-term issues affecting the union. This was only the first union member to be involved in the grand jury's investigation, which was not likely to be over anytime soon. Ray told him it was too complicated to discuss over the phone; it was a very serious situation. He told the union chief to keep the subpoenaed member in his office and that he would be right over.

When he arrived at the union chief's office, the story from the union member had changed. During the fifteen minutes it took Ray to drive across town, the union member had confessed to routinely taking bribes from a number of construction supervisors over the past several years. Ray had barely sat down when he was told the "new" facts, and that what they now wanted from him was advice about how to put the best spin on the facts without admitting guilt and without creating undue negative publicity. Ray raised his hand to stop the conversation and quietly asked the union member to wait outside the office. Surprised by Ray's suggestion, the two men protested, but Ray insisted. When the other man had left them alone, Ray looked at the chief. In a controlled, deadly serious tone, he told the union chief to arrange immediately for a good, criminal defense lawyer to work on the case, and that he, Ray, wanted no part of it, at least not as it was being currently discussed. The union chief's poker face irritated Ray. He banged his fist on the table and stood up, saying, "Do you realize by telling me these facts you have involved me in this case? I'm now in the position of aiding and abetting a cover-up—guilty of misprision—a felony! Thanks a lot! You're in serious trouble. Get that fellow outside a good lawyer, now, immediately. Get yourself a good lawyer. Then call me, if you still want my advice." Ray then shifted his tone to that of a confidant and gave the union chief the names of a few lawyers. Ray shook the man's hand and told him, "Take good care of yourself. Listen to your lawyer. Then, give me a call." As Ray walked out the office, the union chief was dialing the telephone. The anxious union member was down at one end of the hallway, pacing by the cigarette machines. Ray walked in the opposite direction, out of the building.

The next day, the union member admitted to the grand jury that he had been taking bribes. The union chief called Ray and asked him to help work on the case, which he said was now being handled by one of the lawyers Ray had recommended. Ray said he would have to think about it. He called a federal judge who was a personal friend, and they discussed the grand jury investigation in general terms. He also called a prosecutor in the district attorney's office whom he respected, and they, too, discussed the investigation. Both conversations convinced Ray that many union members, including quite possibly the union chief, were involved in bribery and kickbacks. Sensing what Ray was concerned about, the federal judge had warned his friend, "I know you've worked for the union before. But I'd stay away from them this time. They are in it deep. It's a lot bigger and messier than it appears." Later that day, Ray called the union chief and said that, because of previous commitments and his heavy workload, he would not be able to work on the case. When the union chief asked Ray for recommendations for other public relations counselors, he declined by suggesting the chief work more closely with the newly retained lawyer in selecting an appropriate team of advisors.

. . .

MANY FACTORS AFFECT ETHICAL DECISION-MAKING IN PUBLIC RELATIONS

This vignette, based upon an actual incident, illustrates a fact of life for a public relations professional: sometimes, the best solution to an unethical situation is to walk, even when it means walking away from a job. The vignette also highlights the fact that public relations practitioners are legally and professionally vulnerable if their clients or the organizations they work for engage in unethical or illegal activities.

The wise public relations practitioner is well aware not only of all the various factors that can create professionally dangerous situations, but also of how to manage them systematically and ethically. In the previous chapter we discussed intrapersonal, interpersonal, small group, and other internal organizational factors affecting ethical decision-making in public relations. We also explored effective strategies for dealing with ethical dilemmas created by these factors. In this chapter, we will discuss factors outside the immediate control of the focal organization and how these factors affect the management of public relations programs and campaigns.

DEFINING FACTORS OUTSIDE THE CONTROL OF THE ORGANIZATION

Outside the immediate control of most complex organizations are dozens—if not hundreds, sometimes thousands, even millions—of individuals and publics with a stake in the operation of the organization. Some of these stakeholders wish the organization continued success; others wish it would stop or change its ways. Despite their numbers, it is not likely that any of these "external" individuals, acting alone, could affect significantly the ethical behavior of any complex organization. Only individuals aligned as members of publics can dramatically affect ethical decision-making in public relations. As we have discussed in previous chapters, a group of individuals is not necessarily a public. A group is any clustering of individuals; but unless these people are aware of themselves and act collectively, they do not constitute a public, and they are not likely to influence organizational decision-making. Publics may be simply aware of themselves and their issues, but not organized in any way to do anything about the issues. Or, they may be activist publics, organized to satisfy the needs of their members. Employees and, some would argue, vendors and suppliers are internal publics who are dependent upon the focal organization for their survival. Customers would be considered members of an external public. External publics are groups of people who are aware of themselves, who are faced with a common issue or problem, and who are outside the immediate control of the focal organization.

Also outside the control of most organizations are laws and public policies. Laws are principles and rules established by governments to help regulate society. Public policies are courses of action or procedures which conform to public expectations about how society should be regulated.

Surrounding all organizations and affecting all ethical decision-making in society are cultural values and beliefs. Values are concepts, ideals, customs, habits, and traditions within a society—or within an individual, small group, organization, or public—which arouse strong emotional responses, either for or against them. Beliefs are attitudes and opinions that reflect confidence in the truth or existence of something not easily proved.

These factors—external publics, laws and public policies, and cultural values—constitute the three "higher" levels of the six-tiered systems framework used in previous chapters.

External Consumer and Activist Publics

Each organization has consumers of its products or services. These consumers may or may not be organized into activist publics. If the consumers are not organized, then they are not likely to have a significant impact on ethical decision-making within the organization unless members of the organization choose to make consumer-desired decisions. However, unorganized consumers, as a ready and eager market, can "pull" or elicit decisions from an organization that wants to satisfy its consumers. If, on the other hand, an organization is not market oriented or responsive to its consumers, then activists groups are likely to form to force decision-makers to give consideration to consumer demands.[1]

An example of an activist public formed around a consumer product would be the incident a few years ago involving a group of women who protested the advertising produced by a certain manufacturer of lingerie and women's apparel.[2] From the manufacturer's point of view, the female models wearing lingerie whom they photographed in provocative poses were presenting the company's products in a very logical, attractive way—as they would be worn. The activist group, however, considered the poses pornographic and initiated a public relations campaign against the company that included calling a press conference and giving the manufacturer a dubious achievement award for excellence in sexist advertising. Both sides viewed the same set of ads and perceived different images—one saw positive stereotypes, the other negative stereotypes. The incident was a classic example of ethical relativism.

Activist groups can also organize around issues, such as consumer product safety, civil rights, community development, labor-management relations, government actions, or the environment.[3] An example of a single-issue activist group would be the Sierra club which focuses on environmental issues. Research indicates that the people most likely to join such an activist group are concerned about a wide variety of issues relevant to the group. These all-issue activists do not join in order to gain personal benefits; rather, they join because they agree with the group's philosophy, and because it is a way for them to delegate their social responsibility to an organization dedicated to benefiting all of its members.[4]

A special type of single-issue activist public is a labor union. It is special because it has the force of law behind it. Backed by legislation such as the U.S. National Labor Relations Act and the U.S. Labor Management Relations Act, this activist public can require employers not only to meet specific expectations, but also to safeguard the rights of labor unions to exist. For example, employers must not prevent dissemination of labor news to its employees; they cannot publish biased information about labor-management relations; and, they must allow their employees to vote in a fair election for union representation. Labor unions, with their own public relations specialists, lobby for effective labor legislation at national, state, and local levels. They also serve as corporate watchdogs, often providing private and public channels of influence for whistleblowers.[5] Other examples of activist publics and special-interest groups with the force of law defining and protecting their rights include political action committees, philanthropic organizations, and public relations agents representing foreign governments.

The underlying philosophy supporting the role of activist groups in society has been called "interest-group liberalism," which makes the assumption that what is good for special-interest groups dedicated to the common good must be good for society.[6] The assumption does not address two ethical problems: 1) that the definition of what is good for society depends upon the values, principles, and loyalties of each special-interest group, and 2) that there are so many types of groups.

Radical and Mainstream Activist Publics

There are radical and mainstream activist publics and scores of variations in between. Activist publics which have adopted radical, some would say "terrorist," tactics have been accused of conducting unethical public relations campaigns designed to psychologically and physically harm their target audiences.[7] There are activist publics representing every political and economic philosophy, from the far right to the far left. For every major organization in society, there are several activist publics that are focused on it, trying to influence its social performance. Similar to saying that people are best known not so much by their friends as by their enemies, some have said the position of an organization on political or economic issues can best be determined not so much by the types of suppliers, vendors, and consumers it has, but by the types of activist publics it has attracted.[8]

Even mainstream activist publics and special-interest groups have been criticized because of their overall impact on society. Olson has argued that the special interests of activist publics often are in conflict with the general welfare, even though most of the activist publics are interested in collective rather than individual goods.[9] His argument is that organizations, especially governments, when threatened in just the "right" way, will meet the immediate needs of special interest groups and not meet either the long-range goals of the organizations or of society. For example, Olson's research correlated the decline of economic power of nation-states with the rising power of special-interest groups.[10]

Competitors

Competitors are definitely outside the control of the focal organization, and they exert significant influence on ethical decision-making. The actions of competitors are often used to justify the ethics and performance of an organization. Because competitors threaten vital interests, they want to know as much as possible about each other for two main reasons: 1) they don't like to be surprised, and 2) they want to win in the marketplace. In order to track the competition, among other matters, public relations practitioners often engage in environmental scanning—what some have called the gathering of "marketing intelligence."[11]

There are legal and ethical distinctions between industrial espionage, marketing intelligence, and environmental scanning. Espionage is the practice of spying, clandestinely collecting information to gain an advantage over someone, especially the person or organization from whom the information was gathered. It is illegal when it involves breaking and entering or stealing tangible and intellectual properties. It is always unethical because it involves duplicity and invasion of privacy.

Professionals involved in environmental scanning and marketing intelligence are very much concerned about the ethics of how they gather information. Public relations law scholar Morton Simon reported on one study that indicated:

> *". . . businessmen believe that ethical considerations are important in gathering information; company policy is the main force that assures ethical methods; state and federal laws are the second most important deterrent from illegal information-gathering; espionage—pirating of personnel or information secured through a business intermediary such as a common customer—is the most objectionable practice in the gathering of information; marketing-information acquisition is not inherently unethical; most intelligence work is generally overt; information gathered surreptitiously is not an important part of the information flow; covert practices are costly and they are effective only in the short run."*[12]

From another point of view, most public relations activities give away information, even to the competition. For this reason, public relations practitioners have been described as being in perpetual jeopardy when they try to ethically scan the environment, protect corporate secrets, and meet corporate disclosure requirements.[13] Because there are so many points of view from so many stakeholders, public relations practitioners will be damned if they do communicate effectively, and damned if they don't.

Investors and Ethical Corporate Decision-Making

Another set of organizations with an indirect but significant impact on the ethics of publicly-owned corporations includes investment firms, brokerage houses, and financial institutions—and the thousands of investors they represent. Based on literature reviews of empirical studies correlating the two factors, an investment specialist concluded that socially responsible organizations are the most likely to make long-range profits.[14] While this can be considered a positive finding, the cynical implication is that the best investment for short-term profits may be earned from the least socially responsible organizations.

Another study correlating profits and ethics found that senior managers of the most profitable corporations tended to be more ethical—in the sense of being more favorably predisposed toward minorities, the poor, and other aspects of human rights—than were executives in the less profitable firms.[15] The optimistic implication is that the greater the slack resources in the organization, the more ethical the decision-making by senior managers. The pessimistic implication is that "lean machines" are "mean machines" because tight budgets and severe economic constraints increase unethical decision-making.

Professional Associations

A professional association is an excellent example of an activist public; it is a group of individuals who are engaged in similar activities, faced with common problems and opportunities, and very much aware of each other. Peer pressure plays an important role in defining a profession. Professionals are dedicated to a common set of principles, and they encourage ways of enforcing adherence to those principles. Professionals often have to demonstrate mastery of an identifiable body of specialized knowledge that allows them to perform special services or earn special privileges. As a consequence of their privileges, professionals often have special responsibilities to meet specific obligations to others in society. Social scientists have identified five major characteristics of professionals:

1. A common set of values.
2. A common set of principles.

3. A common set of loyalties.
4. Membership in a strong professional association.
5. Mastery of an identifiable body of knowledge, and a commitment to the development of this knowledge.[16]

In public relations, there are scores of professional organizations worldwide, some of which have hundreds of individual chapters. Some professional associations have regional, national, and international memberships. Others are organized to serve certain industries or specializations within public relations. Still others are single-issue activist publics serving professionals interested in specific ethnic, religious, political, economic or gender issues.

State Licensing of Professions For a wide variety of occupations, entry into a profession is regulated by the state. For example, the state controls who can practice as lawyers, doctors, plumbers, and beauticians. The state's compelling interest is to protect the public from some potential harm: for example, injustices, poor medical services, unsafe buildings, or chemically scorched heads of hair. The ethical rationale is that the restrictions imposed on these few individuals by the state when it licenses certain professions is more than offset by the total good achieved for the greater number of individuals in society. The more restrictive the state-imposed guidelines on a profession, the greater the economic consequences; the more restricted the number of individuals who can perform state-sanctioned functions, the more likely it is that they will be able to demand and receive higher rewards either in status or remuneration, or both.

In public relations, the merits of state licensing have been debated for years. One of the founding fathers of the profession, Edward Bernays, organized an activist public dedicated to helping achieve licensing in public relations because, he has argued, it is essential to the attainment of full professional status.[17] A number of public relations practitioners and scholars have argued that to license public relations practitioners would not be constitutional in the United States because it would violate the First Amendment, which guarantees freedom of the press.[18] The argument against public relations licensure is that all individuals in society should be allowed access to the media and should have a right to influence and participate in public debates. To license public relations practitioners would limit individual freedoms of expression and of the press, which are especially important for those without the resources to engage the services of a licensed public relations professional. Consequently, the limited good achieved by licensing practitioners and requiring high professional standards would be offset by the greater harm done to the large number of individuals who would want and benefit from unrestricted access to the media, a free press, and open public discussions.

Voluntary Professional Associations Voluntary professional associations have difficulty justifying to others that they are a profession because practitioners working in the field are not required to be members. Based on memberships in the two largest professional associations in public relations, approximately ten percent of all practitioners are involved in professional associations. Research indicates that public relations practitioners who are members of professional associations hold significantly different values and principles than do practitioners not associated with professional organizations.[19]

The primary reasons people join voluntary professional associations are to meet their colleagues and to "network"—to make contact with other professionals who can assist each other in their career development. In addition to sponsoring forums for meeting people and exchanging ideas, many professional associations also conduct contests to identify outstanding examples of professional work and accreditation examinations to ascertain and document a member's professional status.

Award Programs Recognize Professional Norms Two of the largest professional organizations with major award programs are the Public Relations Society of America (PRSA) and the International Association of Business Communicators (IABC). In 1990, a third organization, the International Public Relations Association (IPRA), established an awards program for its members.

At their competitions, both PRSA and IABC solicit, from members and non-members, descriptions of public relations programs and campaigns. These are judged against others within such categories as special events, investor relations, employee communication programs, public service, feature length video programs, communication audits and research, newsletters, public affairs, marketing communications, international public relations, publications, corporate advertisements, annual reports, speeches, photography, and many more.

Panels of peers are used to select award-winning entries. For the major award programs of both PRSA and IABC, judges focus on how well practitioners executed the four basic steps in the public relations strategic planning process: research, planning, implementation and evaluation. PRSA refers to these stages as research, planning, execution, and evaluation. IABC refers to them as the need, goals and objectives, execution, and evaluation and results.[20]

Accreditation of Professionals Both PRSA and IABC accredit qualified practitioners who pass written and oral examinations. Approximately twenty-five percent of the members of PRSA are accredited, and approximately five percent of IABC members are accredited. The examinations are designed to test the members' understanding of the body of public relations knowledge and their ability to apply that knowledge in practice. The examination also tests the members' knowledge of the association's code of ethics, and of techniques and principles of allied disciplines that affect the practice of public relations.[21] Because the written and oral exams are judged by peers, the accreditation process tests a practitioner's knowledge of professional norms.

Professional Codes of Ethics   While the vast majority of professional associations have codes of ethics, only half of them have strong enforcement policies. This lack of enforcement is especially true for associations with corporate members within a single industry, because strong, enforceable codes invite antitrust proceedings and lawsuits.[22]

In this chapter, we will analyze the codes of ethics from three of the world's largest public relations associations: PRSA, IABC, and IPRA. While each code outlines enforcement procedures, including guidelines for processing complaints and criteria for selection of judges, the harshest sanction against any "convicted" violator of any of the codes is the revocation of membership. Each association stresses the educational, rather than punitive, function of their ethics codes.

SYSTEMS-BASED COMPARISON OF PUBLIC RELATIONS CODES OF ETHICS

Not considering statements in preambles and introductory sections, there are seventeen principles in the PRSA Code of Professional Standards for the Practice of Public Relations, seven principles in the IABC Code of Ethics, and thirteen principles in the IPRA Code of Athens. These thirty-seven principles have been placed into the following systems framework to help identify similarities and differences, and possible areas of improvement. Some principles have been repeated because they applied to two or more levels. (In parenthesis is the number assigned to the principle in each association's formal code, which can be found in the Appendix.)

Practitioner's Relationship with Cultural Values, Beliefs

PRSA: A member shall conduct his or her professional life in accord with the public interest. (1)

PRSA: A member shall exemplify high standards of honesty and integrity while carrying out dual obligations to a client or employer and to the democratic process. (2)

PRSA:	A member shall deal fairly with the public, with past or present clients or employers, and with fellow practitioners, giving due respect to the ideal of free inquiry and to the opinions of others. (3)
PRSA:	A member shall adhere to the highest standards of accuracy and truth, avoiding extravagant claims or unfair comparisons and giving credit for ideas and words borrowed from others. (4)
IPRA:	Each member shall refrain from subordinating the truth to other requirements. (10)
IPRA:	Each member shall endeavor to contribute to the achievement of the moral and cultural conditions enabling human beings to reach their full stature and enjoy the indefeasible rights to which they are entitled under the United Nation's "Universal Declaration of Human Rights." (1)
IPRA:	Each member shall endeavor to establish communication patterns and channels which, by fostering the free flow of essential information, will make each member of the group feel that he/she is being kept informed, and also give him/her an awareness of his/her own personal involvement and responsibility, and of his/her solidarity with other members. (2)
IPRA:	Each member shall undertake to observe, in the course of his/her professional duties, the moral principles and rules of the United Nation's "Universal Declaration of Human Rights." (5)
IPRA:	Each member shall undertake to pay due regard to, and uphold, human dignity, and to recognize the right of each individual to judge for himself/herself. (6)
IPRA:	Each member shall undertake to establish the moral, psychological and intellectual conditions for dialogue in its true sense, and to recognize the right of the parties involved to state their case and express their views. (7)

Practitioner's Relationship with Laws and Public Policies

PRSA: A member shall adhere to the highest standards of accuracy and truth, avoiding extravagant claims or unfair comparisons and giving credit for ideas and words borrowed from others. (4)

PRSA: A member shall not knowingly disseminate false or misleading information and shall act promptly to correct erroneous communications for which he or she is responsible. (5)

PRSA: A member shall not engage in any practice which has the purpose of corrupting the integrity of channels of communication or the processes of government. (6)

IABC: Communication professionals will abide by the spirit and letter of all laws and regulations governing their professional activities. (3)

IABC: Communication professionals will not condone any illegal or unethical act related to their professional activity, their organization and its business or the public environment in which it operates. (4)

IPRA: Each member shall refrain from circulating information which is not based on established and ascertainable facts. (11)

IPRA: Each member shall refrain from taking part in any venture or undertaking which is unethical or dishonest or capable of impairing human dignity and integrity. (12)

Practitioner's Relationship with Publics Outside the Immediate Control of the Sponsoring Organization or Client

PRSA: A member shall deal fairly with the public, with past or present clients or employers, and with fellow practitioners, giving due respect to the ideal of free inquiry and to the opinions of others. (3)

PRSA: A member shall, as soon as possible, sever relations with any organization or individual if such relationship requires conduct contrary to the articles of this Code. (17)

PRSA: A member shall not intentionally injure the professional reputation or practice of another practitioner. (14)

PRSA: If a member has evidence that another member has been guilty of unethical, illegal, or unfair practices, including those in violation of this Code, the member is obligated to present the information promptly to the proper authorities of the Society for action in accordance with the procedure set forth in Article XII of the Bylaws. (15)

PRSA: A member called as witness in a proceeding for the enforcement of this Code is obligated to appear, unless excused for sufficient reason by the judicial panel. (16)

IABC: Communication professionals will uphold the credibility and dignity of their profession by encouraging the practice of honest, candid and timely communication. (1)

IABC: Communication professionals will respect the confidentiality and right-to-privacy of all individuals, employers, clients and customers. (5)

IABC: Communication professionals should uphold IABC standards for ethical conduct in all professional activity, and should use IABC and its designation of accreditation (ABC) only for purposes that are authorized and fairly represent the organization and its professional standards. (7)

IPRA: Each member shall undertake to establish the moral, psychological and intellectual conditions for dialogue in its true sense, and to recognize the right of the parties involved to state their case and express their views. (7)

IPRA: Each member shall endeavor to conduct himself/herself always and in all circumstances in such a manner as to deserve and secure the confidence of those with whom he/she comes into contact. (3)

IPRA:	Each member shall undertake to act, in all circumstances, in such a manner as to take account of the respective interests of the parties involved: both the interests of the organization which he/she serves and the interests of the publics concerned. (8)
IPRA:	Each member shall refrain from using any "manipulative" methods or techniques designed to create subconscious motivations which the individual cannot control to his/her own free will and so cannot be held accountable for the action taken on them. (13)

Practitioner's Relationship with the Sponsoring Organization or Client

PRSA:	A member shall deal fairly with the public, with past or present clients or employers, and with fellow practitioners, giving due respect to the ideal of free inquiry and to the opinions of others. (3)
PRSA:	A member shall be prepared to identify publicly the name of the client or employer on whose behalf any public communication is made. (7)
PRSA:	A member shall not use any individual or organization professing to serve or represent an announced cause, or professing to be independent or unbiased, but actually serving another or undisclosed interest. (8)
PRSA:	A member shall not guarantee the achievement of specified results beyond the member's direct control. (9)
PRSA:	A member shall not represent conflicting or competing interests without the express consent of those involved, given after a full disclosure of the facts. (10)
PRSA:	A member shall not place himself or herself in a position where the member's personal interest is or may be in conflict with an obligation to an employer or client, or others, without full disclosure of such interests to all involved. (11)

PRSA:	A member shall not accept fees, commissions, gifts or any other consideration from anyone except clients or employers for whom services are performed without their express consent, given after full disclosure of the facts. (12)
PRSA:	A member shall scrupulously safeguard the confidences and privacy rights of present and former clients or employers. (13)
PRSA:	A member shall, as soon as possible, sever relations with any organization or individual if such relationship requires conduct contrary to the articles of this Code. (17)
IABC:	Communication professionals will respect the confidentiality and right-to-privacy of all individuals, employers, clients and customers. (5)
IPRA:	Each member shall endeavor to conduct himself/herself always and in all circumstances in such a manner as to deserve and secure the confidence of those with whom he/she comes into contact. (3)
IPRA:	Each member shall undertake to act, in all circumstances, in such a manner as to take account of the respective interests of the parties involved: both the interests of the organization which he/she serves and the interests of the publics concerned. (8)
IPRA:	Each member shall undertake to carry out his/her undertaking and commitments, which shall be so worded as to avoid misunderstanding, and to show loyalty and integrity in all circumstances so as to keep the confidences of his/her clients or employers, past or present and of all publics that are affected by his/her actions. (9)

Practitioner's Relationship with Other Individuals and Small Groups within the Sponsoring Organization or Client

PRSA:	A member shall deal fairly with the public, with past or present clients or employers, and with fellow practitioners, giving due respect to the ideal of free inquiry and to the opinions of others. (3)

PRSA: A member shall, as soon as possible, sever relations with any organization or individual if such relationship requires conduct contrary to the articles of this Code. (17)

IABC: Communication professionals will respect the confidentiality and right-to-privacy of all individuals, employers, clients and customers. (5)

IPRA: Each member shall undertake to pay due regard to, and uphold, human dignity, and to recognize the right of each individual to judge for himself/herself. (6)

IPRA: Each member shall undertake to conduct himself/herself always and in all circumstances in such a manner as to deserve and secure the confidence of those with whom he/she comes into contact. (3)

Practitioner's Relationship with the Self

PRSA: A member shall exemplify high standards of honesty and integrity while carrying out dual obligations to a client or employer and to the democratic process.

PRSA: A member shall not knowingly disseminate false or misleading information and shall act promptly to correct erroneous communications for which he or she is responsible. (7)

IABC: Communication professionals will not use any confidential information gained as a result of professional activity for personal benefit or for that of others. (6)

IPRA: Each member shall endeavor to bear in mind that, because of the relationship between his/her profession and the public, his/her conduct—even in private—will have an impact on the way in which the profession as a whole is appraised. (4)

IPRA: Each member shall refrain from subordinating the truth to other requirements. (10)

Similarities and Differences

In this six-level systems framework, most of the principles in these three codes focus on: 1) relationships between the practitioner and the client/employer, and 2) relationships between the practitioner and publics outside the immediate control of the sponsoring organization or client. An analysis of complaints to PRSA's Grievance Board has indicated that most alleged and actual violations of these principles occur at these same two levels of analysis. Most complaints have fallen into the following specific categories: abuse of media discounts and complimentary rates for purchasing media; ownership of campaign materials, documents, and records produced for the sponsoring organization; guarantees for media placement; blind solicitation of business from organizations with in-house specialists or outside counsel; and disclosure of a potential client's plans to a competitor.[23] The PRSA principles cited most often in complaints registered with the association over the past thirty years have been: #1, dealing fairly with clients, employers, fellow practitioners, and the general public; #7, using care to avoid communication of false or misleading information; #2, conducting professional life in accordance with public interest; #3, adhering to truth and accuracy and to generally accepted standards of good taste; and #6, engaging in practices that tend to corrupt the integrity of communication or governmental processes.[24]

Each of the PRSA, IABC, and IPRA codes stresses the values of truth and honesty, and each emphasizes discretion and loyalty, which are potentially conflicting principles. Each code, however, resolves any potential contradiction by explaining that in situations where these principles are in conflict, the professional should always tell the truth.

All codes underscore the importance of obeying the law.

Neither the PRSA nor the IABC code contains very many principles relating to cultural values and beliefs. PRSA principles encourage upholding standards of good taste and conducting a professional life that is in accord with the public interest. IABC principles do not directly address cultural values. The IPRA code contains several principles focused on belief systems, notably those supporting values stated in the United Nation's Universal Declaration of Human Rights (which is included in the Appendix). While all of the codes insist on the importance of accurate communication, only the IPRA code deals directly with the importance of two-way symmetrical communication, which the IPRA code calls "dialogue in its true sense."

Although PRSA, IABC and IPRA have professional development programs, including the accreditation examinations mentioned previously, none of the codes quoted above requires members to make a commitment to continuing education in their field, as do many codes governing the conduct of other professionals, such as certified public accountants, lawyers, doctors, and educators.[25] The "Declaration of Principles," or preface, of the PRSA code does call for members, "To improve our individual competence and advance the knowledge and proficiency of the profession through continuing research and education." Appropriate language for a more specific code regarding continuing education might be:

> *Public relations professionals will demonstrate an understanding of the body of knowledge in public relations, and will actively pursue and encourage the development of this knowledge.*

PRSA, IABC, IPRA, and other professional associations of public relations practitioners, have committees which regularly review and revise their codes of ethics.

LAWS AND PUBLIC POLICIES

For the ethical public relations practitioner, obeying the law is considered a base level of operations; it's the floor. If a public relations program or campaign drops below this base level, both the practitioner and the employer or client are open to legal liability.[26] The ethical public relations manager operates well above the base level, because the law may not address certain issues or may not declare illegal certain actions which the practitioner considers to be unethical. For example, the public relations field is infamous for making exaggerated statements not intended to be taken literally ("the greatest show on earth") and for staging attention-getting pseudo-events as significant news events. Neither activity is illegal, per se, except in extraordinary cases, but both are considered unethical by most public relations professionals.

It is beyond the scope of this book to describe in detail the legal issues which affect the practice of public relations. However, we will highlight the basic legal considerations important to a public relations professional. The wise public relations manager will meet on a regular basis with lawyers who specialize in commercial speech and communication issues and discuss the specific legal environment within which their organization or client operates. With that caveat in mind, the following statements about the major legal issues affecting the practice of public relations are presented in the form of principles:

1. A public relations professional understands what constitutes the rights of individuals and corporations to experience free speech and open public discussions.[27]
2. A public relations professional understands that national, state, and other jurisdictions often require registration and financial disclosure of lobbyists representing special-interest groups and, especially, foreign governments.[28]

3. A public relations professional understands that national, state, and other jurisdictions often establish ethical standards for elected officials, and that when a practitioner is lobbying these officials, these ethical standards must be honored.[29]
4. A public relations professional understands and complies with laws and regulations enforced by a variety of government agencies at national, state, and local levels that deal with truth in advertising, package labeling, testimonial techniques, promotional games and contests.[30]
5. A public relations professional understands that certain government agencies can be required to release information pertaining to government decisions—except matters directly affecting national security, trade secrets, and personal privacy—to individual and corporations requesting that information through the Freedom of Information Act and similar legislation.[31]
6. A public relations professional understands and respects copyrights, not only because materials produced for programs and campaigns may be copyrighted, but also because "works for hire" supplied by freelance writers, artists, and producers also may be protected by copyrights.[32]
7. A public relations professional understands that if trademarks and trade secrets are not properly and consistently protected in all official corporate communications the courts may rule that others may use this information as they see fit.[33]
8. A public relations professional understands the difference between research and industrial espionage, and between research and sales promotion.[34]
9. A public relations professional recognizes the rights of employees which have been established by national and state governments and regulatory agencies; these rights include regular reports from management, fair union elections, equal employment opportunities, affirmative action, and occupational safety—as well as the employee's right to "blow the whistle" on employers who violate these and other employee rights.[35]
10. A public relations professional understands the risks and responsibilities involved in corporate disclosure of information that may have a "material impact" on the buying and selling of a corporation's stock, and most importantly, that such disclosures should be accurate, mention bad news before good news, and be widely disseminated within minutes of when the information was recognized as being of material value to investors.[36]
11. A public relations professional understands the special financial relationships and income reporting procedures that are required of organizations engaging in philanthropic activities.[37]

12. A public relations professional understands that postal service regulations address numerous aspects of communication activities using the mails—from the size and weight of allowable pieces of mail, to the truthfulness of solicitations.[38]
13. A public relations professional understands that organizations can form political action committees by soliciting contributions from employees and others, that these solicitations cannot be coercive, and that the size of individual donations from givers and the size of contributions to specific political candidates are limited and closely monitored.[39]
14. A public relations professional understands that truth is the best defense against charges of libel; that persons claiming they were libeled must prove that they were identified, that they were damaged by the libelous statements, and—if they are public figures—that there was malice on the part of the communicator.[40]
15. A public relations professional understands that truth may not be a defense in cases alleging an invasion of privacy; rather, there are two other defenses: 1) proving that the communication is about a newsworthy event, and 2) having prior written consent from the individuals involved.[41]
16. A public relations professional understands that a legal consent from someone—for example, for the use of a picture or creative product—should name all parties involved (including heirs and personal representatives) and describe in writing an exchange of something of value for the consent, the intended use of the information, and the length of time the consent is valid.[42]
17. A public relations professional understands that the relationships between public relations practitioners, employers, and clients are governed by contract law, that public relations practitioners act as agents for their clients or employers, and, consequently, that an illegal action by either party in the relationship makes both open to legal liability.[43]

Cultural Values

When human culture is broadly defined as the synergistic set of lifestyles of a recognizable group of people, it is possible to identify a wide variety of cultures. For example, one community may have standards of living, including ethical standards, that differ dramatically from those in another community. These cultural differences can exist between communities located side-by-side within one small regional area. Obviously, such differences can exist between people living in different countries and in different parts of the world. For example, business ethics have been found to vary dramatically from country to country. In recent years, Germany was perceived as the most ethical country in which to conduct business, followed by the United

Kingdom, the United States, and France; Mexico was ranked the least ethical of the countries surveyed.[44] The researchers found that consistent ethical behavior based on a common set of principles was strongly linked to economic development within a culture.

As global changes sweep through cultures, the practice of public relations is affected.[45] Transnational consumerism, international marketing, expansion of free market economies, new alliances among nations, multinational corporate mergers, organizational specialization and diversification are trends that offer both public relations opportunities and problems. In one way or another, public relations practitioners find themselves, for a variety of clients and employers, either working to achieve these changes or working to resist such changes and maintain the status quo.

Public relations practitioners work on a regular basis with two different cultures: the internal, organizational culture of the sponsoring organization or client; and the broader culture within which the organization or client operates. Both types of cultures have shared problems and opportunities; shared resources; shared transformational processes and technologies; shared values, principles, and loyalties; shared languages and communication channels; shared learning experiences; and shared boundaries of concern.

Public relations managers are involved in each of these cultural issues: defining problems and opportunities; gathering, monitoring, and controlling resources; working with others to transform these resources into goods and services; identifying and clarifying appropriate values, principles, and loyalties; using common languages and communication channels; creating shared learning experiences, from specific mass media to general educational programs; and distinguishing areas of interests and boundaries of concern. How these factors are explained to others and put into context—how the "right" and "wrong" ways of looking at these factors are presented—are ethical questions for public relations practitioners to answer.

Broader questions of ethics in public relations emerge when models of cultural change are considered.[46] There are three basic models. One model assumes that individual personalities, in all their complexities, generate change within societies. The assumption is that culture does not dictate human personality; rather, human personality is basic and universal. The public relations professional operating under these assumptions will question the ethics of campaigns designed to change the personalities of individual members of the target audience. A public relations practitioner making the opposite assumption might design a campaign aimed at changing basic personality traits.

Another model of cultural change assumes that patterns of relationships among collective enterprises, not individual differences, account for most structural-functional changes in society. The assumption is that an individual's contribution is not nearly as important as that of groups and organizations. The ethical dilemma for public relations practitioners is whether or not to design campaigns aimed at activist publics, including organizations, or at individuals.

A third model of cultural change assumes that conflict is inevitable between individuals, groups, and organizations in society. The assumption is that the source of the conflict can be either within the human personality or within collective enterprises, with the same result: change. The question for public relations managers is whether or not it is right to design campaigns that do not attempt conflict resolution.

SOLUTIONS TO ETHICAL DILEMMAS IN PUBLIC RELATIONS

Professional communicators should be aware of the United Nation's "Universal Declaration of Human Rights" (see Appendix E) and its implications for ethical communication within and across cultures. The preamble to this declaration, passed by the United Nations in 1948, calls for "a world in which human beings shall enjoy freedom of speech and belief." Article 18 states, "Everyone has the right to freedom of thought, conscience and religion." Article 19 states, "Everyone has the right to freedom of opinion and expression; (this) right includes freedom to hold opinions without interference and to seek, receive and impart information and ideas through any media and regardless of frontiers." Article 27 states, "Everyone has the right freely to participate in the cultural life of the community . . ." Public relations professionals who recognize these basic rights will work to ensure their organizations and clients are engaged in ethical communication.

There are a number of ways public relations practitioners can resolve ethical dilemmas:

1. Use the contingency model of ethical decision-making in public relations that was explained in the previous chapter. This model will help to identify and clarify factors affecting the practitioner's choices.
2. Use the Potter Box that was explained in the previous chapter.
3. Use systems theories, and other theories in public relations, to recognize factors that affect ethical decision-making, and change these factors—recognizing that one of the most important factors a public relations practitioner can change is the perception of the members of the dominant coalition.

SURVEY RESULTS

To identify values, principles, and loyalties of public relations practitioners faced with ethical dilemmas, more than twenty-five personal interviews were conducted with public relations professionals who had participated in the mail survey discussed earlier. A modified Delphi technique was used: the initial set of personal interviews was conducted; case studies were prepared (fictionalized to protect the confidentiality of the participants); and, copies of the cases were distributed by mail and reviewed by the practitioners, who were asked to clarify the values, principles, and loyalties associated with each case.

Three case studies are presented below that describe how factors outside the control of the focal organization affect ethical decision-making. At the end of the chapter there are additional case studies based on these personal interviews. Each of the case studies reported in this and the previous chapter involves a different type of public relations activity, such as holding a press conference, editing a publication, or engaging in issues management.

HOW CULTURAL VALUES AFFECT ETHICAL DECISION-MAKING IN PUBLIC RELATIONS

CASE 10.1:

Shock Radio Advertising on TV, and a Calculated Public Relations Response

The problem: Should a radio station have used television commercials that created controversy and public outrage in other markets? Some claimed the ads were tasteless and offensive, but radio stations using the TV ads in other markets dramatically boosted their ratings.

The situation: A popular local radio station, broadcasting in a highly competitive market, was offered a successfully test-marketed television promotional campaign that many viewers considered offensive. The commercials were parodies of nationally distributed public service announcements about the abuse of drugs. Using a theme of "this is your brain before listening" to the radio station, and "this is your brain after listening," the series of 10-second television commercials featured a variety of live, dead, and toy animals in various cute "before" postures and patently gross "after" poses. The producer of the commercials had sold market-exclusive rights to several other radio stations in other parts of the country. Each radio station airing the commercials had received numerous irate calls, particularly from animal rights groups. However, the ratings of listeners for each radio station using the commercials increased, sometimes quite dramatically. The local station's general manager signed a contract to have the commercials produced and aired in the local market. The general manager told the director of promotions to prepare an appropriate advertising and public relations campaign to support the commercials.

Values: The following values were identified as being relevant to the director of promotions in this case:

To be profitable.

To be outrageous.

To be polite when receiving criticism.

To be a good employee.

To be creative and innovative.

Principles: The following principles were considered by the director of promotions.

It's better to be listened to and hated than not be listened to at all.

Love your enemies; it confuses them.

Community standards are impossible to define.

Professional communicators do not corrupt channels of communication.

Do no harm.

Loyalties: The following loyalties were important to the director of promotions.

To the radio station.

To animals and animal rights advocates.

To television viewers.

To the community at large.

To himself: the director of promotions.

The solution: Before the commercials were aired, the director of promotions prepared a plan to respond quickly to irate callers. The switchboard operator was instructed to place all irate calls through to one staff member, who was instructed to apologize "on behalf of the station" and to send to each caller a formal letter of apology plus a T-shirt. The station also produced its own set of radio and television commercials calling on listeners and viewers to send in their own ideas for a "better" TV commercial. The creator of the winning commercial was to receive a $10,000 cash award and a promise from the station to produce and air the winning commercial as soon as possible. The station waited until there was a public outcry about the original set of offensive ads before announcing the contest for the better commercial.

Analysis: The advertising campaign was designed to test the limit, if not go over the line, of acceptable behavior within the community. It was designed to shock those with certain values. The public relations campaign was designed to deal efficiently with the public outcry, and to turn it to the advantage of the radio station. Had the radio's management not wanted an outrageous image, it would not have used the campaign. Had management misjudged the outer limit of acceptable community standards, more protests would have resulted, with the potential that certain advertisers would not buy commercial time on the station. Had the public relations director been involved in the initial decision to purchase the controversial ad campaign, the practitioner—and the station—probably would have had more options.

HOW LAWS AND PUBLIC POLICIES AFFECT ETHICAL DECISION-MAKING IN PUBLIC RELATIONS

. . .

CASE 10.2:

Releasing Public Information about a Top-Secret Organization

The problem: How to release information about a top-secret organization when the public had a right to know certain information, but the essential work of the organization had to be kept secret. How could these two conflicting principles be resolved when information was released to the media?

The situation: The nature of much of the corporation's work was conducting top-secret research and testing state-of-the-art defense systems. For this reason, most information was kept confidential, and the public relations director had to be very cautious when releasing information to the public. According to one spokesperson, "Our hands were tied much of the time." The director could not be as forthright with the public as most public relations specialists. For example, the organization was once audited by the U.S. Environmental Protection Agency which found hazardous waste containers on the premises. This, in turn, created a large public protest requiring immediate attention. However, an exact reason for using certain chemicals at the facility could not be given to the press, because their use at the facility was considered top-secret.

Values: The following values were identified as being relevant to the public relations practitioner in this case.

- To be operating within the law at all times.
- To be honest and accurate, but not to disclose properly classified, secret information.
- To be technologically sophisticated and conduct state-of-the-art research for clients.
- To make money.
- To be sensitive to the public's right to know.

Principles: The following principles were considered by the public relations practitioner.

- National security is more important than the public's right to know.
- Do not lie.
- The public has a right to know about environmental safety issues.
- Always obey the law.
- When making difficult decisions, choose the option that does the least amount of harm.

Loyalties: The following loyalties were important to the public relations practitioner in this case.

- To the public, especially regarding public safety.
- To the corporation.
- To national security.
- To the media.
- To professional colleagues in public relations.

The solution: Before any information was released, it had to be approved by both the director of the research at the organization and public affairs officers with the Pentagon. In addition, the public relations practitioners had to learn how to speak in general terms. They had to address the problem and demonstrate genuine concern for the public without offering the types of details that would disclose top-secret information. It was always a thin line they had to walk, but they only walked it after clearing information with superiors.

Analysis: Government contract and procurement procedures, and laws protecting national security, limited the options of the public relations professionals. The public's right to know and the practitioner's desire to tell the truth had to be balanced with the legal requirements of conducting top-secret research and the principle of national security which, properly defined, protects the rights of the greatest number of people. If the series of clearances for press releases had not been used, certain information might have been released to the public that would have satisfied the press but would have jeopardized the top-secret research, the government contracts, and national security.

HOW EXTERNAL PUBLICS AND OTHER ORGANIZATIONS AFFECT ETHICAL DECISION-MAKING IN PUBLIC RELATIONS

CASE 10.3:

Hype Versus Solid News Value—How to Get the Media to Pay Attention

The problem: The executives of a small advertising and public relations agency felt that to compete successfully with larger agencies for media placements in their markets they had to hype up press releases and create pseudo-news events to generate publicity for their clients.

The situation: Two professionals comprised the staff of the agency, with billings that placed it somewhere in the top 40 or 50 agencies in their metropolitan Southwest market. Most of their clients had local or regional business interests; only one was a national account. One of their clients had renamed an existing service, which was a computerized listing of new home owners in the community derived from public records of new home sales. The client was dissatisfied with current sales, so the decision was made to reposition it as a unique research service. The client did not conduct any market research to ascertain either current customer satisfaction or potential customer reaction to the name change. The decision was simply made and the public relations agency was told to prepare an appropriate campaign to introduce the "new" service.

Values: The following values were identified as being relevant to the public relations practitioner in this case.

To be successful and make money.

To be creative.

To be better than other agencies at gaining the media's attention.

To generate lots of publicity for the client.

To satisfy the needs of the customer.

Principles: The following principles were considered by the public relations practitioner.

The client is always right.

The media always are interested in human interest stories.

You can fool some of the people some of the time—and those are pretty good odds.

Client monies are better spent on sure-fire publicity than on what-if research.

Take only those actions which would be viewed as proper by a disinterested panel of professional colleagues.

Loyalties: The following loyalties were important to the public relations practitioner.

To the public relations agency.

To the client.

To the media.

To current and potential customers.

To members of the community.

The solution: The agency distributed press releases describing the computer listing as a one-of-a-kind research service, claiming it was unique because it was timely and because the names could be presented in a variety of mailing label formats. The agency also designed a scavenger hunt that involved teams from local high schools. Using the most current list of new residents, students went from home to home, asking homeowners for old household items from their previous residences and for comments about why they chose to move to their current new home. The team with the most outlandish set of "old" household items and the best set of "new" quotes won a cash prize. Following the scavenger hunt, the agency invited local media to a press conference, where the "loot" was displayed, scholarships were awarded to the winning high school teams, and press releases were distributed with the best quotes from people who had recently moved into the community. Prominently mentioned throughout all these activities was the "new" research service of the client.

Analysis: The agency's small market share of public relations business put the two professionals who ran the agency in a vulnerable position: they could not easily afford to lose the account. They did not question the lack of market research or the duplicity of changing the name of an old product, calling it a new product, without making substantive changes in the old product. Had the agency a broader client base, then they might have raised additional issues during the early planning stages of the campaign.

ALTERNATIVE EXPLANATION

According to Canadian public relations scholar Ron Pearson, public relations practitioners who understand systems theories face a special dilemma: to use this knowledge to facilitate the selfish interest of one organization, or client, or to use this knowledge to facilitate all relationships.[47] For public relations practitioners this dilemma means asking a very difficult question: Do you focus your professional energies on protecting and facilitating relationships important to one organization or client, or do you focus your energies on protecting and facilitating all essential relationships within the system?

Pearson's concern was that much of the application of systems theory in the social sciences, including public relations, has been focused on systems functioning to maintain the status quo—or, at least, a comfortably moving, manageable equilibrium. He argued that most discussions of systems theories place too much emphasis on images of organizations as organisms with special needs that must be satisfied. He expressed concern that images of mechanical and organic organizations make practitioners see the focal organization as the center of the system. The result, he predicted, of such a narrow application of systems theory, was that practitioners would emphasize management by egocentric objectives, encourage self-turned system maintenance, establish selfish environmental controls, and engage in one-way or two-way asymmetric communication with stakeholders and key publics.

Pearson argued that systems theories do not need necessarily to lead to egoistic functionalism, if the concept of the system is broadened beyond a focal organization (or set of organizations) to embrace all decision-makers within the system. The functional view of a system is that it is a set of components operating to maintain a steady state. Pearson, and others, argued that a holistic view of a system prevents egoism because it views systems as decision-making bodies. From this perspective, the function of a human system is not to maintain the status quo but to provide a forum for rational discussion. Pearson argued that public relations practitioners using a holistic systems framework would focus on interrelationships within the broadest possible definition of the system, on fair and just exchanges among decision-makers, and on dialogue, mutual understanding and symmetrical two-way communication among all within the system.

IN SUMMARY . . .

The professional codes of PRSA, IABC, and IPRA offer valuable guidelines for ethical behavior in public relations. Compliance with laws governing the practice of public relations is a minimum expectation for public relations professionals. Ethical decision-making by public relations practitioners is affected by external publics, the competition, professional associations, laws, public policies, and cultural factors—factors outside the immediate control of the focal organization. By understanding how the forces operate, a public relations practitioner is in a better position to predict and explain how these factors will or will not influence the conduct of a specific public relations program or campaign.

Study Questions

1. What factors outside the control of an organization affect ethical decision-making within the organization?
2. Discuss the assumption that what is good for a special interest group dedicated to serving the public good is necessarily good for society.
3. What is the difference between effective public relations research and industrial espionage?
4. What are five characteristics of professions? According to these criteria, does the public relations practice qualify as a profession?
5. Discuss the advantages and disadvantages of state licensing of public relations practitioners.
6. Describe what you consider to be the most important sets of ethical principles espoused by public relations professional associations at each of the following levels: intrapersonal, interpersonal, small group, organization, external publics, public policies and laws, and cultural values and beliefs.
7. Do you consider yourself to be a professional? Why? Be as specific as you can.
8. True or false: truth is the best defense in cases alleging invasion of privacy. Discuss your answer and give an example.
9. How are public relations practitioners involved in cultural issues? Give several examples.
10. Discuss three different ways public relations practitioners can resolve ethical dilemmas.

ADDITIONAL CASES

CASE 10.4:

When a Local Catholic Church Wants to Support a Pro-Life Political Candidate

The problem: The leaders of a local Catholic church wanted to help pay for and help run a political advertising and public relations campaign for a particular candidate they liked—and who also happened to be a member of the church. To do so might have jeopardized the church's tax-free nonprofit status with the U.S. Internal Revenue Service.

The situation: A local Catholic church had a pro-life state senator as a parishioner. The senator was up for re-election and was being seriously challenged by a pro-choice advocate. The abortion question promised to be one of the major issues in the election. However, as a nonprofit tax-exempt organization, the church could not directly support political candidates. The volunteer church leaders wanted to support actively their fellow parishioner, who was also the only pro-life candidate in the race. The duties of public relations for the church are handled by one of the priests who, prior to entering the priesthood, worked as a reporter. The lay leaders turned to this priest for advice.

Values: The following values were important from the point of view of the public relations practitioner (the priest) in this case.

- To be supportive of others who share your beliefs.
- To keep the church's tax-exempt status.
- To be faithful to the church's teachings and beliefs.
- To be law abiding.
- To get the pro-life candidate elected.

Principles: The following principles were important from the point of view of the public relations practitioner (the priest) in this case.

- Life begins at conception; life is precious.
- The church's teachings are dogma and should be followed.
- The church should be involved in setting social agenda, not necessarily politics, but issues management.
- There is a domino effect in issues management: if you set the social agenda, the political agenda is sure to follow.
- There are absolute truths; it's not all relative.

Loyalties: The following loyalties were important from the point of view of the public relations practitioner (the priest) in this case.

- To the parishioner/candidate.
- To the local church parishioners.
- To the Archbishop and, through him, the Pope.
- To the U.S. Internal Revenue Service.
- To the community at large.

The solution: The priest set up a meeting with the lay leaders, the archbishop of the diocese, and other top church leaders, to discuss how to deal with the upcoming election. The archbishop said the Catholic Church would have to follow its own teachings as well as the laws set out for non-profit tax-exempt organizations. He said that the church could not outwardly support any one political candidate without giving equal support to the other candidates, and the church did not want to give even tacit support to any of the other candidates. However, he said, the church could support issues, urging all voters to give serious consideration to the church's point of view. They decided to hire a public relations agency to run a pro-life issue-oriented campaign during the election period.

CASE 10.5:

Balancing Customer Confidentiality with the Public's Right to Know and the Organization's Best Interests

The problem: The reporter from the local TV station's consumer affairs department called to ask why the organization had refused service to an apparently deserving customer. But responding to the media inquiry could have jeopardized that customer's confidentiality—and made an awkward situation appear even worse.

The situation: The father of a ten-year-old boy dying of cancer had a family policy with an insurance company that covered the cost of standard but not "experimental" treatments. The company offered many other health plan options, but the father was not enrolled in any of these other plans. The boy's doctor, after discussions with the insurance company, told the family the treatment would be covered by their insurance company. With the family's consent, the doctor performed experimental bone marrow transplants. When the insurance company refused to pay for the experimental treatment, the father contacted the local TV station. The TV reporter asked for an on-camera interview, indicating that the feature story would be aired the next day. The publicly owned insurance company had an established policy against discussing specific customer accounts with the media unless there was written authorization from the customer.

Values: The following values have been identified as being important from the point of view of the public relations practitioner in this case.

To do a good job.

To be fair.

To be law abiding.

To be forthcoming and timely with the media.

To make a profit.

Principles: The following principles have been identified as being important from the point of view of the public relations practitioner in this case.

Do no harm.

Obey the law.

The customer is always right.

The end justifies the means.

The squeaky wheels get oiled.

Loyalties: The following loyalties have been identified as being important from the point of view of the public relations practitioner in this case.

To the company.

To the policy holder.

To the media.

To potential customers.

To current customers.

The solution: The director of public relations for the insurance company told the reporter that she would get back to him within the hour. She contacted the head of the in-house medical review committee to ask that this case be reviewed as soon as possible to make sure the claim had been processed properly. She called the boy's father, expressed sympathy and asked that the father give written permission for the company to discuss the case with the media. The father agreed, and a copy of the agreement was hand-delivered to the father and returned to the company that afternoon. The head of the in-house review team was scheduled to review the case but indicated to the public relations director that it would take time; it could not be completed until much later that afternoon. The director of public relations called the reporter and said a decision about the on-camera interview would be made before ten o'clock the next morning and that she would call to inform him of the decision. She wrote a one-page memo to the CEO alerting him to the situation. Her memo outlined four options: reaffirm the initial decision to deny coverage and refuse the on-camera interview; reaffirm the initial decision and conduct the on-camera interview; alter the initial decision and conduct the on-camera interview; and alter the decision and decline the on-camera interview. She recommended no decision be made until the in-house review committee completed its investigation. The CEO asked that the head of the review committee and the director of public relations meet when the investigation was completed. At this meeting, the CEO decided to reverse the initial decision and conduct the on-camera interview. The three agreed that the following points should be made during the interview: 1) the company was concerned not only about the welfare of the young boy but also about the fair treatment of their customer; 2) there was some confusion and misunderstanding between the doctor and the insurance company; therefore, 3) the initial decision would be reversed and the boy's treatment would be covered; furthermore, 4) additional efforts would be made by the company now and in the future to explain to their customers, and specifically to doctors, what options are covered and what options are not covered by the company's health care plans. Concerned customers and doctors were encouraged to call a special 800 number with any immediate questions.

. . .

CASE 10.6:

When a Vendor Fires a Very Popular Employee

The problem: Two separate companies—a very large corporation and a very small coffee shop—had separate rental agreements in one building. The ethical dilemma occurred when corporate employees became upset about the operation of the coffee shop; yet, legally, they had no right to tell the shop owner how to run his business.

The situation: A major company had a separate rental agreement with the owners of the building in which their corporate headquarters was located. The proprietor of the small coffee shop located inside the corporate headquarters also had a separate rental agreement. The coffee shop owner dismissed a very popular short-order cook and eliminated a favorite concession—fresh-made donuts. This was done despite informal advice from both the director of corporate personnel and the manager of public relations, who daily came into the shop and often discussed business matters with the owner. The popular employee had been working at the shop for the past fifteen years and was a few years from retirement. The customers of the coffee shop—95 percent of them corporate employees—staged impromptu demonstrations in the lobby of the building, put up banners, and distributed leaflets protesting the changes.

Values: The following values have been identified as being important from the point of view of the public relations practitioner in this case.

   To be loyal to old friends.

   To make everyone happy.

   To be fair.

   To be persistent in working for a just conclusion.

   To be helpful.

Principles: The following principles have been identified as being important from the point of view of the public relations practitioner in this case.

   The heavy-handed version of the Golden Rule: he who has all the gold gets to rule.

   The traditional version of the Golden Rule: do unto others as you would have them do unto you.

   Longevity has its place: respect old people.

   Loyalty over years should be rewarded.

   Big is better.

Loyalties: The following loyalties have been identified as being important to the public relations practitioner in this case.

- To the big organization.
- To the small organization.
- To the vendor's employee.
- To the vendor's customers; the big organization's employees.
- To #1: self-respect.

The solution: The corporate legal department ordered security to remove all banners and to stop the distribution of the leaflets, which was done promptly. Some employees complained to the head of personnel that their right to free speech had been violated. The public relations manager offered to help the shop owner write a memo or leaflet for distribution to customers that would explain the reasons for the changes, but the shop owner refused, saying, "It's none of your business." The director of public relations then told the owner that the company was going to sponsor a going-away party for the short-order cook, which was arranged with the permission and appreciation of the cook. The public relations manager wrote a memo which was distributed electronically and as hard copy to all employees, informing them of the cook's going-away party. The CEO attended the party and presented the short-order cook with a small gift of appreciation. The director of personnel, through his contacts, helped the man secure another position, which turned out to offer him more money and better benefits. The CEO wrote a letter to the building owner detailing the incident and recommending that another tenant be considered when the shop owner's contract came up for renewal. A short notice was put in the company newsletter about the cook's new job. No other mention was made of the incident in any company publication.

. . .

CASE 10.7:

When a Hospital Cancels Its Treatment Program for the Homeless

The problem: How to close the hospital's Indigent Care Unit, which took care of the homeless, without causing undue negative publicity. How, by publicizing this decision to close the unit, could the hospital make the general public, through the media, understand that health care needs of the homeless should be addressed by all hospitals in the region—not just by one?

The situation: The privately owned hospital was the area's oldest and was one of three in a densely populated county that bordered a major metropolitan area. The newest of the three hospitals opened within the year. Over the previous five years, the hospital's costs had been rising, and the number of beds occupied had remained steady until this past year when there was a marked decrease in the number of patients. Because of these pressures, the hospital's board decided to cut back on certain programs and to investigate funding options for its special homeless program. The board proposed to the new hospital's board that the two institutions share the administration and operating costs of the homeless program; it was rejected. The board also asked the county government for assistance, but no decision from the county board could be promised within the next twelve months. Consequently, the board voted to close the homeless program. The public relations director recommended holding a press conference with senior administrators and doctors present to answer questions and to make the major points the hospital wanted the public to know.

Values: The following values have been identified as being important to the public relations practitioner in this case.

- To make money, or at least to stop losing money.
- Not to be, or appear, insensitive to the homeless.
- To be flexible in considering options.
- To be candid and aboveboard with all parties.
- To protect the long-term interests of the hospital.

Principles: The following principles have been identified as being important to the public relations practitioner in this case.

- Do no harm.
- Give the greatest good to the greatest number.
- Common problems should be shared by all concerned.
- Avoid extreme actions: seek moderation.
- To negotiate in good faith means to be willing to compromise—to give up some things to gain other things.

Loyalties: The following loyalties have been identified as being important to the public relations practitioner in this case.

- To the homeless.
- To the media.
- To the community at large.
- To the owners of the hospital.
- To local government and other funding sources.

The solution: When asked to justify the decision to close the unit, the senior administrator made the following points at a press conference: This hospital cannot take care of all of the region's homeless; there are two other, larger hospitals in the region; any solution to the homeless problem must be made at a regional level and not addressed unilaterally by only one hospital; therefore, either all hospitals in the region will address the homeless problem, with appropriate government support, or none will.

CASE 10.8:

Putting a Money-Losing Fund-Raising Event in a Favorable Light by Shading the Truth

The problem: Through its hundreds of local chapters, a national association for the prevention of a major disease raised a significant amount of funds by sponsoring special events at the local level. One of the local fund-raising events, coordinated by an eager volunteer, grossed $15,000 but cost more than $20,000 to stage. The dilemma for the local chapter's director of public relations was how to put the best light on the money-losing event.

The situation: The national association annually conducted a nationwide telethon and fund-raising drive, which generated the majority of the association's funds. The association was proud of its fund-raising skills and administrative abilities. Annually they raised millions of dollars, and less than 15 percent of the funds were used for administration expenses; all other funds went to support research and educational programs. Local chapters were advised by national officers on how to conduct successful fund-raising events. For one chapter, a socially well-connected and eager volunteer offered to coordinate a fund-raising event which took place on a pleasure boat. Billed as a night of dining and dancing "under the stars with the stars" while cruising the area's coastal waterways, the event included movie actors, TV personalities, athletes and local celebrities at a buffet dinner and dance held on a large pleasure boat. Although tickets to the event sold out, the ticket sales could not cover expenses; several corporate sponsors were necessary to make the event profitable. The volunteer was unable to secure more than one corporate commitment to underwrite part of the expenses and did not tell the chapter president until the night of the event. When the president learned this, she realized the loss was going to be more than $7,000. During the event, she discussed the matter with the chapter's director of public relations.

Values: The following values have been identified as being important to the public relations manager in this case.

- To be organized.
- To be profitable.
- To be a loyal employee.
- To be in charge of the situation.
- To be responsive to media demand for timely news.

Principles: The following principles have been identified as being important to the public relations manager in this case.

- The best defense is a good offense.
- The spin given to the first set of "facts" sets the agenda for how a topic will be reported in the media, and how the public will perceive the situation.
- Never tell a lie.

You can fool some of the people some of the time, and those are pretty good odds.

Not telling all the facts is not necessarily lying.

Loyalties: The following loyalties have been identified as being important to the public relations manager in this case.

To the association.

To current contributors and participants.

To the media.

To those affected by the disease.

To her boss.

The solution: The staff photographer was told to take an extra number of pictures of those in attendance, to make sure he had complete identifications for all those in the pictures, and to have the pictures ready for distribution by 4 a.m. the next morning. Before 6 a.m., the director of public relations wrote captions for the pictures that included the figure of $15,000 gross revenue generated by the event; she did not mention the net loss. She had messengers hand deliver the pictures and press releases to the major media within the market before 7 a.m. She told the president she did this for several reasons: to make sure the positive news about the event was published before the media picked up on rumors that the event lost money; so that participants would feel proud that they attended the event; so that potential contributors and corporate underwriters would not be hesitant to contribute to future events. She also suggested to the chapter president that one or two regular corporate sponsors of previous events be approached with the facts of the current situation and asked to underwrite retroactively the pleasure boat expenses, so that eventually the event could be reported as making money for the association.

. . .

CASE 10.9:

Reciprocity between an Organization and a Local Television Station

The problem: Over the years, the biggest television station in the market had given outstanding coverage to special events sponsored by the county's Parks and Planning Agency, and the agency had grown to depend on it. Should the public information officer (PIO) have jeopardized this ongoing relationship by offering exclusive features and coverage of certain events to other local TV stations?

The situation: Each year, the Parks and Planning Agency, primarily through its recreation division, sponsored numerous special events—such as bike races, farmers' markets, ice skating, softball leagues, dances, and senior citizen activities. Over the years, the area's most powerful television station consistently aired the agency's public service announcements and made special mention of the agency's events on air. One of the station's major TV personalities was a regular emcee at the annual Fourth of July festivities. This one station provided more than 70 percent of the market's television coverage of agency activities, even though there were several other television outlets in the market. This lopsided coverage was partly the fault of the public information officers; in the past few years, they had not actively sought out coverage by the other media outlets. On the other hand, the community affairs director at the big station, and many of their producers, managers and on-air talent, genuinely liked Parks and Planning activities. But, the status quo was not to be. At a staff meeting of heads of county agencies, the newly elected county executive told the head of the Parks and Planning Agency, in private, to develop a plan for diversifying the television coverage of agency events. The county executive explained, in confidential tones, it seemed to him that "one station in this town has a lock on Parks and Planning. Let's get other stations involved, shall we, particularly the cable companies." (It was well known that a local cable company had contributed not only funds to the county executive's campaign but also "loaned" a senior public relations executive with the company for six months to work on his campaign.)

Values: The following values have been identified as being important to the public information officer in this case.

- To be politically expedient.
- To be loyal to the boss.
- To be efficient.
- To be a good friend.
- To be candid with the media.

Principles: The following principles have been identified as being important to the public information officer in this case.

- When the political winds change, go with them.
- Never tell a lie.
- Do unto others as you would have them do unto you.
- Take care of your friends.
- Professional communicators do not corrupt channels of communication.

Loyalties: The following loyalties have been identified as being important to the public information officer in this case.

- To the county executive.
- To herself: the PIO.
- To taxpayers.
- To the big TV station.
- To other media outlets.

The solution: For the upcoming season of activities, the agency public information officer prepared a calendar of events, which she took with her to one-on-one meetings with the assignment editors and public affairs directors for each of the area's television outlets (independents, network affiliates and cable companies). She began her round of visits with the hardest one: she explained her plan to her long-time friend, the head of community relations for the big TV station. She offered the station exclusive coverage of Fourth of July events, but stated clearly that other stations in the market would need to be given their fair share of exclusive features and options to cover popular events. The reactions to her plan varied: her friend at the big TV station was surprisingly nonchalant and noncommittal; one manager at a cable company expressed some interest; and the other media outlets were less than enthusiastic—basically they said, "Tell us about it when you get it ready, and we'll decide then whether or not to cover the event." In the next year, overall television coverage of agency activities dropped significantly, primarily because the big station did not make announcements about or cover as many agency activities.

. . .

CASE 10.10:

Informing the Public about a Product's Harmful Side-Effects

The problem: How should a small manufacturer of tanning equipment have informed customers about potential harmful side-effects of the equipment—beyond that which was required by law?

The situation: A manufacturer of tanning equipment assembled various components into attractive units, which were sold to small businesses which, in turn, charged individuals a small fee for tanning "sessions" using the equipment. Federal and state regulations required warning labels on the equipment to indicate that certain exposure levels might be harmful to the eyes and to the skin of individuals using the equipment. The manufacturer's marketing director asked the public relations specialist on staff to prepare brochures for sale in bulk quantities with the equipment. The marketing director wanted to include quantities of these brochures with the equipment so that small business owners would have available good-looking brochures to give to potential users. The cost of the brochures would be included in the sale price of the equipment.

Values: The following values have been identified as being important to the public relations practitioner in this case.

  To be forthright and honest.

  To be a manufacturer who provides solutions, not problems, to customers.

  To be socially responsible.

  To be profitable.

  To be innovative.

Principles: The following principles have been identified as being important to the public relations practitioner in this case.

  The best defense is an offense.

  Third-party endorsements are very convincing.

  Always deal fairly with the public.

Organizations do not need to disclose payments to "outside" experts.

Not telling all the truth is not necessarily lying.

Loyalties: The following loyalties have been identified as being important to the public relations practitioner in this case.

- To the manufacturer.
- To the small business owners who purchased equipment.
- To individuals using the equipment.
- To others in the public relations profession.
- To #1: the public relations manager.

The solution: The public relations director prepared a four-color brochure using a question-and-answer format. He reviewed various technical articles about the safety issues and created a list of six key questions. For each answer he cited a different expert who had published explanations elsewhere about how the equipment could be used safely. He contacted each expert and secured approval of a new quotation, a release form, and a studio color portrait. He negotiated separate fees with each expert. At the end of the brochure he used the "mug" shots of the experts and listed their credentials under their pictures. The brochure also contained color photographs of professional models using the equipment safely.

CASE 10.11:

Informing the Public about an Unsafe Bridge

The problem: When do you inform the public about a four-lane bridge that has failed newly revised safety standards? Do you do it immediately, which means during the middle of rush hour, or do you wait a few hours, after appropriate detours and signs have been installed and when fewer travellers will be affected?

The situation: The highway department of a midwest state had recently revised safety requirements for bridges. Under the old standards, one of the state's most traveled bridges passed inspection; under the new regulations, it didn't quite, despite a 20–year-long outstanding safety record. The inspecting team's official report recommending that the bridge be shut down for repairs was delivered to the head of the agency at 3:30 p.m., thirty minutes before the rush hour. If the agency were to close the bridge immediately, it would result in hours of delays for thousands of commuters.

Values: The following values have been identified as being important to the public relations practitioner in this case.

- To be legal.
- To be a team player.
- To be deliberate about making the decision.
- To be timely in informing the media.
- Not to be seen as being afraid of making hard decisions.

Principles: The following principles have been identified as being important to the public relations practitioner in this case.

- Do no harm to others.
- Always comply with the law.
- Play it safe.
- Do the greatest good for the greatest number.
- When in doubt, don't do it.

Loyalties: The following loyalties have been identified as being important to the public relations practitioner in this case.

- To the traveling public.
- To the organization.
- To professional engineers.
- To taxpayers.
- To the boss.

The solution: Present in the room when the head of the inspecting team made his report to the CEO were senior safety engineers and the director of public information. Some in the room voiced the opinion that placing detour signs would take some time, and that the best time to close the bridge would be during the night. Others pointed out that the probabilities of a disaster happening in the next few hours were very remote. Still others warned that, should something happen, they, as managers, might be accused of malfeasance and be subject to criminal and civil charges. They decided to close the bridge immediately. The public affairs officer issued a press release about the closure describing the new inspection standards and stating that the state's new inspection process was being used as a model in seventeen other states.

. . .

CASE 10.12:

Disclosing Donor Information to Third Parties in a Fund-Raising Campaign

The problem: How much information should be disclosed about a potential donor to a third party who would be asked to encourage the donation?

The situation: Since state institutions relied heavily on private donations, they actively sought potential donors, usually through current contributors. They used special researchers to find out information about potential donors, such as their salary and property values. These figures were used to estimate an appropriate and affordable amount the donor would be able to give. Then, they contacted a current donor who knew the potential contributor, and they asked the current donor to help motivate the other person to give the predetermined amount to the institution. Sometimes, the motivating, third party wanted to know how the institution derived the predetermined amount of donation. But, sharing this information would be unethical and could jeopardize the relationships, not only between the institution and the two donors but also between the two donors, who are friends.

Values: The following values have been identified as being important to the public relations practitioner in this case.

> To be confidential and discrete.
>
> To be trustworthy.
>
> To be thoughtful of others' feelings.
>
> To be successful; to raise a lot of money.
>
> Not to offend anyone.

Principles: The following principles have been identified as being important to the public relations practitioner in this case.

> The customer is always right.
>
> Never offend a donor.
>
> Don't burden someone you like with unnecessary, troublesome information.
>
> Take 'em for all they're worth.
>
> Donors benefit by helping others succeed: they gain self-esteem and pride by sharing their good fortune with others.

Loyalties: The following loyalties have been identified as being important to the public relations practitioner in this case.

> To potential donors.
>
> To current donors.
>
> To third-party solicitors.
>
> To professional fund raisers.
>
> To the institution.

The solution: The institution's development specialist convinced the third party of the appropriateness of the predetermined donation by using public information, such as the average salary of a person in the potential donor's position of employment, and the average property value in the potential donor's neighborhood. No personal information about the potential donor was disclosed to the third party.

Endnotes

1. Grunig, Larissa S., "Activism and organizational response: Contemporary cases of collective behavior," paper presented to the Association for Education in Journalism and Mass Communication, Norman, Oklahoma, 1986.

2. Ferrell, O. C., "Implementing and monitoring ethics in advertising," in *Marketing Ethics,* edited by G. R. Laczniak and P. E. Murphy (Lexington, MA: Lexington Books, 1985) pp. 26–40.

3. Boyte, H. C., *The backyard revolution: Understanding the new citizen movement* (Philadelphia: Temple University Press, 1980).

4. Grunig, James E., "Sierra Club study shows who become activist," *Public Relations Review,* Vol. 15, No.3, 1989, pp. 3–24.

5. Simon, Morton J., *Public Relations Law* (New York: Appleton-Century-Crofts, 1969) pp. 714–726.

6. Lowi, T. J., *The End of Liberalism: The Second Republic of the United States* (New York: Norton Publishers, 1979).

7. Rada, Stephen, "Terrorism as public relations," *Public Relations Review,* Vol. 10, No.1, 1985, pp. 25–33.

8. Tesh, S., "In support of 'single issue' politics," *Political Science Quarterly,* Vol. 99, 1984, pp. 27–44.

9. Olson, Mancur, *The Logic of Collective Action* (Cambridge, MA: Harvard University Press, 1971).

10. Olson, Mancur, *Rise and Decline of Nations* (New Haven: Yale University Press, 1982).

11. Kitchen, Philip J., "Developing use of PR in a fragmented Demassified Market," *Marketing Intelligence and Planning,* Vol. 9, No. 2, 1991, pp. 29–33.

12. Simon, Morton J., *Public Relations Law* (New York: Appleton-Century-Crofts, 1969) pp. 553–554.

13. Patrick, Kenneth G., *Perpetual Jeopardy* (New York, NY: MacMillan, 1972).

14. Abratt, Russell, and Diane Sacks, "The marketing challenge: Toward being profitable and socially responsible," *Journal of Business Ethics,* Vol. 7, 1988, pp. 497–507.

15. Sturdivant, Frederic D., and James L. Ginter, "Corporate social responsiveness: Management attitudes and economic performance," *California Management Review,* Spring 1977, pp. 30–39.

16. Grunig, J. E., and Todd Hunt, *Managing Public Relations* (New York: Holt, Rinehart and Winston, 1984) p. 64.

17. Bernays, Edward L., "The case for licensing PR practitioners," *Public Relations Quarterly,* Spring 1983, p. 32.

18. Kalupa, Frank B., and C. G. Seivers, "Public relations licensure: Practitioners and educator attitudes," paper presented to the Association for Education in Journalism and Mass Communication, 1986; Lesley, Philip, "Why licensing won't work for public relations," *Public Relations Review,* Vol. 12, No. 4, Winter 1986, pp. 3–8; and Cutlip, Scott M., Allen H. Center, and Glen M. Broom, "Toward a profession," *Effective Public Relations,* 6th edition (Englewood Cliffs, NJ: Prentice-Hall, 1985) pp. 449–473.

19. KcKee, Blaine K., Oguz B. Nayman, and Dan L. Lattimore, "How PR people see themselves," *Public Relations Journal,* 31, Nov. 1975, pp. 47–52.

20. Broom, Glen. M., and David M. Dozier, *Using Research in Public Relations* (Englewood Cliffs, NJ: Prentice-Hall, 1990) p. 25.

21. *Accreditation Study Guide* (New York: Public Relations Society of America); *How To Become an Accredited Business Communicator* (San Francisco: International Association of Business Communicators).

22. Special report prepared by the Ethics Resource Center, *Implementation and Enforcement Codes of Ethics in Corporations and Associations,* (Princeton, NJ: Opinion Research Corporation, 1980).

23. McCammond, Donald B., "A matter of ethics." *Public Relations Journal,* Nov. 1983, pp. 46–47.

24. Wilcox, D., and Warren Ault, *Public Relations Strategies and Tactics* (New York: Harper and Row, 1989), p. 121.

25. Gorlin, Rena A., editor, *Codes of Professional Responsibility* (Washington, D.C.: The Bureau of National Affairs, 1986).

26. Walsh, Frank, "Legal considerations," in Reuss, Carol, and Donn Silvis, editors, *Inside Organizational Communication* (New York: Longman, 1985) pp. 291–314.

27. Brebbia, John Henry, "First Amendment rights and the corporation," *Public Relations Journal,* Dec. 1979, p. 18.

28. Simon, Morton J., "Lobbying" and "Activities and control of foreign agents," *op.cit.,* pp. 801–842.

29. Kleeman, Rosslyn, "Gray areas of federal ethics law," *Bureaucrat,* Vol. 18, No. 1, Spring 1989, pp.7–10.

30. Simon, Morton J., "Deception and unfair trade practices," "Testimonial techniques," and "Contests and lotteries," *op.cit.,* pp. 381–466.

31. U.S. Freedom of Information Act, enacted in 1966 and amended in 1974 and 1976.

32. Walsh, Frank, "The new copyright law: Stronger and more specific," *Public Relations Journal,* August, 1977, p. 6.

33. Corley, Robert L., and O. Lee Reed, *The Legal Environment of Business* (New York: McGraw Hill, 1981).

34. Simon, Morton J., *Public Relations Law* (New York: Appleton-Century-Crofts, 1969) pp. 550–554.

35. Simon, Morton J., "Corporate employee relations," *op.cit.,* pp. 697–729.

36. Newson, Doug, Allan Scott, and Judy Van Slyke Turk, *This is PR: The Realities of Public Relations,* 5th edition (Belmont, CA: Wadsworth, 1989) Chapter 14.

37. Thompson, K. W., editor, *Philanthropy: Private Means, Public Ends* (Lanham, MD: University Press of America, 1987).

38. Aronoff, Craig, and Otis Baskin, *Public Relations: The Profession and the Practice* (Dubuque, IA: Wm. C. Brown Publishers, 1988).

39. Alexander, Herbert E., "Political action committees and their corporate sponsors in the 1980s," *Public Affairs Review,* 2, 1981, pp. 27–38.

40. Walsh, Frank, *op.cit.,* pp. 292–296.

41. Ibid

42. Ibid

43. Simon, Morton. J., "Legal relationships and liabilities of public relations counsel," *op.cit.,* pp. 27–64.

44. Fritzche, David J., "Ethical issues in multinational marketing," in *Marketing Ethics: Guidelines for Managers,* edited by G. R. Laczniak and P. E. Murphy (Lexington, MA: Lexington Press, 1985) pp. 85–96.

45. Black, Sam, editor, *Public Relations in the 1980s,* Proceedings of the Eighth Public Relations World Congress (New York: Pergamon Press, 1980).

46. Triandis, Harry and Rosita Albert, "Cross-cultural perspectives," in *Handbook of Organizational Communication,* edited by Frederick Jobin, et al, (Newbury Park, CA: Sage, 1987) pp. 264–296.

47. Pearson, Ron, "Ethical values or strategic values? The two faces of systems theory in public relations," in *Public Relations Research Annual,* edited by L. A. Grunig and J. E. Grunig, Vol. 2 (Hillsdale, NJ: Lawrence Erlbaum Associates, 1990) pp. 219–234.

CHAPTER ELEVEN

How to Get a Good Job and Advance in the Field of Public Relations

*T*he room was full of people attending the annual holiday dinner sponsored by the area's three largest public relations professional associations. In the narrow hotel ballroom it was especially crowded by the cash bar and along the buffet table. So many conversations were going at once that it was hard to hear the person next to you, yet it was exhilarating.

Feeling anxious about being on her own in such a large room full of strangers, Maria, 20, leaned toward the woman she had just met and asked, "How long have you been a member?"

"About three years," Kathryn responded. In her mid-thirties, Kathryn was a publications editor with a large corporation. "How about you?" she asked.

"This is my second meeting," Maria said. "I liked the speaker at last month's luncheon. This one looks like a party. Is there a speaker?"

"I think so," Kathryn said. "Yes, a funny man from a radio station, one of their DJs. Tonight's not serious. Tonight's for fun, and to meet people."

"That's why I'm here," Maria said. "I'm looking for a job. I graduate next semester."

Kathryn smiled broadly at Maria, and looking about the room, raised her glass in a grand gesture to those about her, offering a toast. "To all of us this season, a good job. Maybe a new job, or at least a better job—and lots of money, and a happy new year!"

"Here, here," George said, as he stepped up to Kathryn and touched the rim of his cocktail glass to hers. "May we all find, if not more money, at least good friends." As senior vice president of public affairs for the region's only electric utility, and one of the few black public relations professionals in the area, George had the grey hairs, barrel chest, understanding eyes, and bearing of a dignified grandfather. Kathryn liked him a lot.

She asked him, "What kind of practical advice can you offer Maria here, who graduates in a few months? She speaks fluent Spanish. Her parents are from Mexico. And she likes to write."

"Do what you are doing. Let people know you're looking," George said to Maria. *"Talk to as many people as possible. Always stay alert to new job possibilities. That's what we do, isn't it, Kathryn?"*

Kathryn laughed in agreement. Then in a loud stage whisper, George said, "Always keeping our options open, right, Kathryn?"

He then asked Maria to tell him what kind of work she was looking for. While he listened, George found himself thinking about the difficulties minorities have advancing in public relations. He reached out and caught the arm of one of his colleagues passing by.

"Charlie, Charlie," George said, "happy holidays, my friend. Listen, I want you to meet a new member of our profession, a soon-to-be college graduate. She's got some great credentials."

. . .

TODAY'S JOB MARKET

In these past few years, one of the most dramatic shifts in the profession has been the increasing numbers of women; today, more than half of all those practicing public relations are women.[1] An equally dramatic trend is reflected in the vignette; many more people of color are entering the profession. Not only are more individuals of all ethnic backgrounds educating themselves and preparing for careers in public relations, but also, and more importantly in the long run, there is a greater "pull" in the employment marketplace for these individuals. Multinational, multicultural, and multiethnic organizations are aggressively searching for skilled communicators and public relations specialists who are multilingual and culturally sophisticated.

While the overall employment picture may be rosy, there are thorns. Fifteen years ago, men earned an average twenty percent more than women performing comparable work in public relations. Today, the gender salary gap has increased to approximately thirty percent.[2] While the number of nonwhite practitioners has been increasing, the proportion of nonwhite members of professional associations in public relations (and, by extension, of the total work force) continues to be significantly less than the proportion of nonwhites in the total population.[3] It is still rare today to see a public relations executive of color.

Entry-Level Public Relations Positions

The basic skills of entry-level public relations positions are writing, editing, designing and producing communication materials, in all media, but primarily in print and television. Word processing skills are essential. Desktop publishing skills are highly valued. Entry-level practitioners are expected to work closely with printers, photographers, design and layout artists, and other providers of creative services.

They are expected not only to write press releases but also to contact media representatives, particularly reporters and editors. Knowledge of AP style, journalism principles and ethics is essential. Creative flexibility also is important. New employees should be eager to learn. It will be understood that they will be starting at the bottom of a learning curve within the organization, learning its technology and standard operating procedures, but they will be expected to learn this information quickly. They should be detail oriented and willing to do routine (sometimes menial) tasks. Entry-level practitioners today most often have a college education in journalism, public relations, or communication, earning a degree in the liberal arts; many have a college minor in business, with some knowledge of statistics and a foreign language. The annual salary range for entry-level positions $15–$30,000, depending on the industry.

While the senior vice president of Giant Food Inc., in Case 7.1, made the major decisions about the employee publications, entry-level practitioners did all the writing and editing. Two communicators, each with a college degree in journalism, were expected to collect information from everywhere and to get to know everybody—other entry-level employees, supervisors and senior managers. They were expected to write articles, take pictures, instruct photographers, work with design and layout artists, coordinate with printers, and make sure the publications were distributed on time to employees. In addition to planning, writing and editing on a daily basis, they occasionally conducted readership surveys and informal focus groups with employees to get their feedback about the publications.

Almost all entry-level professionals at Manning, Selvage and Lee /Washington who worked on the economic development campaigns (Cases 4.5 and 4.6) had previous work experience in public relations before joining the agency. New college graduates who were hired by the agency had professional experience through internships and had solid portfolios to present of their work. On the economic development campaigns, these junior account executives were expected to write press releases and feature stories, and to create public service announcements and advertising copy for print, radio and television. They were expected to help determine appropriate media placements and media buys. They prepared press kits and helped stage special events. While most of their time was spent writing campaign materials, some of their time was spent tabulating responses to surveys and conducting content analyses of newspapers and magazines in the local communities.

Middle-Management Public Relations Positions

To advance to middle management, a practitioner is expected to have mastered all entry-level skills, plus have demonstrated leadership and management skills. Considered staff professionals and project managers, they know how to budget and plan public relations programs and campaigns; they know how to monitor and control resources; and they have the ability to design and conduct research, which most often means knowing how to procure and supervise contracts with research firms. They are consensus-builders who are able to work with a variety of different managers and to understand other peoples' time pressures and work expectations. Employers prefer their mid-level public relations managers to have had five to ten years professional experience before promoting them to this level, and to have an advanced education, preferably a master's degree with a specialization in organizational behavior, management and public relations. The annual salary range at this level is $25–$50,000, depending on the industry.

As a mid-level manager within Blue Cross Blue Shield (Case 5.1), the director of communication for the Custom Service Department supervised a staff of two. There were three levels of managers between her position and that of the Chief Executive Officer. She was expected to know all the technical aspects of her department and to delegate the majority of the technical work to her staff, while she devoted almost half of her time to planning, budgeting, and managing the more than half dozen programs in various stages of completion that were being generated by her department at any one time. She spent more than half of her time writing and producing various elements of communication programs. She received numerous awards from her colleagues at local professional public relations associations. She was especially good at making presentations to clients; she enjoyed it a lot. She spent the majority of her time making sure client needs were being satisfied and that her staff understood what the clients wanted. She did this primarily one-on-one with different staff members and at staff meetings which she chaired. She said she was frustrated that the profits she knew she generated for the company were not credited to her department but allocated to a general revenue account, so she was working to change that so her efforts and those of her staff would have greater visibility within the company.

The senior account executive with Porter/Novelli who was responsible for the campaign for the International Apple Institute (Case 6.3) was so skilled at budgeting that he conducted in-house seminars for junior account executives and his colleagues on an annual basis. He discussed the need for the campaign with the client and with the help of two of his colleagues wrote the agency's winning proposal. He participated in almost all creative sessions the staff held in developing the campaign. Although he wrote some of the campaign material, he delegated much of the writing and creative production to specialists on his staff. In addition to the International Apple Institute account, he was responsible for more than a half dozen other "working" accounts, and he was responsible for generating new business. Each year he was expected to generate several times his annual salary in profits from accounts he supervised. He and many of his colleagues at the agency had earned master's degrees prior to obtaining their middle management positions.

Senior-Level Public Relations Positions

Senior-level public relations practitioners have highly visible leadership positions in their organization and are specialists in strategic management. They not only have the ability to define problems and opportunities, they have the gift of being able to help others see and understand complex issues. They know how to coordinate and manage complex programs and campaigns. They interact frequently with senior-level managers, often are considered a member of the dominant coalition, and spend more than half their time relating to others outside their organization. They have a great deal of knowledge about their industry, the economy, and public policies, particularly those relating to corporate disclosure, financial relations and government affairs. Most senior-level public relations positions are filled with people who have had more than ten years experience. Many have advanced degrees and hold leadership positions in professional and industry associations. The median annual salary for senior executives in public relations is in the $50–$100,000 range. The high end of the salary range in public relations, earned by senior vice presidents of corporations and senior partners of agencies, is $100–$250,000, with some earning much more.

The president, senior partner and founder of SmithMead and Associates was the man who designed and executed the Job Corps campaign (Case 3.2). A senior executive for a major corporation, he had an outstanding reputation and more than twenty years professional experience in all phases of public relations before he established his public relations agency. He was considered a specialist in strategic management. An excellent writer, he wrote daily, not only business proposals and planning documents, but also press releases, feature articles and communication materials for client campaigns. Each partner managed certain sets of clients; his were major government contracts and associations. Plus, he had overall responsibility for managing the agency. It was not unusual for him to put in 60–70 hour work weeks.

Before becoming the senior public relations executive for the company, the vice president for public affairs of Martin Marietta (Cases 5.3 and 5.4) served for several years as public relations director for one of the company's most significant business units. Prior to joining Martin Marietta he was head of public relations for another major corporation in the defense industry. Before entering the public relations profession, he had worked as a reporter and editor for a major suburban newspaper. As an indication of the scope of his responsibilities as the senior public relations officer for Martin Marietta, here are goals he established for his department for one particular year:

1. Develop and implement an advertising program that is strongly linked to corporate strategy and business development goals.
2. Develop and implement a media relations campaign that targets and uses national publications of prominence to promote key corporate messages.
3. Improve the employee publication and increase employee input.
4. Strengthen the speech writing function and increase the use of speeches.
5. Conduct community relations programs that respond to requests in timely and effective ways, and that closely serve the strategic interests of the corporation.
6. Update and revise the corporation's gifts and grants policy.
7. Formalize quality-of-service requirements within the department in accordance with budgetary resources.
8. Organize and implement career development plans for all public affairs employees.
9. Improve the quality of relationships within the organization, and between the department and field organizations, by promoting greater teamwork and cooperation.
10. Continue strong support of the corporation's ethics and affirmative action policies.

EXPERIENCED PROFESSIONALS OFFER CAREER ADVICE

In-depth personal interviews were conducted with ten experienced public relations professionals who were asked a series of questions about successful strategies for entering and advancing in the field. These professionals had the combined experience of giving advice to, hiring, and promoting hundreds of public relations practitioners throughout the United States. The following are representative comments and suggestions from these professionals.

For Women Entering the Field

What problems do you think women have entering the field of public relations, beyond the problems that might be encountered by men entering the field? What strategies would you recommend these women use to deal successfully with the problems you have identified?

Responses from the professionals included:

> *"The field is pretty fair game for both men and women these days. Employers are really just looking for whoever has the most experience, whether it be a man or a woman."* (Andrea Just, public relations manager with CSX Transportation, Baltimore, Maryland)

"Employers are always looking for experience; therefore, it is important for women—and men—seeking a job in this field to develop their skills and learn how to best sell themselves." (Abbey Lazarus, director of public relations for the March of Dimes, Baltimore, Maryland)

"Women get lower salaries, are not respected as readily as men, and are not able to find entry level positions as quickly as men. To avoid this, women need to form coalitions among themselves and talk to managers and others about their feelings." (Marilyn Kern-Foxworth, university professor specializing in public relations, Texas A&M University, College Station, Texas)

"There seems to be a credibility factor for women starting out. Men tend to be more aggressive, which helps when getting a job. Women get paid less. A woman needs to be sensitive to these issues, and make sure she is educated and informed about equity issues in the workplace." (Marguerite Gee, fundraiser and communications consultant, Oakland, California)

"There seems to be an attitude in the field that women are not as capable. Women have a hard time making it as managers because the field itself is not highly respected. Women need to demonstrate that they are as capable as men—yet, sometimes, they work harder and do more than their male counterparts, only to be judged equal." (Jodie Hier, marketing communications consultant, Chicago, Illinois)

For Minorities Entering the Field

What problems do you think minorities, such as African-Americans, Hispanics and Asians, have entering the field of public relations, beyond the problems that might be encountered by white men in the field? What strategies would you recommend these minorities use to deal successfully with the problems you have identified?

Responses included:

"At the entry levels, I don't believe there is a problem; in fact, blacks and minorities could have an advantage if they are equally qualified and the company is actively looking for minorities." (Abbey Lazarus)

"A black woman has a double advantage in today's job market, if she has marketable skills." (Zack Germroth, public information officer, Baltimore Department of Housing and Community Development, Maryland)

"Some minorities are thought of as not knowing as much as their white counterparts. To change this, professional minorities need to be promoted to more visible positions in both corporations and community organizations so that people can see that minority practitioners are just as qualified as others in the field." (Janet Tom, publicist, San Francisco, California)

"Minorities in public relations carry excess baggage: negative stereotypes. Multi-ethnic practitioners have a hard time becoming part of "good old boy" networks made up of all white males. To overcome this, they need to inform their managers and colleagues of potential problems—and, to align themselves with people who are experiencing similar problems." (Marilyn Kern-Foxworth)

For Any Individual Entering the Field

What problems do you think any individual, regardless of race or sex, would have entering the field of public relations? What strategies would you recommend these individuals use to deal successfully with the problems you have identified?

Responses included:

"Getting experience—that's the biggest problem facing people entering this field. To get this experience, they may have to do volunteer work or take an unpaid college internship—or both. The key is persistence: do whatever it takes, but get the experience." (Janet Tom)

"People entering the field do not have a lot of contacts. They should network through such organizations as the Public Relations Society of America, the International Association of Business Communicators, and other professional associations." (Abbey Lazarus)

"The biggest problem is the lack of experience. To conquer this, network, go on informational interviews, and find a mentor who will teach you the ropes." (Annette Saxon, public relations professional, Baltimore, Maryland)

"Entry-level people have limited on-the-job experience. Assuming you have the basic skills, you need to hone them. Seek out jobs that give you broad responsibilities, so that you can identify your strongest skills." (Marguerite Gee)

"Each employer has a set of biases or perceptions about what a public relations person ought to be. To deal with this, entry-level people need to learn to define their strengths in a number of different ways—and, to continue their job search—by going through several job interviews before making a decision." (Zack Germroth)

"New, young people to our business do not understand or appreciate all the politics that goes on. They need to learn the political nature of our business by keeping their eyes and ears open." (Jodie Hier)

For Entry-Level Applicants

If someone with appropriate qualifications was seeking an entry-level position in the field of public relations, what advice would you offer that person?

Responses included:

"Make as many contacts as possible, pursue every job lead, and be willing to accept a less-than-ideal job to get your foot in the right door." (Debby Butcher, account executive and public relations specialist, Blue Cross Blue Shield of Maryland)

"Know what geographic areas interest you, study all you can about the industry in those areas, then connect with local professional public relations associations." (Marilyn Kern-Foxworth)

"Explore all areas of the profession—nationally and globally—that interest you, and conduct informational interviews with people you respect in those areas." (Marguerite Gee)

"Have your resume reviewed by one or two professionals in the field. Use your discussions with these professionals to identify job leads and more contacts in the field." (Jodie Hier)

"Know how to sell yourself—just as you would a product, or a service, or an idea. An employer will think if you can't sell yourself as the best person for the job you won't be able to sell ideas to others once you get the job—so, you just might not get the job." (Andrea Just)

"Have a professional portfolio filled with the best of your work and lots of good-looking samples of public relations projects you have worked on. Know how to present yourself. Do not be a plastic-looking public relations person. Get your priorities straight. Know what you are about. Look professional." (Annette Saxon)

For People Wanting to Leave an Entry-Level Position

What negative factors account for people wanting to leave an entry-level position in public relations? What career strategies would you recommend to anyone affected by these negative factors?

Responses included:

"It's often the stress. They're not suited for the pressures of the job. They're unable to work beyond a 40–hour work week, juggle a half dozen public relations responsibilities at once—and keep their sense of humor. What to do about it? Get organized, work hard—and loosen up." (Zack Germroth)

"Low pay is a problem. But, the biggest problem is realizing you can't deal with certain pressures. There are so many conflicting expectations on you in public relations. Too many bosses; too little time. It's hard for a new person to stand up under that pressure. Mentors can help. But, the best solution may be to look for a new job." (Marguerite Gee)

"Low pay and a lack of respect for public relations people in general are the biggest problems; but, there is not much a person can do about either one—particularly when you're new to the field. Always keep an eye out for that better job." (Marilyn Kern-Foxworth)

"Sometimes the job becomes too narrowly focused, and there is a lack of opportunity to advance. To get around this, move to a larger company, or find another job—even within the same company—with more opportunities. Don't become disillusioned by one frustrating experience; move on." (Debby Butcher)

"Some people get in over their heads. They lose control of their job and a sense of direction. They feel pushed around and frustrated. An effective strategy would be not to jump too quickly into a new job without first asking a lot of questions, researching the company, and talking with people who have held the position before." (Annette Saxon)

For Women Advancing in the Field

What problems do you think women have advancing in the field of public relations, beyond the problems that might be encountered by men advancing in the field? What strategies would you recommend these women use to deal successfully with the problems you have identified?

Responses included:

"Some women have problems advancing through middle management because they are, at this stage in their careers, also at the age of having children. Women tend to lose their status if they leave the field, even to work part-time, during this time. Once a woman has gone through these years—either with or without children—it becomes much easier to advance in the field." (Annette Saxon)

"It really depends on the company. Where management has been predominantly white males—and they choose to promote other white males—it is a problem for a woman to advance. The strategy is to find a company where there are more women throughout management." (Marguerite Gee)

"Women do not have enough support from mentors. Men more often have mentors who give them guidelines—hints, and clues and suggestions—about how to advance in their careers—whom to see, what to do, that kind of thing. Or, the mentors steer certain projects and opportunities their way. To overcome this, women need to network, to assert themselves—seeking out mentors and participating in training programs that will help them move into higher management positions." (Marilyn Kern-Foxworth)

"Women need to gain the acceptance of all their colleagues, especially the men *and* women *they supervise, before they can advance very far in this field."* (Jodie Hier)

For Minorities Advancing in the Field

What problems do you think minorities, such as African-Americans, Hispanics and Asians, have advancing in the field of public relations, beyond problems that might be encountered by a white man advancing in the field? What strategies would you recommend these minorities use to deal successfully with the problems you have identified?

Responses included:

"There are still a lot of personal prejudices and hateful stereotypes in the workplace today. Sometimes, all you can do is seek legal help. There are those times when a minority would feel prejudice in the workplace. I would urge this individual to deal with the problem quickly, honestly and with integrity." (Abbey Lazarus)

"It is the command of the English language that is essential, not someone's race. If minorities have problems with English—if anyone in this field has problems with English—they will not advance very far." (Zack Germroth)

"All multi-ethnic professionals who want to advance need the resources that come from mentors. To get these kinds of resources, they need to network, assert themselves and prepare themselves to be effective managers." (Marilyn Kern-Foxworth)

"Minorities deal with issues of discrimination all the time; it's nothing new. What is new are the rules and regulations that can be brought to bear. Minorities need to stay abreast of changes in the laws and regulations. And, they need to help educate people in the workplace about these changes." (Marguerite Gee)

For Any Individual Advancing in the Field

What problems do you think any individual, regardless of race or sex, would have advancing in the field of public relations? What strategies would you recommend these individuals use to deal successfully with the problems you have identified?

Responses included:

"The big problem is the narrowing of the field: there are simply fewer and fewer positions the higher you go up the corporate ladder. And, the competition is fierce. To climb the ladder, keep a high profile, demonstrate daily that you're good, and don't stop." (Andrea Just)

"Getting recognition is key. You have to take some risks—stick your neck out—and be right. You have to maintain high visibility." (Jodie Hier)

"You have to be good at what you do. If you are not, either take the time to get the necessary training or get out of the field." (Debby Butcher)

"Sometimes there are no opportunities to advance within one organization. The solution is to move to a higher position with a different employer." (Zack Germroth)

"It's politics: you have to be intelligent enough to see that, to know not only who's who and what to do, but when to do it." (Marguerite Gee)

For Someone No Longer Satisfied at an Entry Level

If someone with appropriate qualifications, who was no longer satisfied at an entry-level position, was searching for career advancement in the field of public relations, what advice would you offer that person?
Responses included:

"Start preparing to advance while you are in your entry-level position: be aware of what skills are required for the next position you want; recognize your assets and liabilities; and, when you have offset those liabilities with proper training, and you have the skills, go for it." (Marilyn Kern-Foxworth)

"Learn how to do your boss's job—document it with portfolio materials, and wait for an opportunity to move up." (Zack Germroth)

"Don't stay where you are not happy, or your unhappiness will affect your work. Go somewhere else. Network, see the bigger picture, and make sure your portfolio is targeted toward the position you want." (Annette Saxon)

"Join professional associations, get involved in their activities, and go on as many interviews as possible." (Abbey Lazarus)

"Know who you can trust, and talk to them. Keep your eyes open. Get a handle on trends in the field. Let people know you are looking—network." (Andrea Just)

For People Wanting to Leave Middle and Senior Management

What negative factors account for people wanting to leave a middle or senior management position in public relations? What career strategies would you recommend to anyone affected by these negative factors?
Responses included:

"A lot of people in middle and upper management get frustrated and dissatisfied. They should spend time reassessing their careers—thinking about learning new skills and seeking something new and challenging." (Janet Tom)

"People leave because they have a sense of futility—they can't make the changes they want, or receive the salary they want—they get discouraged. The best strategy for personal success at this level is just as it is at the entry-level: know how to sell yourself; don't sell yourself short; and, don't get so discouraged that you stop trying." (Abbey Lazarus)

"Burnout from stress is the leading factor. One strategy would be to seek a less stressful position—maybe even at a lower salary. Or, maybe try another field for a few years. Take a break from it, somehow." (Zack Germroth)

"The big factors are the job pressures and winding up in a job doing tasks you don't want to do. Obviously, you have to learn to cope, but you also need to communicate your concerns to senior management." (Debby Butcher)

"Stress, burnout, and the job turning into something it was not thought to be—these are the big problems. The key is to communicate candidly with superiors; and, if that doesn't help, to leave." (Annette Saxon)

ETHICAL GUIDELINES AND CAREER ADVICE

The following comments were given by professional public relations practitioners who responded to a confidential mail survey that asked three questions, each one focused on ethical issues affecting entry-level, middle-management, and senior-management public relations positions:

1. What ethical guidelines or career advice would you recommend for someone to consider who is in an entry-level public relations position?

    "Keep in mind that there are many facets and considerations relating to the operation of your organization of which you may not be aware. Don't be too quick to judge some action as unethical. Be cautious, listen, and learn the ropes of your organization, especially the political and other implications of any action you may propose. Study your boss to see how he or she handles various kinds of situations."

    "Always check with the public relations director before releasing any information to the media. And, in his or her absence, check with the highest and/or most knowledgeable person in the organization. Once information is out, it is difficult to alter or retract. When in doubt, do what is or may appear to be on the conservative side. While timeliness is important—it is one of the most important criteria by which reporters are rated—correctness is always the stronger element of rating for the public relations practitioner."

    "Be honest. Make friends with other public relations professionals—you're going to need them."

    "When in doubt, talk to your supervisor."

    "Never tell a lie. Be loyal to your boss and your organization."

2. What ethical guidelines or career advice would you recommend for someone to consider who is in a middle-management public relations position?

   "You're an advocate for your organization, and there's nothing wrong with that; it's your job to put the best face on your organization. Often it's the press's job to ferret out unfavorable facts about the organization. And, too often, the press often doesn't bother to mention the good aspects of your organization. So, you must act as a balance, giving a fair picture of the situation. This doesn't mean hiding bad news that is necessary for the public to know."

   "You may find yourself teaching non-public relations superiors, and often the media, what good public relations and ethics are all about. As a public relations practitioner, you are looked to as the opinion leader in these matters. Develop trust/openness, and you will get the same in return."

   "Be honest. Keep in touch with your colleagues on a regular basis."

   "Transfer ethical problems on the job to your personal life—hypothetically, that is: if you would consider the situation unethical in that context, then it most likely is also unethical on the job."

   "Never tell a lie. Be loyal to your boss and your organization."

3. What ethical guidelines or career advice would you recommend for someone to consider who is in a senior-management public relations position?

   "By the time you have reached a senior-management public relations position, you have the wisdom and experience to act as an advisor to senior management. You should speak out if you think some action is unethical, and advise management that acting unethically for short-term gain can very well backfire in the long run and cause the organization more trouble than it's worth."

   "Remember the basics: double check your information, no matter how high up your source, before releasing information to the public. Remember that many reporters seem to have a need to report some sort of controversy in the best of articles. You will need to learn to live with this. Don't forget: a half-truth, puffed or excessively-colored information will catch up with you and may cause you and your organization harm. Truth be known: the public relations person is often a reporter's only or final word on a topic. It is, therefore, your ethical duty to make sure that what you release is accurate in every sense."

   "Do not be afraid to ask difficult questions. Do not compromise your personal integrity. Do not do anything illegal or that you cannot support."

> *"It is your role to bring unethical situations to the attention of senior management. If you fail to do so—and fail to offer solutions at the same time—then, you are failing in your job."*
>
> *"Never tell a lie. Be loyal to your boss and your organization."*

FACTORS AFFECTING ETHICAL DECISIONS VARY FROM LEVEL TO LEVEL

Gary Edwards, executive director of the Ethics Resource Center in Washington, D.C., identified a number of factors affecting ethical decisions for public relations practitioners at different levels within an organization:

> *A major ethical problem at the entry-level is not having all the facts, yet having to do what you are told.*
>
> *At the mid-management level, it's agreeing to meet certain quotas—signing up to do something—and, then, not being able to deliver. Supervisors are always signing up to do something, agreeing to get people to do something or other, and then, finding themselves unable to deliver. Most organizations pay lip service to management-by-objectives, especially at the supervisory level. In too many organizations, people at these levels don't set goals; they are told what their goals are, and they have to agree to them. Then, they have to figure out the means of meeting those goals—and, sometimes, they think that means by any means necessary.*
>
> *At the senior-management level, the ethical dilemma is having most of the facts, yet knowing that some of those facts are not good—and that you have to put a good face on it all, somehow, and deal with the consequences.*
>
> *Ethical issues arise when there is not enough information, and when there is not enough time to make a proper decision. The best strategy for dealing with the lack of information is to get more, if at all possible, and to verify what information you do have. The best strategy for dealing with the lack of time is to insist on more—to resist being pressured unreasonably. The alternative—for we rarely have all the information we want, and genuine time pressures do occur—is to prepare yourself, ahead of time, to imagine various scenarios, and to train yourself for various possible situations. What you need to do is to think out, in advance, what would be an appropriate, ethical decision.*
>
> *Another ethical problem arises when people think of ethical situations in simplistic terms—that it's this or that, either A or Not-A. People should be more imaginative: they should stop and reflect on the situation and think of more options.*[4]

APPLYING FOR THE JOB

Advice on How to Prepare a Resume

Three forms of resumes are used most often in public relations: functional, chronological, and a combination of these two.[5] The functional resume is used most often by individuals with a variety of work experience who want to cluster these different jobs in a way that allows a potential employer to see the specific functions that the person can perform—for example, TV production or technical editing. The chronological resume presents a person's work history in sequence—for example, from the most current to the earliest relevant job experience. The combination resume highlights both job skills and employment chronology—for example, under TV production an employment history relevant to those job skills will be presented. Each form of resume has its advantages and disadvantages.

The key to the success of any resume is knowing how to describe accurately and succinctly your education, training, and work experience in language that appeals to potential employers. One of the best ways to prepare a resume is to write a variety of different short sentences or phrases that describe your education and work experience. Do not write whole paragraphs, but write separate, short descriptive phrases—incomplete sentences—that describe what you have done. Try out a variety of phrases and select the best, then integrate the best phrases into coherent sentences and persuasive paragraphs. Here are powerful, action words you may be able to use to strengthen your resume:

achieved	administered	advised	analyzed
applied	arranged	budgeted	carried out
classified	communicated	completed	computed
conceptualized	coordinated	cut	delegated
determined	developed	devised	directed
established	evaluated	executed	formulated
gathered	generated	guided	implemented
improved	initiated	instituted	instructed
introduced	invented	issued	launched
lectured	litigated	lobbied	managed
negotiated	operated	organized	overhauled
planned	prepared	presented	presided
programmed	promoted	recommended	researched
reviewed	revised	reorganized	regulated
selected	solved	scheduled	supervised
systematized	taught	tested	traced
trained	updated	worked	wrote

Good resumes are short—one to two pages. Unless the employer has specifically requested otherwise, keep your resume as short as possible. A resume for a remarkably accomplished individual can be presented on one page and, because it is so brief, be a very powerful document. Remember: the purpose of a resume is to secure an invitation to an initial interview. If an employer wants to know more details about certain points on a resume, then that will come up during the initial interview. Having an interested employer say, "Tell me more about this. . . ." works to the advantage of the potential employee.

All resumes by public relations specialists should be of the highest professional appearance: error-free, graphically pleasing, and printed on quality paper.

Functional Resume Functional resumes work best for individuals with a wide range of experience that they want to cluster and succinctly present to a potential employer. The assumption is that the employer is looking for specific skills and experiences, and finding a person's skills clustered in this way will please the employer. The kind of functional resumes employers like includes dates of employment so an interviewer can reconstruct a chronological employment history. Some applicants, though, use the functional resume to highlight job skills and present little or no information about when the job skills were acquired. For this reason, many employers do not like functional resumes because it is difficult for them to see sequential patterns in the development of a person's career.

See Figure 11.1 for an example of a functional resume. The major advantage of a functional resume is that it allows someone with an employment history that lacks an apparent direction or focus to cluster various job skills together, so the potential employer can see that the person does have a significant set of experiences in a certain functional area—despite the fact that the experiences were gained at different times and at different jobs. For this reason, functional resumes are especially useful in public relations for people without an extensive employment history in the field but who have gained relevant communication and management skills in other fields. Communication and management skills gained in voluntary organizations can be presented in a functional resume, along with other work experience, to show the potential employer the true scope of the person's practical experience.

Chronological Resume A chronological resume is more than a list of your education and work experiences. The chronological resume, like a functional resume, should highlight a person's skills and experiences most relevant to a potential employer. It should not describe in detail all jobs and educational experiences—only the relevant ones. (Omit your driver's training course, and that two-week summer job you had

FIGURE 11.1

Example of a functional resume

John P. Jones
8822 Rossfield Drive
Houston, Texas 77005
Home phone: (713) 982–7176

Career goals:	To serve on a management team skilled in the use of public relations and corporate communication; to write and edit publications; to produce corporate videos; and, to be involved in community relations.
Education:	Bachelor of Science, University of Texas at Austin, May, 1992. Honors in journalism. Major: Journalism. Minor: Business.
Writing skills:	As a general assignment reporter for "The Houston Chronicle," (1989–90) and as a technical writer for Oilfield Supplies, Inc., (1990–present) wrote news stories, feature stories, technical articles, and scripts for corporate video training programs; helped write sales brochures and advertising copy for technical publications in the oil industry.
Editing skills:	With Oilfield Supplies, and as an intern with XYZ Corporation (1991), edited and helped design and produce employee publications, sales literature, and other print material; pay envelope stuffers; worked with artists, designers, and printers.
TV production skills:	With Oilfield Supplies, and as class projects at the university, wrote and produced video training programs, company news programs, and video news releases.
Public speaking:	Wrote and delivered numerous speeches and presentations, primarily as class exercises, but also for in-house audiences at Oilfield Supplies.
References:	Available upon request.

---

as a teenager at a car wash.) Because many employers like to see a continuous employment history in a potential new hire, they prefer a chronological resume to a functional resume: it is easy to scan the list of jobs to see the pattern of employment. Consequently, if there is a time during which no employment occurred, there should be some brief explanation in a chronological resume of what the person was doing during this time period. It is also possible on a chronological resume to list relevant volunteer work experiences.

The chronological resume is the most commonly used resume in public relations. See Figure 11.2 for an example. The best chronological resumes present not only the basic facts in sequence, they present these facts with a freshness and clarity that demonstrate the person's professional writing and presentations skills.

Combination Functional/Chronological Resume A growing trend in resume writing is combining the functional and chronological formats so that the potential employer sees relevant job skills of the applicant

FIGURE 11.2

Example of a chronological resume

John P. Jones
8822 Rossfield Drive
Houston, Texas 77005
Home phone: (713) 982-7176

Career goals:	To serve on a management team skilled in the use of public relations and corporate communication; to write and edit publications; to produce corporate videos; and, to be involved in community relations.
Education:	Bachelor of Science, University of Texas at Austin, May, 1992. Honors in journalism. Major: Journalism. Minor: Business.
Work experience:	
Fall, 1991	Public relations intern, XYZ Corporation. Wrote and helped produce company publications and sales brochures. One of the sales brochures was cited by the Sales Manager as being "one of the most effective we've ever had."
1990–present	Communication specialist, part-time, with Oilfield Supplies, Inc. Wrote articles for the employee publication, helped produce video news releases, and assisted in production of audio-visual presentations. Article in employee publication has been reprinted in sales literature for distribution to customers.
1989–1990	General assignment reporter, "The Houston Chronicle." Wrote news articles and feature stories. Received bonus from city editor for Sunday feature story.
References:	Available upon request.

---

clustered together and is presented an employment history that is easy to scan. The combination of the function and chronological formats is especially useful for entry-level and middle-level public relations specialists who have had a variety of work assignments that are not accurately reflected in job titles. The combination resume becomes an extremely persuasive document when the applicant's job skills are tailored to the specific job requirements of an employer. See Figure 11.3 for an example of the combination functional/chronological resume.

The best resumes accurately reflect not only the person's qualifications but also the person's personality. The best resumes not only provide basic information about education and work experience that any potential employer would need, they do it with dignity, style and flair. The best resumes reflect the uniqueness of the individual; they make the employer want to know more about that person. Here's good

FIGURE 11.3

Example of a functional/chronological resume

John P. Jones	8822 Rossfield Drive Houston, Texas 77005 Home phone: (713) 982-7176
Education:	Bachelor of Science, University of Texas at Austin, May, 1992. Honors in journalism. Major: Journalism. Minor: Business.
Job skills	
Writing:	As a general assignment reporter for "The Houston Chronicle," and as a technical writer for Oilfield Supplies, Inc., wrote news stories, feature stories, technical articles, and scripts for corporate video training programs; helped write sales brochures and advertising copy for technical publications in the oil industry.
Editing:	With Oilfield Supplies, and as an intern with XYZ Corporation, edited and helped with the design and production of employee publications, sales literature, and other print material: worked with artists, designers, and printers.
TV production:	With Oilfield Supplies, and as class projects at the university, wrote and produced video training programs, company news programs, and video news releases.
Public speaking:	Wrote and delivered numerous speeches and presentations, primarily as class exercises, but also for in-house audiences at Oilfield Supplies.
Work experience:	
Fall, 1991	Public relations intern, XYZ Corporation.
1990–present	Communication specialist, part-time, with Oilfield Supplies, Inc.
1989–1990	General assignment reporter, "The Houston Chronicle."
References:	Available upon request.

---

advice for anyone writing a resume: Listen to all the advice you can get; then, write a resume, and cover letter, that accurately reflects you and best serves your needs at this particular time in your career.

Advice on How to Write a Cover Letter

Research any organization before you apply for a position or inquire about career opportunities. Find out as much as you can by reading:

  two years of annual reports.

  recent company publications.

  current magazine and newspaper articles about the employer, especially in the trade press.

Libraries in the area where the organization is located often will have copies of these materials. Many organizations will send copies of these publications to individuals applying for public relations positions.

The opening paragraph of a good cover letter includes the reason you are writing and, if at all possible, some background information you have gathered about the organization. If, for whatever reason, no information is available—for example, if the identity of the organization is unknown because the job announcement is in a "blind ad" in a newspaper—then the first paragraph of the letter should state why you are writing and restate key points in the job description.

The second paragraph should mention some interesting fact not in the resume, or it should highlight some fact in the resume that may be of special interest to the employer.

The third paragraph should indicate why you are impressed with this company and why you want to work for them. Do not be self-centered. Do not explain what you want the company to do for you. Do not mention salary. In the third paragraph you should answer the employer's question, "What can you do for us?"

The last paragraph should ask for an opportunity to meet with the employer, at their convenience, within a certain period of time, and it should explain when you will be getting back in touch with them to set up an appointment for an interview. It should also express thanks and appreciation.

Keep your resume cover letter all on one page. See Figure 11.4 for an example.

Advice on How to Have a Successful Job Interview

Throughout the interview process, be sincere. Do not put on a false front. Act as you would on the first day of the job: curious, interested, and respectful of those you meet. Listen closely to what is said to you; in fact, it would be appropriate, at different points during an interview, for you to take notes. Be sure to dress for success. Don't dress for a fashion show. If you are not sure about what to wear to the job interview, ask in advance, or go by the organization and watch people entering and leaving the building. When in doubt, dress conservatively, in understated, professional business attire. Arrive for your interview rested and alert after a good night's sleep.

Prepare answers to questions most likely to be asked of you during the interview. You might write out your answers to these questions beforehand. Don't memorize your answers, but think through all the issues. Anticipate the following questions:

Why do you want this job?

Why do you think you'll be successful in this position?

FIGURE 11.4

Example of a resume cover letter

8822 Rossfield Drive
Houston, Texas 77005
December 1, 1992

Edward F. Donovan
Director of Public Relations
International Oil Corporation
Bakersfield, California 92102

Dear Mr. Donovan:

As a specialist in corporate communication, with experience in the oil industry, I am interested in the employee publication position recently advertised in "Overseas Oil" magazine. Enclosed is my resume.

Not mentioned in the resume are my overseas travels. I accompanied my father, who is with The Oil Tool Company, on two business trips to Saudia Arabia and to the Persian Gulf region during the summers of 1987 and 1989. Last summer, I toured England, France, and Spain. I am fluent in Spanish.

The range of overseas operations of International Oil Corporation impresses me. I understand that the majority of your employees are based in the United States and that you have foreign subsidiaries. I have read several of your corporate publications. I would like very much to work for your company because it has a fine reputation in the oil industry, and its share of the market is growing. Given my experience and skills, I know I could make a contribution to your organization.

Next month, January 20th–25th, I will be in Southern California on business. Would it be possible to meet then? I hope so. I will call you in a few days to discuss these matters with you. In the meantime, please call me, if you have any immediate questions at (713) 982-7176.

Sincerely,

John P. Jones

Enclosure: Resume

Why did you choose this company?

What can you do for us?

What are your strengths and weaknesses?

What are your career goals?

What jobs have you held and why did you leave them?

What are your salary requirements?

Tell me about yourself.

Do you have any questions?

Be prepared yourself to ask the right questions of those who are interviewing you. The types of questions you ask will depend, in part, on the level of job you are applying for—the more advanced the position, the more probing the questions you will ask. The type of questions you ask also may depend on when, during the interview or series of interviews, you are given an opportunity to ask questions. You should choose an appropriate time to ask these questions so that both you and the potential employer are comfortable discussing the answers.

Consider asking the following questions:

What will my typical day be like?

What happened to the last person who had this job?

What does it take to be a success in this job?

How would you characterize the management philosophy of your firm as it relates to public relations?

How would you characterize the working relationship between the public relations staff, the chief executive officer, and other members of senior management?

What is the relationship between various departments in the organization that deal with communication issues, such as marketing, advertising, human resources, and public relations?

How are budgets for public relations programs and campaigns determined?

Is there a trend in the role of minorities and women in management? What factors are behind this trend?

What are the profiles of the most important publics this organization deals with?

What are this organization's strengths? What aspects of the organization could be improved?

Why did you come to work here? What keeps you here?

If you were in my shoes today, would you take this job and come to work for this organization? Why?

Given my qualifications and what you know about the company, what do you estimate are my chances for career advancement?[6]

AN ALTERNATIVE EXPLANATION FOR THE "GLASS CEILING" IN PUBLIC RELATIONS

In this chapter, we have presented a variety of strategies and career advice from both men, women, and minorities in public relations. Implicit in some of their comments, and explicit in research on the impact of women in public relations, is the notion that a "glass ceiling" exists that blocks women and minorities in public relations from advancing into the senior ranks of management.[7]

Public relations scholar Elizabeth Lance Toth of Syracuse University has described the area above this invisible glass ceiling as the domain of general managers and not of public relations specialists.[8] She contends that the technical function of public relations—producing and disseminating messages which occur below the glass ceiling—may be more important to an organization than the "higher" functions claimed by some public relations managers, because the problem-solving roles of public relations managers are very much like those of any general manager. To document her argument, Toth points out that when corporate downsizing affects a public relations department, it is often the communication technician roles, and not the public relations problem-solving roles, which remain.

Toth wonders if men overemphasize the role of conflict resolution and negotiation in public relations because it supports masculine myths about the function of management. She thinks that women may be especially good at fulfilling technician roles because women possess a distinct set of nurturing, empathetic values and a greater appreciation of communication processes than do men.

Toth is concerned that questions about equity among men, women, and minorities in public relations take the spotlight away from what she considers to be more profound questions about the role of gender in public relations. For example, she argues, we need to look at gender not as the biological sex of a person—an independent variable—but as a dependent variable, an aspect of a public relations role that is dependent on a number of factors in addition to a person's biological sex, including role expectations, individual personality, socialization, and organizational factors.

IN SUMMARY . . .

We have stressed throughout this book that complex systems possess certain characteristics that need to be understood before they can be properly managed. And, we have argued that systems concepts and theories help to explain and predict organizational behavior, including public relations.

Systems theories help explain the criteria by which organizations hire and promote individuals to the highest ranks of management, including public relations. Organizations, because they strive to be rational, do not promote into senior management men over women, whites over blacks, young people over old people, so much as they promote competent managers over incompetent managers. Rational organizations throughout the world seek out effective, ethical managers, and promote them to the highest ranks, because these individuals provide the greatest good to the greatest number of people over the longest period of time.

The call for equity in the workplace should be taken seriously, especially in public relations, for the inequities are real and worrisome. But, we should recognize that at the highest levels of management, the issue of "Equity for Whom?" shifts: at the senior ranks of management, organizations look for competent, effective, ethical managers, regardless of their technical background, gender, or other individual differences. The implication for public relations practitioners wishing to get a good job and advance in the field is: Don't be stymied by all the sexism, the racism, the ageism, the whateverism—they are just some of the factors and forces in this world that need to be managed.

Public relations professionals should not be overwhelmed by all the pressures and ethical dilemmas that come with the job. They should recognize that all individuals, in all walks of life, face pressures and make ethical decisions based on their values, principles and loyalties. Unfortunately, knowing how ethical decisions are made only eases the process somewhat; it does not lessen the pressures or make the dilemmas any less difficult to resolve. Ethical public relations managers recognize their responsibilities; they understand that their decisions have the potential to affect the lives of others in a variety of ways, and they act accordingly. Fortunately, for those interested in getting a good job and advancing in the field, the demand for ethical, effective managers in public relations is great, and is likely to continue, as societies and organizations become more complex, decentralized, and interdependent.

Strategies for getting a good job and advancing in the field of public relations vary from entry-level to senior-level positions; yet, certain strategies apply to all pursuing careers in public relations:

know what you want—and, be persistent;

gain the skills and knowledge you need;

be a creative, persuasive communicator—but, above all, be a good listener;

develop a network of professional friends—and, find a mentor, or two;

work hard;

learn how to handle stress, laugh, and keep it in perspective; and,

be honest and fair with yourself and with others.

As we approach the 21st century, the challenges and oppotunities are there for the management of systematic, ethical public relations to enhance our lives—to improve how individuals, organizations, and publics relate to and, most importantly, understand each other. To have impact, ethical public relations professionals will need to continue their education to stay abreast of the rapidly expanding knowledge in this field, and to learn how to apply this knowledge not only with creativity and flexibility but also with vision and leadership.

Study Questions

1. True or false: Men earn an average of 20–30 percent more than women performing comparable public relations jobs. Explain your answer by briefly discussing salary trends in public relations.
2. Write an ideal job description for yourself as an entry-level person, a middle-management practitioner, and a senior-level manager. What skills do you have now and what do you need to advance?
3. What problems do you think women have entering and advancing in the field of public relations, beyond problems that might be encountered by men entering the field?
4. What problems do you think minorities have entering and advancing in the field of public relations, beyond problems that might be encountered by white men entering the field?
5. What problems do you think any individual, regardless of race or sex, would have entering and advancing in the field of public relations?
6. What factors affect ethical decisions at entry levels, middle-management levels, and senior-management levels in public relations?
7. What are the advantages and disadvantages of chronological, functional, and combination chronological-functional resumes?
8. Write a cover letter and resume for yourself, in response to a specific job you know about or one that you would like to have.
9. Prepare a list of questions you would ask during the initial set of (you hope, successful) interviews you have for the position described in Question 8.
10. List at least a half dozen strategies you have for getting a good job and advancing in the field of public relations.

Endnotes

1. Hon, Linda Childers, Larissa Grunig, and David Dozier, "Women in public relations: problems and opportunities," in *Excellence in Public Relations and Communication Management,* edited by James Grunig (Hillsdale, N.J.: Lawrence Erlbaum Associates, 1992) pp. 419–438.
2. Jacobson, David Y., and Nicholas Tortorello, "Fifth annual salary survey," *Public Relations Journal,* Vol. 46, No. 6. 1990, pp. 18–26. According to these authors: "Among public relations practitioners who are 35 years of age

and younger, the male median salary is 24 percent higher than the female median. Among those over 35, the gap widens to 35 percent—and the median bonus size for men is 114 percent higher."

3. Kern-Foxworth, Marilyn, "Minorities 2000—The Shape of Things to Come" *Public Relations Journal*, 45, 8, August 1989, pp. 14–22.

4. Personal interview with the author, January, 1991.

5. *Public Relations Career Director*, edited by Ronald W. Fry (Hawthorne, NJ: The Career Press, 1988) p. 252.

6. Based on "Questions for You, Questions For Them," in *Public Relations Career Directory*, edited by Ronald W. Fry (Hawthorne, NJ: The Career Press, 1988) pp. 259–264.

7. Cline, Carolyn G., Elizabeth L. Toth, Judy VanSlyke Turk, Lynn Masel Walters, Nancy Johnson, and Hank Smith, *The Velvet Ghetto: The Impact of the Increasing Percentage of Women in Public Relations and Business Communication* (San Francisco, CA: International Association of Business Communicators, 1986).

8. Toth, Elizabeth Lance, "The gender balance argument," *Mass Communication Review*, Spring-Summer, 1989, pp. 70–76.

APPENDIX A

How to Use *Systematic Public Relations Software* (sPRs)

Designed to generate checklists, project flow charts, budgets, cost-benefit analyses, complete proposals and reports, and other planning documents that aid in the management of public relations programs and campaigns, sPRs is a database management program for public relations professionals, educators, and students. sPRs supplements information in *Managing Systematic and Ethical Public Relations.*

sPRs is available for IBM or IBM-compatible computers with hard disk drives and at least 640K memory. sPRs will be available in Windows and for Macintosh and Apple environments.

To install sPRs, insert the diskette that contains the installation program into Drive A. From the C: prompt, type A: and hit return. Type INSTALL and hit return. Then, follow the instructions on the screen. With sPRs installed, hit F2 at any time for help.

Here is what you will find on sPRs:

A report writer that generates presentation-quality customized documents containing the following optional sections:

Title page

Statement of the Problem

Goals and Objectives

Target Audience Profiles

Media Characteristics

Themes and Strategies

Timeline

Budget

Evaluation Options

    Research design

    What-if-not-funded scenarios

Appendix A How to Use Systematic Public Relations Software (sPRs) Version 1.0

      Shadow pricing
      Cost-compensation estimation technique
      Expected value analysis,
  Statement of Benefits
  Appendix

Useful checklists—each of which can generate sequential lists of activities; assignment lists, with spaces for filling in the names of persons responsible, start and due dates for each activity; and, assignment lists with project flow diagrams (Gantt charts). sPRs includes checklists:

  Defining problems
  Building theories
  Establishing goals
  Specifying objectives
  Using the nominal group technique
  Conducting a force field analysis
  Defining key publics
  Analyzing publics
  Planning process
  Creating Gantt charts
  Drafting PERT diagrams
  Preparing narrative budgets
  Estimating costs
  Writing what-if-not-funded scenarios
  Determining shadow prices
  Using cost-compensation estimation techniques
  Performing expected value analysis
  Negotiating budgets
  Conducting research
  Selecting research designs
  Using a master evaluation checklist
  Evaluating publications
  Evaluating media relations
  Conducting a Delphi survey
  Investigating priority research questions
  Making ethical decisions
  Facilitating cooperation
  Preparing corporate codes of ethics

Using a contingency model of ethical decision-making

Writing your own professional code of ethics

Understanding legal principles

Preparing an effective resume

Writing an effective cover letter

Preparing for an effective job interview

A resume writer.

Scores of study questions based on information in *Managing Systematic and Ethical Public Relations*.

For educators—sample syllabi, learning exercises, discussion points, and more than 200 examination questions, on a special version of sPRs.

sPRs Version 1.7 price: $59.95 each for professionals. Educators' version of sPRs: free with student bulk orders. Students: $25 each in bulk orders of fewer than a dozen; $20 each in bulk orders of a dozen or more. Add 10% for shipping and handling. Local sales tax, when applicable, also must be included. Bulk order only by certified check or money order for the total amount due. When ordering in bulk, indicate total number of students, and specify size and number of diskettes: 5 1/4″ or 3 1/2″. Network and multi-site license agreements available. To order, or for more information, write: sPRs, Box 183, Greenbelt, Maryland 20768.

APPENDIX B

Code of the Public Relations Society of America

This Code was adopted by the PRSA Assembly in 1988. It replaces a Code of Ethics in force since 1950 and revised in 1954, 1959, 1963, 1977, and 1983.

Declaration of Principles

Members of the Public Relations Society of America base their professional principles on the fundamental value and dignity of the individual, holding that the free exercise of human rights, especially freedom of speech, freedom of assembly, and freedom of the press, is essential to the practice of public relations.

In serving the interests of clients and employers, we dedicate ourselves to the goals of better communication, understanding, and cooperation among the diverse individuals, groups, and institutions of society, and of equal opportunity of employment in the public relations profession.

We pledge:

To conduct ourselves professionally, with truth, accuracy, fairness, and responsibility to the public;

To improve our individual competence and advance the knowledge and proficiency of the profession through continuing research and education;

And to adhere to the articles of the Code of Professional Standards for the Practice of Public Relations as adopted by the governing Assembly of the Society.

Code of Professional Standards for the Practice of Public Relations

These articles have been adopted by the Public Relations Society of America to promote and maintain high standards of public service and ethical conduct among its members.

Appendix B Code of the Public Relations Society of America

1. A member shall conduct his or her professional life in accord with the public interest.
2. A member shall exemplify high standards of honesty and integrity while carrying out dual obligations to a client or employer and to the democratic process.
3. A member shall deal fairly with the public, with past or present clients or employers, and with fellow practitioners, giving due respect to the ideal of free inquiry and to the opinions of others.
4. A member shall adhere to the highest standards of accuracy and truth, avoiding extravagant claims or unfair comparisons and giving credit for ideas and words borrowed from others.
5. A member shall not knowingly disseminate false or misleading information and shall act promptly to correct erroneous communications for which he or she is responsible.
6. A member shall not engage in any practice which has the purpose of corrupting the integrity of channels of communications or the processes of government.
7. A member shall be prepared to identify publicly the name of the client or employer on whose behalf any public communication is made.
8. A member shall not use any individual or organization professing to serve or represent an announced cause, or professing to be independent or unbiased, but actually serving another or undisclosed interest.
9. A member shall not guarantee the achievement of specified results beyond the member's direct control.
10. A member shall not represent conflicting or competing interests without the express consent of those concerned, given after a full disclosure of the facts.
11. A member shall not place himself or herself in a position where the member's personal interest is or may be in conflict with an obligation to an employer or client, or others, without full disclosure of such interests to all involved.
12. A member shall not accept fees, commissions, gifts or any other consideration from anyone except clients or employers for whom services are performed without their express consent, given after full disclosure of the facts.
13. A member shall scrupulously safeguard the confidences and privacy rights of present, former, and prospective clients or employers.
14. A member shall not intentionally damage the professional reputation or practice of another practitioner.
15. If a member has evidence that another member has been guilty of unethical, illegal, or unfair practices, including those in violation of this Code, the member is obligated to present the information promptly to the proper authorities of the Society for action in accordance with the procedure set forth in Article XII of the Bylaws.

16. A member called as a witness in a proceeding for enforcement of this Code is obligated to appear, unless excused for sufficient reason by the judicial panel.
17. A member shall, as soon as possible, sever relations with any organization or individual if such relationship requires conduct contrary to the articles of this Code.

OFFICIAL INTERPRETATIONS OF THE CODE

Interpretation of Code Paragraph 1, which reads, "A member shall conduct his or her professional life in accord with the public interest."

> The public interest is here defined primarily as comprising respect for and enforcement of the rights guaranteed by the Constitution of the United States of America.

Interpretation of Code Paragraph 6, which reads, "A member shall not engage in any practice which has the purpose of corrupting the integrity of channels of communication or the processes of government."

1. Among the practices prohibited by this paragraph are those that tend to place representatives of media or government under any obligation to the member, or the member's employer or client, which is in conflict with their obligations to media or government, such as:
   a. the giving of gifts of more than nominal value;
   b. any form of payment or compensation to a member of the media in order to obtain preferential or guaranteed news or editorial coverage in the medium;
   c. any retainer or fee to a media employee or use of such employee if retained by a client or employer, where the circumstances are not fully disclosed to and accepted by the media employer;
   d. providing trips, for media representatives, that are unrelated to legitimate news interest;
   e. the use by a member of an investment or loan or advertising commitment made by the member, or the member's client or employer, to obtain preferential or guaranteed coverage in the medium.
2. This Code paragraph does not prohibit hosting media or government representatives at meals, cocktails, or news functions and special events that are occasions for the exchange of news information or views, or the furtherance of understanding, which is part of the public relations function. Nor does it prohibit the bona fide press event or tour when media or government representatives are given the opportunity for an on-the-spot viewing of a newsworthy product, process, or event in which the media or government representatives have a legitimate interest. What is customary or reasonable hospitality has to be a matter of particular judgment in

Appendix B   Code of the Public Relations Society of America

specific situations. In all of these cases, however, it is, or should be, understood that no preferential treatment or guarantees are expected or implied and that complete independence always is left to the media or government representative.

3. This paragraph does not prohibit the reasonable giving or lending of sample products or services to media representatives who have a legitimate interest in the products or services.
4. It is permissible, under Article 6 of the Code, to offer complimentary or discount rates to the media (travel writers, for example) if the rate is for business use and is made available to all writers. Considerable question exists as to the propriety of extending such rates for personal use.

Interpretation of Code Paragraph 9, which reads, "A member shall not guarantee the achievement of specified results beyond the member's direct control."

The Code paragraph, in effect, prohibits misleading a client or employer as to what professional public relations can accomplish. It does not prohibit guarantees of quality or service. But it does prohibit guaranteeing specific results which, by their very nature, cannot be guaranteed because they are not subject to the member's control. As an example, a guarantee that a news release will appear specifically in a particular publication would be prohibited. This paragraph should not be interpreted as prohibiting contingent fees.

Interpretation of Code Paragraph 13, which reads, "A member shall scrupulously safeguard the confidences and privacy rights of present, former, and prospective clients or employers."

1. This article does not prohibit a member who has knowledge of client or employer activities that are illegal from making such disclosures to the proper authorities as he or she believes are legally required.
2. Communications between a practitioner and client/employer are deemed to be confidential under Article 13 of the Code of Professional Standards. However, although practitioner/client/employer communications are considered confidential between the parties, such communications are not privileged against disclosure in a court of law.
3. In the absence of any contractual arrangement, the client or employer legally owns the rights to papers or materials created for him.

Interpretation of Code Paragraph 14, which reads, "A member shall not intentionally damage the professional reputation or practice of another practitioner."

Blind solicitation, on its face, is not prohibited by the Code. However, if the customer list were improperly obtained, or if the solicitation contained references reflecting adversely on the quality of current services, a complaint might be justified.

AN OFFICIAL INTERPRETATION OF THE CODE AS IT APPLIES TO POLITICAL PUBLIC RELATIONS.

Preamble.
In the practice of political public relations, a PRSA member must have professional capabilities to offer an employer or client quite apart from any political relationships of value, and members may serve their employer or client without necessarily having attributed to them the character, reputation, or beliefs of those they serve. It is understood that members may choose to serve only those interests with whose political philosophy they are personally comfortable.

Definition. "Political Public Relations" is defined as those areas of public relations that relate to:
  a. the counseling of political organizations, committees, candidates, or potential candidates for public office; and groups constituted for the purpose of influencing the vote on any ballot issue;
  b. the counseling of holders of public office;
  c. the management, or direction, of a political campaign for or against a ballot issue to be determined by voter approval or rejection;
  d. the practice of public relations on behalf of a client or an employer in connection with that client's or employer's relationships with any candidates or holders of public office, with the purpose of influencing legislation or government regulation or treatment of a client or employer, regardless of whether the PRSA member is a recognized lobbyist;
  e. the counseling of government bodies, or segments thereof, either domestic or foreign.

Precepts.
  1. It is the responsibility of PRSA members practicing political public relations, as defined above, to be conversant with the various statutes, local, state, and federal, governing such activities and to adhere to them strictly. This includes, but is not limited to, the various local, state, and federal laws, courts decisions, and official interpretations governing lobbying, political contributions, disclosure, elections, libel, slander, and the like. In carrying out this responsibility, members shall seek appropriate counseling whenever necessary.
  2. It is also the responsibility of members to abide by PRSA's Code of Professional Standards.

Appendix B Code of the Public Relations Society of America

3. Members shall represent clients or employers in good faith, and while partisan advocacy on behalf of a candidate or public issue may be expected, members shall act in accord with the public interest and adhere to truth and accuracy and to generally accepted standards of good taste.
4. Members shall not issue descriptive material or any advertising or publicity information or participate in the preparation or use thereof that is not signed by responsible persons or is false, misleading, or unlabeled as to its source, and are obligated to use care to avoid dissemination of any such material.
5. Members have an obligation to clients to disclose what remuneration beyond their fees they expect to receive as a result of their relationship, such as commissions for media advertising, printing, and the like, and should not accept such extra payment without their client's consent.
6. Members shall not improperly use their positions to encourage additional future employment or compensation. It is understood that successful campaign directors or managers, because of the performance of their duties and the working relationship that develops, may well continue to assist and counsel, for pay, the successful candidate.
7. Members shall voluntarily disclose to employers or clients the identity of other employers or clients with whom they are currently associated, and whose interests might be affected favorably or unfavorably by their political representation.
8. Members shall respect the confidentiality of information pertaining to employers or clients past, present, and potential, even after the relationships cease, avoiding future associations wherein insider information is sought that would give a desired advantage over a member's previous clients.
9. In avoiding practices that might tend to corrupt the processes of government, members shall not make undisclosed gifts of cash or other valuable considerations that are designed to influence specific decisions of voters, legislators, or public officials on public matters. A business lunch or dinner, or other comparable expenditure made in the course of communicating a point of view or public position, would not constitute such a violation. Nor, for example, would a plant visit designed and financed to provide useful background information to an interested legislator or candidate.
10. Nothing herein should be construed as prohibiting members from making legal, properly disclosed contributions to the candidates, party, or referenda issues of their choice.
11. Members shall not, through use of information known to be false or misleading, conveyed directly or through a third party, intentionally injure the public reputation of an opposing interest.

AN OFFICIAL INTERPRETATION OF THE CODE AS IT APPLIES TO FINANCIAL PUBLIC RELATIONS

This interpretation of the Society Code as it applies to financial public relations was originally adopted in 1963 and amended in 1972, 1977, 1983, and 1988 by action of the PRSA Board of Directors. "Financial public relations" is defined as "that area of public relations which relates to the dissemination of information that affects the understanding of stockholders and investors generally concerning the financial position and prospects of a company, and includes among its objectives the improvement of relations between corporations and their stockholders." The interpretation was prepared in 1963 by the Society's Financial Relations Committee, working with the Securities and Exchange Commission and with the advice of the Society's legal counsel. It is rooted directly in the Code with the full force of the Code behind it, and a violation of any of the following paragraphs is subject to the same procedures and penalties as violation of the Code.

1. It is the responsibility of PRSA members who practice financial public relations to be thoroughly familiar with and understand the rules and regulations of the SEC and the laws it administers, as well as other laws, rules, and regulations affecting financial public relations, and to act in accordance with their letter and spirit. In carrying out this responsibility, members shall also seek legal counsel, when appropriate, on matters concerning financial public relations.

2. Members shall adhere to the general policy of making full and timely disclosure of corporate information on behalf of clients or employers. The information disclosed shall be accurate, clear, and understandable. The purpose of such disclosure is to provide the investing public with all material information affecting security values or influencing investment decisions. In complying with the duty of full and timely disclosure, members shall present all material facts, including those adverse to the company. They shall exercise care to ascertain the facts and to disseminate only information they believe to be accurate. They shall not knowingly omit information, the omission of which might make a release false or misleading. Under no circumstances shall members participate in any activity designed to mislead or manipulate the price of a company's securities.

3. Members shall publicly disclose or release information promptly so as to avoid the possibility of any use of the information by any insider or third party. To that end, members shall make every effort to comply with the spirit and intent of the timely-disclosure policies of the stock exchanges, NASD, and the SEC. Material information shall be made available on an equal basis.

Appendix B   Code of the Public Relations Society of America

4. Members shall not disclose confidential information the disclosure of which might be adverse to a valid corporate purpose or interest and whose disclosure is not required by the timely-disclosure provisions of the law. During any such period of non-disclosure members shall not directly or indirectly (a) communicate the confidential information to any other person or (b) buy or sell or in any other way deal in the company's securities where the confidential information may materially affect the market for the security when disclosed. Material information shall be disclosed publicly as soon as its confidential status has terminated or the requirement of timely disclosure takes effect.
5. During the registration period, members shall not engage in practices designed to precondition the market for such securities. During registration, the issuance of forecasts, projections, predictions about sales and earnings, or opinions concerning security values or other aspects of the future performance of the company, shall be in accordance with current SEC regulations and statements of policy. In the case of companies whose securities are publicly held, the normal flow of factual information to shareholders and the investing public shall continue during the registration period.
6. Where members have any reason to doubt that projections have an adequate basis in fact, they shall satisfy themselves as to the adequacy of the projections prior to disseminating them.
7. Acting in concert with clients or employers, members shall act promptly to correct false or misleading information or rumors concerning clients' or employers' securities or business whenever they have reason to believe such information or rumors are materially affecting investor attitudes.
8. Members shall not issue descriptive materials designed or written in such a fashion as to appear to be, contrary to fact, an independent third-party endorsement or recommendation of a company or a security. Whenever members issue material for clients or employers, either in their own names or in the name of someone other than the clients or employers, they shall disclose in large type and in a prominent position on the face of the material the source of such material and the existence of the issuer's client or employer relationship.
9. Members shall not use inside information for personal gain. However, this is not intended to prohibit members from making bona fide investments in their company's or client's securities insofar as they can make such investments without the benefit of material inside information.
10. Members shall not accept compensation that would place them in a position of conflict with their duty to a client, employer, or the investing public. Members shall not accept stock options from clients or employers nor accept securities as compensation at a price below market price except as part of an overall plan for corporate employees.

11. Members shall act so as to maintain the integrity of channels of public communication. They shall not pay or permit to be paid to any publication or other communications medium any consideration in exchange for publicizing a company, except through clearly recognizable paid advertising.
12. Members shall in general be guided by the PRSA Declaration of Principles and the Code of Professional Standards for the Practice of Public Relations of which this is an official interpretation.

COUNSELORS ACADEMY'S INTERPRETATIONS TO THE PRSA CODE OF PROFESSIONAL STANDARDS

Members of counseling firms have a specific responsibility to maintain the highest standards of ethics in the practice of public relations. Counselors embrace the many responsibilities of serving the interests of clients and the public at large, while considering their own personal interests and those of their firms. There are several key relationships in every public relations counseling business, and they involve:

Clients we serve;

Each other, as employees and competitors;

Media with whom we work;

Suppliers with whom we work;

Communities where we live and work.

Members of the Counselors Academy, and each member's employees, are expected to practice his or her profession in the most responsible, reliable, truthful and cooperative way.

The Counselors Academy advocates the following precepts:

1. Counselors have an overriding responsibility to carefully balance public interests with those of their clients, and to place both those interests above their own.
2. Counselors must operate in an open and truthful manner at all times.
3. Counselors have a responsibility to protect the integrity of certain elements of public relations practice, including:

    - contracts and non-compete agreements between counseling firms and their employees;
    - contracts and agreements between counseling firms and clients;
    - confidential client information;
    - confidential agency information.

4. It is incumbent on counselors to understand the requirements of their clients and to exert best efforts to satisfy those requirements by submitting realistic proposals on performance, cost and

Appendix B Code of the Public Relations Society of America

schedule. Counselors will employ the highest ethical business practices in source selection, negotiation, determination of awards and the administration of all purchasing activities.

5. Counselors must not work for more than one client or employer whose goals may be in conflict, without the express consent of those concerned, given after a full disclosure of the facts. Members must be particularly sensitive to alleviate situations where a conflict of interest or even a perception of such a conflict could originate.
6. Counselors must not collect fees for services based on guaranteed results of any kind with media or other third parties.
7. Counselors have an obligation to clients to disclose any remuneration beyond their fees that they expect to receive as a result of their relationship, and should not accept such extra payments without their client's consent.
8. Counselors shall respect the confidentiality of information pertaining to present, former and prospective clients, and avoid future associations wherein insider information is used that would give a desired advantage over the counselor's previous clients.
9. In no instance may counselors use or share inside information, which is not otherwise available to the general public, for any manner of personal gain as might be realized, for example, through trading in the stock of a client company.
10. We consider that it could be a breach of our standards for any counseling firm to seek a competitive advantage through the payment or receipt of extraordinary gifts, gratuities, or other favors.
11. Counselors shall not personally, or in the interests of a client, intentionally injure the public reputation of another practitioner.
12. Counselors must move quickly to present evidence of unethical activity by other counselors to the proper authorities of the Society.
13. Counselors shall in general be guided by the PRSA Declaration of Principles and the PRSA Code of Professional Standards for the Practice of Public Relations of which this document is an interpretation.

The Committee On Business Practices, The Counselors Academy, Public Relations Society of America, October, 1990

APPENDIX C

Code of the International Association of Business Communicators

The IABC Code of Ethics has been developed to provide IABC members and other communication professionals with guidelines of professional behavior and standards of ethical practice. The Code will be reviewed and revised as necessary by the Ethics Committee and the Executive Board.

Any IABC member who wishes advice and guidance regarding its interpretation and/or application may write or phone IABC headquarters. Questions will be routed to the Executive Board member responsible for the Code.

COMMUNICATION AND INFORMATION DISSEMINATION

1. *Communication professionals will uphold the credibility and dignity of their profession by encouraging the practice of honest, candid and timely communication.*

   The highest standards of professionalism will be upheld in all communication. Communicators should encourage frequent communication and messages that are honest in their content, candid, accurate and appropriate to the needs of the organization and its audiences.

2. *Professional communicators will not use any information that has been generated or appropriately acquired by a business for another business without permission. Further, communicators should attempt to identify the source of information to be used.*

   When one is changing employers, information developed at the previous position will not be used without permission from that employer. Acts of plagiarism and copyright infringement are illegal acts; material in the public domain should have its source attributed, if possible. If an organization grants permission to use its information and requests public acknowledgment, it will be made in a place appropriate to the material used. The material will be used only for the purpose for which permission was granted.

STANDARDS OF CONDUCT

3. *Communication professionals will abide by the spirit and letter of all laws and regulations governing their professional activities.*

    All international, national and local laws and regulations must be observed, with particular attention to those pertaining to communication, such as copyright law. Industry and organizational regulations will also be observed.

4. *Communication professionals will not condone any illegal or unethical act related to their professional activity, their organization and its business or the public environment in which it operates.*

    It is the personal responsibility of professional communicators to act honestly, fairly and with integrity at all times in all professional activities. Looking the other way while others act illegally tacitly condones such acts whether or not the communicator has committed them. The communicator should speak with the individual involved, his or her supervisor or appropriate authorities—depending on the context of the situation and one's own ethical judgment.

CONFIDENTIALITY/DISCLOSURE

5. *Communication professionals will respect the confidentiality and right-to-privacy of all individuals, employers, clients and customers.*

    Communicators must determine the ethical balance between right-to-privacy and need-to-know. Unless the situation involves illegal or grossly unethical acts, confidences should be maintained. If there is a conflict between right-to-privacy and need-to-know, a communicator should first talk with the source and negotiate the need for the information to be communicated.

6. *Communication professionals will not use any confidential information gained as a result of professional activity for personal benefit or for that of others.*

    Confidential information can not be used to give inside advantage to stock transactions, gain favors from outsiders, assist a competing company for whom one is going to work, assist companies in developing a marketing advantage, achieve a publishing advantage or otherwise act to the detriment of an organization. Such information must remain confidential during and after one's employment period.

PROFESSIONALISM

7. *Communication professionals should uphold IABC's standards for ethical conduct in all professional activity, and should use IABC and its designation of accreditation (ABC) only for purposes that are authorized and fairly represent the organization and its professional standards.*

   IABC recognizes the need for professional integrity within any organization, including the association. Members should acknowledge that their actions reflect on themselves, their organizations and their profession.

A SYSTEM OF ENACTMENT

To guide communication professionals in ethical matters and assure professional consistency, an ethical philosophy and code must have a means of enactment. The code must reinforce the observance of all civil and criminal laws and regulations, yet be flexible enough for situational considerations and for seeking reform through legitimate channels.

Therefore, the following steps should be undertaken to enact the IABC Code of Ethics:

Communication

The code should be published, along with supplementary materials and a brief reference bibliography, in a folder given to each member on a one-time basis. New members should automatically receive a Code on joining.

Include a sentence on all application and annual renewal forms stating "I have reviewed and pledge to uphold IABC's code of ethics and standards of professional communication."

In all IABC application materials and introductory brochures, include the principles of the code.

Communication World should run an article on a topic of professional ethics relevant to IABC's philosophy at least annually. A variety of themes can be chosen from the code's principles and explanations. Different approaches and case examples can increase editorial options.

At least one session about ethics should be scheduled at the IABC annual conference to assist newer professionals in developing and refining their communication ethics, education and professional development. Ethics should also be supported in IABC's professional development seminar series and sessions at district conferences. Names of speakers on ethics should be made available and shared among districts and local chapters.

IABC ethics must be participatory. In the development of a communication ethos, two-way communication is essential; therefore, the proposed IABC ethics documents should be submitted for review by all chapters with feedback collected and discussed by the districts and sent to IABC. Clarification, specific questions and concerns with accompanying recommendations are important in developing a document that fairly and honestly represents the ethical perspective of its membership. Above all, the opinions and concerns of members in *all* countries must be given full consideration.

Review Committee

Establish an ethics review committee of at least three accredited members. Non-accredited members may be appointed upon special approval by the IABC Executive Committee and the director representing ethics on the Executive Board.

The first function should be to offer an IABC member service in assisting with general ethical questions related to the profession. The committee would not provide legal opinions. Opinions on questions would be solicited from an additional two accredited members and one member at random, and these would be factored into the review committee's summary opinion. Names of those requesting and giving opinions would be confidential.

The second function of the review committee would be the professional development of members on the subject of ethics, working in conjunction with IABC's professional development committee. Efforts should be made to inform and educate membership on matters of ethics, focusing on helping individuals develop ethical decision-making skills that are interdependent with IABC policy.

The third function should be to review and sanction violations of ethical conduct among members as they reflect on IABC and the communication profession. If a member's conduct is deemed by the director responsible for ethics to violate IABC's ethical code in a way that jeopardizes the credibility of the organization and profession, then the matter would first be discussed with the individual to determine the facts of the situation. Then, if circumstances warrant, the matter would be taken up by the ethics review committee. The individual's name would be kept confidential. In addition to the committee's deliberation, at least three additional opinions would be sought in any decision. Two opinions would be solicited at random from the pool of accredited members and one from a member-at-large. The IABC director representing ethics on the Executive Board would be an ex-officio member of the process.

Members of the ethics review committee would serve staggered, three-year consecutive terms to ensure internal consistency. They may serve more than one term but not consecutively. Members of the committee will be IABC accredited as a means of objective evidence that they have a working knowledge of communication ethics which meets the organization's standards of professionalism. Non-accredited members may be appointed upon special approval by the IABC Executive Committee and the director representing ethics on the Executive Board.

SANCTIONS

It is recognized that while the code may apply to communication professionals generally, sanctions would apply only to IABC members.

For a first violation, unless criminal activity is involved, the sanctions would be informative and educational. They would share concern over the situation, rendering opinions with the intent to help guide the member toward more professional performance.

A second violation for the same or related offense would bring a warning, again with the intent of information and education.

A third or subsequent violation could involve a further warning, or if the situation was flagrant without serious commitment of improvement, an alternative sanction of suspension for up to one year could be given. *Any decision of suspension or reinstatement must be reviewed and approved by the IABC Executive Committee and the executive board director responsible.*

APPENDIX D

Code of the International Public Relations Association

INTERNATIONAL CODE OF ETHICS
CODE OF ATHENS
English Version
adopted by IPRA General Assembly at Athens on 12 May 1965 and modified at Tehran on 17 April 1968

CONSIDERING that all Member countries of the United Nations Organisation have agreed to abide by its Charter which reaffirms "its faith in fundamental human rights, in the dignity and worth of the human person" and that having regard to the very nature of their professions, Public Relations practitioners in these countries should undertake to ascertain and observe the principles set out in this Charter;

CONSIDERING that, apart from "rights," human beings have not only physical or material needs but also intellectual, moral and social needs and that their rights are of real benefit to them only in so far as these needs are essentially met;

CONSIDERING that, in the course of their professional duties and depending on how these duties are performed, Public Relations practitioners can substantially help to meet these intellectual, moral and social needs;

And lastly, CONSIDERING that the use of techniques enabling them to come simultaneously into contact with millions of people gives Public Relations practitioners a power that has to be restrained by the observance of a strict moral code.

On all these grounds, the undersigned Public Relations Associations hereby declare that they accept as their moral charter the principles of the following Code of Ethics, and that if, in the light of evidence submitted to the Council, a member of these associations should be found to have infringed this Code in the course of his/her professional duties, he/she will be deemed to be guilty of serious misconduct calling for an appropriate penalty.

Accordingly, each Member of these Associations:

SHALL ENDEAVOUR

1. To contribute to the achievement of the moral and cultural conditions enabling human beings to reach their full stature and enjoy the indefeasible rights to which they are entitled under the "Universal Declaration of Human Rights";
2. To establish communication patterns and channels which, by fostering the free flow of essential information, will make each member of the group feel that he/she is being kept informed, and also give him/her an awareness of his/her own personal involvement and responsibility, and of his/her solidarity with other members;
3. To conduct himself/herself always and in all circumstances in such a manner as to deserve and secure the confidence of those with whom he/she comes into contact;
4. To bear in mind that, because of the relationship between his/her profession and the public, his/her conduct—even in private—will have an impact on the way in which the profession as a whole is appraised.

Shall Undertake

5. To observe, in the course of his/her professional duties, the moral principles and rules of the "Universal Declaration of Human Rights";
6. To pay due regard to, and uphold, human dignity, and to recognise the right of each individual to judge for himself/herself;
7. To establish the moral, psychological and intellectual conditions for dialogue in its true sense, and to recognise the right of the parties involved to state their case and express their views;
8. To act, in all circumstances, in such a manner as to take account of the respective interests of the parties involved: both the interests of the organisation which he/she serves and the interests of the publics concerned;
9. To carry out his/her undertakings and commitments, which shall always be so worded as to avoid any misunderstandings, and to show loyalty and integrity in all circumstances so as to keep the confidence of his/her clients or employers, past or present, and of all the publics that are affected by his/her actions.

Shall Refrain From

10. Subordinating the truth to other requirements;
11. Circulating information which is not based on established and ascertainable facts;
12. Taking part in any venture or undertaking which is unethical or dishonest or capable of impairing human dignity and integrity;
13. Using any "manipulative" methods or techniques designed to create subconscious motivations which the individual cannot control of his/her own free will and so cannot be held accountable for the action taken on them.

APPENDIX E

International Bill of Rights of the United Nations

. . . . . .

UNIVERSAL DECLARATION OF HUMAN RIGHTS

Preamble

Whereas recognition of the inherent dignity and of the equal and inalienable rights of all members of the human family is the foundation of freedom, justice and peace in the world,

Whereas disregard and contempt for human rights have resulted in barbarous acts which have outraged the conscience of mankind, and the advent of a world in which human beings shall enjoy freedom of speech and belief and freedom from fear and want has been proclaimed as the highest aspiration of the common people,

Whereas it is essential, if man is not to be compelled to have recourse, as a last resort, to rebellion against tyranny and oppression, that human rights should be protected by the rule of law,

Whereas it is essential to promote the development of friendly relations between nations,

Whereas the people of the United Nations have in the Charter reaffirmed their faith in fundamental human rights, in the dignity and worth of the human person and in the equal rights of men and women and have determined to promote social progress and better standards of life in larger freedom,

Whereas Member States have pledged themselves to achieve, in cooperation with the United Nations, the promotion of universal respect for and observance of human rights and fundamental freedoms,

Whereas a common understanding of these rights and freedoms is of the greatest importance for the full realizations of this pledge,

Now, therefore,

The General Assembly

Proclaims this Universal Declaration of Human Rights as a common standard of achievement for all peoples and all nations, to the end that every individual and every organ of society, keeping this Declaration constantly in mind, shall strive by teaching and education to promote respect for these rights and freedoms and by progressive measures, national and international, to secure their universal and effective recognition and observance, both among the peoples of Members States themselves and among the peoples of territories under their jurisdiction.

Article 1

All human beings are born free and equal in dignity and rights. They are endowed with reason and conscience and should act towards one another in a spirit of brotherhood.

Article 2

Everyone is entitled to all the rights and freedoms set forth in this Declaration, without distinction of any kind, such as race, colour, sex, language, religion, political or other opinion, national or social origin, property, birth or other status.

Furthermore, no distinction shall be made on the basis of the political, jurisdictional or international status of the country or territory to which a person belongs, whether it be independent, trust, non-self-governing or under any other limitation of sovereignty.

Article 3

Everyone has the right to life, liberty and security of person.

Article 4

No one shall be held in slavery or servitude; slavery and the slave trade shall be prohibited in all their forms.

Article 5

No one shall be subjected to torture or to cruel, inhuman or degrading treatment or punishment.

Article 6

Everyone has the right to recognition everywhere as a person before the law.

Article 7

All are equal before the law and are entitled without any discrimination to equal protection of the law. All are entitled to equal protection against any discrimination in violation of this Declaration and against any incitement to such discrimination.

Article 8

Everyone has the right to an effective remedy by the competent national tribunals for acts violating the fundamental rights granted him by the constitution or by law.

Article 9

No one shall be subjected to arbitrary arrest, detention or exile.

Article 10

Everyone is entitled in full equality to a fair and public hearing by an independent and impartial tribunal, in the determination of his rights and obligations and of any criminal charge against him.

Article 11

1. Everyone charged with a penal offence has the right to be presumed innocent until proved guilty according to law in a public trial at which he has had all the guarantees necessary for his defence.
2. No one shall be held guilty of any penal offence on account of any act or omission which did not constitute a penal offence, under national or international law, at the time when it was committed. Nor shall a heavier penalty be imposed than the one that was applicable at the time the penal offence was committed.

Article 12

No one shall be subjected to arbitrary interference with his privacy, family, home or correspondence, nor to attacks upon his honour and reputation. Everyone has the right to the protection of the law against such interference or attacks.

Article 13

1. Everyone has the right to freedom of movement and residence within the borders of each State.
2. Everyone has the right to leave any country, including his own, and to return to his country.

Article 14

1. Everyone has the right to seek and to enjoy in other countries asylum from persecution.
2. This right may not be invoked in the case of prosecutions genuinely arising from non-political crimes or from acts contrary to the purposes and principles of the United Nations.

Article 15

1. Everyone has the right to a nationality.
2. No one shall be arbitrarily deprived of his nationality nor denied the right to change his nationality.

Article 16

1. Men and women of full age, without any limitation due to race, nationality or religion, have the right to marry and to found a family. They are entitled to equal rights as to marriage, during marriage and at its dissolution.
2. Marriage shall be entered into only with the free and full consent of the intending spouses.
3. The family is the natural and fundamental group unit of society and is entitled to protection by society and the State.

Article 17

1. Everyone has the right to own property alone as well as in association with others.
2. No one shall be arbitrarily deprived of his property.

Article 18

Everyone has the right to freedom of thought, conscience and religion; this right includes freedom to change his religion or belief, and freedom, either alone or in community with others and in public or private, to manifest his religion or belief in teaching, practice, worship and observance.

Article 19

Everyone has the right to freedom of opinion and expression; this right includes freedom to hold opinions without interference and to seek, receive and impart information and ideas through any media and regardless of frontiers.

Article 20

1. Everyone has the right to freedom of peaceful assembly and association.
2. No one may be compelled to belong to an association.

Article 21

1. Everyone has the right to take part in the government of his country, directly or through freely chosen representatives.
2. Everyone has the right of equal access to public service in his country.
3. The will of the people shall be the basis of the authority of government; this will shall be expressed in periodic and genuine elections which shall be by universal and equal suffrage and shall be held by secret vote or by equivalent free voting procedures.

Article 22

Everyone, as a member of society, has the right to social security and is entitled to realization, through national effort and international cooperation and in accordance with the organization and resources of each State, of the economic, social and cultural rights indispensable for his dignity and the free development of his personality.

Article 23

1. Everyone has the right to work, to free choice of employment, to just and favourable conditions of work and to protection against unemployment.
2. Everyone, without any discrimination, has the right to equal pay for equal work.
3. Everyone who works has the right to just and favourable remuneration ensuring for himself and his family an existence worthy of human dignity, and supplemented, if necessary, by the other means of social protection.
4. Everyone has the right to form and to join trade unions for the protection of his interests.

Article 24

Everyone has the right to rest and leisure, including reasonable limitation of working hours and periodic holidays with pay.

Article 25

1. Everyone has the right to a standard of living adequate for the health and well-being of himself and of his family, including food, clothing, housing and medical care and necessary social services, and the right to security in the event of unemployment, sickness, disability, widowhood, old age or other lack of livelihood in circumstances beyond his control.
2. Motherhood and childhood are entitled to special care and assistance. All children, whether born in or out of wedlock, shall enjoy the same social protection.

Article 26

1. Everyone has the right to education. Education shall be free, at least in the elementary and fundamental stages. Elementary education shall be compulsory. Technical and professional education shall be made generally available and higher education shall be equally accessible to all on the basis of merit.
2. Education shall be directed to the full development of the human personality and to the strengthening of respect for human rights and fundamental freedoms. It shall promote understanding, tolerance and friendship among all nations, racial or religious groups, and shall further the activities of the United Nations for the maintenance of peace.
3. Parents have a prior right to choose the kind of education that shall be given to their children.

Article 27

1. Everyone has the right freely to participate in the cultural life of the community, to enjoy the arts and to share in scientific advancement and it benefits.
2. Everyone has the right to the protection of the moral and material interests resulting from any scientific, literary or artistic production of which he is the author.

Article 28

Everyone is entitled to a social and international order in which the rights and freedoms set forth in this Declaration can be fully realized.

Article 29

1. Everyone has duties to the community in which alone the free and full development of his personality is possible.
2. In the exercise of his rights and freedoms, everyone shall be subject only to such limitations as are determined by law solely for the purpose of securing due recognition and respect for the rights and freedoms of others and of meeting the just requirements of morality, public order and the general welfare in a democratic society.
3. These rights and freedoms may in no case be exercised contrary to the purposes and principles of the United Nations.

Article 30

Nothing in this Declaration may be interpreted as implying for any State, group or person any right to engage in any activity or to perform any act aimed at the destruction of any of the rights and freedoms set forth herein.

INDEX

Accreditation, 378–79
Action Oriented Theories, 70
Agenda Setting Theory, 112–13
Alberta Government Telephones, 77
Altruism, 297, 312
Anti-Trust Legislation, 9

Bank of America, 79–82
Benefit Cost Ratios, 186
Benefit Cost Remainders, 186
Benefit Shadow Pricing, 179–82
Baltimore Gas & Electric Company, 61
Black & Decker, 240
Blue Cross & Blue Shield, 169–70
Boundary Spanners, 14, 338
Budgets
    Definition of, 158
    Factors associated with, 193–94
    Narrative, 164–68
    Reasons for unsophisticated, 159
    Standard categories within, 161
    Standard types, 162

Calendarizing, 130
Campaign vs. Program, 4
Career Advice, 419–26
Checklists
    Master, 159–64
    For media relations, 11–12, 15, 32
    For publications, 274–76
    Strengths and weaknesses of, 158–59
Codes of ethics
    Comparison of, 379–86
    International Association of Business Communicators, 454–58
    International Public Relations Associations, 460–62
    Public Relations Society of America, 444–53
Cognitive Growth/Stability Theory, 119
Community Power Theory, 116
Control Groups, 206
Content Analysis, 232–34

Coorientation Model, 96–97
Cost Benefit Compensation Estimation, 183–86
Cover Letter, 433–35
Cultural values, 389–91

Delphi Technique 88
    Definition of, 298
District of Columbia Campaign, 58–61, 243–46
Dominant Coalition
    Definition of, 14
    Relationship to practitioner, 22
    View of organization, 33
    View of world, 56–57
    View of publics, 109

Egoism, 323
Elaboration Likelihood Theory, 110–11
Ethical Decision-making
    Basic model of, 327
    Contingency model of, 349–51
Ethical Relativism, 324–25
Ethics
    Definition of, 54
    Evolution of Consciousness and Conscience, 359
    Factors outside organization's control, 372–77
    Guidelines and career advice, 426–28
    Interpersonal factors affecting, 332
    Intrapersonal factors affecting, 332
    Meta-ethics, 321
    Moral Development 330–31
    Organizational factors affecting, 320, 335
    Small group factors affecting, 335
    Sociobiology and, 358
    Strategies for improving, 342–43
Expected Value Analysis 188–93
Evaluations
    Alternative approaches, 291

Focus Groups
   Examples of, 227–32
Freddie Mac's Campaign 102–3
Force Field Analysis, 88

Gantt Chart, 130–31
Garbage Can Theory, 89–90
General Systems Theory
   Definition of, 13
Giant Food's Publications 264
Glass Ceiling, 437
Goals
   Assigning priorities to, 86
   Definition of, 53
   Developing, 65
   How to write, 83
   Outcome, 54, 159
   Process, 53
   Theory based, 69–70
Grunig's Situational Model, 119

Hierarchy, 387–89
Hierarchy of Effects, 79

International Bill of Rights
   of the United Nations, 391, 464–69

Job Descriptions
   Entry-level, 415
   Middle-management, 416
   Senior-level, 418

Job Interviews, 434, 436
Job Corps Campaign, 104–6

Legal principles 387–89

"McGruff" Crime Prevention Campaign, 247–48
Markets vs. Publics, 99
Martin Marietta, 345, 419
Media Relations, 278, 280–85
   Checklist for, 285–290

National Coffee Association Campaign, 277
Nominal Group Technique, 87, 229
Nonvariables
   Definition of, 70
Norrell, 75–76

Objectives
   Assigning priorities, 86
   Definition of, 53
   How to determine, 84–85

Opportunities
   Definition of, 12–13
   Vs. problems, 52–53
Organizational Flexibility, 23
Organizational Size
   To public relations, 17, 19–20, 25–27
Organizational Types 20, 31–32
   Mechanical, 20, 38
   Mixed Mechanical/Organic, 21, 40
   Organic 21, 29
   Traditional, 20, 37

PERT Diagram, 132–33
Plan Book, 118, 151, 194–95, 252, 290–91
Planning
   For nonroutine events, 132, 135
   For routine events, 126, 132
Porter/Novelli Campaigns, 172–73, 224
Potter Box, 326–28
Priority Research Questions, 297–98, 303–8
   How conducted, 298–302
Prisoner's Dilemma, 340–41
Project Flow Charts. *See* Gantt Chart, PERT Diagram
Publics
   Active 96, 204
   Defining key, 108
   Definition of, 95, 204
   External, 22, 327
   Equivalent, 207
   Latent, 95, 204
   Non equivalent, 207
   As nonvariables, 99
   As variables, 99
   Vs. markets, 99
Public Relations
   Brief history, 6–13
   Definition of, 4
   Roles, 337–38

"Quality of Service" Campaign 61–64

Research
   Alternative reasons for, 252–53
   Basic/Applied, 200
   Checklist for conducting, 248–50
   Confirmatory, 199
   Definition of, 199
   Ethics in, 253–54
   Evaluative, 205, 291
   Exploratory, 199
   Formal/Informal, 200
   Qualitative, 199

Quantitative, 199
Quasi-experimental, 247
Samples, 238–40
Research Designs 200, 203, 209–23
Research Process 200–202
Resume 429
Chronological, 430–32
Combination functional/chronological, 431–32
Functional, 430
Roman Catholic Pope's Tour (Papal Visit), 170–72, 277

Scientific Theoretical Statements, 70
Social Exchange Theory, 76–77
Social Learning Theory, 74–75

Structural Functionalism, 16
Systematic Public Relations Software (sPRs), 422–23

Technology, 336
Timeline. *See* Gantt Chart
Towson State University's Publications, 264

Variables
Definition of, 70
Dependent, 203
Independent, 203, 204
Intervening, 203, 204
Moderating, 203–4

What-If-Not-Funded-Scenario, 174–78